SHAKING THE CHAINS

A Personal and Political History

by

FRED WESTACOTT

Published by
Joe Clark, 14 Woodland Way, Old Tupton, Chesterfield S42 6JA

ISBN 0-9543549-0-7

Typeset in Times New Roman 11pt on 13pt

Printed and bound in Great Britain by
Antony Rowe Limited, Chippenham, Wiltshire

To my grandchildren,
hoping that their lives will be as interesting as mine
and their world a better one.

Rise like Lions after slumber
In unvanquishable number -
Shake your chains to earth like dew
Which in sleep had fallen on you -
Ye are many, they are few.

P. B. Shelley

CONTENTS

FOREWORD

by TONY BENN

Fred Westacott's life story is, in every sense, a truly remarkable one that should be read by everyone in the labour movement.

It gives his readers a very full account of his long and memorable life and work, from his childhood in Wales, through his time as a toolmaker, wartime soldier and Communist Party organizer, to his last years as a major figure in the Chesterfield Trades Council, where I first met him in 1984. His near photographic memory of every detail makes it both readable and unforgettable. Unlike some autobiographies, which are mainly about the author's personal achievements, this one is modestly written and contains the warmest account of his family and friends, especially his beloved wife Kath to whom he was absolutely devoted and whose death he felt most acutely until the end.

But this book is also one of the very best political histories of the whole period. It describes and analyzes the events through which he lived and the industrial struggles in which he was involved, from the poverty of his youth, through the general strike, the depression in the thirties and all the developments in Britain and the world during the cold war.

Experience, they say, is the best teacher, and Fred certainly learned from his own, studying its meaning and drawing his own conclusions through reading and discussion with his comrades. His openness about the doubts he had, and his refusal to fall back on hindsight to justify views he held which he subsequently developed, give this book a quality of honesty that stands out on every page. He was a genuine intellectual in the way he thought out the deeper meaning of the many challenges of his own life, but he never allowed this to divert him from intense activity aimed at improving the lot of those he represented - the working class.

He was originally a member of the Labour Party, but losing confidence in it as a serious instrument for bringing in socialism, he moved to the Communist Party. Yet he retained his respect for those who did not follow that path but whom he believed were genuine in their own work, a wholly non-sectarian approach that characterizes the very best tradition of a whole generation of Communists who were so falsely demonized for their faith.

I am very proud to have known him over the last few years of his life, and I shall never forget his many kindnesses and the inspiration which he gave to me and everyone who knew him, all of which came out so clearly at his funeral, where the tributes paid by comrades and friends were moving and heartfelt.

By any standards Fred was a great man. His final gift to us is this book which will help us to see what has to be done now as we enter the Dark Ages again, with rampant capitalism (now described as globalization) and crude imperialism dominating the world and being presented to this generation as both inevitable and beneficial – a claim that is false on both counts.

We shall need a lot more people like Fred, with vision and courage to see us through to a better and more peaceful future; and those who read this book will be encouraged to understand how it can best be done.

INTRODUCTION

H. G. Wells once wrote, "Everyone has a story to write, the story of his life." Women, as well as men, of course. This is true in the sense that everyone's life is unique. It adds something to the total record of human experience. Yet we do not live in isolation from one another, nor from society. By definition, an autobiography is bound to concentrate on the writer, but the defect of so many is that the fundamental qualification that "No person is an island" is ignored or minimised. The role of the individual is so exaggerated as to be artificially detached from the encompassing circumstances. Often, such narratives become simply ego-trips.

I hope I have avoided this. My life is only interesting to others because of the remarkable period in which I have been fortunate enough to live and because of the struggles that have taken place in which I have participated. This, therefore, is not only about myself, but also about the unfolding political and social developments over the past seventy years and my reaction to them at the time. I have tried to summarise the more important events, using contemporary material. It might, therefore, be of interest to those who want to know more about what happened and what life was like, even though they may not be particularly interested in the reminiscences of the writer.

Today, much is written by academics about the 1920's, 1930's and 1940's, and I confess to being irritated by the trash so many of them write, and realise how true is the comment of the historian, W. G. Hoskins:

"The older one grows in the practice of writing history, the more sceptical one becomes about the truths embodied in books and documents; and the more one comes to realise that history is about people, and they are escaping our net if we merely fish in muniment rooms and libraries."

Unfortunately, this "fishing" is precisely what most modern historians seem to spend their time doing. When I read some of the learned treatises dealing with my times, I sit back and wonder if I was really alive then, or whether, perhaps, I existed in a parallel universe peopled by the same characters but in a different social and political environment! So many historians seem incapable of imagining what things were like in the three decades before the war, yet imagination is surely one of the essential qualities a professional historian should have.

Orthodox writers, conditioned as they are by the dominant ideology of the time, tend to interpret history from the point of view of the capitalist establishment – thus they say it was Churchill, and not the political left that led the fight against appeasement. Regrettably, however, many progressive historians, including some who regard themselves as Marxists, are also guilty of distortion, mainly by moulding the past to fit the conceptions they have today – for example, condemning outright what they see as the "sectarianism" of Communists and others in the labour movement over much of the period. This also reflects an inability to project their minds into past reality and view things from the standpoint of those who lived in a radically different society.

There is another reason why I have written this autobiography. It isn't "leaders" who have built our labour movement. It is the hard work and dedication of many thousands of men and women whose sole aim has been to improve the conditions of their class and to change society. They are largely unsung and their personal contributions unrecorded. Usually, only the famous (and the infamous) get written about or write about themselves – another way history is distorted. During my life I have known so many wonderful comrades who have given so much to the cause and to whom I owe so much. This story is also about them, and even if it bores the reader to have so many names mentioned and 'potted' biographies inserted, I make no apologies. At least it places their names in labour's roll of honour, in the records for posterity.

But, of course, this is primarily the story of my life. It is by no means all politics, but the political struggle is central. It has been my good fortune to have lived through one of the most eventful periods of history and to have done so most of the time alongside such a truly grand comrade as my wife, Kath. True, the 20th century is not ending with the victory of socialism, as we had hoped. The Communist movement is in disarray. However, the basic ideas of socialism are more valid than ever.

The "gleam" of the new society has not been extinguished. It will grow brighter as another generation takes up the torch, as capitalist society proves incapable of solving the problems facing humankind and as the lessons of the past are learned. It is a race to ensure that this will come before all is destroyed either by war or by the irreparable damage to the earth's life-supporting environment. I hope this account of past struggles will be some little help to those who have far greater battles to fight and to win.

Fred Westacott

CHAPTER I

1916-1931: EARLY MEMORIES

1. ROOTS

We called them "the people from the hills." Strange, as Tredegar where I lived was itself a thousand feet above sea level. But they came down to us, across the high moorland to the north of the town from where we could sometimes see in the distance the blue-grey peaks of the Brecknock Beacons. They came on horseback, riding side-saddle and with bulging bags. Sombre women in dark long dresses, high boots and broad-brimmed hats, selling butter, cheese, eggs and other fresh farm produce. When all had been sold they would ride away, and we wouldn't see them again for another week or so.

Later, I learned from where they came, from small farms in the beautiful Dyffryn Crawnon, a small, isolated and unspoiled valley at the edge of the Brecon mountains, where I and my pals were to spend many happy days during those warm and delightfully long summer holidays of our school years. To my friend Cyril and me this was our escape world, remote from the real one in which we were forced to live, our Shangri-la, our small taste of paradise. We would start out early in the morning and walk over the high moorland to the top of the Dyffryn from where we could look down on the patchwork quilt of small farms in the valley far below. The descent was down a narrow, steep and rocky path, intersected near the top by a stream flowing from a high waterfall, which we loved to climb. We would wander along the track serving the farms, drink from the mountain brooks when we were thirsty or ask at a farm house for a glass of milk, always freely given.

On at least one occasion, to the great anxiety of our parents, we stayed out all night, lying under a hedge listening to the hooting of the owls and the other strange nocturnal whistles, rustles and murmurs of this alternative existence. Sometimes in the evenings, weasels, stoats and hedgehogs would shuffle by, disdainfully ignoring the presence of strangers, and on one occasion a pair of badgers with their cubs passed within a few feet of us. Another time, a fox ambled across our path with a chicken, the victim of its latest forage, slung over its shoulder. Birds there were in great variety, in the Dyffryn and in the country around it. Walking over the moorland we would sometimes disturb grouse, which would fly close to the heather, making raucous protest cries at being disturbed, or lapwings would dive down on us with their angry "pee-weet" call as we came near to their nests. One year Cyril and I identified the nests of over thirty different species of birds.

Sometimes, on our travels, we would nervously watch a herd of wild mountain ponies gallop towards us, with a stallion, head high and mane flowing, in the lead, but invariably they would veer to one side before reaching us. There were always new, alien experiences. Another of our favourite spots was a tiny, rock-strewn, uninhabited valley called "The Dingle", with an ivy-covered stone archway at one end through which flowed a fast moving mountain stream, in the icy waters of which we used to splash around, build dams or sail improvised model boats. We considered getting there something of an adventure, for we had to pass through a farmyard and face a gaggle of ferocious geese which would advance towards us aggressively hissing and with necks outstretched. How brave we thought ourselves as we manoeuvred around them; what spice it added to the afternoon's enjoyment!

If we were not in the valleys, we would be high above them, exploring the remote Chartists' Cave, so named because it was there, in 1839, that the Chartists stored their weapons in preparation for their march down the industrial valleys in their ill-fated attempt to seize Newport. The cave was so rocky and deep that we never penetrated to its limit, being content to accept the wildly far-fetched story that it went all the way to Abergavenny, ten miles away.

Considering that we lived in one of the wettest parts of Britain, it's odd that, looking back to those far-off days, I find it difficult to recall a summer holiday that wasn't sunny and wasn't warm! Memories of the wet, cold days that there must have been in abundance have been mercifully buried deep in my sub-conscious.

Our trek through the Dyffryn would end where the little valley stream joins the River Usk. Near it is the village of Llangynidr, once a straggling collection of farm labourers' cottages and isolated until the intrusion of civilisation in the form of a tarmacked road brought the motor car and immigrants from nearby towns. It was from here that my mother's family came. She used to boast that it could be traced back three hundred years in the village church records, although this is a claim I have never confirmed. Her father, my grandfather, John Gunter, died before I was born, but a strong impression of his personality has emerged from the many stories that formed part of the family lore upon which I and my brothers were brought up. He was a farm worker, proud and stern, a typical bearded Victorian patriarch, whose forbidding glance would be enough to silence the slightest capriciousness on the part of his daughters. Woe betide any of the girls if they nibbled at meals before grace was said, or if they spoke a word at table without first asking permission.

Subsequently, the inheritance of the "Gunter Frown" became something to be looked for in his grandchildren. "You've got that Gunter frown again", my mother would say, most often to my brother Arthur, who apparently had many of the characteristics of her father. Not surprisingly, John Gunter was a pillar of the local Welsh chapel, and took his duties as a deacon so seriously that even when the family moved to Tredegar, each Sunday he would walk the seven miles over the mountain to Llangynidr to attend early service.

Sarah Ann, my mother, was the youngest of the four girls born to his first wife, Margaret, a gentle woman and a good mother, who died when the girls were quite young. She came from a cultured Welsh-speaking working-class family, and two of her brothers, William and David Williams were awarded Bardic crowns for their poetry. Their Bardic titles were "Myfyr Wyn" and "Myfyr Dddu." After their father was killed in a pit accident, William was compelled, when only nine years old, to start work in the Sirhowy Iron Works, where he eventually became a blacksmith.

My mother and her sisters always spoke of their mother with great tenderness and feelings of regret at losing her so early, no doubt with memories enhanced by the contrast they drew with the woman who replaced her. They didn't particularly like their step-mother, not because she was the "bad stepmother" of pantomime tradition, but because she was more severe than their real mother, and they felt, I suppose, that one stern parent was about as much as any children should be asked to endure.

Welsh was the first language they spoke when they were children, but already the dominant English establishment in Wales had gone a long way towards suppressing their native tongue and imposing its own. My

17

mother would recall how pupils would be punished if they were heard speaking Welsh in school. The sad consequence of growing up in what had become an almost totally English-speaking area was that she gradually lost her aptitude with the language, although she retained a repertoire of Welsh phrases – "ych a fi" she would scold us if we had been playing in the mud or had done something equally disgusting. And she often used to sing Welsh songs to us.

It was the inevitable lot of most working-class girls when they reached their 'teens, to go into domestic service, and my mother was no exception. She spoke little of this, but the accounts of others testify that it wasn't a particularly easy life. The one position she did often recall was when she was a servant in the house of a leading local Liberal, where the maids were treated better than was usual.

At that time, Tredegar was a Liberal stronghold, with a government minister, Sir William Harcourt, as its M.P. Many well-known Liberal politicians used to stay at her employer's house and she was fond of telling of her meeting with Lloyd George. "He came into the kitchen, with his finger all covered in blood, where he had cut it with a knife. I fetched a piece of cloth to bandage it with, and he was so pleased that he gave me sixpence!" Probably it was the sixpence that impressed itself on her memory more than the eminent donor, for in those days it was a rich bonus indeed for a servant.

It was when she was a servant girl that she met my father. He was a bricklayer doing a job near where she worked, a dashing young "card" (as he was for most of his life) who soon started up a flirtation with her. I can well understand why, because she must have been a very pretty girl, buxom, with long raven-black hair streaming down her back, which in later years we children used to love to help her comb, but which, as she grew older, she would roll up in a bun at the back of her head.

George Henry Westacott came from Newport, the only son and the youngest of the six children of George Henry and Catherine Westacott. His father was a skilled journeyman mason who, as a young man facing hard times in his own area, had tramped from Barnstaple in North Devon, around Gloucester to Newport, looking for work. We only discovered this just before my father died, when, as so often happens, early memories flood to the front of consciousness. Many years later, I visited North Devon with my wife and our children and we came across the village of Westacott. It is a sufficiently uncommon name to set us wondering whether there is a family connection. In Newport, my grandfather met a girl from the valleys, wed her, and settled down there.

My clearest recollection of Grancher Westacott was of a tall, bearded, distinguished-looking man standing in front of a roaring coal fire, one hand grasping his lapel, before a roomful of guests, giving powerful renderings of "Thora" and other Victorian ballads at his Golden Wedding. Grandma was a life-long Co-operator, well respected in Labour circles in Newport. She never believed her grandchildren ever grew up, and well into my teens I would get a child's toy on my birthday – which she never forgot. She was eighty-seven when she died in 1937, a good old age in those days. Although Newport was only twenty miles away it used to be a rare treat for us all to go by train down the valley to do the rounds of my father's relatives – he had five sisters. What excitement there was in preparing for such an expedition. Clean clothes, shoes polished, scrubbed shining faces and the mile walk to Sirhowy station. Then the journey itself! The thrill of poking one's head out of the window, the friendly "chug-chug" of the engine and the hasty pit-a-pat of the wheels on the line, the delicious smell of the acrid smoke and feeling the wind on one's face, even though the inevitable consequence was a speck of grit in the eye and a stern parental admonishment.

There was also the inevitable crisis with one or another of us, arising from the fact that there was no corridor or toilet on the train.

Our first visit would be to Gran and Grancher, after which we would start on the round of our various aunts and uncles who lived in different parts of the town. Each house visited had its own special fascination for us. There was Uncle Walter, who had only one arm but who made exquisite models and ornaments out of fretwork, Uncle Jim who bred guinea pigs, and another uncle who worked on a tug and was always promising to take us with him on a trip around Lundy Island, but never did.

There was also a plentiful supply of cousins to play with. As a special treat, my father would sometimes take us to see Newport's main landmark, the Transporter Bridge, or sundry aunts, uncles and cousins would pile into a horse-and-trap to have a picnic at the Lighthouse.

We usually stayed with my Auntie Florrie, who kept a boarding house at the back of Newport station. The railwaymen's leader and later Cabinet Minister, J. H. ("Jimmy") Thomas used to stay there on his visits to Newport and – existing as we did largely on cast-off clothes – I once had the doubtful distinction of having as part of my motley wardrobe a pullover that had belonged to Jimmy Thomas and a cap previously worn by Aneurin Bevan.

19

2. CHILDHOOD

The world was going through one of its periodical bouts of madness when I first came on the scene. The "war to end wars" was half way through, and in September 1916, far away from Tredegar, the greatest carnage in human history was taking place. On the Somme, 23,000 British and Allied soldiers had been slaughtered in a few days to gain a few yards of mud: on the nineteenth of the month Field Marshall Haig decided to "gamble" (his word) the lives of the survivors in another futile offensive.

This happened to be the day I decided to put in an appearance – not such a momentous event as the one taking place on the Western Front, but I daresay it was the one that wholly occupied the attention of my mother and father. They, like other proud parents of those years, were fortunately blissfully unaware that they were producing the babies who, twenty-three years later, were to be the participants in a repeat of the bloody conflict then being fought out with such ferocity.

I was the sixth of eight children – six boys and two girls. We lived in a privately rented terraced house in Nantybwch on the northern outskirts of Tredegar, fronting on to the main road to Merthyr Tydfil. The origin of the name Nantybwch becomes clear when it is translated into English; it means "Goat's Brook" and presumably referred to a small stream that ran nearby. Now it is a built-up suburb of the town, but then it was mainly green fields and grassed-over nineteenth century mine workings interspersed with a few short rows of cottages. Our street was called Birchgrove, but the planners had clearly not been very good at identifying trees, because a few years later it was renamed Ashvale! At the far end of a field at the back of the house was a single-track railway line with a steep gradient.

Every afternoon the "colliers' train," filled with miners returning from work, would noisily and laboriously crawl its way to Nantybwch Station at the top of the valley. Sometimes, if there were too many coaches, the strain would be too great for one engine and its wheels would emit an agonising scream as they failed to grip the rails, whereupon the driver would whistle for help and another engine would come puffing to the rescue by pushing from behind.

This is where I started life, but most of my brothers and sisters had already arrived before my mother and father moved to their new home. My father had been a bricklayer on the houses when they were built and they were regarded as being a cut above the usual run of miners' cottages. In addition to the living room we had a small front room, the "parlour," which was only used on special occasions. Off the living room was a tiny pantry and a scullery with a cold-water tap over an earthenware sink. In the scullery was a cast-iron boiler which could be heated by lighting a fire underneath it and which was used for washing clothes (by hand, of course) and boiling the puddings at Xmas time. The "cwtch" under the stairs – a small cupboard – was where odds and ends were kept alongside the gas meter, and was where we kids often used to hide.

The W.C. was outside in the back yard with a coalhouse opposite. There were two small bedrooms and a tiny "box room" which was always used as an additional bedroom by most families. It wasn't called a bedroom because it was smaller than statutory dimensions allowed. Carpets were, of course, unheard of except in the houses of the well-to-do. The living-room floor was made of red earthenware tiles, the coldness of which was softened by coconut matting which had an amazing propensity to collect dust and which had to be beaten regularly, particularly as the coal fire produced a great deal of soot.

Linoleum covered the floor of the parlour and the stairs. The fireplace in the living room was part of a black cast-iron range with an oven at the side in which all the baking was done. There was none of the thermostatically controlled heating that seems so essential for modern cookery. Indeed, many years later when we bought Mama a gas cooker we had great difficulty in getting her to use it. Meals were, of course, much simpler and less varied than today; but even so, the cakes my mother made and meals she prepared were – and in my unprejudiced opinion still are – unsurpassed. The smell and taste of just-from-the-oven home-made bread, spread in the rare affluent days with "best butter" (for some reason butter was always "best") and a scraping of jam, remains with me and makes my mouth water after all these years. And I doubt whether she read a recipe book in her life. On the hob above the oven rested the cast-iron kettle, the cast-iron "iron" for pressing clothes, and the earthenware tea-pot, while above the fireplace was a high mantelpiece on which reposed a "Kardomah" tin tea-caddy and an assortment of other containers and ornaments.

The only upholstered furniture in the house were two small fireside chairs in the parlour. The centrepiece in the living room was a bare whitewood table which was scrubbed regularly and which was covered with newspapers at meal times, except on Sundays or special occasions, when a linen tablecloth would be put down. Mama had a wooden rocking-chair and my father an upright wooden arm-chair reverently reserved for his use alone. What we called "the couch" was a plain wooden bench-settee with one or two loose cushions, and there were four plain kitchen chairs to go along with it. Every Saturday morning Mama would be on her hands and knees scrubbing the tiled floor right out to the front door, ending with cleaning the door-step with a "brick-block", and the fire-range would be polished with "Zebra" black-lead. Monday was traditionally the day when the main washing was done, in the boiler and by hand, of course, with a scrubbing board and a bar of soap.

Looking back, it seems incredible that she did all the housework, all the washing and cooking for a family that included six growing lads, without the use of any modern devices like a washing machine, cooker or Hoover, and that she did it all so cheerfully – as most working class women did. For a few weeks before and after my brothers were born and if my father was working at the time, a girl who lived nearby was paid to come in and help for a few hours each day. But for most of the time Mama would be nursing one or other of the younger children at the same time as doing the housework. When Emrys was far from being a baby and must have been quite a weight, she carried him around in a shawl while doing the daily chores because he was recovering from pneumonia. It was the custom for the baby to be wrapped tightly around the mother with a large, woollen "Welsh Shawl" which would be firmly tucked in, thus allowing the mother the full use of her hands while she got on with other jobs. The effectiveness of this so impressed my wife that she adopted it when our children were small.

As was the custom then, the woman also did any decorating that was needed, white-washing the ceilings with "whiting powder" and water, and papering the walls usually with floral-patterned wallpaper, stuck on with paste made from flour and water. My father helped very little with the housework, even when he was unemployed, not because he was lazy – far from it – but because it was "not a man's job", a convention neither of them ever questioned, and, to be honest, neither did we boys until we were into our teens. If my two sisters had lived, they would have been expected to share the burden, but Gwen died in the 1918 influenza epidemic, and Lily was killed through falling off a railway bridge on which she was playing, when she was about twelve.

The enduring memory I have of my mother is her natural, unsophisticated cheerfulness. She loved to gossip with the neighbours, would play and laugh with us, and tell us stories or sing a Welsh song. She was

22

totally unselfish in her attitude to life and to people, and her children were well and truly the apples of her eyes. Apart from the occasional half-hearted slap if we were doing something naughty, she never used corporal punishment; her main threat was "wait 'till your father gets home," but when he did she usually forgot to tell him – and if she did all that happened was a good telling-off. There were occasions when her cheerfulness would depart, usually because of an immediate acute and insoluble problem of "how to make ends meet." And there were occasions when she would sit in her rocking chair with a far-away look on her face and with moist eyes, and we knew she was thinking of her girls who had died and who would, had they lived, have been such a help and comfort to her.

In the early years, the only lighting was by a paraffin hand lamp which stood in the centre of the table and around which all reading, writing and school homework in the evening had to be done. This is how I remember my brother, Arthur, helping to teach me to read. Later, we progressed to a "hanging lamp;" still an oil lamp, but suspended from a hook in the ceiling and balanced by a weight. Once the hook gave way and the lamp fell with a great crash on to the table when we were having a meal. In time, the oil lamp was superseded by gas, operated by putting pennies in the meter, and in the 1930's the wonder of electricity came to Tredegar.

The most precious decoration was a striking pendulum wall clock with a big dial and a wonderfully majestic "tick-tock." Today, television and radio have banished the pleasure of real silence from most homes and it's hard for most people to imagine how soothing it can be in a quiet room in the evening to hear nothing but the comforting "tick-tock" of a pendulum clock. Modern battery clocks, when they can be heard, emit a fussy, frantic, disagreeable ticking which irritates rather than comforts. We children were never allowed to touch the clock. All important documents were placed in a space below the pendulum and every day Dada would religiously wind and set it, usually ten minutes fast. There were a few pictures on the walls, and pride of place was given to a painted photograph of Lily that was greatly cherished by my mother.

We slept three to a bed on a straw or flock mattress. In the days before electricity we used a candle to light the way upstairs and during the winter the beds were warmed by wrapping the cast-iron shelf from the oven, or a heated brick, in an old piece of blanket. The bedclothes were sometimes augmented with coats. Fleas positively thrived in the mattresses, and every morning our bodies would be marked with bites. Mama fought a continuous and unsuccessful war against them, for effective insecticides like D.D.T. just didn't exist. A favourite expedient of hers was crushed camphor sprinkled between the blankets, which had no noticeable effect on the fleas but almost asphyxiated us children!

When times were good we would all be given a spoonful of "Cod Liver Oil and Malt" or "Parish's Food" after our usual cup of OXO or cocoa before going to bed, and every Friday evening the tin bath that hung on the wall in our yard was brought in, gallons of water heated in saucepans on the open fire and we boys subjected to our weekly scrubbing.

Of course, there were none of the labour-saving products that are so commonplace today that we never even think about them – so much do we take them for granted – such as washing-up liquid, washing powder or aerosols. Torn-up newspapers served as toilet paper. Nor was there the wide range of pre-packed products that are now a normal part of our existence. In our corner shop such things as sugar, tea, flour, butter and dried fruit were delivered to the grocer loose, and would be either packed by him (sugar was always in blue bags) or simply laded out in the amount required by the customer. Quick food and drinks were unheard of, as were frozen foods – no-one possessed a fridge, anyway. Fresh milk was delivered daily by "Robins the Farm" in his horse and cart, and would be measured out straight from the churn into a jug. We had an old cat that seemed to have an uncanny sixth sense and would run to the door to greet the milkman long before the rattle of the churns heralded his arrival at our house. The supermarket was still in the distant future, but there were some grocery chain stores in the towns, such as Liptons and the Home and Colonial. The bulk of the shopping, however, was done in the corner shop, not only because of its convenience but because goods could be bought "on tick" and paid for weekly.

Bricklaying was a somewhat precarious occupation being dependent on whether houses were being built, the weather and the time of the year. Winter was the hardest period, and my father used to augment his dole money with any odd repair job that came his way. Long-term work was dependent on the two small local building firms or council work. When work was available, he stood a good chance of getting a job, for he had a reputation of being a hard worker and a fine craftsman – not just someone who laid bricks, but a mason of the old type who could do anything in brick or stone.

His pride in his craft often brought trouble, for he strongly resisted "skimping" a job at the behest of a profit-orientated employer. On one occasion he was sacked because he publicly exposed the deliberately shoddy work being done by a private firm contracted to build council houses and which was giving a "back-hander" to the council clerk-of-works to persuade him to turn a blind eye to it. This craftsmanship was passed on to three of his sons, Clarence, Emrys and Bert, who also became bricklayers.

In those days there were no contracts of employment, and building workers could be, and usually were, laid off with only an hour's notice. My mother's face would show her dismay if he walked in on a Friday with his tool bag in his hand and the disastrous news that he had been sacked. All his life he was a staunch trade unionist, and for many years he was secretary of the local branches of both the Amalgamated Union of Building Trade Workers (the brickies' union) and the National Federation of Building Trade Operatives, which linked all unions in the industry and which subsequently became U.C.A.T.T. When, in later years, my father read that great socialist classic, The Ragged Trousered Philanthropists, he was thrilled by it, for Robert Tressell described so accurately what conditions were like in the building industry as he had known it.

He was slightly below medium height, always neatly dressed and walked briskly with a soldierly bearing – as a young man he had been in the Territorial Army Reserves. He very seldom went into pubs and never swore, but this didn't mean that he was in any way straightlaced. On the contrary, he had a great sense of fun and a reputation on the job for being a practical joker. It was he who would always send the new apprentice to the stores for "a new bubble for the spirit level," or play some prank on one of his mates.

He was also a great bluffer. There was one occasion when he was on the dole and had the opportunity of doing a job "on the side," re-building a chimney stack on one of a couple of houses when the tenants were away. I had just left school without a job, so I was conscripted as his labourer. The job lasted about a week, but when he went to collect the money due he discovered to his horror that he had worked on the wrong house – it was next door that needed the new stack! Even worse, the house was owned by the manager of the labour exchange – and Dada had drawn his dole for that week! Praying that the manager wouldn't know this, he went to him and told him of the mistake, but presenting it as if

25

he had done him a great favour. "It was lucky for you I was there," he said, "because that stack was just on the point of collapsing, and if it had, someone would certainly have been hurt, perhaps killed, and you would have been held responsible." The ploy paid off and the manager paid up not cottoning on that Dada was supposed to be unemployed (or maybe not letting on that he knew). Moreover, there was a bonus of an additional week's work doing the original job.

Like most working class families, everything new, such as clothes, blankets and furniture, was bought on the "never-never," and as a consequence my parents were continuously in debt due to inability to keep up the instalments. There was a routine we were all very familiar with – demands for payment, final demands, threats and ultimately a court order for payment. When this produced no response, the inevitable climax would be reached, the "bums," which is what we called the court bailiffs, would arrive on the doorstep and at the last moment some token payment would be made to stave off imprisonment. It was a cynical establishment fallacy that no person could be imprisoned for debt – that, we were assured, belonged to the days of Dickens. But you could be imprisoned for "contempt of court," that is, failing to respond to a court order to pay up – a fine legal distinction which was lost on working-class families!

There was one occasion when Dada tried to bluff it out past the usual last point. He said he had no money and couldn't pay. "Come on, George," one of the "bums" pleaded – of course they knew each other; it was all like a game – "give us something. We don't want to, but you know we'll have to take you to Newport if you don't pay" (Newport was where the jail was). Dada gravely collected the clothes he would need in prison and marched off between them to catch the bus to Newport. Then, just as the bus was about to start, he capitulated, accepted that his bluff had failed this time, and paid the minimum acceptable amount. The one weekly payment that was seldom allowed to get into arrears was the penny-a-week funeral insurance on each member of the family, collected by the man from the Prudential.

The weekly rent was twelve shillings and sixpence (65p), a crippling burden for a skilled bricklayer on £3, whose family income dropped to about half that when my father was on the dole. Inevitably, the rent was always in arrears, and there was a continuous flow of threatening letters from the solicitor acting for the landlord.

These sometimes led to action, in the form of a Court Order, and when this extremity was reached, something had to be paid off the arrears regardless of what sacrifice had to be made.

A time came when it seemed we had reached the point of no return and an eviction order was served. We had a fortnight to get out of the house. There was no way by which my parents could raise the £30 arrears demanded, so we began looking for somewhere else to live. Unfortunately, any prospective landlord would want to see the current rent book – and sight of it, showing the arrears, would damn our chances. The only way out was to buy an empty rent book from Woolworths and fill it in ourselves, forging a landlord's signature and demonstrating what impeccable tenants we were! But even using this expediency, we could find nowhere to go, not even in the most derelict part of the town, and the day came when we had to be out the next morning. In desperation it was arranged for the family to move into a lean-to glass outhouse attached to the home of Auntie Gwen, my mother's sister.

The morning arrived and we had packed everything ready to move. My father's pride had forced him to spend much-needed money on the few repairs to the house that needed doing; he had even fixed new handles to all the doors. "We must leave the house as it was when we first moved in," he declared. We waited, but the removal van was late in coming. The postman arrived first, with a letter from the landlord's solicitor lifting the eviction order for a month to give us an opportunity to pay something off the arrears. In the empty house we held a family meeting. Should we accept this respite and unpack everything, or having gone so far, should we go to my Auntie Gwen's – I think it was the thought of all of us trying to live and sleep in the small outhouse that clinched the issue.

Both my parents had a great love of Dickens, whose novels they had read many times. Dada also had a detailed knowledge of Dickens' life. On Sunday evenings we often used to gather around the fireside and, while my mother sat in her rocking-chair knitting or patching our clothes, he would read chapters from one of the novels. We sometimes extracted great amusement from comparing people we knew to Dickens' characters. Hall Caine's Manx sagas were also favourites. This was, of course, when prepacked entertainment, even radio, was still in its infancy and entertainment had to be self-made. Today, it sometimes seems that most families would not be able to survive without "the box."

Apart from Dickens and Caine, my father was not a great book reader, but Mama was an avid reader of romantic fiction until she died. Jane Eyre she read many times, and she would look forward with impatience

27

to Tuesday's delivery of the "Red Letter" and the latest instalment of "Maria Martin and the Murder in the Red Barn" or other such melodramas. Ethel M. Dell, the then equivalent of Barbara Cartland, was one of her favourite authors. I had a feeling that she had once had a love of poetry, but the only ones she could remember and would sometimes recite to us were parts of "The Wreck of the Hesperus" and "After Blenheim." Books were all obtained from the free lending library. The only exception, at least in the early days, was a huge tattered family bible that sat on a small table in the parlour and contained wonderful drawings that gave me endless enjoyment. Our daily newspaper was Labour's *Daily Herald,* and the Co-operative paper, *Reynold's News* on Sunday, and there were times when we had periodicals – *Tit-Bits, Answers* or *John Bull.*

Dada used also to regale us with stories of the old Music Halls. In his younger days he was a regular frequenter of the Newport Empire, and he would tell us about Dan Leno, Little Tich, Marie Lloyd, George Robey and the other great stars of those days whom he had often seen. Sometimes he would sing some of the songs, intermingled with Victorian ballads and jingoist songs of the Boer War. One tear-jerker began, "The Boers have got my daddy, my soldier dad . . . " and ended "I'm a going to fight the Boers, I am, and bring my daddy back to me." Draughts was one his great interests. He was a champion player and when out of work he would spend the best part of every day playing the game with his cronies in the Workmen's Hall. He travelled to other towns in South Wales playing for the Tredegar Draughts Team.

The main outside entertainment was the cinema – silent films, of course. The first I can remember going to see was with my father. It was Charlie Chaplin and Jackie Coogan in "The Kid." Chaplin was a great favourite of us children and we saw him in most of his early films – "The Gold Rush," for example. Mama would usually go with one of her sisters, especially to the highly sentimental films starring Mary Pickford, Lilian Gish, Rudolph Valentino and their contemporaries. Talkies were to come much later, first to Merthyr, seven miles away. It was a great thrill when we all went to see Al Jolson in "Sonny Boy," and the novelty of the new magic of sound far outweighed the banality of such a tear-jerker. Certainly, my mother and aunts wept buckets during the performance. Apart from the cinema, there was one event which we hardly ever missed – the annual performance of light operas by the Tredegar Operatic Society.

My formal education, from five to fourteen, took place entirely at Dukestown Council School, which embraced both infant and junior school. The day I started school is still one of my most vivid memories. It was soon after my fifth birthday, and my mother literally dragged me along, accompanied by my best friend who was being just as unwillingly pulled along by his mother. The school was half a mile from home, and we howled all the way. We were pacified somewhat when we arrived and found that the teacher was Beryl, the girl who lived next door to us, particularly when she introduced us to a wonderful rocking-horse.

I liked school, probably because I was a bright pupil and, being painfully shy and reserved – something my friends today find hard to believe – gave little trouble to the teachers. No doubt they were as competent as other teachers, but I cannot recall them with any great affection. The headmaster, "Dai Donkey" to us, was a somewhat remote figure who used occasionally to appear in the classroom and ask a few questions, or tell us the only two jokes he seemed to know – which we would dutifully laugh at even though we had heard them many times before. One teacher, who was a bit of a bully and whose idea of keeping order was to shout and use the cane freely, met his deserts one dark winter's day when he was waylaid and roughed up by some of the older children. Then there was young and pretty Miss Andrews, who, to the great amusement of her heartless pupils, would inexplicably faint every few weeks in front of the class and have to be revived with a glass of water.

But the most influential teacher, even more than the head, was Eli Meyrick, who taught the top class – "Standard Eight." He was a good teacher, with a sense of humour and a good rapport with his class. He boasted he had never used the cane, but he did what was probably more hurtful – ridicule offenders in front of the class. I can see him now, warming his backside in front of a roaring fire, while we unfortunates in the back of the large classroom would be shivering with cold. He conducted the choir in Ebenezer chapel, so music was a favourite subject of his. When he led us in singing, he would move around the class with his head down and his ear stuck out, and if he detected anyone singing out of tune there would be a sharp tap on the head with a pencil, meaning "shut up." I always received a tap. However, I was good at English, and to my intense embarrassment, my compositions were usually read out to the class as an example to my fellow pupils, and even taken around other classes. On the wall was a map of the world, with one third of it – the British Empire – coloured in red. I was thrilled when I read G. A.

29

Henty's tales of the famed Empire builders – Under Drake's Drum, With Clive in India, With Rhodes in Africa, With Wolfe in Canada, and also the wonderful adventure stories of R. M. Ballantyne. Without making any conscious effort, I memorised very many poems, including Macaulay's "Horatius," a large part of Longfellow's "Hiawatha" and some of Shakespeare. Indeed, I found I could memorise the written word without a great deal of effort, and although that ability didn't persist, I can still, seventy years later, remember much of what I then read. Drawing, science and woodwork were also favourite subjects, but arithmetic I detested; nor was I very good at sports. Welsh was taught rather desultorily and made little impact on me. One of the disadvantages of following your brothers up the same school, with the same teachers, is that they can compare you with your predecessors – which, in my case, they often did, usually to my detriment.

Almost the only occasions I was caned were for being late. The first school bell would ring out about fifteen minutes before the start of lessons, and this was the signal for everyone to start from home. Woe betide any pupil who hadn't arrived before the "second bell" had ended. We then had to line up in the school yard with one hand held out. "Dai Donkey" would move along the line giving each offender a hefty thwack on the palm with his cane. Thus, many a morning started with a painfully stinging hand, not in the least eased by putting a hair on one's hand beforehand – a stratagem that was supposed to make the cane less painful! The main reason for being late in my family arose from the logistics of getting us all off to school at the same time. We each had to wash – in a bowl of cold water – be breakfasted, usually with porridge, and examined to see that we were properly dressed. An exciting event I can remember with clarity was the total eclipse of the sun in 1927. I'm afraid there was none of the panicky advice that abounded on the next such occasion in 1999. We were, of course, told not to look at the naked sun, but to blacken a piece of glass with soot over a candle flame. It was early in the morning and for some reason we were told to go to the top of Sirhowy Hill to view it – we thought it was probably because it took us a couple of hundred yards nearer to the sun! It was quite impressive and eerie, although we were disappointed because, being just outside the area of totality, the darkness was not as deep as we hoped for.

My mother was the only member of the family who took religion seriously. She was a member of the English-speaking Baptist chapel, Carmel, and she sometimes used to take me with her to the Sunday service.

We sat in a tall pew, which I could hardly see over the top of. The minister, "Evans Carmel," was a kindly, but typically narrow-minded Welsh preacher who used to visit his flock regularly but in the pulpit was full of hell and damnation. He refused to attend a performance of the religious oratorio, Belshazzar's Feast, put on by some of the other chapels, because there was dancing in it! There was great rivalry between Carmel and nearby Tabernacle, where my Uncle Charlie was a leading figure and led the choir. Although he spoke Welsh fluently and had great pride in Wales, I learned later that he was, in fact, English, hailing from Shropshire. When I was about fourteen I was persuaded by a friend to go with him to the Church of England Sunday School, but I soon gave it up in disgust when I discovered that our teacher firmly believed that God had made the earth the centre of the universe and that the sun orbited around it!

3. HARD TIMES

Poverty was, of course, endemic in South Wales in the 1920's and 1930's, and we felt no stigma about being poor because most people were in the same boat; indeed many were far worse off than us. There was not the sharp contrast between those in good jobs and those who were less fortunate that is the case nowadays. Unemployment was widespread, and most of those who did work received miserable wages as miners. Nor was there the continuous pressure-advertising on T.V. that we now get, which socially stigmatises those who are not able to buy the latest gadget or keep up with the latest fashion.

Vitamin D deficiency, due to poor diet, resulted in rickets being common among children, and we were well-used to school-pals with bow legs or wearing leg-irons. But the great killer was T.B. (tuberculosis or consumption), a disease caused by poor living conditions and lack of nourishment. It was almost wiped out after the war, but now, as I write this in Tory Britain, it is beginning to show itself again in our inner cities. "The White Scourge" particularly attacked the young, and many of my school-mates, including one of my best friends, died from the disease. The consumptive children could be clearly identified by their pale faces and the dark rings around their eyes. In seven years, 17,222 died from T.B. in South Wales and Monmouthshire. The death rate among young women in nearby Merthyr Tydfil was two and half times as high for women of fifteen to thirty than in the rest of Britain. There was a direct co-relationship between T.B. and poverty. So many families lived in grossly overcrowded conditions, and at the time, 173,000 persons in Wales existed on the totally inadequate scales provided by the unemployment authorities. Almost as many had to live on even less – on Parish or Public Assistance Relief. 140,000 miners lived on an average weekly wage of less than £2.15. This was at a time when the British Medical Association and the eminent nutritionist, Sir John Orr, declared that ten shillings (50p) a week for each person in a family for food only was the very minimum needed for adequate nutrition. It is a reflection on the system under which we live that war rationing resulted in working-class children being better nourished than before the war, and that children of the same age in South Wales were on an average two inches taller at the end of the war than at the beginning.

Of course, there was no National Health Service although Tredegar was in advance of the rest of the country in having a Medical Aid Society, to which everyone subscribed and from which they received treatment when needed (including free medicines and hospital treatment). It also had salaried G.P.'s, something we haven't got today. The writer A. J. Cronin was one of the doctors for a time and used his experiences as a background in some of his books. The Medical Aid Society had been started by Walter Conway, and Aneurin Bevan, when he became Minister of Health, used it as the pattern for the N.H.S. But in the early years of my childhood, we had a family doctor, Dr Smith, solemn, stately and awe-inspiring. He lived in a large, dingy house with a mysteriously smelling dispensary attached, and used to do his house calls in a horse-and-trap, a most dignified figure wearing a top hat and always sitting bolt upright in the front of the buggy.

Life for us was a succession of booms and slumps, depending on whether my father was working or not. When he was, we ate reasonably well and there was a greater variety of food – we would have cakes and cheese as well as the standard bread, marge and jam for tea. At such times we possibly ate more meat than is usual in many poorer working-class homes today, because it was relatively cheaper. Fish of various kinds was also a favourite meal. Mama would sometimes miraculously whip up quantities of Welsh cakes – small flat cakes with currants, baked on a griddle – which she would produce in a few minutes. Supper was, and to some extent still is, a tradition in Wales and usually for us children it consisted of a cup of Oxo, with bread broken up in it. But if Friday was a payday, one of us would be sent to the nearby fish and chip shop for "six penn'th of chips and six penny fish." The joy of such occasions made up for the many more days of far less sumptuous fare!

But even when a wage was coming into the house, things were far from easy for my mother. More often than not, debts piled up during the period of unemployment, and these had to be paid. Groceries were bought from the local shop supposedly on a weekly credit basis, but when customers couldn't afford to pay, Mr Jervis, the grocer, would usually allow bills to mount. However, when he knew circumstances had improved he not unreasonably expected payment of the arrears. This flexible personal relationship between the local grocer and his customers arose from their being members of a closely-knit and mutually dependent community. Although my mother and the neighbours were always "knocking" Lew Jervis, it would have been infinitely harder if they had lived in this age of the cash-only supermarket which has squeezed out most of the family corner shops.

The only rows I can remember between my parents were over money. My father always handed over his pay packet unopened on a Friday, and often it contained far less than Mama had anticipated and had planned for. He would remind her that he had "subbed" during the week ("subbing" was the practice of drawing out some pay before the end of the week). Or he might need more than his usual "pocket money" to pay union arrears. Compared with most husbands his financial demands were small. Although not a teetotaller, he seldom drank, nor did he have expensive pastimes. But, like so many building workers, he was a heavy smoker.

Some families were reduced to a pitiable existence because the husband sought a temporary escape from responsibility by spending most of the dole money or pay in a pub. During the hard times, often long periods and during the winter, when there was no work available, things could be very tough indeed, but my parents tried to ensure that we children suffered least of all. Dada would give up his cigarettes and tobacco, but he couldn't stop the craving for a smoke, so in desperation he would try all manner of dried leaves in his pipe. A common recourse was orange peel, dried in the oven and then flaked like tobacco. After gas was installed there was a much-appreciated bonus. When the man called to empty the meter he would hand back a rebate, based on the cost of gas and how much had been used. It was only a couple of pence in the shilling, but how we welcomed him! Sometimes, if we worried Mama for pennies to buy sweets she would say, "Wait till the gas-man comes," Football Pools had not yet arrived to instil exciting dreams of becoming

33

rich overnight. The nearest equivalent was the crossword puzzles in the Sunday papers, with their tantalising offer of "£1,000 or £5 a week for life." There was a year when my father and my Uncle Charlie were hooked on *The People* crossword. Competitors could send in as many entries as they liked, but it meant copying the entire crossword on blank sheets of paper, and, not having the convenience of photo-copiers, this meant doing it by hand. Every Sunday, with loud protests, Emrys, Bert or I was conscripted for the tedious task of copying out twenty or thirty crosswords. Of course, they never won anything: the number of alternative answers to clues made the chances a million to one.

Food, fuel and clothes replacements were the biggest problems, especially during the winter. An entry in my diary for Thursday, 28th January 1932: "I didn't get up until one o'clock today, there being no food in the house." I can remember on another occasion Mama giving me a jam sandwich and telling me to take it upstairs to eat in case my younger brother, who had already had his share, saw me and wanted more. We did have a small garden in which some years my father grew a few vegetables, mainly potatoes. When we were out of coal for the fire, we boys would scour the back-lanes for odd pieces of wood, and delve among the cinders thrown out by others to retrieve any coke that could still be burned. On one bitterly cold day my father, in desperation, even burned the rungs off the stairs banister – which, of course, had to be replaced when he found work.

Active, boisterous boys were hard on clothes, and keeping us reasonably dressed must have been my mother's biggest headache. Whenever she was not doing household chores she would be knitting – she was extremely fast at it – or making or mending clothes for the children. Like other kids, our coats and trousers were festooned with patches, put on for necessity, not for decoration as is the fashion among youngsters today. She would work particularly hard in the weeks before the annual Whitsun chapel "walk out," when children and their parents would walk through the town behind their respective chapel choirs singing hymns. It was a matter of pride to see that the children were neat and well-dressed. We enjoyed the "walk out" not only because we were proud of our new clothes, but mainly because it ended with a children's garden party in the grounds of the vicarage, with plenty to eat and games to play.

Of course, like most working-class children in those days, we existed to a great extent on "hand-me-downs," either from within the family, or from relatives or better-off friends. Shoes were a special problem. My

34

father used to try and repair them, but couldn't keep up with the speed at which they wore out. More often than not our shoes had big holes in the soles, so before going to school each morning a fresh piece of cardboard would be put inside the shoes in a not very effective attempt to protect the feet. One of my enduring memories of schooldays during the winter was having permanently cold feet. On one occasion my mother saw some cheap children's shoes advertised in the daily paper, and sent for them. They turned out to be made of soft moulded rubber, and I endured torture wearing them for a few weeks. During the summer we wore plimsolls – what we then called "daps."

At the beginning of the depression years, the Lord Mayor of London launched an appeal for boots and shoes for children living in the depressed areas. So it was that one day I was sent to the Council Offices, where a huge heap of shoes was piled on the floor in one of the rooms and I had to pick a pair that fitted and were a reasonable match.

This picture might appear overwhelmingly depressing, but that would be a distortion. At least for us children, most of the time we had no feeling of deprivation and hardship. This was because everyone was in the same boat and there was no significant contrasting group who were greatly better-off. It was also due to the fact that we were a close and happy family. I get impatient when I hear so-called advanced social thinkers, even some who claim to be Marxists, condemn the family out of hand as being a totally reactionary organisation that needs abolishing as quickly as possible. This is a hopelessly simplistic analysis which fails to recognise the dialectics of the situation. While the modern monogamous family clearly reflects capitalist society in some respects, including its property relations, the working class family often also serves as a collective protective shield against many of the most oppressive features of society. It makes capitalism more bearable for many who suffer most from it. This was certainly the case so far as we were concerned, and our family was fairly typical.

However hard up we were, there were many things our parents did to make us happy. For example, I cannot remember a time when we didn't have weekly comics or boy's papers – *Chick's Own* for the youngest, *Film Fun* or *Comic Cuts* for the older boys and *The Children's Newspaper* for many years. George and Arthur used to have *Boy's Own* or *Sexton Blake*, while I would take *The Wizard* or *The Rover*. And what a joy it was to go to the Saturday afternoon children's matinee at the local cinema. This, of course, was in the silent days and the film would

35

be shown against a cacophonous background of yells, shrieks and general hubbub from an audience of boisterous youngsters shouting at one another and encouraging the hero on the screen. Every so often the film would be halted and the cinema manager would threaten not to start it going again unless we behaved ourselves, an appeal that was ignored and a threat that was never carried out – as we knew full well it wouldn't be. There was always a serial, each episode of which ended with the hero either hanging over a cliff or about to be eaten by a lion. If we had twopence left when we came out, we would regale ourselves with "peas and faggots."

When money was coming into the house Mama would go shopping to town on Saturdays, and always brought back small presents for us. This is how I came by my first real book, a sixpenny edition of Lord Lytton's *The Last Days of Pompeii*, which I cherished for years. In anticipation of these presents we children would set-to and make the living room spick and span before she came home – the younger ones being bullied to help.

The community we lived in was one of poverty, but a strongly welded community nevertheless. As was usual in South Wales in those days, doors were seldom locked. This was not only because there was no point in guarding against thieves because there was nothing to steal, but also because it was alien to the community tradition. Neighbours would walk into one another's houses with only a perfunctory tap on the door, to gossip, to borrow something or just for company. And help was always there if someone was ill.

Every Thursday evening my Auntie Gwen and Auntie Maggie would pay a visit and the three sisters would sit by the fire exchanging the gossip of the week and drinking cups of tea. If the story being told was particularly scandalous, they would glance furtively at the children, sitting reading or listening with headphones to the wireless, and their heads would come together and their voices drop to a whisper so that our innocence would be protected. And we would pretend, of course, not to notice or hear anything. Mama was always a soft touch for tramps. They would come to the door with hard luck stories and invariably would be invited in for a cup of tea and a slice of bread and jam, in return for which they would tell her tales of their experiences on the road.

For those who had a gramophone (as we did for a time) the records were almost common property – they were the old 78 records, of course, played on a wind-up gramophone. We had collected about a dozen records, and would play them over and over again. When we wanted a change we would take them to someone else who had a gramophone and exchange our records for theirs, to a point when it was sometimes difficult to know who the original owners were.

Because Tredegar was a relatively small town, it was well-nigh impossible for anyone to shelter behind anonymity. Often, in the Welsh manner, people were known more by their occupation or where they lived than by their surnames – a custom that probably arose because of the large numbers with the same surname. In addition to those already mentioned, I can remember "Jones Ty-Bryn" (the name of the house), "Jones Top-House," "Jones the Milk" and "Jones the Bakehouse." Then there was "Evans the Farm," "Griffiths the Shop," "Griffiths the Post Office," "Pask the Bobbie," "Jimmy Oil" (who delivered paraffin), "Billy Jones Monkey" the chimney sweep, "Cookie the Ragman," "Tom Peg-Leg." One of the oddest, and understandably the most malicious, was "Dai Back Rent," who used to buy back debts cheaply and then try and collect them.

We knew our neighbours intimately, as most people nowadays do not. We shared their tragedies – and their comedies. Like our next door neighbours, for instance. The mother was obsessively tidy and spent all her time cleaning, tidying and polishing, or shouting at her husband and children for walking on the parts of the floor she hadn't yet covered with newspapers. The parlour was a hallowed domain that no one was allowed to enter. Her husband, Tom, was normally a quiet man who most of the time suffered in silence. But on Saturday night, after a few drinks too many at the local pub, the Mr Hyde in him would emerge. He would return home after closing time and proceed noisily to eject his wife and family from the house. Having done this, he would lock the door, go into the parlour, and play hymns on the organ until after midnight, while my father and other neighbours, including Mr Pask, our neighbourhood "bobby," would be knocking on the door and window, appealing for him to restore normal relations.

The hidden bonds that existed in communities such as ours stemmed not only from tradition but also from the fact that there were no significant social divisions and that almost everyone was up against the same enemy – poverty and insecurity. It's as if when there is a common threat, a danger in the face of which the individual feels powerless, the collective instinct asserts itself; self-preservation demands that people move closer together. We had a powerful example of this during the war, when,

37

in face of the air-raids, shortages and the threat of invasion, there developed a real spirit of comradeship among most sections of the people.

The communal – and anti-establishment – attitude of our people in the time I'm writing about was expressed in another way. Although Tredegar was built on abundant coal, such is the nature of capitalism that lack of it in their homes was a continuous problem for most families. Denied of work digging coal for the coalowners, many of the unemployed logically enough considered that there was nothing wrong in digging it up for themselves. Just above our house was a stretch of moorland called "The Patches," covered with grass-grown hillocks of what had once been small mine workings and where there was still outcrop coal fairly near the surface. The men used to get at this coal by digging "levels" or small shafts, to supply their own needs and to sell it cheaply to their neighbours at sixpence a bag.

But it was, of course, illegal. The coalowners owned all the mineral rights, and even though they didn't need the outcrop coal, they were determined to stop others having it. The local bobbies usually turned a blind eye to what was going on, but every so often the owners would instigate a police raid and ten or twenty of the men would be up before the magistrates and fined for "stealing coal." It was no deterrent, and immediately afterwards the alleged miscreants would be mining again. The openings to many of the workings were usually well camouflaged, but, more important, was the protection of the community. In addition to the "lookouts" always posted, it was recognised as an unwritten communal duty on the part of anyone who saw a policeman acting suspiciously to immediately pass the information on to the workers. The only time I can ever remember our coalhouse being full was when my brother, Clarence, was one of a Patches team. Eventually he had a nasty accident, because, of course, the work was extremely hazardous. The Patches have now been landscaped into an attractive park and it is difficult for a visitor to imagine what it was like in those days. It was the site of the 1990 Welsh National Eisteddfod.

In most towns at this time there was one grim reminder of your ultimate destination if you lost the fight against poverty – that most dehumanising of all institutions, the workhouse. Its usual position in the South Wales valleys meant that it couldn't be ignored, for it was usually in an elevated position overlooking the town – a forbidding, brooding, red-brick building more comparable to a prison than a final home for the elderly and infirm. Tredegar was no exception. Our workhouse was situated on a high point of the valley-side to the south of the town. Ending up in the workhouse was the spectre haunting so many people, particularly as they came near to old age. It was the last indignity, life's final cruel blow to respectability and pride. Fortunately, the extended family was more usual then than now, even in homes where it was a difficult struggle just to exist. In far too many cases, however, the problems of living became so great that the workhouse became the only answer, particularly for old people with no relatives to help support them. So they were compelled to end a hard life by surrendering all hopes and sacrificing all pride – a damning indictment of the system.

4. DIVERSIONS

As children, we spent most of our time playing games, quarrelling, getting bored, getting into mischief, annoying the adults, skiving out of running errands or doing household tasks and generally being a constant worry to our parents – indeed, acting as normal children the world over always have and probably always will act. There were no children's playgrounds with slides and swings: our playground was usually the "back lane" at the rear of the street, or sometimes the road at the front of the house. Some evenings we would play "Fox after Hounds," a game that covered a big area and many streets. Two or three of us would act as "foxes" and go off and hide while the others, the "hounds," counted up to one hundred. Then the chase would be on. If the pursuers completely lost track of the pursued they would yell "whistle or 'oller, the hounds cannot follow," upon which the "foxes" would let out a howl and the chase would be on again.

A favourite pastime was running behind lorries. They moved very much slower than today, and we would hang on to the back of one of them and see how far we could run before having to let go. The most satisfactory were the lorries slowly trundling to and from the brewery of "Buchan's Rhymney Beers" in the next town. The greatest hazard in our eyes was being seen by a teacher, for then it would mean a severe caning the next morning. Bogey-racing was also popular, with crude vehicles made from salvaged wood and pram wheels, and another indication of the different road conditions compared with today is that we used to race down a steep road, "Lambert's Hill," directly on to the main road. During the winter home-made sledges took the place of the bogeys.

In the same way that memory deludes us into thinking that all summers were warm and sunny, remembrance of winter is of wonderfully

39

deep, clean snow. True, Tredegar being so high up meant that we did have more than our fair share of snow and there was one memorable year when the snow drifted over the front door. We had to dig a tunnel out to the centre of the road and the telegraph poles in the street came down like ninepins. There was also the winter of the great snowball battle, when after school the children of Dukestown clashed with the Ashvale crowd. For hours the two sides, about fifty children in all, lambasted each other, and it only ended – indecisively – when darkness came and it became dangerous because some desperate participants started escalating the conflict by putting stones in the snowballs.

At school we played the traditional games of boys, such as marbles, jack-stones, fighting, wrestling and various ball-games. The girls played hop-scotch, skipping, tag and the various 'heeny, meeny, minee more' type of knock-out game; we all played with whips and tops. If one of us was fortunate enough to be given an unexpected penny, or more usually a halfpenny, we would all hive off to the nearby shop and spend a delectable few minutes there trying to make a collective decision on what to buy. During the dark evenings we would sometimes arm ourselves with sticks and vainly try hitting the bats that would be darting about among the trees in the grounds of the isolation hospital opposite our house. They nested in an old derelict stone building nearby which was supposed to be haunted.

My brothers and I liked to visit my Auntie Gwen and Uncle Charlie who lived at Dukestown, about three miles away. A major attraction was the large garden surrounding their house, in which there was fruit in abundance – particularly gooseberries – and plenty of bushes and undergrowth in which to play about. And there were always the large slices of rich home-made fruit cake generously handed out by Auntie Gwen. Their only child, Oenwen, was the closest we had to a sister, and she would join us in our games – being particularly welcome because she had a high swing that her father had made for her.

There were the usual diversions of a community such as ours; collecting jam-jars when the rag-and-bone man came round (for which he would put his grimy hand into a jar and give us a few unwrapped sticky sweets), following the hurdy-gurdy man when he visited the street with his barrel organ and pathetic little monkey, or exchanging repartee with "Jimmy the Oil" when he called every week with his horse and cart delivering paraffin for the lamps. Sometimes we would get a whiff of foreign parts when "Spanish Onion Men" travelled door-to-door, wearing black berets and striped shirts, and with long strings of onions hanging around their necks. I always thought they came from Spain, but they were probably Bretons and the term "Spanish" described the type of onion they were selling rather than the nationality of the sellers. Then, two or three times a year, a circus would come to town, usually either Lord John Sangers or Bostock and Wombals, and if we didn't have the money to get in to see the show – which was usually the case – we would wander around the Big Tent drawing in the strange, exotic smells of the animals and trying to get a glimpse of them.

Special festivals were celebrated much more than they are today. On Hallowe'en, 30th October, we would hollow out turnips, cut holes for eyes, nose and mouth, and walk around with a candle inside the head. We called the evening "ducking-apple night" because of the practice of "ducking" for apples floating in a bowl of water or we would try, with hands behind us, to take a bite off an apple hanging from a string. On New Year's Eve we were allowed to stay up to welcome the new year. At the stroke of midnight the hooters from the local pits and works would sound and this would be the signal for my mother to open all the outside doors "to let the New Year in." She would then go out the front and exchange greetings with the neighbours and passers-by. We children would be up early next morning and go up and down the street knocking on doors asking "please for a New Year's gift." The tradition was that we could only do this until noon, and then we would compare the booty of sweets and fruit we had collected.

As we got older, our horizons broadened. We would spend much of our time wandering around The Patches and playing in the local streams. We progressed from fishing for minnows with a bent pin in the Nant, and Cyril and I became expert at "tickling" perch, illegally, from the nearby "Mile Pond." Sometimes some of us would spend the whole day crawling among the heather picking whinberries to take to our mothers – if we were able successfully to complete the perilous journey home without being ambushed by older boys lying in wait to steal our hard-won pickings. But the whinberry tart, particularly as baked by my mother, made it all well worth while.

Cricket was our obsession and Jack Hobbs, Herbert Sutcliffe, Wally Hammond, Don Bradman, Harold Larwood, Len Hutton and the other contemporary giants of the game, our great heroes. We played wherever and whenever we could: in the back lane, sometimes across the main road (it was not very hazardous in those low-traffic days), or more fre-

41

quently on an improvised pitch of hard clay near the school, with piled stones as wickets. The star player among us was a gypsy boy, who we called "Jimmy the Van." To us he was a veritable Larwood, and on the hard, uneven pitch it was dangerous indeed to be in front of the wicket when Jimmy was the bowler. Being part of a travelling family, Jimmy would be with us for only a few weeks every summer, but the news that the gypsies had arrived would be the signal that our cricket season had commenced in real earnest. Arthur was also a keen cricketer, but being older he played in a real local team. On one sad occasion he was badly hit in the eye by the ball, and to add to his misery on the way home a suspicious dog gave him a nasty bite!

During the summer we would often voluntarily help some of the local farmers, doing odd jobs about the farm, cleaning out, feeding the animals or sometimes bringing the cows in for milking. At harvest time, many of the grown-ups would be bribed with a limitless supply of cider to lend a hand in the fields. On one occasion the cider was mistakenly put in a paraffin drum and was undrinkable – that is to all except our neighbour, Tom, who obviously thought it sacrilege to waste so much alcohol simply because it was adulterated. During the day he drank the lot. We children would make our doubtful contribution to bringing in the harvest, and I still find the smell of new-mown hay very evocative.

About once a week we would walk to town along the "Tram Road," a disused small-gauge railway track along which limestone from Trefil quarries used to be transported to Tredegar Ironworks. Being at the head of a valley, Tredegar is somewhat different from the typical South Wales mining town. The valley is much shallower, only deepening out at its southernmost end. It also has several distinctive features, such as the Town Clock, a cylindrical steel tower erected in memory of the Duke of Wellington. Nearby is the Workmen's Hall, which at that time housed the library, games rooms and a cinema-cum-meeting-hall – all run by a workmen's committee. Sadly, this has now changed. There was another cinema, the Olympia, and a small market. The two shops we liked looking around, especially if we had some money, were the Penny Bazaar, which sold a multitude of delightful things for only a penny or two, and Woolworth's, which proudly proclaimed below its name, "Nothing Over 6d in the Stores."

But our pride and joy was Bedwellty Park, an oasis of greens, woods and lily ponds, among which we loved to play "cowboys-and-indians." The park was a "gift" from Lord Tredegar, who was a direct descendant of the infamous pirate, Henry Morgan, the terror of the Caribbean in the seventeenth Century. He was bribed by the British government to turn against his fellow buccaneers and rewarded by being given a knighthood and made Governor of Jamaica. However, his descendants did not give up the family occupation. Instead of pillaging defenceless sailing ships they shifted their attention to extracting tribute from Britain's coal industry and the miners. Royalties had to be paid to the Tredegar family for every ton of coal carried by the railways over a small part of their land on the way to Newport docks. Much safer and probably more remunerative.

Our daily routine was sometimes enlivened by the excitement of a pigeon race. Everyone in the street was infected, even those who couldn't tell a pigeon from a sparrow. No derby crowd or motor racing fan could beat our enthusiasm. The suspense of waiting for the first bird home was almost unbearable. Urgent jobs had to wait undone and meals put on one side until our local feathered champions were safely back home.

Keeping and racing pigeons was, and indeed still is, a popular working-class pastime in many parts of Britain. This was certainly the case in Tredegar in the 1930's. Our street boasted several "lofts" in the back gardens, built with loving care and skill out of scrounged wooden boxes, old railway sleepers or pit props, and strips of felt. My eldest brother, Clarence, was one of the enthusiasts, and two doors down was another loft, one of the biggest. The men, with plenty of time on their hands, used to congregate in one of the lofts and, against the background chorus of the pigeons cooing, argue about the merits of their birds and anything else they had a mind to, over a fag or a cup of tea. Loving care was lavished on a favourite "blue" or "brown," the finer parts of its beautiful body inspected for flaws and the evenness of its outstretched wings admired. It's a serious criticism of our sociologists that up to now pigeon lofts have not been accorded the recognition they deserve as important social centres of the depression years alongside pubs, cafes, billiard halls, chapels and churches.

The more ambitious fanciers entered their best birds for the big races organised by the British Homing Pigeon Association. The great events were from San Sebastian, in Spain, and Thurso, in Scotland – "South or North Roads." Competing pigeons would be collected by the local Association and transported to the starting venue where they would be released at a pre-determined time. It was only possible to make a rough estimate as to when they would arrive home, for so much depended on weather conditions. Pigeons don't fly at night, but at first light in the

43

morning they were most optimistically expected. The anxious owners would be seen in their back gardens peering intently at the sky and hoping they would not have to be there again the following day. As the morning progressed, anxiety would increase. Had the birds lost their way, as occasionally happened – had they been shot down or caught by a hawk? Wives had strict instructions not to hang clothes on the lines for fear of distracting the returning birds, and we children were threatened with dire penalties if we made too much noise. By midday, the excitement would be great. The men would all be outside, chatting in groups; the wives would steal a minute from doing the household chores to pop out and check if anything was happening; and we would be clouted for shouting out false alarms whenever we saw a swallow in the distance.

Then would come the great moment. "There it is!" someone would shout, and all eyes would be turned sky-wards. Sure enough, what was unmistakably a pigeon would appear as if from nowhere, to be recognised immediately by its owner as the bird on which his hopes – and his money – were placed. One of the tests of a good racer is that it doesn't waste time hanging about outside the loft, but even so the pigeon would first warily land on the roof of the house. These were the crucial minutes when no one in the street dared cough as the distraught fancier tried to entice his bird home by rattling Indian corn in a metal dish, at the same time reassuring it by calling with his own special words of endearment which he hoped the pigeon would recognise. The bird would be tired and hungry, and it didn't usually need much coaxing before it would drop down, first on to the roof of the loft and then through the trap door that led to the interior. Immediately it would be unceremoniously seized and the rubber racing ring detached from its leg. This would be the start of the final act of the drama, as noisy and rumbustious as up to then it had been subdued. Pent-up emotions could now be released with a vengeance.

To understand this, it is necessary again to delve into the technicalities of pigeon racing. There being no winning post to pass, and with birds flying from different areas and different distances, it is all a question of time and handicaps. A rubber ring with an identifying number is attached to the leg of the bird. When the bird arrives home, this ring is detached and put into a sealed clock, which registers the time. I daresay nowadays all serious racing fanciers own their own clocks, but it wasn't so in poverty-ridden Tredegar at the time. The local Association would own a few clocks which would be located at strategic points throughout the area. Unfortunately, the nearest clock to us was about a mile away over rough ground, so there was the big problem of getting the ring to it as quickly as possible. The heavy responsibility for doing this fell on the fittest man in the street, a lodger called Jim who lived next door but one to us. Jim would have been waiting all day for his great moment. While the owner was enticing the bird down, he would be limbering up for a lightning start.

Then he would get on his mark, the ring would be handed to him, and off he would go, to the accompaniment of such a roar of encouragement as all Rome is reputed to have let forth when Horatius's bridge collapsed in front of the invading Tuscan army. After which, life in Ashvale would return to its normal unexciting run – until the next race.

I was always an onlooker, never a participant. But when we were about fifteen or sixteen, Cyril and I did build a loft in his garden and for a time owned a motley collection of pigeons. We did nothing with them but exacted a great deal of pleasure simply from looking after them.

Apart from Christmas, the great treat of the year was the family's day visit to the seaside – in our case, Barry Island. This was before the extended holiday and holiday pay, so it, too, had to be paid for in advance by weekly savings in a "club." We were luckier than some children. Although Tredegar was only twenty-five miles from the coast I knew many who were in their 'teens before they had their first sight of the sea. Then there were the rare charabanc outings, usually around the Wye Valley, with everybody happily singing "Show Me The Way To Go Home" and the wind blowing in our faces – charabancs were the precursors of the modern motor coaches, with soft collapsible tops that were usually folded down. Unless the trip was being organised by the Rechabites or some other temperance organisation there would be a stop at a pub, but only the men went in; the women and children would stay in the charabanc and have drinks brought out to them. Sometimes, on a warm Sunday, Mama would announce that we were all going on a picnic, and we would excitedly help pack the food we needed and walk to the picnic site, usually the side of a small stream running underneath a railway viaduct called the Nine Arches, in which we would paddle and sail home-made boats until, all too soon, we were marshalled for the walk home and bed.

But it was Christmas that we looked forward to most of all. As most children do, we entered into the preparations with excited anticipation, making decorations from tissue paper with flour paste and helping to

45

hang them up, watching Mama make the Christmas pudding and taking turns to stir the ingredients and watch the puddings bubbling away in the boiler, and being unaccustomedly and self-consciously well-behaved in case any naughtiness on our part would somehow delay the climax we were so looking forward to. Mama would make large fruit cakes in bread baking tins – four or five, for they would be expected to last well over the Christmas period. As they were too large to be baked in our oven, on Christmas Eve we would take them up the road to Jones the Bakehouse to be baked in his large oven. The neighbours would be doing the same, so there would be dozens of cakes in all, and each had to be identified with a distinguishing mark and a piece of paper stuck on with a stick, so that there would be no mistake when we collected them later in the day. If we had a duck or – rarely – a goose for Christmas dinner, this would be taken to the bakehouse on Christmas morning and would be collected, piping hot, in time for dinner. The cakes were not coated with icing, as is the custom now.

Of course, the thrilling finale of all this was Christmas morning when we received our presents. It seems remarkable now that however difficult were the times our parents were going through, even when no wage was coming in, they always contrived somehow to give us a good time, with a main present for each of us and our stockings comfortably filled. Meccano sets, a clockwork Hornby train and a steam engine were presents that I remember. The older boys had books – Arthur always *The Greyfriars Holiday Annual* and George *The Boys' Own Annual*. Dada would feign disappointment at finding his stocking stuffed with potatoes and onions, particularly as he had taken great care to leave out a mince pie and a glass of sherry for Father Christmas. Christmas was the only time when the luxury of a bottle of port or sherry was bought.

The mechanism for paying for the presents and the Christmas fare was the weekly savings club, with the Xmas Club starting as soon as the summer holiday was over. Many were the lengths my father would go in order to ensure that nothing was lacking to make it a really festive occasion. Sometimes his ingenuity was dubious, to say the least. There was, for instance, the year when he answered a number of adverts asking for agents to get orders for Christmas cards. He replied to all of them, and received back albums of sample cards that were supposed to be for display only. Instead, he carefully prised the cards out of the albums – and sold them. Despite threats, the card companies never got back their albums, or any money! A few days prior to another Christmas he acquired a small box of oranges which had been carelessly "mislaid" by a building employer he had visited looking for work. He saw no contradiction between this and the fact that he regarded himself, quite rightly, as a respectable, honest and highly moral person. Although he wouldn't have seen it as such, his was a working-class morality; he would have been revolted by the thought of taking anything from a fellow-worker, but bosses were fair game.

Some years we kept a couple of chickens, and once we even kept ducks, in the small back garden. The "duck pond" was an old boiler, about two feet across, filled with water on which the poor ducks could only sit one at a time. One Christmas my father decided he would kill one of the chickens himself. Unfortunately for him and the chicken, he had no idea how to do it. Not wanting us to witness him carry out the gruesome execution, he took the bird to the shed at the bottom of our garden . . . equipped with a pair of scissors. For some time strange noises came from the shed. Half an hour passed, and then he tottered out. Apart from losing all its neck feathers, the chicken was still very much alive, but Dada, with a face as white as a sheet, was on the point of collapse. It was decided to transfer the task to a neighbour who was an expert at dispatching poultry.

Poultry was as far as we went in livestock husbandry, but a neighbour a few doors away kept pigs, which half the street would help to feed with vegetable peelings and other scraps. Every so often, when the piglets were old enough, the quiet calm of our Sunday mornings would be rent with their agonised squeals as they had their snouts pierced with a red hot poker so that they could be ringed – an operation which, to our chagrin, we were never allowed to witness.

There was another Christmas when we tasted our first turkey. It was also the one Christmas dinner none of us enjoyed eating. The previous summer, Cyril and I had been wandering around the countryside near our homes, when I found this large, speckled egg provocatively resting on a low wall on its own. We took it home, and a neighbour pronounced it to be a turkey's egg and offered to put it under one of her broody hens. As it took longer to hatch than the chickens' eggs, it was then transferred to another neighbour's hen, and eventually we became the proud owners of a healthy turkey chick. We called it "Biddy" and tended it with loving care. Biddy became a family pet; it would come when called, and often wandered about the house, attacking anything that glistened. But, of course, keeping a turkey as a pet was a luxury a family such as ours just

47

couldn't afford, especially with Christmas approaching and the festivi-
ties to be paid for. My father had other plans for Biddy, and these came
to fruition on the Christmas dinner table. We children were horrified; we
felt like cannibals, and Emrys vowed he would never eat meat again – a
vow he kept to for several months. Of course, we used to go carol-
singing at Christmas time, but the ancient folk- practice of performing
the "Mummers Play" in people's houses had died out when I was a child,
although my elder brothers used to do it when they were children. They
would knock on someone's door and one would cry, "Open the door and
strike a light, for in this house there's going to be a fight!" They would
then rush in, pretending to fight until one would fall. The play would
continue until another of the group would appear crying "In comes I, old
Dr Brown, the finest doctor in the town!" He would treat the injured
combatant, who would jump to his feet, cured, and peace would be
restored all round – and a collection taken. People who claim to know
something about folk-lore say such plays go back into antiquity and are
supposed to represent earth's awakening from the death of winter.

5. 1926 – THE GENERAL STRIKE AND MINERS' LOCKOUT

The universe of a child is normally limited to the family, the school and
the immediate surroundings. There is at most only a hazy awareness that
there are mysterious outside forces operating which cause your dad and
so many other dads to be out of work or lie behind the perpetual struggle to make ends meet. I was no exception. Yet I suppose understanding
developed faster because of the area in which I lived and because my
first conscious experience of working class-struggle came when I was
only ten.

Tredegar was a typical South Wales mining town and most of the men
who had jobs worked at Ty Trist colliery, or travelled daily in the
"colliers' train" to pits down the valley. It had once been an important
iron town, part of the "Iron Belt" that stretched across the northern parts
of the Monmouthshire and Glamorgan valleys which brought enormous
riches to the great iron masters like Crawshaw-Bailey, the Guests and the
Baldwins, and upon which, along with coal, Britain's Industrial
Revolution was based. The masters drew great fortunes out of the industry, but the heritage left to the people who produced the wealth was
unemployment, hardship and poverty. Ironically, the very localities that
contributed most to England's industrial supremacy became the
"distressed areas" a century or so later.

Almost all that remained of the iron works when I was a boy were melancholy rusty skeletons slowly being earthed over, but often when the nights were overcast we could look up at the sky and be reminded of Tredegar's former glory, for the clouds would be afire with a brilliant, shimmering orange light, a magnificent artificial Aurora Borealis – the reflection of steel being tapped at the works still operating at Merthyr Tydfil to the west and Ebbw Vale to the east. Whiteheads, the one small remaining foundry in Tredegar, closed in the 'thirties.

Thus it was that when the post-war slump developed in the early 1920's, Tredegar was hit badly, for it was by then a one-industry town, and coal was that industry. And it was the industry that bore the brunt of the crisis. The men who owned the mines were the most ruthless, heartless group of employers in a capitalist class not worried overmuch by humane considerations, and their solution to all problems was a simple one: reduce wages, increase hours, lower safety standards. There thus began a decade of the most vicious attacks on the living standards of any one section of the working class since the early days of capitalism. Of course, the miners fought back. The Miners' Federation united the various miners' area unions and was acknowledged to be the most powerful section of the trade union movement. It also had a well-deserved record of solidarity and militancy, as well as capable and experienced leaders.

The confrontation came to a head in 1925. The post-war boom had been short-lived and on top of the general crisis developing in the capitalist world, British capitalism was being hit particularly hard by loss of markets, arising mainly from the growing economic challenge of the United States. Predictably, the working class was expected to shoulder the burden of capitalism's crisis. Tory Prime Minister, Stanley Baldwin, of the iron and steel family, gave the signal with a speech in which he said that "the wages of all workers must come down," a message enthusiastically taken up by the coalowners, who announced a reduction in miners' wages and an increase in working hours. But they were a bit premature. Not only did the miners' union make it clear that it would fight this onslaught to the bitter end, but other unions declared that they would back the miners. Baldwin had to eat his words; at the last moment he announced a subsidy to the coalowners in order to maintain wages as they were for a year. This day became known as "Red Friday."

There was natural jubilation, but Communists and others warned that confrontation was only postponed. Faced with the determined resistance of the trade union movement, the government and the coal-owners wanted

49

more time to prepare for the battle they knew was inevitable – and the date set was when the subsidy came to an end at the beginning of May, 1926. With the slogan "not a penny off the pay, not a minute on the day," the miners refused to work under the new terms the owners then tried to impose. Such was the feeling of solidarity among trade unionists that the right-wing dominated T.U.C. General Council was reluctantly forced to call a General Strike. The response was electrifying. Industry was brought to a standstill as workers poured out of the factories and workplaces in their millions. Fleet Street could not produce a single newspaper. In every locality "Councils of Action" were set up by local trade unionists which took over the running of the towns. The right-wing leaders of the T.U.C. were so badly frightened by these developments that they ignominiously called off the strike after only nine days, and despite the fact that the momentum of the strike was increasing. This betrayal meant that the miners had to fight alone, and for seven months they suffered enormous privation and sacrifices before they were literally starved back to work on the employers' terms.

Of course, I learned all this many years later. Being only ten at the time, I only had an inkling of what it was all about, but the bitterness of the conflict and the fact that the entire community in which I lived was involved could not but leave a lasting impression on my young mind. There was no question which side my school pals and I were on. We reflected the attitude of our parents: the coalowners were the blackest of villains and the miners' leader A. J. Cook was our great hero. How indignant we were when a story circulated that the coalowners had tried to get rid of him by sending him a loaded revolver and a poisoned cake – an early piece of imaginative elementary school propaganda!

What made it particularly thrilling was the fact that our house was right in the local front line. Tredegar's Council of Action (a young man called Aneurin Bevan was one of its leading members) took over complete control of the town from the word go, and one of its first measures was aimed at preventing coal being moved from the area. Our house was on the main road out of the town to the north, and opposite was a small park surrounding an isolation hospital. The miners chopped down one of the biggest trees and fixed it by pulleys and ropes to another tree, so that it could be easily lowered on to the road. Lookouts were posted about half a mile down the road and as soon as a car or van approached they would give a signal to the squad in charge of the tree. The tree would then be lowered, forcing the vehicle to stop. It would then be searched and if there was no contraband coal on board, the barrier would be raised and the driver could proceed. But if it carried coal, this would be unloaded and, if the driver was lucky, he could go on his way. It was highly organised right around the clock, and you can imagine the time we kids had in helping with the good work. It was like a Western come to life!

An interesting point I only learned about many years later, and which may contain a good political lesson, was that one of the most enthusiastic of the men in charge of the squad lowering the tree was that very rare anachronism at the time, a miner who was also a Tory. Clearly, at a time of sharp struggle in which he was involved, his class loyalty proved to be greater than his party political allegiance.

It was around this time that I attended my first public meeting – if attended is the right word for a kid sneaking in behind the backs of the grown-ups. A familiar figure in those days and in the years that followed, was the miners' 'crier,' a man with a particularly loud voice who would come around the streets ringing a bell and summoning union members employed at Ty Trist or some other pit to a meeting later in the day, usually in the Workmen's Hall. One day, being near the hall and curious to know what it was all about, some pals and I surreptitiously crept into a meeting; we soon crept out again, however, when we found it all so boring.

But during the seven months of the miners' lockout it was the jazz bands we kids revelled in. Having lots of time on their hands, the miners formed improvised street bands that would march around the town and continuously compete with each other. The basic instruments were the same – kazoos, mouth organs, tin whistles and usually a tea-chest covered with a cloth improvising as a drum. But what they lacked in instruments they made up for in costumes and make-up. Their imaginations ran riot: cannibals, clowns, tramps (rags were easily come by!), Red Indians; each area of the town had its own distinguishing band, and the competition was fierce. Every few weeks there were galas in which all participated and which included more serious turns. Sometimes, bands would come from Ebbw Vale, Rhymney, Blackwood, Brynmawr and other nearby towns and there would be a wonderful mixture of jazz bands playing popular music, other bands playing more serious stuff like "Poet and Peasant," Sousa marches, all combined with Welsh choral singing and individual performers. And it was all taken very seriously. Like the children of Hamelin, we would follow the band spellbound for miles, wearing out many a flimsy shoe in the process.

CHAPTER II

1931-1936: ADOLESCENCE

6. THE 1930's: LEAVING SCHOOL IN THE GREAT SLUMP

I have dealt in some detail with my life as a child for two reasons: first, because every age is unique, and it might be of some interest to my grandchildren and their generation to know what it was like to live and grow up in a fairly typical working-class family in a depressed South Wales community in the second decade of the twentieth century (my children have already heard it all ad nauseam!). And second, because "the child is father of the man," my roots, my early experiences and the environment in which I lived were the main influences on my future life, determining the political and philosophical outlook I adopted and the political road I took. There is, of course, nothing special about this; it applies to a great many other people.

What makes the description of life in the 1920's and 1930's particularly interesting is the staggering contrast between then and now. Developments in science and technology since the Second World War have been breathtaking, and the rate of progress increases all the time – exponentially, so we are told. It has been worked out that three-quarters of all the scientists who have ever lived are living today and that the great majority of all the scientific discoveries made since people first appeared on the earth have been made during the past forty five years. Computers have spread to all corners of life, electronics penetrate everywhere, we have lasers, nuclear energy and space travel. The possession of a car is no longer a sign of great affluence, a T.V. set is a necessity and a video player or even a computer quite commonplace. The great contrast between people's way of life, technically and socially, before and after the war is staggering; it is almost as though we are talking about two different planets. And this, despite the fact that the technical and scientific revolution has not been matched with a social revolution of the same magnitude, affecting the way society is organised. Poverty, homelessness, injustice and war remain, and new problems, like the threat to the environment, have intensified.

During school years my understanding of what politics was all about was nil or extremely rudimentary. To me, the experiences I've related about the 1926 miners' lockout were no more than interesting incidents, the significance of which I only dimly appreciated at the time. I knew that almost everyone in the community seemed to be "Labour" – one exception being the couple who lived two doors from us, who were "Tories." I only had an elementary idea what these creatures were supposed to be. He was an overman at the pit – "a company man," my father would say contemptuously. When the Duke and Duchess of York, the later King George VI and Queen Mary, once swept past on a tour of South Wales, Mrs Evans was the only person in the street to feebly wave a small paper Union Jack.

Political consciousness began to take form in my last years at school and was helped when I left with the realisation that there was no job to go to and that I was destined to fritter away my life in idleness. It happened to coincide with another shattering event, one that was to profoundly influence my future. One evening, as we sat down to "tea," which is what we called our early evening meal, from the crackling loudspeaker of our wireless set in the corner of the room came the announcement that the Prime Minister was to make an important statement. Silence, and then . . . "My friends: the wor-r-r-ld is in the midst of a grave financial crisis."

After almost sixty years, these words still ring in my ears: the rolling, sombre voice of Ramsey MacDonald. The first words of a Judas speech. An attempt to justify the unjustifiable: the betrayal of the people and the movement which two years before had so proudly put him in power. The speech he gave was the prologue to the most vicious offensive against working people this century. A few days later it shook me to see for the first time a grown man shed tears. Like thousands of others, he had placed a lifetime of hopes on the election of a Labour government and had worked and sacrificed so that it would come about. MacDonald was his Moses who was to lead the working class into the promised land. This Labour activist just could not believe that his great hero had feet of clay, and when the truth could no longer be denied . . . he simply broke down and wept. And he was not alone. The heaviest blow delivered by MacDonald and his cabal of traitors was to the faith and confidence of the labour movement.

53

In 1929 the second Labour Government had been elected. True, it was a minority government and depended on Liberal support, but after five years of Tory rule people were justified in expecting at least some radical differences in policy. Instead, apart from some mild reforms, the same platitudes were uttered, the same old arguments put forward, almost the same policies advanced, only by MacDonald instead of his Tory predecessor, Baldwin. After the General Strike, the right-wing Labour and trade union leaders had joined forces with the Tories and leading industrialists in advocating "class peace," best exemplified in the Mond-Turner talks (Sir Alfred Mond, later Lord Melchet, was a powerful capitalist tycoon; Ben Turner represented the T.U.C.).

MacDonald, Philip Snowden, Arthur Henderson and Co. carried forward this same policy of collaboration into government. It saw itself as "representing the nation," capitalists included, rather than the workers who had put it in power. In response to demands for socialist policies, socialism was either redefined into a meaningless platitude, or presented as a dream to be achieved in the distant future after the country was "on its feet again." The Empire was sacrosanct: "we must defend the jolly old Empire," Herbert Morrison was to say later. In India thirty leading trade unionists, including two British Communists, were arrested on a trumped-up charge of conspiracy (they were to spend four years in prison under the most appalling conditions, followed by further incarceration after they were found guilty at their trial at Meerut).

Objectively, the Labour Government served the interests of capitalism at a difficult period for the capitalists, and it quite unashamedly saw its role as making capitalism more profitable. And if this could only be done by workers having to make sacrifices and accept increased exploitation, well, so be it; the "good of the nation" demanded it.

When Labour was elected there were already signs that the brief period of capitalist stabilisation after the slump of the early 1920's was coming to an end. There was mounting pressure on the government from the banks and industrialists to reduce spending on the social services, and for "economy measures" to be taken, mainly by cutting wages and benefits. Succumbing to this pressure, MacDonald set up a Royal Commission on Unemployment (the May Commission) and a Committee on National Expenditure, packed with people totally unsympathetic to the working class and the labour movement. Predictably, both committees called for drastic economies, but the real aim of the reports was undoubtedly to frighten the country and destabilise the government.

The great crash in the United States produced panic throughout the capitalist world. America, which had been held up by the "new realists" of the day as the example of a new kind of capitalism which was emerging, proved to be a bankrupt colossus. And because of its dominant position in the world and the much greater international ramifications of capital, the crisis there quickly spread to the entire world capitalist system. So we had the worst slump in history. Mass unemployment soared in all capitalist countries. Stocks of goods that couldn't be sold were destroyed on a massive scale, including foodstuffs that the impoverished people badly needed, such as wheat, potatoes, butter and coffee. Putting the Luddites to shame, the governments of these countries demolished the very means of producing goods: factories, mills, shipyards and machines. The world seemed to have gone mad.

It was exactly what many socialists had been predicting. Here was a golden opportunity to hammer home the socialist message, and for the Labour Government (which still called itself socialist) to challenge the system that had manifestly failed and which was bringing about such anarchy and suffering. The people would have rallied behind a leadership determined to challenge capitalism and fight for an alternative way forward. Instead, the majority of the Labour leaders ignominiously caved in. They accepted the capitalist interpretation of events and adopted its remedies, which were to place the burden of the crisis on the shoulders of the working class. The proposals of the May Commission and the Committee on Public Expenditure were accepted. On some issues the Cabinet was divided, particularly the proposal to cut unemployment benefit – in total abandonment of Labour's election promises. Even on this, MacDonald had a small majority, but he used the split as a pretext for dismissing the Cabinet. The next day, after consultation with the King, he formed a "National Government" containing the leaders of the Tory and Liberal parties.

In the panic election that followed, with blood-curdling warnings of the danger of economic devastation, with the Tories, Liberals and MacDonaldites in alliance and with Labour split and totally discredited, the "National" Government was endorsed and the number of Labour MP's fell from two hundred and eight nine to only forty six (although in terms of votes it was only two million down on 1929). Such was the consequence of right-wing betrayal. "Every Duchess in Britain will want to kiss me tonight," MacDonald was reported as saying.

The offensive against the people had already begun. On the plea of national emergency the National Economy Act had been rushed through Parliament, giving dictatorial powers to the Government to rule by Orders in Council. A ten per cent cut in unemployment benefit and an increase in National Insurance contributions were imposed. Benefit was limited to twenty six weeks, following which claimants would be subjected to a rigid Household Means Test, to be administered by Public Assistance Committees. The pay of teachers, civil servants, the police and the armed forces was cut. There were big reductions in the amounts spent on health, education and other sections of the social services. Special Acts of Parliament were passed to enforce the destruction of shipyards and textile mills.

Resistance was immediate and widespread. Three days after the announcement that there would be one shilling a day reduction in the pay of all naval ratings below the rank of warrant officer, 12,000 sailors of the British Navy North Atlantic Fleet, stationed at Invergordon, mutinied and refused to obey the orders of their officers. A shilling a day doesn't seem a lot today, but then it represented twenty five per cent of the pay of general ratings. This action was a staggering blow for the government, which hastily retreated and revised the original decision. Feeling among the police also ran high. At a mass rally in the Albert Hall, 12,000 policeman passed a resolution protesting against the cuts in their pay (although, as the leader of the unemployed, Wal Hannington, ruefully remarked, their indignation at the way they were being treated had no effect on their conduct towards unemployed demonstrators).

The main resistance to the ruthless policies of the National Government came from the unemployed, particularly from the National Unemployed Workers Movement (N.U.W.M.) which organised demonstrations and marches throughout the country. In 1930, and particularly 1932, great National Hunger Marches were held, with contingents from all over Britain converging on London. More than anything else, these marches focused public attention on the attacks being made on the poorest section of the community and made the treatment of the unemployed a burning issue that the government could not ignore. This was especially important because in two years the number of unemployed had more than doubled, reaching almost three million by 1932.

7. POLITICAL AWARENESS

When, in August 1931, I listened with my family to MacDonald describing the measures he proposed taking for tackling the greatest slump in

Britain's history, I little appreciated what it presaged for me personally. I had stayed at school as long as was allowed after my fourteeth birthday. The future already seemed bleak enough, with no job to go to and no hope of one, and the economic crisis made it still more grim, even in a South Wales already ravaged by unemployment and poverty. Yet, with the benefit of hindsight I can now appreciate how fortunate I was to be launched into adult life at the beginning of one of the most momentous decades in modern history. The great struggles provoked by the attacks on the unemployed and on the living standards of the people, the rise and threat of fascism, the anti-war movement and the fact that I lived in an area which was a hotbed of socialist thought and political activity, combined to create a greenhouse environment which could not but force the pace of my political awareness.

My brother, George, had already introduced me to socialist ideas, although my main interest at this stage was in science. The few "science" lessons we had at school were nothing more than demonstrations by the teacher of apparently magical tricks. The entire stock of science equipment took up two shelves of a cupboard and consisted of a vacuum pump (which the school was very proud of and which we weren't allowed to touch), one bunsen burner, some test tubes, half a dozen small containers of the more common chemicals and a pickled snake in a large jar.

After I left school I attended some "night school" classes at which we were taught simple scientific facts relating to coal mining – the job it was assumed we would all end up in. So it was to the lending library I had to go to satisfy my thirst for scientific knowledge. The books borrowed were old books on "natural science," but I found them absorbing reading. With scrounged copper wire and magnets, nails and a dexterous use of my mother's scissors on old tins, I tried to reconstruct Faraday's famous experiments with electro-magnetism, make a Volta's Pile (the first battery) and electroscope, and copy the experiments of some of the other early physicists. I constructed my first wireless set and even started making a primitive Baird television receiver. At one time I raised a little pocket money by making simple toy electric motors and selling them to acquaintances. My attempt to raise some more cash by embarking into journalism failed: an article on how to make a hot-wire ammeter was rejected by a hobbies magazine.

The great physicist Michael Faraday was, and still is, one of my heroes because I could appreciate a little the obstacles he had to overcome as a young man. He was brilliant and passionately devoted to science, yet, because he had no academic qualifications, he found it difficult to break into the scientific establishment of the day. A blacksmith's son who left school at twelve with little formal education, he had a single-minded passion for acquiring scientific knowledge, which he had to satisfy the hard way, by self-study. At twenty two, he managed to get a job in the laboratory of Sir Humphrey Davy, but he had to use the back door, do menial tasks like scrubbing floors, and was never allowed to eat with the family!

He subsequently succeeded his master as the head of the Royal Institute and was showered with the highest honours. Probably remembering his own childhood, he inaugurated and took part in the famous Royal Institute Popular Lectures on science, directed towards youngsters and now televised every Christmas. His experiments concerning electricity and magnetism were the start of the electronics revolution, and his invention of the dynamo, the electric motor and the transformer laid the basis for the mighty electrical power industry we have today.

Our house was one of the first in Tredegar to have radio (or wireless as it was then called). My elder brothers, George and Clarence, were both interested in this new technical marvel, and graduated from a crystal set, with headphones that were passed around the family, to a two-valve receiver which filled an alcove and used the early "bright emitter" valves which lit up the room. They had to make the batteries themselves, and as matchsticks were essential components, I would be bribed to scour the gutters for used ones, for which I was paid a halfpenny a hundred. As time went on, the sets got more powerful and the horn speakers larger. This, of course, was in the days of the Marconi Company and Savoy Hill, before the B.B.C. as a public corporation had started. The room would often be full of neighbours come to experience for themselves the marvel of radio, and on the occasion of the opening by George V of the Wembley Exhibition in 1924 the audience not only filled the room, but crowded the passage right out to the front gate.

As I grew older, I used to listen a lot to the wireless, especially talks and plays, and, oddly enough, boxing – probably a reflection of the enthusiasm at the time arising from the fact that South Wales had a reputation for producing champions like Jimmy Wilde ("The Mighty Atom") and, later, Tommy Farr. Some of us would stay up all night listening, amidst the crackles, to live commentaries from America of the championship fights of Dempsey, Tunney, Carpentier, Carnera and the other great heavyweights of those years. Most exciting were the two clashes between Joe Louis and Max Schmelling because of what they represented – the blonde Aryan, Schmelling, feted by the Nazis as the personification of the "master race," and Joe Louis, the black worker who, against all odds, had fought his way through the racist barriers set up by the boxing control body and who had come to be a symbol for black Americans. We were bitterly disappointed when Schmelling won the first fight in 1936, but overjoyed when he was thoroughly trounced by Louis two years later.

Of course, the international rugby matches, particularly if Wales was one of the contestants, held the enthusiastic attention of most of the family and any neighbour who should drop in. As cricket was the sport we youngsters were most interested in, we naturally listened to the commentaries of the test matches between England and Australia and followed avidly the fortunes of our cricketing heroes. An enduring memory is listening every evening over supper to the music of the great dance bands of that era: Jack Payne, Henry Hall, Ambrose, Lew Stone, Roy Fox, etc., with vocalists like Al Bowley and Elsie Carlyle. It is strange how the songs of those days have survived and even experienced something of a revival, partly, no doubt, because the tunes and lyrics are so easily remembered, and helped, perhaps, by the popular T.V. musical plays of Dennis Potter.

I was a prolific reader of all kinds of books, and much to my father's annoyance used to do most of it during the quiet hours when the rest of the family were in bed, often staying up until after dawn. As well as grumbling at me wasting electricity and coal, he would say, "all this reading will damage your brain." Maybe he was right!

But there was another factor that was a great stimulant to thinking. A group of us who had gone through school together and whose interests were broadly the same kept up a close friendship afterwards. Our friendship was not only based on us having grown up together, but arose even more from a common intellectual urge to know and understand. Indeed, argument seemed the raison d'être of our existence. Being out of work, we would stroll interminably around the streets or the nearby hills, and sometimes sit for hours over a cup of tea in Berni's, one of the two Italian cafes, under the benevolent eye of the proprietor, who would occasionally join in the discussion. (A cafe run by an Italian emigré was a standard feature of every South Wales mining town). If it was too wet or too cold to walk about, or if Berni's was closed, we would sit in one of the billiard halls, sometimes playing, if we could afford it, or for free if a

59

table was empty and the proprietor was in a good mood.

We would discuss everything under the sun: politics, religion, atheism, astronomy, science, half-baked philosophy, poetry, books we had read, wireless programmes we had listened to, sex, sport (particularly Welsh rugby and cricket), popular music, films we had seen, the iniquities of the Government or the coalowners, the misdeeds of the local council, what the world was going to be like in ten, fifty, a hundred, a thousand years time, our plans for the future, and just plain gossip about our contemporaries. That we were socialists went without saying, although the basis for our beliefs was emotional, a gut class reaction to the situation we were in. In contrast with our immediate circumstances, we were sublime optimists and had supreme confidence in the correctness of our ideas to set the world aright, and assumed that this would be revealed in the not too distant future. Most of the time we were not bitter: we were angry, yes; we hated the system that produced the poverty and injustices that we saw around us and from which we suffered; we knew we were being hard done by; but there wasn't the corrosive, negative bitterness that eats away at one's spirit like a canker, undermines idealism, paralyses action and often leads to disillusionment and despair. Life was far too interesting. We thought we understood what was happening, and we were quite sure that the wrongs of society could and would be righted, and that it would not be long before reason would prevail. Naïve, perhaps, but it was a sustaining naïvety that supported us as we moved into a more realistic appreciation of the world in which we lived. This was the difference between us and the "angry young men," the "rebels without a cause" of post war years. Because they did not know what they were fighting for or where they were going, most of them came to terms with the established order of things, some even becoming Tory politicians and M.P.'s. Others withdrew into an apolitical wilderness.

Today, young people are hammered quite a lot and their anti-social conduct roundly condemned by their elders. Men and women of my generation are fond of saying "there wasn't the hooliganism and vandalism when we were their age." True, although we were not the lily-white goodies some try and make out. We were not averse to damaging property, minor though it might be, taking pot shots at telegraph pole insulators, smashing the odd lamplight, stealing swedes and turnips from fields or fruit from stalls, putting nails or pennies on railway lines to flatten them, breaking into empty buildings – all actions to which I must plead guilty. And if paint aerosols had been invented, I daresay plenty of walls would have been generously adorned with graffiti. But there's no gainsaying that there is a big difference, both in attitudes and scale. Condemnation alone, however, is not enough: we need to get to the root causes of the increase in anti-social behaviour among young people since before the war.

This is far too big a subject to deal with at length here, and all I can do is to venture a few admittedly arguable suggestions. The conscious feeling of being alienated from society is probably greater now than it was when I was a lad. True, we felt put down by the system and isolated from society as a whole, but it didn't have the same impact that it does today when T.V. and mass advertising emphasise the schisms between those who can afford to buy and those who cannot, and when macho-individualism and the cult of violence connected with it is projected on a massive scale as something to be emulated. Young people leaving school and the unemployed are generally not organised or associated with organised resistance to the establishment as expressed particularly through the trade union and labour movement. They are left to their own devices, with no aims and little hope, so they take their frustrations and resentments out on society. Whereas in the 1930's, the nation was largely divided into regions of the poor and regions of the not so poor, today the divisions and the contrasts are more evenly spread across the country. The importance of this is that those of us who lived in the depressed areas might have felt isolated from society in general, but we never felt alienated from our community. On the contrary, we felt part of it. And when the youth of today are being judged, let us not forget to put on the scales the positive contribution that many, many thousands are making in the peace movement, the struggle against apartheid, on environmental issues and in the war on want throughout the world.

We were a motley group of self-confident youngsters who sought to put the world of the 1930's aright. Cyril I have already mentioned. He was my closest school friend and our friendship endured until his death in 1992. We shared many common interests outside of politics and at one time, his house was a second home to me. His mother died when he was about fifteen and it was Ivy, his younger sister, who stepped into her shoes and had to give up a promising secondary school education to take on most of the heavy responsibility of managing the family of three boys, two girls, their father and uncle – a task she performed efficiently and with remarkable cheerfulness.

Gordon, studious and knowledgeable, and with a quirky sense of humour, lived in an isolated old house on the hillside overlooking Tredegar. His father, a miner, was an amateur astronomer who had built himself a large telescope in a sort of shed-observatory in the garden, which was sacrosanct but through which occasionally we were permitted to look at the moon. Gordon had nocturnal habits and sometimes, at around midnight, there would be a knock on our front door and invariably it would be he, wanting to go for a stroll and have a discussion.

Doug was the quietest member of our circle, in contrast to Monty, who was extremely argumentative and reputed to be a brilliant scholar. His parents belonged to the small group of Jewish shopkeepers in Tredegar. Many years later Monty became editor of *Challenge*, the national paper of the Young Communist League.

Glyn took everything very seriously and was a somewhat delicate lad – he died of T.B. a few years later. These were the hard core of our group, although there were others who came and went. It was not in any way a formal group, but simply a loose association of lads who had become friends and had the same interests.

I have often been asked what made me a socialist. The simple answer is that I was never conscious of being anything else. Hatred of the established order and the need to replace it with a better one was part of the very air we breathed. Later, George began imparting a rationale to this gut feeling. But it was during my last years at school and just afterwards, that I felt the need for more substantial explanations. A book by H. G. Wells, called *New Worlds For Old*, had a great influence on me. He showed the stupidity of people going without shoes while shoe factories were standing idle and leather workers were out of work – a simple point that had obvious relevance to our situation. I recall how indignant I was when I read in the *Daily Herald* that 30,000 oranges had been dumped in the sea off Liverpool to keep up the price, and that the owners had refused to sell them cheaply to the local unemployed. This at a time when for youngsters such as myself an orange would have been a luxury.

Fortunately, in Tredegar we had what was proudly claimed to be one of the finest working class political libraries in Britain, started and run by a workers' committee, all of whom were active socialists. So there was no shortage of books. My mates and I read many of the early socialist novels, such as Jack London's *The Iron Heel* and *The People of the Abyss*, Edward Bellamy's *Looking Backwards*, William Morris's *News From Nowhere*, Upton Sinclair's *The Jungle* and *Oil*, and we would discuss them at length. (An appalling act of cultural vandalism in recent years has been the selling off of South Wales' workers' libraries for peanut money, most of the books to be pulped).

As our political understanding grew, we felt the need to do something about it. We came to the conclusion that what was wanted was some form of organisation for young socialists; the questions were what and how. The existence of a dominant local Labour Party we took for granted and its leaders were household names. But we had little direct contact with them or the movement, with a few exceptions. In 1929, Aneurin Bevan had been elected M.P. for the Ebbw Vale constituency, which comprised the three towns of Tredegar, Ebbw Vale and Rhymney, and he was beginning to make a name for himself nationally. In the election of 1931 he had been returned unopposed and was regarded locally, not just as the leading figure in the local labour movement but as the undisputed leader of the entire community. His sister kept the sub-post office two doors away from us, and his brother, Bill, moved next door, and this neighbourly relationship with the Bevan family, plus the fact that my father was on the Trades and Labour Council, meant that we were fairly well informed about what was happening in Labour circles. My brother George was an active member of the Labour Party in Oxford, and Arthur had become secretary of the Stretford, Manchester, Labour League of Youth. When they came home at holiday time, they would discuss what they had been doing, and I began to think of joining the Labour Party myself.

Another close contact we had with the local movement was through Gwyn, whose father, Jack Evans – known as "Jackie Snip," because he had his arm cut off underground in a mining accident – was a Labour Councillor and Chairman of the Tredegar Unemployed Workers Organisation. He had been a member of the "Query Club," an organisation of socialists which included Aneurin Bevan and which, in the 1920's, had set itself the tasks of breaking the grip of the coalowners on the council and town affairs, winning a socialist majority on the council and getting a left M.P. elected for Ebbw Vale. It had been called the "Query Club" not only because it questioned established beliefs but out of a half-serious desire to mystify people, particularly its opponents. If anyone asked a member what the query-mark badge meant, the answer would be, "Aye, that's the question!" Gwyn's father convinced him that he should join the Labour Party.

However, other members of the group were suspicious of the restrictions party membership might impose on our freedom of thought and actions, and chary of being dominated by our elders. In the end we decided to set up an independent Youth Socialist Society, condescendingly agreeing that we would be prepared to work with, but not become part of, the Labour Party.

In fact, it never got past the first meeting. News of it had obviously been passed on, and one day a few of us were asked to meet Archie Lush, Bevan's agent, and a local Labour councillor, Oliver Jones. They suggested that we help set up a branch of the Socialist League in Tredegar and become a "Junior Section" of it. The Socialist League was a national left-wing organisation within the Labour Party which had just been started by Frank Wise, Sir Stafford Cripps and others with the avowed aim of combating right-wing policies and strengthening the socialist content of the party. In 1932 the majority of the Independent Labour Party (I.L.P) broke away from the Labour Party, ostensibly because of the imposition by the right-wing of a rigorous Parliamentary discipline, and many of those remaining joined other left-wingers in the party to form the Socialist League. Archie and Oliver proposed that we form a junior section of the League when it was established. We put this to the others, and it was agreed.

Thereafter, much of my life revolved around the League. A large room was rented in a former warehouse behind the Central Surgery in Church Street, accessed by means of a rickety iron staircase. We enthusiastically cleaned it up, decorated it, equipped it with donated furniture, including a table-tennis table, and pasted up some Soviet posters. In pride of place at the front was a large poster of Lenin speaking in front of a red flag, with the slogan "We Must Electrify, says Lenin." It meant that we now had premises which could serve as a centre and where we could meet whenever we wanted to.

It was our university. Each week there would be an organised discussion on a theme – not necessarily a political one. Of crucial importance, I was introduced to Marxism for the first time, through classes run by Oliver Jones. Oliver was a wise and remarkable man, a genuine working-class intellectual who combined theory with his work as a councillor and an activist. He had been a wagon-repairer, but had lost the sight of one eye, so during the 1930's he was unemployed. He, also, had been a member of the 'Query Club.' Over fifty years later, at the 1987 Labour Party Conference, Neil Kinnock, who hailed from Tredegar and had recently become the Leader of the party, publicly acknowledged the help he had received from Oliver. He confessed to the Conference that whenever he was confused on an issue it was to "a wise old socialist, Oliver Jones," he had always gone for advice. I could not help writing a letter to *The Guardian*, which was published, with a cartoon.

> Neil Kinnock described to the delegates of the Labour Party Conference how he visited an old socialist to clarify his ideas at a time when they were confused. This was commendable, and the advice he received from Oliver Jones was typically sound. It's a pity, however, that Neil was not more influenced by Oliver. For Oliver Jones was a committed Marxist who dedicated himself in the 1930's to introducing youngsters like myself to Marxism, giving classes twice a week and aiding us in our studies. He helped to collect in the Tredegar Workingmen's Library probably the finest collection of socialist, particularly Marxist literature in Britain. He was a miner who was also a brilliant intellectual and one of the group around Aneurin Bevan that led to Nye entering Parliament – the kind of person who achieved much, left an indelible mark, but is ignored by biographers.
>
> Oliver Jones died some years ago, but I cannot help wondering what he would make of Neil Kinnock's latest attempt at ideological gymnastics – using an honourable word "socialism" to describe a re-vamped kind of capitalism. I have a pretty good idea, however, for Oliver often warned about the "new definitions" of the word that regularly arise to confuse the movement. He believed that socialism unambiguously meant ownership of the means of production and distribution by the working class in the interests of the people, to be achieved through struggle. Old-fashioned? – maybe, but still correct – and not as archaic as much of the "new thinking," masquerading as socialism now again being dredged up and which is confusing so many Labour supporters.

We have seen, since this was written, the damage Kinnock's ideas have done to the Labour Party, taking it towards being a U.S.A. Democratic Party type of organisation, and weakening the traditional ties with the trade unions. Kinnock's gymnastics have taken him to a full acceptance of the basic ideas of capitalism, but like others before him seeks to disguise it by calling it "Ethical Socialism."

Oliver's abiding interest was philosophy, and for a year, twice a week, in addition to Marxism we studied the ideas of Plato, Hegel, Kant, Descartes, Berkeley and the other great classical philosophers. He was particularly interested in the German worker-philosopher, Joseph Deitzgen, who developed many of the ideas of Marxism independently of Marx and Engels – a fact that was generously acknowledged by Engels in Anti-Dühring. To me, these classes were a revelation, the opening up of a new world of knowledge. Oliver was always provocative and stimulating, and never allowed one to get away with a woolly or illogical statement. Yet, he always treated us as equals and never talked down to us. He insisted that we respect and try to understand ideas that we might not agree with, and sometimes he would act as "devil's advocate" or insist that we defend such ideas. It was largely his attitude to learning that instilled in me the belief I have always tried to abide by, that nothing should ever be taken for granted, that every new idea should be looked at objectively but critically, and that even when one is convinced, one must still try to guard against dogmatism, the ossification of one's own ideas which so often leads to intolerance.

Marxism seemed so much the answer to the questions we had been arguing about for so long that I was impatient to absorb it all as quickly as possible. So down to the library I went and got out the three volumes of Capital. Imagine my disappointment that night when I found it was all totally incomprehensible to me. Similarly with the Communist Manifesto. Later I came to realise what a remarkable pamphlet it is and how universal and rich are the concepts advanced by Marx and Engels. But this very fact, and the concentration of so many ideas in so few pages, made it difficult to grasp, particularly as many of the words used were strange to me. Fortunately, I had a good tutor in Oliver. It is a sad fact that so many youngsters today become inspired by taking part in a great class action, such as the miners' strike, thirst for understanding and plunge into Marxism at the deep end, only to get frustrated because there's no-one around to help them or no classes they can attend – or, indeed, often no books easily available.

In this last respect we were indeed fortunate in have a lending library that contained almost everything written on socialism and associated subjects. Indeed, it was our proud boast that it was the finest political library in Britain. I can remember reading Paul Lafargue's *The Right to be Lazy* and *The Evolution of Property*, Kautsky's *Class Struggle*, Labriola's *Historical Materialism* and many other books now no longer available, as well as the ones that it is still possible to get hold of. The writings of Marx and Engels were only obtainable in the American Kerr editions, which I subsequently learnt were bad translations, but which served us well, nevertheless. The reading room also had a wide range of socialist periodicals, and when each issue came out we would collect the previous issue; this is how I started collecting *Labour Monthly*, with Palme Dutt's wonderful Marxist interpretation of events which served as our main guide on the contemporary situation. The very first book I purchased, bought out of my first week's pay from a temporary job, was Anti-Dühring, and after that I collected a number of The Thinkers Library, one-shilling books published by the Rationalist Press Association.

Modern though our library was, would-be borrowers had to go through an elaborate procedure to get a book out. There was none of the browsing among the shelves that is normal today. In a small ante-room, usually crowded, one had to wait to get hold of one of the dog-eared catalogues of books which were constantly being perused. The reference number of the required volumes had to be noted, and then looked up on dividing panels around the room. Under each number was a slit, and if a book was available, a piece of card would be inserted in the slit. If you were lucky, you then had to take the number to the attendant at the counter, who would fetch the desired book. A few years later this system was changed to the more convenient system that is now used everywhere.

A few months after the formation of the Socialist League, Oliver passed on a message that Aneurin wanted to see Gwyn, Monty and myself. It was like being summoned before God, and it was with some trepidation that Gwyn and I (Monty wasn't available) went to Bevan's house at the top of Queens Street. He complimented us on what we were trying to do, but suggested that it would be useful if we formed a branch of the Labour League of Youth in Tredegar. At that time the League was having one of its many battles with the right-wing leadership of the party, but in any case he felt that it would be best if we were part of the mainstream of the socialist youth movement. We agreed to this, and soon afterwards reconstituted ourselves as a branch of the L.L.Y. We soon had over sixty members.

With evangelical fervour we tackled the job of spreading the word to

67

the rest of the people of Tredegar. Our main method was open-air street meetings. A venue would be decided, and the day before, equipped with large lumps of chalk, we would decorate the roads around with details of the meeting. When the time came, one of us would knock on the door of the nearest house and ask to borrow a chair that could be used as a platform. I cannot remember anyone ever refusing us. Then we would speak in turns, each in his own particular style. As a mark of defiance we would sometimes end the programme by holding a meeting outside the house of the colliery manager – with no audience, no noticeable impact, but wonderfully satisfying nevertheless! I have kept full notes of my speeches, and find re-reading them an interesting revelation, not surprisingly revealing a deal of naïvety, supreme confidence that the revolution was just around the corner, but also a satisfying political soundness in dealing with the issues of the day. There is one thing we always did, which has sadly gone out of fashion nowadays. It was to include in every speech the basic economic, political and moral arguments for socialism.

We in the L.L.Y. were not always as progressive as we liked to think we were. The minute book of the branch reveals that at the inaugural meeting it was decided to debar girls from being officers. True, it was soon rescinded and Ivy was elected our chairperson, later also becoming chairperson of the Socialist League. After a time I became Secretary of the L.L.Y.

In case it might be thought that the lives of my pals and myself was always deadly serious and just one round of political activity, let me hasten to put the record straight. We enjoyed the diversions of all healthy teenagers, although we did, perhaps, regard them as of secondary importance. All of us had our own special interests. For some time, as has already been mentioned, Cyril and I were greatly preoccupied with pigeons and built a loft in his back-garden. And there were the usual flirtations; although I was generally shy of girls, I did have several short-lived attachments – it would be an exaggeration to call them romances. In today's permissive society it's difficult for young people to imagine how strong were the social taboos on us and the pressure to maintain at least an outward show of what was regarded as respectability, and this was particularly so in areas like South Wales. People would be shocked at the public kissing and petting that goes on today. It had to be done surreptitiously, in the back seats at the cinema, in the front-room at home (if parents approved), at parties or on walks out of sight of houses. Hypocritical? – maybe. But any judgement must take into account the culture of the time. I must confess, though, that I cannot help envying the easy, unselfconscious atmosphere in sex relations enjoyed by the present generation – and wishing it had come sooner!

Although we liked to think of ourselves as sophisticated in all things, our understanding of sexual matters was most elementary. I can remember when someone – I think it was Edith, Nye Bevan's niece – managed to get hold of an illegal copy of Radcliffe Hall's *The Well of Loneliness*, which was banned because it dealt with a lesbian relationship. We were terribly disappointed and couldn't understand what the fuss was all about (having read it again since I'm not all that surprised, because its treatment of the subject is quite obscure and wouldn't make the eye of a born-again Christian blink today!). Oliver shook us at one of our meetings when he decided to devote the whole of the evening to a discussion of birth control.

In every town and village there was at least one dance hall and a billiard hall, and in Tredegar there were several. The Friday or Saturday "hop" was the accepted method of men and women intermingling socially. Pubs were, of course, the exclusive preserve of men, but even among men it was not customary, in Tredegar at least, for young teenagers to habitually frequent public houses, probably partly due to the pervading influence of nonconformism. If this were the case, the influence gradually diminished, because drunkenness among adults was not uncommon. In any case none of us were particularly interested, even if we had been able to afford visiting pubs. The little alcohol we imbibed was at parties held on special occasions at one another's houses. We had our own well-attended dance every Friday evening at the Socialist League room, but – to my great regret later, and especially that of my wife – I was content to disdainfully watch and never learned, despite strenuous appeals by Stan Beynon, the League's Secretary, who was an accomplished ballroom dancer. A few of us were interested in billiards and snooker, and played when we could afford it.

For a time I was hooked on a new sport that had come to Tredegar. Originating in Australia, speedway racing had been introduced into Britain, and one of the first tracks was in Tredegar. We called it "dirt-track racing" and I never missed a meeting. The smell of the fuel used by the Norton machines is still with me.

But all this was subsidiary to our political interests. It was around this that our lives mainly revolved.

In Michael Foot's excellent biography of Bevan, he refers to a quasi-

69

military organisation of young people, the Workers' Freedom Group, which Nye was supposed to have started in the early 1930's as the danger of fascism in Britain increased. Foot states that there was a Tredegar branch of the Group, which went on route marches and did physical training, and that Nye worked with young communists in setting it up. I am completely mystified by this story and highly sceptical of it, for it seems incredible in the extreme that such an organisation could have existed without any of us active young socialists being involved, particularly as we were working closely with Nye's nearest associates, including his agent and his sister Ariadne (who was a leading member of the local branch of the Socialist League). Nor were there at the time any young communists in Tredegar. I have checked with some of my contemporaries who stayed in Tredegar after I had left in 1936 and continued to be active young socialists. They, also, know nothing at all about it. Foot also says that the Query Club was still active in the 1930's, but in fact it ceased its activities in the late 1920's.

8. UNEMPLOYED STRUGGLES

There was no job to go to when I left school. My headmaster and my mother tried to persuade me to go to the "County School," as the local secondary school was called, but I had a deep-rooted antipathy to examinations and point-blank refused to sit the entrance exam. My father believed I would be better off trying to get a job, thinking, no doubt, of the problems of having to maintain me for a few more years. Unfortunately, there were no jobs around. It looked as if I was destined to follow in the footsteps of George and Arthur. George had left school before he was thirteen to go down the pit, but it had so impaired his health that he had to give it up. He had bought himself some volumes of *The Harmsworth Self Educator*, and with the help of these and the radio, became an accomplished linguist, being able to read and speak several European languages. After a period of unemployment, he was forced to leave home at eighteen and ended up working for the Pressed Steel Company at Oxford, part of the Morris motor works complex. Arthur had a job for a time delivering tea with an old horse-and-cart before he, also, was forced by the Labour Exchange to go to Manchester, working first at the Universal Stores and, later, in A.V. Roe's aircraft factory. In both cases they "graduated" via a Government Training Centre at Bristol – a path I was destined to follow a few years later.

Most of the time I was out of work, but there was the occasional job.

My first was delivering handbills to all the surrounding villages for a local clothes shop, for which I was paid the princely sum of 2s 6d a day (12p in today's money). After doing what I considered a fair day's work, I had no compunction about dumping the rest down disused mine shafts. Another job I had was making firelighters, frozen to the marrow in an unheated broken-down old shed in the middle of winter. There was no set wage; at the end of the week the owner, a dour Lancashireman, would dip his hand in his pocket and give me and my mate whatever he had a mind to – which was never very much. The longest periods of work were as a builder's labourer with the firms where my father was employed.

I get angry today when I hear people criticising the apparent aimlessness of youngsters, some in their twenties, who have never worked since leaving school. These people seem to have no conception of the frustration and bitterness long periods of unemployment engenders and which is one of the root causes of the passivity and anti-social behaviour of many young people.

Not surprising, one of the most important and hard-working organisations in Tredegar was the branch of the National Unemployed Workers' Movement, a movement that had been initiated by the Communist Party in 1921 and which in the 1930's had great mass support. The Tredegar branch was closely linked with the Unemployed Section of the South Wales Miners Federation. It had a room in a house opposite the Labour Exchange where the local officials, Jim Trevelen, Jack Evans, Fred Francis, Albert Tillings, and other voluntary experts – they were truly experts – were ever ready to answer queries and take up cases. Every Friday, for the entire day, they would sit at a table just outside the door of the Exchange where complaints from men and women who had just drawn their dole or been refused it, could be dealt with on the spot. The weekly voluntary contribution to the branch would also be made, and everyone gave without question, a point I often made in later years when the question of raising money for this or that cause came up: if people are to be won to help they must see clearly what it is they are giving to and approve the purpose of the appeal. Pitiful though the dole was, the unemployed willingly gave their pennies because they recognised the importance of the N.U.W.M., looked upon it as their organisation and saw clearly that the money they were giving was being used on their behalf. It is also worth recalling that all the local officials of the N.U.W.M were unpaid, even though the organisation took up most of their time.

71

Long dole queues were a feature of every town, in South Wales more than anywhere, and no better device could have been contrived to convey information, conduct propaganda and mobilise the unemployed – which is why the Metropolitan Police tried at one stage to use an 1839 Act to ban such activity near Labour Exchanges in London. I am convinced that the post-war switch to sending 'Giros' by post is aimed at making the mobilisation of the unemployed more difficult, as well as to hide from public view the true extent of unemployment.

The full, epic story of the unemployed struggles, the campaigns, especially the great hunger marches to London have been recorded by others, particularly by Wal Hannington, the outstanding leader of the N.U.W.M. It was a struggle of desperate men and women, forced to exist at well below the poverty line, watching their families starve and often broken up, by the operation of the Means Test. There was something indecent about the way supposedly learned people in high places vied with each other in producing statistics purporting to work out the minimum amount it was possible for a family to live on. There was the Board of Trade Standard, the Ministry of Health figures, the B.M.A. Standard and the "Rowntree Minimum." They were all totally unrealistic and assumed that housewives were expert nutritionists with facilities for shopping around to buy food at the cheapest places. Nor was anything ever allowed over the barest minimum needed for food clothes and rent. I have always thought that the very term "the cost of living," used so often today in relation to fixing workers' wages and benefits, reveals a lot about the attitude of the bosses. Anything above what it costs to exist is regarded as an unjustified luxury.

But in the 1930's, "the cost of subsistence" was a favourite term used, and, needless to say, those without jobs, and many with jobs, were compelled to exist well below this level. The full unemployment benefit for a man, his wife and three children after the ten per cent 1931 cuts was £1. 9s. 3d (146p) a week. The British Medical Association brought out a report which stated that the minimum amount needed to feed such a family was 21s. 10d (109p), leaving 7s. 5d (37p) for fuel, rent, clothing, etc. – and this assuming a clinical knowledge and ability to buy the exact nutritive foods at the lowest prices. And, of course, there were thousands of families trying to exist on less even than this meagre pittance.

On top of this was the hated Means Test. This was the brilliant but devilish system worked out by the Government to shift responsibility for maintaining the unemployed from the state to the family and the local community. After receiving unemployment benefit for twenty-six weeks a claimant would be transferred to "public assistance." The local Public Assistance Committee employed officers who would visit the house and make a detailed examination of the "means" of the claimant. They could, and often did, insist that any furniture or household articles over the bare necessities be sold before any benefit was paid. A piano, or a gramophone, for example, could be regarded as an unnecessary luxury. Moreover, not only was the means of the claimant taken into account, but that of the entire household – the family and often others living in the house. The privacy of the family was destroyed because the officers had the power to enter the house at any time, interrogate all members of the household and even question the neighbours.

The weekly standard set varied slightly from area to area because it was based on local Poor Law Relief, but the average allowed was 10s (50p) a head for those over sixteen years of age and 3s (15p) for children below sixteen. The claimant would only get enough public assistance to bring the total income coming into the house up to the standard, and if the income was above it, because, for example, the father or brother – or often a lodger – had a job, no benefit would be paid. So if someone was lucky enough to be in work, the family would be penalised for it! It was a recipe for breaking up families and it was commonplace for someone on the Means Test to leave home and find a place to live where the family income was too low to affect his or her benefit; although, even here, Means Test Officers would spy on them and question neighbours to make sure it wasn't a ruse and that they weren't just sleeping somewhere else but still living at home. The system was humiliating, especially for those families who had all their lives regarded "going on the poor law" as the ultimate degradation.

It was no wonder that the movement of the unemployed grew in strength. "Work or Full Maintenance" was the slogan that united them; the N.U.W.M .the body that led them. To their shame, the right-wing dominated Labour Party and T.U.C. did nothing to build this movement: on the contrary, they condemned as "Communist conspiracies" the N.U.W.M. and the demonstrations taking place up and down the country, and urged the unemployed to have nothing to do with them. They were content simply to issue statements criticising the government, hold occasional meetings, and make speeches in Parliament. This refusal by most of the official movement to join with the unemployed in a united struggle was one of the tragic weaknesses of the movement, although there were honourable exceptions, notably the South Wales Miners Federation.

Throughout 1931 and 1932, as the registered unemployed rose to almost three million, the movement grew, with marches and demonstrations in most towns, usually to the local Public Assistance Offices from which the hated Means Test was administered. Thousands demonstrated outside the Trades Union Congress, but Congress, to its shame, refused to receive a deputation (although there was a sizeable minority of delegates in favour of doing so). So the unemployed took to their feet. Under the leadership of the N.U.W.M. they marched from every corner of Britain to the country's capital. There had been hunger marches before, but nothing like this one. 2,500 marched all the way to London, organised in eighteen contingents, including a special Women's Contingent. Ten times that number would cheerfully have joined in had there not been the need to keep the march to manageable proportions. In every town they passed through the marchers made a great impact, and not only on workers. Sections of the middle-class and particularly students were drawn in. It wasn't only the anti-fascist struggle of those years that radicalised students, as is generally believed. Students everywhere did what they could to help. James Klugman, who later became a leading figure in the Communist Party, was at that time one of the group of Cambridge Marxist undergraduates that later became famous. He has described the traumatic effect meeting and fraternising with unemployment marchers had on them all:

> We, an extraordinarily erudite and arrogant generation of Cambridge students thought that we were the best intellectuals, and that the intellectuals were the wisest of the community, we were still lost at the beginning of the thirties, often with immense knowledge . . . but no purpose. And then we suddenly met up with people who knew where they were going, knew what they were doing, who could discuss a problem in a clearer, more coherent, more logical way than the most advanced 'double first' amongst us. And to do so with a resilient humanity absent from the typical intellectual of the time.

On Thursday, 27th October 1932, at 2.30 in the afternoon, the Hunger Marchers proudly entered Hyde Park, to be greeted by a huge crowd of

100,000, one of the biggest political gatherings ever seen in London. Three days later another demonstration was held in Trafalgar Square, and on 1st November more than 100,000 marched on Parliament to present a petition with a million signatures – to be met by a massive force of 3,700 foot and mounted police, who indiscriminately attacked the demonstrators.

Great days, but days that put the fear of God up the authorities. The revolution had arrived, according to some of the Tories and their scribes. Predictably, the *Daily Mail* led the field with a scaremongering article alleging that "Russian Gold" was behind it all. The Government was forced to hold a three-day debate in the course of which it confirmed its intention to bring in a new Unemployment Bill.

The new Bill was to be based on the report of a Royal Commission that was soon to be published. It came out in November and the majority proposals gave fresh stimulus to the movement, incredibly calling for further cuts in benefits and a strengthening of the Means Test. Because of the intensity of the campaign, the Government was not only forced to delay introducing the Bill, but when it did it left out some of the worst features of the Royal Commission Report, including the cut in unemployment benefit. This was a partial victory, but a greater one was ahead. Part One of the 1934 Unemployment Insurance Act, which dealt with benefits, was to come into operation in July 1934, but Part Two was not to come into force until January 1935. On that date, every person who had exhausted their statutory unemployment benefit period, usually twenty-six weeks, was to be transferred to a new body, the Unemployment Assistance Board (U.A.B) which would have the job of setting and administering the level of Means Test payments.

For seven months before the passing of the Bill, Labour M.P.'s conducted a fierce parliamentary battle against it, led by Aneurin Bevan. It brought out all the oratorical powers, and the invective, that he justly became famous for. I remember hearing him speak to a packed Workmen's Hall in Tredegar when he brilliantly and without a single note dissected the Bill clause by clause, bringing his audience to their feet in their hatred for it and those responsible.

The feeling against it built up and reached boiling point when, the week before Christmas – superb timing – the new U.A.B. scales were announced. Almost everyone over eighteen (which just included me) was to have their benefit reduced. The South Wales Miners' Federation immediately called a conference to discuss action and the N.U.W.M.

called for nation-wide protests on 7th January, when the new regulations were to start.

But it was only on that Friday, when we actually drew our dole, that the full impact of the cuts was brought home to us. I went to the 'dole office', as usual, to find a noisy crowd around the N.U.W.M. table, some arguing that a mistake must have been made in their money, others demanding that something drastic be done – anything short of burning down the Labour Exchange there on the spot, and many wouldn't have been averse to doing just that! Meetings of protest took place throughout the day. The demand was made that the Town Council or the local Trades and Labour Council call an immediate town meeting of protest. An emergency meeting of the Trades and Labour Council was called and it was decided to set up a Council of Action, the kind of organisation that had sprung into being during the 1926 General Strike. Spontaneously, in other towns throughout South Wales, the same thing was happening.

It was a remarkable experience. At our first meeting the atmosphere was electric, and we could see that virtually every organisation in Tredegar had sent representatives; the miners' lodges and other trade unions, the Town Council, most political and non-political organisations, even the Chamber of Trade, the Boy Scouts and many of the Chapels (but not the Church of England!) – a measure of how deeply it affected the entire population. I was one of the three delegates from the Labour League of Youth, and another of our delegates, Monty Cohen, was elected secretary, partly because of his reputation as a scholar.

We met every day, and what meetings they were! They went on for hours, with continuous discussion and argument, often heated, about developing short and long-term resistance to the Act. It was a real forum of debate, but with action the objective all the time. It gave me a glimpse of what the soviets during the Russian Revolution must have been like. The first thing we decided to do was to hold a united march and demonstration on the Sunday afternoon. A measure of the strength of feeling was that many of the Chapels even agreed to cancel their services so that their congregations could attend – truly remarkable, considering the reputation Welsh chapels had for narrow-mindedness!

It was without doubt the biggest demonstration ever held in that part of South Wales. About 50,000 took part – about half the population of the area covered. The marchers came from the towns at the head of three valleys, the main centres of the Ebbw Vale Constituency. After marching six miles the Rhymney contingent joined the men and women from

Tredegar at Sirhowy Bridge; from there we marched up Sirhowy Hill to a place on the high moorland between Tredegar and Ebbw Vale called Waun Pound. It was here, one hundred years before, that the Chartists used to meet, many of them having walked thirty or forty miles. (The memorial to Aneurin Bevan is erected on the spot.) As we neared Waun Pound we could see thousands more marchers approaching us from Ebbw Vale and Beaufort. The main speaker was, of course, Bevan, but there were other national political and trade union speakers whose names I cannot now remember, although I believe Jenny Lee was one. A mighty roar affirmed a pledge from all present to do everything possible to destroy the hated Act.

The campaign grew in intensity. By the middle of January there was hardly a town throughout Britain that wasn't seeing daily demonstrations of some sort, but naturally it was the areas of high unemployment that led the way. 60,000 marched down the Rhondda Valley to Pontypridd and another 40,000 did the same in Merthyr Vale. 1,600 delegates attended the All-South-Wales Conference called by the S.W.M.F. at which the anthracite miners of West Wales announced that they had a mandate to call a strike. Other lodges were taking similar action. In Scotland a Hunger March of 3,000 converged on Glasgow.

While the Government had expected some protest, they were not prepared for action on this scale, and in a debate forced on them in the House of Commons they announced concessions: an easing of Means Test regulations and an increase in some U.A.B. rates. If they thought this would dampen down the campaign, they were soon taught otherwise. Despite a ban on marches, 10,000 marched in North Shields, while on Tyneside 30,000 demonstrated until late into the night. The first weekend of February saw 300,000 on the march in South Wales (*Manchester Guardian* estimate). The following day, with Ethel Horner, the wife of miners' leader Arthur Horner, among them, over a thousand women, supported by 3,000 men, stormed the U.A.B. offices in Merthyr Tydfil, smashed all the windows and doors, and marooned the officials in their rooms. Up and down the country the mood was getting more determined as desperate men and women felt they had nothing to lose by fighting. Clashes with the police were common and in many places there were near-riots.

At last, a frightened Government was forced to give way. On 5th February, Mr Oliver Stanley, the Minister of Labour, announced a "Standstill Order" withdrawing the scales and regulations under Part

Two of the Act, restoring the old scales and even agreeing to repay all cuts made since 7th January.

It was a great and famous victory, yet, now having the bit between their teeth, the unemployed were still not satisfied. Stanley had said that it would take a fortnight before the Order could be put into effect – and the unemployed wanted action at once. The very next day, 40,000 marched on the City Hall in Sheffield demanding immediate payments by the P.A.C., and severe fighting took place with the police. The Government was again forced to capitulate, and in many towns P.A.C. Offices opened all day Sunday to pay out the benefits due.

It was a wonderful demonstration of the power of extra-parliamentary action. The Government had been totally humiliated, and at a victory meeting in Tredegar afterwards, Nye declared, "Your actions on the streets have achieved what seven months of our debating in the House of Commons failed to do."

But there was no room for complacency. The Unemployment Act was still on the statute book and there were plenty of indications that the Government was only waiting for the struggle to die down to re-introduce the measures they had been forced to suspend. Moreover, there were many other sections of the Act that were totally unacceptable. And the Means Test remained. So, throughout 1935 the struggle continued.

9. THE FIGHT GOES ON

At this time I was a member of the Labour Party, Secretary of the Tredegar Branch of the Labour League of Youth and a member of the South Wales Area Council of the Socialist League. Probably because of the left-wing character of the local Labour Party, no Communist Party organisation had developed in Tredegar, even though many of the activists in the N.U.W.M. regarded themselves as closer to the C.P. than to the Labour Party. I had heard the occasional Communist public speaker and regularly read the *Daily Worker* and *Labour Monthly* in the reading room of the library. Possibly because of our not having any direct experience of the Communist Party, there was an element of romanticism attached to it arising from the association in our minds with Lenin and the Russian Revolution, and the fact that its outlook was based on Marxism, the philosophy we had come to accept as the key to the present and the future. We were continuously getting reports of the activities of the Communist Party and the N.U.W.M. in the eastern valleys of Monmouthshire – Nantyglo, Blaina, Abertillery and Pontypool – where the C.P. was strong and had a number of local and county councillors.

Gwyn and I decided to investigate. So it was that one morning in late February 1935 we walked the five miles over the valley tops to Nantyglo, a small mining town near the head of a narrow valley. We had heard that the Communist Party had built its own hall, so it was to there that we went. "Unity Hall" was a wood and corrugated-iron building which also served as the headquarters of the local branch of the N.U.W.M., and we made ourselves known to the officials on duty there. Soon we were introduced to Phil Abraham, the Communist County Councillor for Nantyglo, who seemed impressed by the fact that we were young Labour Party members from Tredegar and had come over to make contact. He invited us to attend the CP branch committee meeting that was being held that afternoon. Looking back, I suppose he saw us as promising youngsters who could be brought nearer to the C.P. politically.

The committee discussed a proposal for an N.U.W.M. march from Nantyglo and the adjoining towns of Blaina and Abertillery to the Public Assistance Committee Offices, situated in Blaina. It was decided to put the proposition to a public meeting, so a comrade was forthwith dispatched with a megaphone, to do the round of the streets and inform everyone that a meeting would be held in Unity Hall that evening. Of course, we stayed for the meeting and were glad we did so. Despite the short notice – literally only hours – Unity Hall was packed and the entire town seemed to be there – men, women and children.

Above the platform was a banner, "Workers of the World, Unite!" while at the back of the stage was a huge painting of Lenin. "How sectarian!" I can hear some saying today. They should remember that we are talking about different historical periods. The class divisions in areas such as South Wales were then stark and obvious. It was a simple issue of 'them' or 'us,' bosses or workers, capitalism or socialism, and any question of alliances with non-committed sections of society, or of there being a long transitory phase before socialism, would not have been easily comprehensible.

Moreover, world capitalism was in a deep crisis and its collapse didn't seem at all improbable, and if this happened the question of socialism would come on the agenda. Socialism was equated in the minds of most politically conscious workers with the Soviet Union. There, for the first time, was a country run by workers, a living proof that the hated capitalist system which was responsible for our miseries, could indeed be ended. So there was a natural affinity with the Soviet people, felt, not only by Communists, but by many thousands of others as well.

It would obviously be wrong to transpose the situation existing in those days, and the policies arising from it, to today, but the converse is just as false – transposing the experiences and knowledge of post-war decades to the twenties and thirties. Yet this is precisely what some present-day Communist, as well as non-Communist, historians seem to do in their simplistic analyses and lack of comprehension as to why so many Communists supported the so-called "Class Against Class" line of the Party in the late 1920's.

That the policy was mistaken, there can be no doubt. It was sectarian, it falsely believed that socialism was on the agenda, it condemned the Labour Party as being "an auxiliary apparatus of the bourgeoisie," ended the campaign for affiliation and urged trade unionists not to pay the political levy to the Labour Party and not to vote Labour. As a result it alienated thousands of Labour supporters. At the time I am writing about, the policy had just changed, yet many of the attitudes still prevailed.

How could this be, if, as these critics argue, the line was "imposed on an unenthusiastic membership" and "produced demoralisation"? I suggest two reasons. Firstly, in many areas the policy was never applied to the letter. There is plenty of evidence of continued good working relations with local Labour Party organisations and individuals throughout the period. Secondly, the policy did have some basis in reality, at least in the worst-hit areas of places like South Wales, where the struggle was sharp and clearly defined, and really was class against class. It might not have been general, but I can only say that, far from there being demoralisation, I have never experienced such optimism and mass enthusiasm as that which then existed in the localities where I was active. The decline in party membership in the "Class Against Class" period is used as evidence of the policy's unpopularity, but a factor that should be taken into account is the particularly stringent attitude to the admission of members in those years. It was not easy to join. I am sure that if the "mass party" concept that came later had been operated in Blaina and Nantyglo, many of the people who voted Communist and supported the Communist Party would have joined. As it was, I knew of at least one active member of the N.U.W.M. in the area who was refused admission because it was considered that he was "not yet ready" for membership!

The meeting decided to go ahead with the march and the date fixed was 21st March. Publicity for it was, as usual, cheap and effective, consisting in the main of open-air meetings outside the Labour Exchanges and at street corners, and chalking or whitewashing the roads with the details. Some days we went across to give a hand. In an unprecedented move, the police declared in advance that any march would be "provocative," and on the day of the demonstration it soon became obvious that they intended using force against it, for throughout the morning busloads of police began to arrive from Birmingham and Bristol. The local force obviously couldn't be trusted.

According to police estimates, well over 5,000 people turned up at Nantyglo alone, to march to the P.A.C. Offices, where they were to meet the other contingents. The N.U.W.M. had requested in advance that the Committee members receive a deputation, and afterwards there was to be a meeting in Blaina Park. However, as we drew near to the rendezvous we found our way barred by a large contingent of police blocking the road. Monmouthshire assistant police chief, Superintendent Baker, was in charge and ordered the N.U.W.M. officials leading the march to call it off, but before they could explain this to the marchers, Baker shouted "Let the buggers have it!" and the police baton-charged the marchers. In the middle of the fighting, 2,000 more marchers appeared from the other direction, from Blaina and Abertillery, and when they saw what was happening to their Nantyglo comrades, they rushed to help them.

The police were sandwiched between the two contingents, immediately panicked, and made a bee-line for a nearby inn, where they locked themselves in. Unfortunately, one couldn't make it. He was shut outside and stood hammering on the door screaming for his colleagues to rescue him, which they were too frightened to do. When the marchers got hold of the unfortunate cop, he really thought he was going to be torn limb from limb, but, probably to his intense relief despite acute embarrassment, they only debagged him. One of my indelible memories is of the women lined up at the side of the road and on the embankment pelting the police with stones. Afterwards, the road was carpeted with the makeshift ammunition they had used.

Warrants were immediately issued for the arrest of Phil Abraham and seventeen other N.U.W.M. members for "Causing a great riot to the terror and alarm of His Majesty's subjects" – ironic, as all of His Majesty's subjects in the locality were taking part in the demonstration, and the only people who showed any terror or alarm were the police arrayed against them! The warrants covered most of the leaders of the movement, and there was a justifiable suspicion that they had been drawn up in advance.

Phil immediately disappeared, materialising every day in different parts of South Wales at meetings called to mobilise support for himself and his comrades, with the police trying hard to discover where he was going to pop up next. In Nantyglo the atmosphere was tense, and even though it had been noticed that none of the local bobbies had drawn their batons when ordered to do so, not one of them was able to appear in public for fear of being stoned by the women. Not long afterwards I was at a packed and emotional meeting in Unity Hall, which was surrounded by police, when, to rapturous applause, Phil dramatically appeared from the back of the stage, and was able to make a short rousing speech before being arrested by the police lying in wait. It was at this meeting that I first heard Idris Cox, Welsh Secretary of the Communist Party, who I came to know quite well in later years. During this period I also first met Communist M.P., William Gallacher, and miners' leader, Arthur Horner.

The trial took place at Monmouth Assizes, with the two most eminent progressive barristers of the time, D. N. Pritt and Dudley Collard, appearing for the defence. The police made great use of the fact that many of the accused were members of the Communist Party and that "revolutionary literature" had been distributed, but Pritt and Collard tore to shreds the police evidence, proving that the whole exercise had been a plot to destroy or weaken the N.U.W.M. in an area where the organisations had mass support. Predictably, there was a "guilty" verdict, but the exposure of the police was so effective that the longest sentence was eleven months, for Phil Abraham. Unfortunately, the police partially achieved their main objective, for the movement in the locality was seriously weakened by the removal of its leadership, and never fully recovered, despite the efforts of Will Paynter (then one of the N.U.M.W. leaders in the Rhymney Valley) who was sent there to help. In later years Will was to become General Secretary of the National Union of Miners.

Unemployment nationally was now beginning to fall, although it remained well above the average in South Wales and the other Depressed Areas (now renamed Special Areas). So in 1936 the N.U.W.M. decided to organise another Hunger March, which was, in fact, to be the last. In some ways it turned out to be the best, particularly in one important respect. For the first time, support for it was not banned by the Labour and trade union leadership, although they still urged non-cooperation. The main reason for this change was undoubtedly the success of the previous marches, but another factor was the changed tactics of the Communist Party which, faced with the threat of fascism, had moved away from its previously somewhat sectarian attitude towards Labour and initiated the movement for a broad united front. The result was that the march received widespread support from sections of the official movement. Five hundred and ninety five delegates from trades councils and local Labour Parties in South Wales decided unanimously to sponsor the march, as did many other trades councils in England and Scotland, and constituency Labour parties, such as Broxtowe in Nottinghamshire.

The 1,500 marchers were more carefully chosen for their fitness than previously, and were generally better equipped. For example, the Tredegar contingent, my brother George among them, had to pass a health test and was well kitted out by the local Co-op. The slogan of the march was "Against the U.A.B., Down with Means Test." As with previous marches, the reception they received en route to London varied a great deal, but in most places they were welcomed and well cared for by all manner of bodies, official and unofficial. Before they arrived in London, the Prime Minister made an unprecedented intervention – going on radio to declare that the government would not receive any deputation and advising the marchers to go home.

According to the *Daily Herald*, 250,000 people welcomed them at Hyde Park, despite the bad weather, and the speakers on the six platforms included Clem Attlee, later to become Labour Prime Minister, Aneurin Bevan and other Labour M.P.s, as well as leading Communists and representatives of the London Trades Council. The overwhelming popular support the marchers received forced the government to do an about-turn and receive a deputation, but with the face-saver that they were receiving "representatives of constituencies." The deputation was led by Aneurin Bevan and the Communist M.P., William Gallacher, and it was able to win some small concessions in benefits.

The week previously, another Hunger March had arrived in London. It was the Jarrow Crusade. If one believes today's media and modern historians, including those claiming to be progressive, this was the only march that took place in the 1930's. It has come to symbolise the unemployed struggles of the decade. In fact, this is quite fictitious. It was neither the first, nor the largest, nor the most important of the Hunger Marches of those years. Why, then, has history been so blatantly re-written and distorted? First of all, it was more "respectable" than the others in that it

83

was organised by the Jarrow Town Council, with the support of both Labour and Tory Parties in the city. The organisers stressed that it was non-political, and as such was separate from the national movement of the unemployed. Secondly, the aim of the Crusade was the narrow one of drawing attention to the plight of Jarrow, rather than demanding jobs and better conditions for all Britain's unemployed.

Nevertheless, the attitude of the N.U.W.M. to the Jarrow Crusade was a positive and helpful one. With seventy per cent of the working population of the town being out of work, there certainly was a particularly acute situation. Despite the fact that the organisers distanced themselves from the N.U.W.M., the town's charismatic and outstanding Labour M.P., Ellen Wilkinson, who led the march all the way to London, asked Wal Hannington for advice, which was, of course, freely given, and the N.U.W.M. did all it could to win support for the Crusade.

Incredibly, the Labour Party nationally disapproved of the march, and in some localities this was expressed practically. Ellen Wilkinson has recounted how the Chesterfield Trades Council refused to host the marchers, who had to be cared for by the local Tories! Local trade unionists have since more than expunged this blot on their good name.

This is only a brief account of the unemployed movement and much is left out. There were, for instance, the imaginative methods, in addition to the marches, adopted by the N.U.W.M. to draw attention to the plight of the unemployed. On one occasion one hundred of its members occupied the dining room of London's posh Ritz Hotel and wouldn't leave until they had been given a meal. At another time, workless men packed the lobby of the House of Commons. On one New Year's Eve a thirty by twenty foot banner was strung from the Monument, near the Stock Exchange, reading "FOR A HAPPY NEW YEAR THE UNEMPLOYED MUST NOT STARVE." The next day there was a mock funeral procession to St. Paul's Cathedral, with "HE DID NOT GET WINTER RELIEF" painted on the side of the coffin. There were many stunts of this sort, staged in London and in other parts of the country, aimed at keeping the issue of unemployment very much alive.

10. ANEURIN BEVAN, THE RISE OF FASCISM AND THE 1935 GENERAL ELECTION

Around March 1935, our experience of working with Communists in the other valleys, a growing respect for Communist leaders we had met and dissatisfaction with the policies and actions of the Labour Party nationally, including its attacks on the Labour League of Youth for being too left-wing, led a few of us to think of forming a branch of the Communist Party in Tredegar. What held us back was the left-wing character of the local Labour Party, our admiration for Bevan and our membership of the Socialist League, which we valued because it had contributed so much to our political understanding. Also, the League in Tredegar was less of a talking shop than it was elsewhere, and contained all the people we admired most locally. At the same time, we were highly critical of the increasingly pacifist policy of the League nationally on many issues. I had recently prepared a paper which I read out to our branch in which I argued that, objectively, the League was in some ways hindering the development of the left by acting as a "safe alternative" to the Communist Party, through holding back left-wingers who would otherwise join the party. Nye's sister, Ariadne, who was close to him and acted as his secretary, asked if she could take the paper to show him.

Our intentions leaked out, and Oliver Jones, and then Archie Lush, had a word with us and tried to get us to dish the idea. Gwen and I were then told that Nye wanted to see us. In notes I made at the time, I commented on how sympathetic Nye's tone was. He said he fully appreciated our feelings and could see how attractive the Communist Party seemed. He himself admired much of what the Party was doing, particularly in the unemployed and anti-fascist struggles, and the dedication of its members; but he believed that the future of socialism in Britain lay in changing Labour Party policy and electing it to power. From the point of view of winning power in the foreseeable future, the C.P. was an irrelevancy and it would be better if its members were in the Labour Party. There was a parliamentary election due, and it was essential that we concentrate all our efforts on winning. He agreed with my point that the Socialist League could act as a barrier to people joining the C.P., and then surprisingly said, maybe tongue in cheek, that if the Socialist League didn't exist, it could well be in the interests of Labour's right-wing to encourage an organisation like it, as a diversion and a safety valve.

This reflected Bevan's cautious approach to the League. He had declined to be a founding member, even though he often spoke on its platforms. Occasionally, he would speak to our branch, and Ariadne was one of our most active members.

With some reluctance, Gwyn and I decided not to join the C.P. – at least for the time being. The enormous esteem in which we held Nye gave his views almost the weight of law, especially to those of my generation in Tredegar who had never been close to him. Older comrades who had worked with him for many years were not so uncritical, and although they respected him, at times they often expressed some irritation, though more on a personal level than with his politics. In later years, for instance, it was felt that he wasn't seen enough in the constituency, that he had become too distant from his old comrades; and there were rumours of his life style in London. But there was never any doubt about his tremendous leadership qualities and the role he was playing as an authentic voice for socialism in the labour movement. It was not only on a platform that Nye was impressive. He had a natural imposing manner, extremely self-confident and articulate, which meant that he dominated any discussion. As a young man he had a bad stutter, which he overcame by sheer hard work and will power, but a trace of it always remained – which he used to good effect when speaking. He had a magic way with words and never used notes. (I once heard him say that when he became a government minister he found it difficult at first having to speak from a brief). Nye was best speaking to his own people, a Welsh working-class audience; and I have been at a meeting in the Workmen's Hall when the enthusiasm he aroused in his listeners was such that I'm sure we would have left the hall and started the revolution on our own if he had demanded it.

Although the unemployed struggle occupied a lot of our attention because it was of immediate importance and very near to us, we were also very concerned with the other big political issues of the day. In 1934, for example, some of us took part in collecting signatures for the National Peace Ballot. This had been organised on the initiative of the League of Nations Union (L.N.U.), and thirty-eight organisations agreed officially to sponsor it, including the Labour and Liberal Parties, the T.U.C., the Co-operative Movement and many religious bodies. It was not, as it is sometimes presented today, a ballot simply against war. True, there was a strong pacifist feeling in the country, for it was only fifteen years after the First World War, the horrors of which were still fresh in people's minds.

But the questions asked on the ballot were whether Britain should remain in the League of Nations, support disarmament by international agreement, abolish military aircraft by agreement, stop the production of arms for private profit and take part in collective economic or military action to stop aggression. As there was no branch of the L.N.U. in Tredegar, the local ballot was organised by an ad hoc committee, mainly

Labour people. A meeting was organised in Tredegar at which the socialist writer H. M. Brailsford exposed the profits being made from arms.
The national result was truly staggering. 11,559,165 voted and the 'yes'
votes ranged from over 11,000,000 to almost 7,000,000, this last being
the vote on whether collective military action to stem an aggressor was
justified.

At this time I was also a member of the South Wales Area Council of
the Socialist League, which met in Cardiff. The meetings were usually
attended by one of the League's national leaders.

However, it was the rise of fascism in Europe, particularly the emer-
gence of Hitler's Nazi Party as the main reactionary force in Germany,
that we became mainly concerned with. The economic factors that led to
the election of the "National" Government in Britain applied also to
Germany, but they were part of a much more complex situation and a
capitalism which was particularly unstable as a consequence of
Germany's defeat in the first World War. For most of the time up to 1932
the country had been governed by a coalition which included the Social
Democrats, and when the world economic crisis hit Germany the government took up a similar position to the MacDonald government in
Britain. Draconian measures were taken against the workers, wages were
reduced and social gains previously won, wiped out. This was the
situation that helped the rise of the Nazi Party.

But there were other, even more important, factors. Only twelve years
before, following the collapse of the Kaiser's regime, the heavy losses
sustained during the war, and the hardships endured afterwards, the
German working class attempted to follow the example of the Russian
workers in carrying through a socialist revolution.

It was brutally crushed, and two of the leaders of the newly formed
German Communist Party, Karl Liebknecht and Rosa Luxemburg, were
murdered, but thereafter the spectre of revolution haunted the German
capitalist class. Substance was given to this fear by the strength of the
German Communist Party – the largest outside of the Soviet Union – and
the fact that its influence was growing. In the 1928 election 3.2 million
people voted Communist, 9.1 million voted for the Social Democrats
and only 800,000 for the Nazis (a drop of over a million in four years).

It was at this stage that many powerful German industrialists and
financiers decided to throw their weight and their money behind Hitler.
In two years the Nazi vote had increased to almost 6.4 million, but the
Communist vote also went up to 4.5 million. Except for one brief

period, the combined Communist and Social-Democratic vote was always higher than the Nazis. Unity could have stopped fascism, but despite repeated appeals by the Communists, the right-wing leaders of the S.D.P. refused even to discuss it – although it must also be said that the sectarian language and tactics of the Communist Party, and the sharp attacks it made on the S.D.P. leaders (reflecting the attitude of the Communist International at that time), was also an important obstacle to unity.

Instead of mobilising the mass of the people against Hitler, the Social Democrats concentrated on parliamentary opposition and pursuing what John Strachey called the disastrous "policy of the lesser evil," first supporting the right-wing authoritarian regime of Brüning, passively accepting the unconstitutional dismissal of the Social Democratic Government of Prussia, and finally refusing to agree to an anti-fascist candidate in the presidential election. Instead, it supported the right-wing general, Hindenberg, as an "alternative" to Hitler, thereby ensuring Hitler's election. In the last free elections the Nazi vote dropped and the Communist vote increased. This was a danger signal for the German ruling capitalist class. Because democracy, even in the limited form it had become, now posed a potential threat to its power, it had to be destroyed. In January 1933, Hindenburg made Hitler Chancellor, democracy was done away with and soon Hitler became Führer. A train of events was set in motion that dominated the 1930's, led to the Second World War and is still having a tremendous impact today.

Of course, this was not so clear at the beginning of the decade as it became later, but we did avidly follow the events in Germany. George was particularly interested because he understood German, and whenever he could he got hold of German newspapers. We would listen to Hitler speaking on German radio and George would interpret the speeches to me. We hardly believed it when the Nazis seized power without a struggle, for the German working-class movement had a long socialist tradition and seemed so well-organised. The one bright light in this dismal scene was the heroic stand put up by the Bulgarian Communist, Georgi Dimitrov, who had been working in Germany and was tried on the fake charge of setting fire to the Reichstag – really the act of the Nazis and the pretext they used for establishing the Hitler dictatorship. In the first, and last, public trial in Nazi Germany, Dimitrov flayed his accusers and turned it into a trial of the Nazis. So great was the international impact that the Nazis were forced to release him, especially when he was made a Soviet citizen. His stand inspired us all. The victory of the Nazis in Germany was the stimulus for the advance of fascism in other countries. The great crisis of 1929-31 had sent shivers down the spine of the ruling classes in all capitalist countries, and important sections increasingly saw democracy as a possible threat to them in their weakened position, especially as, in contrast to capitalism, the Soviet Union was becoming stronger economically. They saw the German experience as a possible way out, as a way of guaranteeing their power and their profits. In February 1934 the French fascists, the Croix de Feu, had stormed the Parliament buildings and almost succeeded in seizing power, and in Britain money was being poured into the coffers of Mosley's British Union of Fascists which was being publicly backed by Lord Rothermere's *Daily Mail* and secretly supported by some industrialists and financiers.

Responding to the threat of fascism and war, and to the experiences of the growing anti-fascist struggle in many countries, particularly France and Spain, the world Communist movement had changed its strategy. Socialism was no longer seen as the immediate next step. First, fascism had to be defeated and peace assured. At the Seventh World Congress of the Communist International, held in September 1934, Dimitrov put forward this strategy and called for a united front of all forces opposed to fascism and war.

By 1936, the "Popular Front" as it came to be called, was making spectacular advances. In February a Popular Front government was elected in Spain, and four months later in France. It looked as if the counter-offensive against fascism was succeeding.

However, this optimism was soon to be dashed. In July, Spanish Generals under Franco rebelled against the democratically elected government and the bitter civil war started. There was a tremendous upsurge of support throughout the whole of Britain, with very broadly based local Aid For Spain Committees being set up everywhere. Volunteers from all over the world went to fight in the International Brigade – including, in the two years of its existence, over 2,000 from Britain, of whom five hundred were to be killed and 1,200 wounded. Child refugees from Northern Spain were brought to this country and were put in camps at various places, including Caerleon and Southampton.

I shall write more about this later. But in the months before leaving Tredegar, I played what little part I could in the political fight to win

89

support for the Republic, and in collecting clothes and food for Spain. One incident I remember was calling on the local Catholic priest and wondering what reception I would get, as the Pope had blessed Franco. I needn't have worried: he gave generously.

While the British Union of Fascists was a disturbing force in parts of London and other cities, in South Wales they had made no headway. The left didn't in any way minimise the necessity to fight Mosley and his thugs and appreciated that there could come a time when the whole weight of the capitalist establishment might be thrown behind the fascists. But we believed that the main danger in Britain at that time came from the reactionary policies of the government and the increasingly authoritarian measures it was adopting.

In my notes of the street-corner speeches I made for the L.L.Y., there are frequent warnings of this danger, with references to the Public Order Act, which limited the right to demonstrate, and what I perhaps exaggeratedly called "the fascistisation of the police" through limiting democratic control and creating a special elite officer class.

This was the backdrop to the General Election that took place in November 1935, the first of the many I have taken part in, including four as candidate and once as agent. In 1929 Nye Bevan had been returned unopposed, but this time the Tories put up a Miss Scarborough as their candidate.

There was little doubt what the result would be, nor were there any illusions that the real objective in putting up a Tory candidate was to stop Nye speaking in other parts of the country. Nevertheless, nothing was left to chance. Archie Lush was Labour's Agent, and he organised the campaign with a verve and efficiency as if it were the closest of marginals. For me, it has been the model I have always measured other election campaigns against.

This was when I made my debut as a speaker at indoor public meetings. Bevan would do several meetings in different parts of the constituency each night, and, of course, there had to be other fill-in speakers at each place to keep the pot boiling until he arrived. This was my role. One day Archie told me to go that evening to Trefil, a village to the north of Tredegar. "Your job," he said, "is a simple one, you have to go on speaking until Aneurin comes through the door – then you immediately shut up!" That was the easiest part. As it happened, although I was very nervous, speaking wasn't a difficult task because Trefil was aggressively hundred per cent Labour and so the audience was totally sympathetic (there was once a rumour that sent shudders through the village that on one occasion someone there actually voted Tory). During the campaign I performed the same role at other meetings – Tavanabach and Troedrhigwair are two I remember. Some time later I was told by Archie that asking me to speak was part of a conscious design to train some of us youngsters.

One could hardly imagine a more unsuitable candidate for a Welsh mining constituency than Miss Scarborough, a well-off, city lady who would obviously be more at home at Mayfair coffee mornings than haranguing working-class men and women living in poverty. Her meetings were hilarious and noisy affairs.

They were always packed with Labour supporters and would invariably end with the entire audience singing "The Red Flag." There were several songs written – the suspicion was by Archie – and distributed to the children, which they used to sing with gusto. One of them was to the tune of "Oh, Oh, Antonia:"

> Oh, Oh, Miss Scarborough,
>   You're going away.
> Not into Parliament – this Government's had its day.
>   We'll put Aneurin back for Ebbw Vale,
> So out you go, Miss Scarborough,
>   With your fairy tale.

And another one, a parody of "Roll Along Covered Wagon:"

> Roll along Labour voters, roll along.
>   Put Aneurin back where he belongs,
> City ladies may be fine,
>   But give me that lad of mine,
> Roll along Labour voters, roll along.

At the time of the election, the Richard Thomas Company was in the process of buying the Ebbw Vale steel works, which had been closed in 1929 with the loss of about 10,000 jobs. The company entered the election fray, using its not inconsiderable clout to try and turn voters against Labour, and using the prospect of jobs as a weapon. *The Western Mail*, South Wales' main daily paper, became its willing propaganda mouthpiece, and Lady Firth, wife of the Chairman of Richard Thomas, actively

91

campaigned for Miss Scarborough. They played their trump card on the eve of the poll. A packed meeting at the Tredegar Workmen's Hall had heard Bevan at his most brilliant, but when we came out we found that the town had been deluged with free front pages of the *Western Mail* containing an interview with Sir William Firth, under the banner headlines, "If Bevan is elected, the Ebbw Vale Works will not open."

There was a quick council of war, and it was decided to get the printer to work right away on a leaflet, to be distributed as soon as they were ready and before the poll opened. The leaflet was brief and to the point: To the People of Ebbw Vale Division:

DON'T TAKE YOUR POLITICS FROM YOUR EMPLOYERS.
The Coal Owners and the Steel Masters have joined hands in a last-minute attempt to stampede you. We warned you they would do this.
It is their favourite trick.

DO YOU EXPECT YOUR EMPLOYERS TO HELP LABOUR?
Remember the *"Western Mail"* is owned by the Coal and Steel employers and can be relied upon to stab the workers in the back every time.

STAND FIRM. VOTE LABOUR. BE STRONG.
Aneurin Bevan.

We didn't go to bed that night, but waited for the printer to get the leaflets out; then, in the early hours of the morning, we distributed them door-to-door throughout the constituency.

Nye had a majority of 17,862, but although the number of Labour M.P.'s increased to one hundred and fifty four (plus four I.L.P. and one Communist), the Tories remained in power, winning four hundred and thirty two seats. Soon after the election, Archie Lush invited a few of us to spend every Thursday evening at his house, a fair-sized, middle-class abode by our standards, and containing what was to us an awesome collection of books – the largest private library I had seen. Those evenings were some of the most pleasant I have ever spent, where, in a relaxed atmosphere over coffee and sandwiches we discussed any subject that came up. Archie was a great raconteur and wit, and used to tell us stories of the earlier years in the movement, of his life at Oxford University and about Bevan – Archie was Nye's longest and closest friend. But mostly we discussed politics, philosophy and literature. He had a love of drama – a few months before I had attended an evening class of his on its history, and had played my first and last dramatic role, as a minor character in the class's performance of Shaw's *On the Rocks*. I discovered later that there was a more serious purpose behind these evenings, and that those of us who were invited had been specially singled out as youngsters with some potential for political development.

Archie occupied a unique position in the labour movement. He was universally respected, and in the local rifts that sometimes arose, he was always a unifying force, looked up to by all protagonists. He could easily have become an M.P., but had no ambitions in that direction. I couldn't help feeling a little sad when, in retirement, he accepted a knighthood, even though it was from a Labour Government, and like to think it was his puckishness and sense of the incongruous that led him to accept it.

Independent working-class education flourished in the South Wales of the 1930's. There were usually W.E.A. (Workers Education Association) classes taking place, but generally it was the courses organised under the auspices of the National Council of Labour Colleges that attracted us. There was widespread suspicion of the W.E.A. among the left because it was partly funded by the establishment, and as such, the syllabuses were carefully controlled and avoided overt political commitment. The N.C.L.C., on the other hand, saw its role as spreading socialist, particularly Marxist, education in the labour movement and the working class in general. It published its own paper *Plebs* and produced a serious of excellent socialist textbooks, as well as running correspondence courses on a wide range of subjects. These courses were free to members of affiliated trade unions, and, taking advantage of this last point, I took courses on economics, English grammar, chairmanship and labour movement history in the name of my father. One class I attended, on Marxism, was taken by Len Williams, who many years later became the General Secretary of the Labour Party. However, at the time he was working for the N.C.L.C. and had written a popular booklet "What Is Marxism." Each week I would meet Len off the bus in Tredegar and we would walk over the steep valley side to Ebbw Vale, where the classes were being held.

Our labour movement owes a great debt of gratitude to the N.C.L.C. for the work it did in politically educating two generations of socialist activists. Its demise, following the T.U.C. taking it over after the war, left a gap that has not been filled. What is offered by the trade union movement today is mainly training in negotiating skills, legal questions and union administration. Necessary though this might be, it does not help

93

workers to understand the true nature of the world in which we live, or give a socialist perspective – the essentials of working-class education. Nor do the courses given by Ruskin College, Coleg Harlech, or even Northern College, truly fill the gap, even though they do give a ground-work in economics, politics and labour movement history. Unfortunately, though perhaps understandably, they are often seen as a means of escaping from the workplace and as stepping stones to new careers as full-time trade union officers, employment managers or social service officials.

Another organisation that was enormously important in the development of young socialists in the thirties was the Left Book Club. This was started in May 1936 by the progressive publisher Victor Gollancz. Its declared aim was "to help in the terribly urgent struggle for world peace and for a better social and economic order and against fascism, by giving all who are determined to play a part in this struggle such knowledge as will immensely increase their efficiency." Members had to agree to take a chosen book each month for a payment of 2s. 6d (15p). Purchase of additional books at reduced prices was optional. It was a great success. 7,000 subscribed in the first month and within a year there were 44,800 members. By 1939 this had gone up to 58,000 and there were 1,200 Left Book Club Discussion Groups throughout the country.

For us unemployed youngsters it was particularly timely. With the limited financial resources at our disposal it enabled us to build our own personal collections of socialist and progressive books on basic and topical political themes. Good though a library might be (and the Tredegar library was one of the best) it isn't the same as having one's own books always ready to hand to be referred to and studied. We avidly looked forward to the monthly "choice," which was usually the basis of a subsequent discussion. The Left Book Club also published some excellent pamphlets and leaflets. At the time of the Munich crisis, two and a half million of a leaflet, "The Hitler Menace," were printed and distributed in three days. One of the most memorable pamphlets was John Strachey's "Why You Should Be A Socialist." It cost 2d. and a quarter of a million copies were sold in the first year. Parallel with the Left Book Club was the Topic Record Club, started by the Workers' Music Association. Members received a record each month, usually songs on a topical or generally political theme.

Of course, during the whole of this period I had to go through the farce of proving that I was always "genuinely seeking work"; farcical because there were hardly any jobs existing and the great bulk of the working population was unemployed. But it was the statutory condition for continuing to draw the dole. So every few weeks I would go to a possible employer and get him to sign a "green card" supplied by the Labour Exchange to prove I had been there looking for a job.

Under the Unemployment Act, several government training schemes for the young unemployed were started. The most notorious were the so-called "Labour Colonies" – popularly known as the "slave camps" – which were directly copied from the Hitler Labour Camps. Youngsters could be drafted into these camps and forced to work on road building, afforestation, land drainage, etc. under a semi-military regime and without wages (they were given three shillings a week "pocket money," reduced by fines for petty offences such as being found outside the camp). I was able to dodge going to one of these, but couldn't get out of going to the "training centres" set up ostensibly to teach skills. In fact, I didn't mind it all that much because they were non-residential and thus enabled me to continue with my political activity. I also liked working with my hands, although there was not always the opportunity for doing so. At one centre I attended, in Ebbw Vale, the principal, a foul-mouthed ex-army officer, would greet us in the morning and tell us he didn't want to see us until it was time to check us off at the end of the day, so we would spend our time wandering around the town, playing football in the park or playing on the children's swings. A much better centre was at Pentrabach, near Merthyr Tydfil, where some effort was made to teach us something.

Going there every morning, we would pass the huge Dowlais steel works, idle and rusted over. It was a fantastic sight, looking as if time had suddenly stopped and everything had frozen over at one moment. Among the buildings and giant converters, steam engines, dark brown with rust and with trucks still attached, silently rested where they had finally stopped. It was looking down on this desolate scene that prompted the Prince of Wales, later the Duke of Windsor, to make his famous remark, "Something will have to be done." It created a sensation at the time, for unlike now, when royals seem to publicly dabble in everything, it was not considered proper for a prince of the realm to make even an innocuous remark like that. Of course, nothing was done, and we know now that if Edward had had his way his solution would probably have been fascism and labour conscription, for he was a secret admirer of Hitler.

95

Just before he stopped off at the Dowlais works, the Prince had visited our training centre at Pentrabach. I was not there to greet him, however, because a number of us had decided to take the day off in protest at his visit.

In March 1936 I left home for the first time to go to one of the principal government training centres at Bristol. There I was to spend the next three months, learning the rudiments of metalwork, the trade which I was destined to follow for a large part of my later life. George and Arthur had preceded me to the Bristol centre, and we later used to refer to it as "our university." While I was at Bristol, I joined the Bristol East Labour League of Youth (Sir Stafford Cripps was the M.P.) and most Sundays we spent with the Bristol Young Communist League holding meetings on Durdham Down (or heckling at other meetings). When I was not doing this or visiting home, I would be tramping over the Mendip Hills or exploring Bath and Wells.

1935 was marked by another sequence of events which only touched me peripherally but which in later years was to assume a much greater personal importance. Following the 1926 lockout, the coalowners, with the support of the Tory government, had engineered a split in the miners' organisation. Based on the Nottinghamshire coalfield, George Spencer, a Labour M.P., had established a so-called "industrial," "non-political" union in opposition to the Miners' Federation. It was correctly stigmatised as a bosses' organization, a scab union. With the help of the coalowners, a determined effort was made to establish a base in South Wales, but this was resisted by a series of strikes throughout the coalfield. One of the most famous of these took place at the Nine Mile Point colliery, 14 miles down the Sirhowy Valley from Tredegar. In response to a provocation on the part of the management, M.F.G.B. members took a new, dramatic form of direct action. They simply stayed down the mine and would not come up.

The stay-down strike immediately aroused national and international interest (subsequently, Montague Slater wrote a play about it), but of more immediate importance was the wave of strikes, sit-ins and other solidarity actions that took place in support of the Nine Mile Point miners. I attended, and photographed, a huge demonstration in Tredegar's Recreation Ground, and 5,600 men at local pits decided to stop work. The "Ghost Trains" was the name given to the transport used by the owners to smuggle scabs from remote areas to some of the pits affected, and at every vantage point they were stoned by miners and their wives. At Wylie, a rock weighing a hundredweight was dropped from a bridge on to one of the trains, damaging the engine and a carriage. Direct action of this sort was taken by men and women driven to desperation by the inhuman conditions under which they were forced to live and work, and as such was totally justified.

The culminating point in the struggle that defeated the Spencer organisation came a year or so later after a famous strike at Harworth, in Nottinghamshire, led by Mick Kane, who went to prison for two years as a result. Mick is one of the great heroes of the miners and the British working class-movement, and in later years I was privileged to be one of his closest friends. But more of this will come later. I have always felt, however, that the sustained struggle of the South Wales miners has not been given sufficient recognition in most accounts of the fight that destroyed Spencerism.

Someone, I think it was J. B. Priestley, once wrote that there are occasions in a person's life when a simple decision has to be made which, although it may not be appreciated at the time, will determine the entire course of one's future: "dangerous corners" I believe he called them. For me, such a point arrived not long after finishing my stint at Bristol. I had been attending W.E.A. classes in Ebbw Vale, and, at the end of one session, the tutor told me that some time before, without telling me, he had submitted my name for a one-year course at Coleg Harlech, the progressive adult education college in North Wales which worked closely with Ruskin College. He had just heard that I had been accepted. Of course, I was pleased and flattered to hear this. However, when I went to sign on at the labour exchange the following morning I was informed that there was a job available for me in an aircraft factory near Southampton. It was under "The Juvenile Transference Scheme" under which youngsters from the depressed areas were deported to more affluent parts of the country. In future years, these poorer areas, particularly South Wales, were to suffer heavily from this bleeding away of their young people which left behind an abnormally older population.

I was faced with a quandary. Going to Coleg Harlech would be very satisfying and enjoyable, but the probability was that when the course was over I would be back on the dole. Southampton was a gamble, but at least it would mean a job, money in my pocket and an end to being dependent, even partly, on parents who had little enough to live on as it was. Furthermore, it offered the prospect of genuinely learning a trade. Asking my father for advice proved to be fruitless, so the decision was

97

left for me alone to make. After a day and a sleepless night thinking about it, I opted for the job. I left Tredegar, with, I must confess, a heavy heart, for in those days Southampton might well have been China, and I knew that it would probably be at least a year before I would see home again. It saddened me to leave so many friends and acquaintances who meant so much to me, although I wasn't aware then of the crucial part they played in moulding my future outlook.

But whilst sadness and apprehension about what lay ahead were my main emotions, there was also excitement at the prospect of a new life and new experiences.

CHAPTER III

1936-1940: A NEW LIFE

11. AIRCRAFT WORKER

Butlocks Heath. A nondescript collection of houses about five miles to the east of Southampton on a road leading to nowhere, deserted during the day, miserably dark at night, and where nothing ever happened. It is where my "digs" were, where I was sent by the Labour Exchange. I was not alone. Three other lads had just arrived, one from Glasgow, a Geordie and a youth from the Rhondda. We shared the same bedroom and out of 28s weekly pay, 25s was handed to the landlady. The remainder was our pocket-money, out of which princely sum we were supposed to pay bus fares to work, replenish our clothes and save up to go home each Christmas – and once in the summer if we were lucky. It made being away from home that much harder to bear, and compelled us to work overtime whenever we could.

One hundred miles from home – not a great distance today when travel abroad is commonplace and when most people are at the end of a phone, but in those days I might just as well have been exiled to a South Sea island. For a lad who had never ever been very far away from home it was a most harrowing experience. Although homesickness is a common enough experience, this is no consolation for what is a very personal misery. As well as the ache of separation from one's family and friends, there was the added pain of isolation, of uncertainty about the future and of being cast into an alien environment – almost an alien culture – with no contact with one's roots. Probably because so many Welsh people have, throughout the ages, experienced this, they have a special word for it – "hireath," the intense longing for one's native land. I felt that first separation more than when I was posted to Italy during the war. Of course, I was not alone: my fellow exiles shared the same feeling.

The overcrowded conditions soon got me down. When I knew the area better I moved to nearby Netley, and was fortunate to find a place in a large house with a pleasant family, with whom I stayed for the rest of the three-and-a-half years I was down south. There were two other lads in lodgings there, as well as two young, middle-class Indian men who had been sent by their parents to train as pilots at Air Service Training, a nearby private flying school.

Mrs Robinson, our landlady, came from a seafaring family. Her father spent most of his time sitting by the fireside smoking a foul pipe and spitting into the flames. When the mood took him he would give us graphic accounts of the hard life he had lived working aboard ship at the beginning of the century. Like most sailors, he knew how to tell a good yarn. A favourite tale was about a trip to Boston one winter aboard a small freighter which also carried a few passengers. "We hit a storm," he would explain, "but it wasn't an ordinary storm. All my life as a sailor I hadn't seen anything like it. It was like hell unleashed, the worst storm the North Atlantic has ever known. Our ship was tossed about like a matchbox in a river. One moment we'd be right at the bottom of a deep valley, with great mountains of water soaring out of sight above us; then we would be on the peak of a high mountain looking down into a bottomless black hole. There was nothing we could do but hang on and pray – and pray we did. We nailed down the hatches to stop the passengers coming on deck and then we tied ourselves to anything firm we could find to stop being swept overboard. We all thought we were goners, but, thanks to God, after three days we were still alive. It was a miracle. The tempest worked itself out and the ship was battered but still afloat. After a pause, he would come to the gruesome conclusion: "When we unfastened the hatches, the stench was awful. The passengers were still alive, but they were all lying helpless on the floor in several inches of water, vomit and shit – it was a terrible sight." And he would puff at his pipe, and relapse into silence at the unpleasant memory, thinking probably of his lucky escape.

His son, Tom, had gone to sea in his dad's footsteps. He couldn't read or write, but he was a fantastic water-colour painter, usually of sea scenes. He and his wife had a teenage daughter with Down's Syndrome, who only had to hear a tune once to recall and sing every note perfectly. The overwhelming concern of her parents was to raise enough money to see that she was looked after when they were gone. Tom's favourite story was a happier one than his father's. When a young man, he and his mate had signed on with the Titanic for its maiden voyage. The night before, however, they celebrated by going on the binge and as a result slept late the next morning. They rushed to the docks just in time to see the ill-fated liner already underway. One of the world's luckiest escapes!

I found it pleasant staying at the Robinsons', the friendly easy-going atmosphere, the arguments, the good food, playing badminton on the lawn . . . and flirting with the daughter, Jo, or her friend, Sheila. It was a new experience living alongside the sea and listening in bed at night to all the sounds associated with it: the rollers when the waters were rough, the hooters of the ships approaching dock and the fog horn of the Calshot lightship. Sometimes I would spend an afternoon beachcombing, searching for odd items thrown or lost overboard from the liners as they approached Southampton. The most common articles were sun-helmets, ritually thrown away by soldiers returning from service in India or some other part of the Empire.

The firm I worked for was at Hamble, and to get there meant cycling alongside the beach, through the grounds of the big Netley Naval Hospital. British Marine Aircraft was a new company that had been set up mainly to do sub-contract work for the big aircraft firms – one of several such factories spread along the side of the Solent. Subsequently it became Folland Aircraft. Folland had been one of the designers of Vickers Supermarine at nearby Southampton, and much of the work we did was for them. With imbecilic lack of planning, in view of the growing danger of war, most of Britain's key aircraft factories were sited in the areas of southern England most vulnerable to bombing – a stupidity which Britain was to pay dearly for a few years later.

I was employed as a trainee fitter and liked the work, even though much of it was repetitive. We were fortunate in having an old charge-hand who genuinely took an interest in us and tried to help us learn the skills of the trade. Probably because he had lost an eye himself, he was always concerned for our safety and often used to come out with the appropriate quip. "Never quarrel with a machine; it's stronger than you are," he used to caution us. "Your hands are more precious than your bonus," was another one. I'm sure that if the management knew what he was telling us, he wouldn't have been a charge-hand for long!

Much to my disgust, I was transferred for a time to the heat treatment department. The fumes from the anodising and plating plant were extremely unpleasant, as was the heat from the nitrate baths used to anneal duralumin sheets and rivets. In fact it was illegal to employ anyone under twenty one in this department, and

101

after a few months I was sent back to the fitting shop.

It was an exciting new world to me. There was still something of the pioneering spirit about the aircraft industry, and although we raw youngsters occupied the lowest possible position in it, we proudly identified ourselves very quickly with all that was going on. The fact that much of the work we were doing was experimental helped to establish this rapport. A revolutionary new aircraft was being developed at Vickers Supermarine based on a plane that had won the international Schneider Trophy race for several years, and some of the work was being done by us. We didn't know at the time, but the plane was to play a vital part in the war that was creeping nearer. It was subsequently to get its famous name, "Spitfire," and I can remember its designer, R. G. Mitchell, being pointed out to me when he was walking around the plant with Folland. This must have been not long before he died in 1937.

We also did the maintenance work on the Short Empire Flying Boats, which were then the basis of Britain's long-haul international air service. They seemed gigantic, but of course were nothing like the modern passenger jets. Our factory had a runway that sloped into the Solent, and I liked to sit on the beach during the lunch break, eating my sandwiches and watching the huge liners moving to dock at Southampton, or the flying boats taking off and landing.

I soon found evidence that there were Communists in the factory, because of the copies of the *Daily Worker* left in the toilets and on the benches during lunch time. It turned out that the guiding spirit was a storeman, Fred Ward, who used to pick up about forty to fifty copies of the paper at the station when cycling to work every morning (for at that time newsagents refused to handle it). Every month, two or three dozen copies of *Labour Monthly* were also sold. But it was the *The New Propeller*, the paper of the Aircraft Shop Stewards National Council, which had the biggest circulation in the factory. Its Editor was a Communist, Peter Zinkin, and it was popular because it contained news of what was happening in aircraft factories throughout Britain. Later, I was to take over responsibility for distributing the paper and became its local correspondent.

It didn't take me long to establish local political connections. I went to a public meeting in Southampton, addressed by D. N. Pritt, and when it was over I met some Communists and Labour Party members. As a result I joined the Labour Party, and was also given details about the Southampton Branch of the C.P. Among the Labour Party members I got to know were two with whom I became very friendly. Fred Blessley and his wife were a middle-aged couple who lived in a delightful bungalow facing the Hamble river, which was always crowded with colourful yachts belonging to those fortunate enough to be able to enjoy such an expensive pastime. Fred was a Parish Councillor and Secretary of the Hamble and District Labour Party. They welcomed me with open arms and I soon became a frequent visitor to their home. They were fine examples of the sort of people who have always so enriched our labour movement: firm socialists, but with convictions stemming probably more from the heart than from the head, dedicated to the cause and giving all their time to it without thought of recognition or reward. They were on the left of the Labour Party, and members of the Left Book Club, which had a very active branch in Southampton and which I also joined. During the war they joined the Communist Party.

The political situation at this time was dominated by the rise of fascism in Europe and the growing threat of war. With the collusion of the British and French governments, Hitler had embarked on a vast rearmament programme in direct defiance of the Versailles Treaty, and in March 1936 the Nazi armies had started to roll across the German borders to occupy the Rhineland. Five months earlier, fascist Italy had invaded Abyssinia (Ethiopia), using poison gas and other barbarous weapons of warfare, against a defenceless population. In November Hitler signed an alliance with Mussolini (the "Rome-Berlin Axis") and with Japan (the "Anti-Comintern Pact"). A massive propaganda campaign was mounted by the Nazis for the inclusion of Austria into a "Greater Germany." The Spanish Civil War was still raging, and crack German panzer divisions were fighting for Franco while the German and Italian navies blockaded Republican ports and their bombs destroyed its cities. Although the main objective was to destroy the Republic and set up a fascist state in Spain, the war was also being used as a training and testing ground for the larger conflict that was to come. The destruction of Guernica, immortalised in Picasso's famous painting, was the first exercise in the mass bombing that was to become a feature of World War Two. This was the truly horrifying picture facing us at the time.

Today, "appeasement" is a dirty word, the supreme example of craven connivance at aggression. No Tory, Liberal or Labour politician today who lived through those years will admit to ever having supported such a policy. The records speak otherwise. Appeasement is the word that accurately describes the line taken by governments of the western

103

democracies in the face of fascist aggression. At every stage of the fascist offensive they capitulated. More than that, they assisted aggression by supplying the aggressors with the arms and materials needed to wage war. This had nothing to do with Britain and France being too weak militarily to stand up to the dictators – the myth that has been created to excuse their craven conduct. It was the Anglo-German Naval Agreement in 1935 that enabled Hitler to rebuild the German navy. Help was given to the re-creation of a powerful Air Force and a blind eye turned to its use against the people of Spain. Every territorial gain Hitler was allowed to make strengthened Germany's military might. Anti-Sovietism was the raison d'être of appeasement. Chamberlain and Daladier were deliberately feeding Hitler, building the military strength of the fascist powers to encourage them to eventually attack and destroy the Soviet Union.

Hitler had many supporters in high places in this country. The Anglo-German Fellowship included among its members powerful industrialists and financiers who openly applauded what the Nazis were doing, even his anti-semitism. Lord Rothermere, owner of the *Daily Mail* and several other papers, made no secret of this. "Why I Back Hitler" was the title of an article he wrote in the *Daily Mail*, which also offered five weekly prizes for the best letters on "Why I Like the Blackshirts" (the Blackshirts being the British Union of Fascists). *The Times*, owned by Lord Astor, was a vociferous advocate of appeasement. It was at the Cliveden home of Lord and Lady Astor that there used to gather leading Tory politicians, including Cabinet Ministers, tycoons of industry and banking, newspaper editors and other manipulators of public opinion. The members of the notorious Cliveden Set had four things in common: their hatred of the Soviet Union, their hatred of the working-class movement, their admiration of Hitler and Mussolini, and their absolute belief that they were the ones chosen by God to run Britain and the world.

In an attempt to re-write history, Churchill is now presented as the heroic figure who struggled alone against appeasement. This, of course, is a blatant lie. True, he, and a group of dissident Tories were extremely worried that appeasing the fascists, helping them to become militarily stronger, was a potential threat to the British Empire. But the real opposition to appeasement came from the left, particularly from the labour movement, but extending over a wide spectrum of liberal and progressive opinion. What was remarkable was the extent of opposition among academics, writers, poets and scientists great and small, and their willingness to participate in the great public campaigns in support of Spain, against fascism, war, and the treacherous policy of the government. The official Labour Party adopted an ambivalent attitude. It had moved from an almost pacifist position to one supporting the League of Nations and collective security against aggression. It refused, however, to join any campaigns involving Communists, and continued the attacks on the left in its own ranks. It argued that fascism was a "continental phenomenon" and not a threat in Britain; and as for Mosley and his Blackshirts – well, people should laugh at them and keep away from their meetings – disturbingly reminiscent of the advice given by the German Social-Democratic leaders in the early days of Hitler. On Spain, it dragged its feet, backing the Republic in words, but opposing "unconstitutional" actions in Britain in its support. Parliamentary opposition and electing a Labour government was its answer to everything. To its disgrace, for a time it even supported the government policy of "non-intervention," which meant refusing any aid to the democratically elected constitutional government of Spain at a time when the fascist powers were pouring in arms and military forces to help Franco and imposing a tight blockade to prevent food and other material getting to the Republic. The honour of the Labour Party was at least partly preserved by the stand taken by many of its best-known members in support of Spain and against appeasement.

The standing of the Soviet Union had never been greater among progressives. It consistently advocated a peace alliance of all democratic powers to curb the fascists. When Italy invaded Abyssinia, Litvinov, Soviet Foreign Minister, at the League of Nations urged the imposition of the only sanction that mattered – oil – but this was rejected. It was there that he made his famous appeal: "Peace is indivisible: an aggression against one must be regarded as an aggression against all." British Foreign Minister, Lord Halifax, showed his contempt by walking out of the Chamber while Litvinov was speaking. The Soviet Union was the only power that rejected the phoney "non-intervention" policy and helped the Spanish Republic, with arms, food, and military and technical advisers. It was no wonder that the Soviet Union's prestige was high, not only with sections of the labour movement but with a large number of middle-class intellectuals who saw the fight for freedom as being of paramount importance.

At the beginning of 1937, the Communist Party, Socialist League and Independent Labour Party agreed to work together in a Unity Campaign against the National Government, fascism and war, and local United Front Committees were set up. Sir Stafford Cripps, James Maxton, leader of the I.L.P. and Harry Pollitt, General Secretary of the Communist Party, spoke at big meetings throughout the country, and other leading left-wingers (including Aneurin Bevan) were drawn into the campaign. In 1938, the Communist Party made an appeal to the Labour Party to join it in forming a People's Front, and to conduct a joint campaign to bring down the Chamberlain government and replace it with an alternative anti-fascist government. This was rejected by the Labour Party, as was a later appeal by Sir Stafford Cripps.

However, the idea of the People's Front caught on and found expression in many ways. Its most dramatic was the political campaign of support for the Spanish Republic and the immensely broad Spanish Aid movement. The movement was truly inspiring, and the most varied organisations and individual were involved: churches, local councils, trade unions, non-political bodies and people of all democratic political viewpoints. A leading part was played by the Duchess of Atholl, one of a small group of Tories who actively supported the Republican cause. In many towns the Mayor was the chairperson of the Aid For Spain Committee. Meetings and rallies were held continually and millions of leaflets were distributed. Clothes, food and money were collected. Southampton dockers loading a Hampshire Food Ship for Spain gave their day's pay to buy more relief. The A.E.U. and other unions initiated Industrial Aid for Spain, and their members built motorcycle ambulances. Doctors organised medical aid; two hundred men and women went out to give medical and other aid on the spot. Of course, much of the support was on humanitarian grounds, but in the main the movement was motivated by a genuine desire to help a people heroically fighting to defend their democratically elected government against brutal fascist aggression.

In May 1937 we experienced a particularly poignant event, one which truly brought out the grim realities of war, but also the warmth and humanity of most people. 2,000 children from the heavily bombed Basque area of Spain, packed tight in every corner of the ship, arrived at Southampton Docks, and 2,000 more came later. It was the biggest influx of refugees in British history and the only one made up entirely of children. The whole community rallied to see that they were looked after. In preparation for their coming, a farmer at North Stoneham, just outside Southampton, freely offered three fields for a camp, the

Co-operative Society helped provide for them (one of its leading members had experience with the Woodcraft Folk); the woodworkers and other unions assisted by offering the specialist skills of their members, and dockers took on the job of digging latrines. There were so many volunteers that it was difficult to organise everyone. I did a multitude of menial jobs, mainly fetching and carrying. The Girl Guides agreed to erect and run a camp for the youngest children, and an empty manor house was given as a sanatorium. The Catholic Church and the Salvation Army accepted a great deal of responsibility for most of the children. Grudgingly, the War Office loaned tents and field equipment – but charged interest on the cost. The city of tents was a spectacular sight.

One thousand people attended a public meeting in the Guildhall, chaired by the Lord Mayor and addressed by the Tory M.P., the Labour Parliamentary Candidate and leaders of the Catholic and Anglican churches, including the Bishop of Winchester. It was an exhilarating, if sad, occasion. The unhappiness of the children was heart-rending. Torn from their homes and families and set down in a strange land where people spoke a language they couldn't understand, what was happening was beyond their comprehension. They were terrified whenever a plane flew overhead, and were even afraid of the media cameras, at first thinking they were guns. Eventually, the children were dispersed to camps and homes in other parts of the country.

Although most of the media supported Franco, or pretended to take a neutral stance, newspapers with reasonable circulations, particularly the *Daily Herald*, the *News Chronicle*, the *Daily Worker*, *Reynolds News* and the *Sunday Referee* supported the Republic. Thankfully, we were not cursed with our modern-day tabloids, nor did we have television. Those on the left had no illusions about what was at stake: it was no less than the future of Europe and the world. As bombs were being dropped on Spain's capital city, many of the banners carried in our demonstrations carried the truly prophetic warning: "Madrid Today – London Tomorrow!" We now know that Spain was, in truth, the first battleground of the Second World War.

There was also the broad movement that developed around the Left Book Club, which grew from a mere book club into a campaigning body with branches all over the country. My very first visit to London was to attend one of its great rallies at the Albert Hall. The speakers were John Strachey and Harold Laski from the Labour Party left; Liberal leader Richard Acland; the eminent barrister, D. N. Pritt, and Communist Party

General Secretary, Harry Pollitt. Every seat of this huge hall was taken. I heard Pollitt speak on numerous occasions in subsequent years and sometimes even shared the same platform, but, great orator though he was, he never thrilled me more than he did on that occasion. He ended his speech, as he frequently did, with a poem, this time from William Morris's "March of the Workers":

> What is this the sound and rumour–
> What is this that all men hear–
> Like the wind in hollow valleys
> When the storm is drawing near,
> Like the rolling of oceans
> In the eventide of fear,
> 'TIS THE PEOPLE MARCHING ON.

As Pollitt uttered these last words, the huge audience rose to its feet as one body in a great emotional demonstration of enthusiasm and solidarity. It was at another Left Book Club Rally in the Albert Hall that I first heard that great singer and fighter for human rights, Paul Robeson. He also brought the house down.

We had an active Left Book Club group in Southampton, run by a professional writer, Alan Jenkins. The range of speakers at our well-attended meetings now looks quite impressive: poets Randall Swingler, Edgell Rickword and Stephen Spender; famous novelist, Sylvia Townsend-Warner; and a host of other men and women whom older readers will remember for the prominent part they played in public life. They included Professors Levi and Betts, Commander Edgar Young, Major Vernon, Palme Dutt, Tom Wintringham, T. A. Jackson, H. B. Lees-Smith M.P., J. P. M. Millar, Fred Copeman, Jurgin Kuczinski. As well as these meetings, we also discussed the monthly "choice" and were active in other ways. One rash decision we made was to accept a challenge to a cricket match at Winchester. It turned out to be a much more formal and serious affair than we anticipated. We were thrashed, and I contributed to the debacle by scoring a duck and dropping a catch.

I soon became deeply involved in the political life of Southampton and the area around: in the Left Book Club, the *Daily Worker* Readers' League (of which I was persuaded by George Allison to become secretary), the Labour Party and also the Communist Party and the Young Communist League. There was any amount of activity going on, and the movement was fortunate in having a number of well-known and able socialists living in the area. David Guest, a Communist and son of a Labour M.P., was a lecturer at Southampton University. He was an active participant in our activities and used to give lectures on Marxist philosophy. David joined the International Brigade and in 1938 was killed on the Ebro, but his book on dialectical materialism, based on the lectures, is a lasting memorial to him. Another comrade who fought in Spain was Bill Alexander, whom I first saw when he came back to Southampton after the Brigade was disbanded. The poet Edgell Rickword was a member of the local branch of the C.P.; I believe he worked in the party bookshop. I have always regretted turning down an invitation to accompany him on a visit to the home of Siegfried Sassoon. We also often saw Hyman Levi, a well-known philosophy professor who was to become a leading Communist intellectual and who lived in the New Forest with his two lovely daughters.

The influence of the left, particularly the Communists, in some of the main workplaces of the area was very significant. The docks was one of the most important in the country. Southampton was Britain's greatest passenger port, but a great deal of freight also passed through it. It became a national focal point for a short time when dockers refused to load Japanese ships because of Japan's brutal invasion of China. I was a member of the Aid China Committee, and we organised meetings and film shows, receiving a great deal of help from the often despised Chinese laundrymen and cafe owners who turned out to be far more politically conscious than we had thought. On another occasion, a dispute arose about the appalling conditions of Indian seamen, and Krishna Menon, the Secretary of the India League who was to become India's first Foreign Minister, came down for a few days. I felt privileged at the time to be invited by his host to have a meal with both of them.

At the end of 1937 I decided to join the Communist Party, and my political involvement thereafter was very much with the Party. It was a lively branch of fifty five members and there was always plenty going on: meetings, poster parades, *Daily Worker* sales, leaflet distributions, chalking, etc. On Sundays I would go to Southampton Common, sell the *Daily Worker* (there were 1,180 daily readers reported in the Southampton area) and listen to and heckle the many speakers always holding forth on a multitude of topics. It was quite an education to me, hearing arguments on so many subjects.

Generally, good-humoured tolerance was shown to the speakers; but

109

there was an exception. The one organisation that popular opposition prevented from holding meetings was the British Union of Fascists. So when it was rumoured that the Fascist leader, Sir Oswald Mosley himself, was going to speak at a rally on the Common, there was an immediate outcry. The Party decided to organise a rival meeting and appealed for support from the rest of the movement. The evenings before the event we were out chalking the roads and walls, calling on everyone to rally against the fascists. When the time came a great crowd had assembled, waiting for Mosley to appear. He came in his armoured van, protected by police and a large bodyguard, which helped the van force its way through the crowd. It was then surrounded by a ring of Blackshirt thugs – in characteristic pose, legs apart and arms folded – and another ring of police, whose sole purpose seemed to be to ensure that Mosley would be able to speak. Meanwhile, a little way off, the anti-fascist meeting had started. As expected, a good proportion of the crowd surrounded Mosley and his cordon, and kept up a continuous barrage of shouting and singing anti-fascist songs, making it impossible to hear what the fascist leader was saying. This was despite the fact that he was no mean orator and had loudspeaker equipment – a rarity in those days.

The crowd became more and more incensed, to the point where the police and the fascists could no longer hold them. There was a surge forward, the van was seized, rocked from side to side and eventually turned over. Mosley managed to jump off and was immediately surrounded by his thugs and the police, who then had the problem of getting him to safety. Inch by inch they forced a way to the nearby road, but could go no further. The police then commandeered a tram, turned all the passengers out and put Mosley aboard. This proved to be no solution, for some enterprising demonstrators immobilised the tram by pulling the conducting pole from the overhead electric wire. With no clear strategy, the crowd then jubilantly pushed the tram towards the town centre, but when it arrived opposite the police station, Mosley and his police escort managed to get off and run for refuge into the station. It was a grand victory, and the anti-fascist meeting continued with a greatly enlarged and enthusiastic audience. I knew two or three B.U.F. members at work and individually they were not bad blokes; the tragedy was that they were taken in by the demagogy of Mosley and the sinister group around him. Of course, we used to argue – I couldn't see any point in boycotting them – and at least one of them saw the error of his ways and later became a good worker in the labour movement.

Although now a member of the Communist Party, I did not sever my connections with the Labour Party. Indeed, contrary to the rules of both organisations I held dual membership, something that I didn't hide but which was accepted as being expedient in the circumstances. The Hamble and District Labour Party barely existed, and it was decided to try and revive it as the best way of developing political activity in the predominantly Tory area it covered. I took over as secretary and also became the branch's delegate to the General Council of the Winchester Constituency Party. Although small and covering a wide area, in time the branch became quite active. There was one occasion when we were involved in a fight against the enclosure of common land, a struggle I thought had ended in the eighteen century. We discovered that fences had been put around the common in one of our villages to prevent people using it – for what purpose we weren't sure, although we had our suspicions. We set about putting a spanner in the works. As well as conducting a public campaign, some of us would stealthily creep out night after night and pull down the fences. Whether we were successful in the long run I cannot say, but we certainly delayed the enclosure for a long time. One wonders how many square miles of common land in Britain have been surreptitiously stolen from the people in this way.

While I was preoccupied with political and trade union activity in Hampshire, Arthur and George were likewise engaged in their respective localities. In the case of George, his activity was punctuated by cycling trips to France and Germany when work was slack. He was very much involved in the Oxford Labour Party and was on the Editorial Board of the *Oxford Labour Weekly* (children's novelist Geoffrey Trease was a fellow Board member). However, he worked closely with the Communist Party and was a friend of Abe Lazarus, the full-time Oxford organiser of the Party, also known as "Jack Firestone" for his part in leading a famous strike at the Firestone tyre factory in London. Abe was a fine orator of the type the Communist Party in those days used to throw up in abundance.

In 1938 an extremely important parliamentary bye-election took place in Oxford in which George was very much involved. Oxford was then a safe Tory seat, and there was a strong feeling among the left and other progressives that the democratic forces should unite behind an acceptable non-party anti-appeasement candidate. The favoured person was Dr. Lindsay, the Master of Balliol, highly respected for his outspoken stand against Government policy. However, this proposal was opposed

111

by the National Executive Committee of the Labour Party which wanted to field its own candidate, Patrick Gordon Walker. It sent its National Secretary and Chairman to a highly charged special General Meeting of the Oxford Party, called to decide the issue. George was a delegate, and spoke and voted in support of Lindsay. Walker refused to withdraw, but the overwhelming view of the meeting was for a democratic unity candidate and the Labour leadership was forced to give way. George played a full part in the subsequent campaign. The Tory candidate, Quintin Hogg (later Lord Hailsham), won, but with a dramatically reduced majority.

I wanted to join the union as soon as I had started work, and there was no barrier to union membership put up by the management. The obstacle was the union itself. Although the A.E.U. was no longer supposed to be the exclusive craft union it had once been, it was still dominated by time-served men who looked down their noses at the semi-skilled and didn't welcome us with open arms. Tool-room workers particularly, being in a powerful position in the factory, were the aristocrats of the workforce and were more concerned with retaining their key bargaining position than unionising the rest of the factory. Then an incident occurred which brought matters to a head. The nitrate baths in which duralumin sheets and rivets were annealed had to be continuously supervised and kept at a steady high temperature. One dinner-time, none of the regular workers being available, an inexperienced fifteen-year-old lad, quite illegally, was put on one of the baths during the break. He obviously hadn't been told that nothing wet should be put in the bath, so he lowered into the extremely hot liquid a rivet pot which contained water. The bath erupted, covering the lad with searing liquid nitrate. He was rushed to hospital, but died in a few hours. The firm immediately disclaimed responsibility, maintaining that the lad had not been authorised to be working on the bath. We were furious at such an obvious lie, and I wrote out a report and sent it the District Secretary of the A.E.U.. As a result, he came to see me, the union took up the case – although the lad had not been a member – and the firm was forced to pay an out-of-court sum to the lad's mother rather than risk going to court.

As a result of this I raised with the union official the position of the semi-skilled in the factory, and a new branch of the union was set up which a good many of us immediately joined. It became a very lively and well-attended branch, and in time I was elected its President. At twenty two I must have been one of the youngest office-holders in the A.E.U.

At that time the main rank and file organisation in the aircraft industry was the Aircraft Shop Stewards' National Council, which had very great support, especially in the big factories around London. Once we had extended our influence in Follands, we regularly sent a delegate to the Council's conferences, more often than not myself. Its paper was *The New Propeller*, and one of my responsibilities was to write a monthly article – anonymously, of course – reporting on happenings in the factories around Southampton. There was an occasion when this almost got me into trouble with the right-wing leadership of the A.E.U. One of the big flying boats was being overhauled when the jig holding it collapsed and the heavy plane dropped several feet. Obviously, it must have badly jarred the fuselage of the plane, but no tests were made and the incident was hushed up. A few weeks later the plane crashed in the Far East, and I speculated on whether there wasn't a connection. The firm was furious, and sent a protest to the national office of the A.E.U. As a result, the District Secretary of the union was asked to try and find out who had written it – he did not succeed – and a statement appeared in the next issue of the union's national journal dissociating the union from the story and urging its members not to read a subversive paper like *The New Propeller*. The union leaders seemed unconcerned about whether or not the story was true, even though lives may have been lost through the action, or lack of it, by the firm. They simply accepted the official explanation.

There was not much future for me at Follands. I had started as a semi-skilled worker and that I would remain, even though I was doing the same work and was as skilled as the men I was working with and had studied many books on toolmaking and the mathematics associated with it. So I decided to make a break. I was encouraged by the foreman of the tool-room, a quiet, studious chap who had written several books about fitting and tool-making (I heard later that he had been sacked for being too easy-going and tolerant). I applied for a job as a toolmaker at the firm of Phillip and Powis, near Reading, giving false qualifications and hoping they wouldn't check. They didn't, so for about six months I was able to have practical tool-room experience. The isolated hamlet where I stayed was even worse than Butlock's Heath, but my spirits were raised when I went to work on the first morning and found a friend of George selling *The New Propeller* outside the factory.

The experience at Phillips and Powis gave me the confidence to return to Southampton, but now as a qualified toolmaker, having succeeded in transferring to Section One – the skilled section of the union. There was no possibility in those days of getting a job as a toolmaker in most aircraft factories without showing a green Section One union membership card or apprenticeship 'papers'. Fortunately, the District Committee turned a blind eye to the fact that I did not fulfil this condition, ostensibly because of my services to the union, although I soon learned there was another reason.

When I called at the A.E.U. District Office to see what jobs were available, the District Secretary told me of a particular problem then being considered by the District Committee. A new firm, Cunliffe-Owens, had opened up at a factory adjoining Eastleigh aerodrome, north of Southampton. Sir Hugo Cunliffe-Owen was the head of the Anglo-American Tobacco Company, and the story that went the rounds was that at a binge in New York, Sikorsky, the owner of the giant American aircraft company, had taken advantage of the intoxicated state Sir Hugo was in, to trick him into signing a contract to develop a somewhat dodgy plane in Britain. So the unfortunate Sir Hugo was placed in the position of having to take over a factory and make an effort to build, under license from Sikorsky, a so-called "flying wing" plane.

Sikorsky was viciously anti-union, and this attitude was passed on to Cunliffe-Owens. As the aircraft industry in Southampton was well organised, the A.E.U. District Committee was particularly concerned to break into Cunliffe-Owens, and jumped at my offer to try and get a job there as this would give them someone on the inside. The firm obviously didn't check on me, for I managed to get started relatively easily and soon became the skilled man in charge of a team of about a dozen mainly semi-skilled fitters.

It was a fantastic set-up, and quite obviously the firm had only a rudimentary knowledge of how to build aircraft. What should have been extremely accurate large jigs forming the framework around which the fuselage and wings of a plane are constructed, were jury-rigged, Heath-Robinson affairs. There were not nearly enough skilled workers – most craftsmen in the area preferring to work in a decent factory – and a good proportion of the workforce were underpaid youngsters with little or no knowledge of engineering. I was able to take advantage of this situation by getting a job for a friend of mine back home who had been a miner but was unemployed. I spun a yarn to the employment manager that Gordon was a skilled fitter, and he jumped at the chance to take him on. So Gordon joined me in Southampton and started work at Cunliffe-

114

Owens. The problem was that he had never been inside a factory in his life and hardly knew what a file or a drill looked like, let alone how to use more sophisticated tools like micrometers and verniers. Fortunately, I persuaded the foreman to put him in my section, and for weeks I simply carried him, doing his job as well as my own. Luckily, Gordon was a fast learner and, more important, a competent actor, so he was able to put on a good show whenever the foreman came near!

Slowly, I succeeded in recruiting some of the workers into the A.E.U., but it had to be done surreptitiously because of the attitude of the management. The union helped by holding regular weekly meetings outside the factory gate and distributing leaflets. The firm had introduced some of the most obnoxious American practices, which would not have been tolerated in any decent union factory. Particularly degrading was a check made on men going to the toilets. Traditionally, in most factories the toilets are hallowed places, the only "free" areas in the factory, the place one went not only to do one's business but also for a short smoke or a read when one felt like a break or during waiting periods between jobs. Not so at Cunliffe-Owens. The cubicles had stable type half-doors, where everyone could see what you were doing, and to add to the indignity, before entering the toilet one's name and the time would be recorded in a book by a man sitting at a table just outside. If one was not out in five minutes he would shout out, and anyone going to the toilet more than a specified number of times a day would be reported, and his pay docked unless he could get a doctor's certificate proving that he couldn't help it!

Understandably, there was a great deal of resentment about these and other practices. What was needed, however, was an issue which would arouse sufficient feeling to unify at least a section of the workers in defiance of the management. It came, but the issue itself was so extraordinary that it deserves a chapter on its own.

12. THE LEEK

Jenkins his name was. A good Welsh name. Well fitted for someone who was to be the central character in the singular event that was to shut down the factory and achieve what poor wages, bad conditions and ceaseless agitation on my part had failed to do. The day was 1st March, which – as all educated people know – is Wales' national day, the day when due homage is paid to the country's patron saint, David. On this occasion, however, Dewi Sant was to have a more direct influence on

115

what happened than being just the distant recipient of the token annual obeisance to his name as a gesture to Welsh national feeling. For one of the great gifts he was reputed to have bestowed on the Welsh people was our national emblem, the leek, and it was this humble, though undoubtedly tasty, vegetable which was to be the main prop in the drama about to unfold at 10 a.m. of the morning in question.

The day had started as tediously as any other. All of my gang were dutifully working away at our prescribed tasks, either preoccupied with what we were doing, or talking about the escapades of the previous night and plans for the evening to come. This was the scene when Jenkins came across to have a word with me. He worked in another workshop, and I could see at once that he was infuriated to bursting point. He soon revealed the reason.

"Millard has sacked me!" Millard was the foreman of his section. "The bastard has ordered me to take my leek off!"

When he had simmered down, he told me the story. The leek he was wearing was one that could not easily be ignored. It was a giant of the species and one that any championship gardener would have envied, measuring eighteen inches from the tip of the leaves to the root, two inches in diameter and with a rich bunch of leaves that covered most of the front of Jenkins' overalls. Indeed, St. David himself would have been proud of it and felt fully justified in bestowing national immortality on its kind.

It was the crux of the trouble. Millard had told Jenkins to remove it because it was inciting a great deal of ribald comment and general larding about on the part of the lads in the section; such a provocation as was Fluellen's leek to Pistol in Henry V. With some justification Millard argued that it was interfering with their work.

It goes without saying that Jenkins refused. He regarded the very suggestion as an affront not just to himself, but to his country and his people.

"If you don't take it off," Millard said, "you can collect your cards at lunchtime," ("Collecting one's cards" was a common euphemism for being sacked).

As well as sharing Jenkins' natural feeling of outrage, I saw this as a wonderful opportunity of developing the united action we so badly needed. "Stop work, lads," I called to my gang, almost all of whom were Welsh. I then explained what had happened, and to a man we put down our tools and starting banging on sheets of metal, the traditional way of attracting

116

the attention of everyone else. I then went around the factory explaining to the men in the other shops what had happened and calling for solidarity. Within half an hour the entire factory was at a standstill, and there was that eerie but comforting drop in the noise level as machine after machine came to a standstill. Not only the Welsh lads, but our Scottish and English workmates also joined the stoppage. In an imaginative act of international solidarity, the Scots went out on to the airfield and collected thistles, their national emblem, which they proudly fastened to the front of their overalls.

I went to see Millard and demanded that he withdraw the threat to Jenkins. When he refused, we held a meeting and appointed a small multi-national deputation to go and see the under-manager – the manager was away – and I was elected spokesman.

As it happened, the under-manager was himself a Welshman who had originated from Tredegar, but even so he refused to countermand Millard's decision, only conceding that Jenkins could work the day out. All our arguments, threats and appeals to his national pride were of no avail. He obviously thought that the strike was a petty affair that would peter out by the end of the morning.

It didn't. When the afternoon came, not a man started work. Instead, they sat on the grass outside the hangar, or played cards. Towards two o'clock a messenger came from the under-manager asking that I go and see him. It is, of course, a sound trade union principle that you do not negotiate with management on your own, so I gathered together the members of our committee and we duly presented ourselves at his office. He was now an obviously worried man, a more chastened person than the one we had seen that morning, but for all that, after an hour's discussion, we had still failed to reach any agreement.

We were leaving the office, and had gone only a few yards along the corridor when he stuck his head out of the office door and called out, "Westacott, can I see you for a moment." I stopped, and he came up to me.

"Look," he said, "I'm in a hell of a predicament, you're right, of course, Millard was an absolute idiot to do what he did; but I'm only prepared to say this to you. Publicly, I have an obligation to stand behind my foremen and I must stick to it. What I'm asking is that we try and work out some kind of formula that will allow me to keep Jenkins on without compromising my duty to support Millard."

I called the committee back, and in a few minutes we had reached

117

agreement. The threat to sack Jenkins was withdrawn, and he was to be allowed to continue wearing his leek for the remainder of the day. The concession we had to make was over the size of the leek. It had to be cut in two. As there was only a hour left before finishing time, I felt this was a justifiable compromise, especially as I had no illusions that by the next day, with Jenkins gone and St David's Day over, it would have been extremely difficult to continue the action. Tempting though it was, we didn't even impose on the under-manager the penalty Fluellen inflicted on the hapless Pistol by forcing him to eat the leek at the end of the day.

This incident, trivial though it might appear, had more important and far-reaching consequences. It helped to unify the workforce in the factory and create a feeling of solidarity, and the victory, small though it was, demonstrated that by acting together we could win victories. Also, for the first time, the management had accepted the idea of negotiating with workers' representatives and recognised me, de facto at least, as a shop steward. These were significant inroads into the anti-union stance of the firm. It was a demonstration of the truth of something Lenin once wrote: that even trivial issues are important if workers feel a sense of grievance, for action around them can often lead to bigger things.

By this time Arthur had moved to London, where, after a brief spell working in a warehouse at Wembley for thirty shillings a week, he got a job as a skilled woodworker at the De Haviland aircraft factory at Hatfield. He made considerable progress there and was one of the small group of workers selected to make the original wooden model of the famous "Mosquito" fighter plane. He was elected a shop steward and later became Secretary of the De Haviland Shop Stewards Committee, as well as being a delegate to the London Trades Council from his union N.U.F.T.O. After the war he was to become the union's Organiser for Wales and the West of England. George was still at Oxford, but used to visit London frequently, so, as Southampton was in easy reach of the capital, the three of us would often meet at weekends.

These meetings are among my most pleasant memories. We would rendezvous at the top of Piccadilly tube station and go for a meal at the large Lyons Corner House at Marble Arch. This was one of George's favourite venues, because, he said, just for the price of a cup of tea you could relax in comfort and enjoy a concert by a live orchestra. Indeed, the Corner Houses were popular, cheap and pleasant restaurants, but the wages and conditions of the workers were abominable.

After eating, we would listen to the multitude of would-be orators at

Speakers Corner and wander around Hyde Park discussing and arguing. In the evening we usually went to Unity Theatre. Unity was a great venture. It didn't have the grandeur of a West End theatre; it was small and in a dingy building; but this was totally eclipsed by the content of the productions, the quality of the acting and the enormous enthusiasm of the audience and players. One of its most memorable productions was *The Babes in the Wood* – (a Pantomime with a Political Point), which contained catchy songs like "Affiliate With Me" (the C.P. affiliation to the Labour Party campaign was at its heights) and "Sing me a Song of Social Significance." Paul Robeson gave the theatre a tremendous boost when he starred in *Plant in the Sun*. Unity Theatre was the nursery that produced many fine actors who were to become household names in the post-war theatre and on television.

Once the three of us spent a grand holiday in Belgium, and on another occasion we went Youth Hostelling in the Isle of Wight, a favourite place I often used to visit. Arthur expressed concern at the number of Germans there appeared to be at every hostel, a concern justified later when it was disclosed that the Nazis used tourists as a means of gathering information.

13. THE OUTBREAK OF WAR

The incident of the leek was not the only demonstration of petty stupidity on the part of the management. Another took place on, of all times, 3rd September 1939, the day the war started. Of course, the outbreak of war came as no surprise and we were already working plenty of overtime, although it was voluntary. Even so, on that fateful Sunday morning when Neville Chamberlain's melancholy voice announcing that Britain was at war with Germany was relayed over the factory loudspeaker system, the atmosphere was unusually sombre and subdued. At lunch time a management statement was pinned to the notice board listing what it now expected of us . . . increased output, less absenteeism, better time-keeping and compulsory overtime every evening, Saturdays and Sundays. It must be said that, despite resentment at the indecent haste of the management and the lack of any consultation, this was accepted by most of the workers, because they recognised the importance of the job they were doing and saw it as a way of bringing the war to an end quickly.

It was the custom, mid-morning and mid-afternoon, for "tea trolleys" to come round at which we could buy a "cuppa" and biscuits to partake of while we got on with our work. However, on this fateful day, three o'clock came and went with no sign of the tea ladies. After fifteen minutes a ripple of unrest spread throughout the factory, and as there was no explanation and the foremen were keeping a canny silence, I felt beholden, being the unofficial workers' representative, to find out was happening. Incredibly, I was told that because someone had drilled a hole in one of the enamel mugs the day before, it had been decided to stop the trolleys as a reprisal! This absurd pretext to get a bit more work out of us was so transparent that a wave of anger swept through the workshops when I reported it; so the firm had another stoppage on its hands. After all, everyone was prepared to do more for the war effort, but to be rewarded by having the simple pleasure of a cup of tea taken away from us – well, that really was too much. It didn't take long for the management to see sense; albeit an hour late, the trolleys were wheeled out – to a mighty roar and a thunderous banging of hammers from all over the factory.

Communists and others on the left had seen the war coming a long time before. When, in September 1938, Chamberlain returned from seeing Hitler, waving that notorious piece of paper, the Munich Agreement, and proclaiming it meant "peace in our time" we saw it not only as a betrayal of Czechoslovakia but as a recipe for world war. The Sudetenland region of Czechoslovakia was ceded to Hitler, and with it the northern defences of the country.

However, at the time most people were genuinely relieved because it seemed that the immediate prospect of war had been averted. The government had deliberately engineered an atmosphere of hysteria, and for weeks before had set soldiers digging trenches, sandbagging important buildings and taking other measures aimed at creating the impression that at any moment bombs would be dropping and we would be at war. Writing in *Labour Monthly*, Palme Dutt astutely warned that this could be a deliberate subterfuge before betrayal, a move to stimulate fear so that any compromise that lifted that fear would be acceptable. And so it proved. There was a feeling of great relief, and in the House of Commons, Labour, and even I.L.P. M.P.'s, joined with the Tories in wildly cheering Chamberlain for having brought peace. Amid the hysteria there was the one lone voice of Communist M.P., William Gallacher, who shouted out, "You haven't brought peace: you've made war more certain." And how true his words proved to be.

In March 1939, in flagrant defiance of the Munich Agreement, the Nazi invaders marched into Prague, and Chamberlain was quick to reveal that the treaty he had signed "guaranteeing the new frontiers of Czechoslovakia" was to him another worthless piece of paper. He, and the French Premier, Daladier, refused to carry out their pledge to go to the aid of the Czechs. In what must be one of the most perfidious speeches of all time, Chamberlain justified their betrayal of the Czechs with the words, "why should the life of one British soldier be sacrificed to defend a far-off country about which most people know nothing?"

Although we expected it, the invasion of Czechoslovakia still came as a shock; hope is a very tenacious attribute of the human condition. A big demonstration on Southampton Common spontaneously became a march down the high street to the offices of the local newspaper, shouting and carrying banners with slogans like "Stand by the Czechs," "Save Peace – Stop Fascism" and "Prague today, London tomorrow." Similar actions were taking place everywhere. We were naturally particularly concerned over the fate of Czech anti-fascists. One of our local comrades who had recently visited the country immediately flew to Prague and married a Jewish communist so that she could come to England as his wife; and his was not a lone action.

The possibility now was not just that there would be a war involving the whole of Europe but also that the appeasers would commit the final act of treachery and connive with Hitler for an attack on the Soviet Union. After all, the prime object of appeasement was to strengthen the fascist powers so that they could do precisely that. This was a very real danger, and increasingly Tory voices were raised joyfully as they anticipated the prospect of a mortal conflict between the Soviet Union and Germany, with Britain looking on.

But there was an alternative. For many years the Soviet government had argued that fascist aggression could be halted and peace preserved if the democratic powers, particularly Britain, France, the United States and the Soviet Union formed an anti-fascist alliance and stood up to Hitler and Mussolini. Together, these powers were economically and militarily much stronger than Germany and Italy, and could easily have stopped aggression when the fascist powers were relatively weak. Even after the Nazis had consolidated their position and grown strategically and militarily stronger, particularly through invasion and expansion, Hitler would have thought twice before taking on such a formidable alliance.

The idea of an Anti-Fascist Peace Pact was enthusiastically taken up by the peace movement in the western democratic countries and received wide support in the labour movement as well as among church people, the democratic movement and many others who were not usually

121

regarded as progressive but were appalled at the prospect of war. So strong was the movement that Chamberlain was compelled to make some gesture. He sent emissaries to Moscow, ostensibly to discuss the Soviet proposal for an anti-fascist front. That it was only an empty gesture was soon demonstrated. Instead of sending a government minister, with power to negotiate, he sent a third-rate Foreign Office civil servant, William Strang, notorious for his pathological hatred of the Soviet Union, and long-retired Admiral Drax. They were given no power to take decisions. As a further insult, they leisurely travelled to Moscow overland, by the slowest route possible. By contrast, the Soviet representatives in the talks were the Foreign Minister, Molotov, and the Commissar for Defence, Voroshilov.

The British – French proposals were breathtaking in their arrogance. The Soviet Union was to agree to go the aid of Finland, Estonia, Lithuania, Latvia and Rumania if they were attacked and aid was needed, but Britain and France were prepared only to give guarantees to Poland and Rumania. In other words, in the event of a German attack on the Soviet Union through the Baltic states, Britain and France would do nothing – a clear suggestion to the Nazis as to which way they should go. Moreover, the neo-fascist government of Poland declared, obviously with the blessing of Britain and France, that it would not allow Soviet troops to pass over its territory in the event of war breaking out. The stark contrast between this and the way Chamberlain and Daladier scuttled off to do a deal with Hitler at Munich was painfully manifest.

It is this that convinced the Soviet Government that Britain and France were not prepared to do anything to stop the onward march of fascism, that they still had hopes that Hitler would turn eastward, and that the war, when it came, would be between Germany and the Soviet Union.

Faced with the failure to establish an anti-fascist alliance, the hostility of the British and French governments, and the increasing inevitability of war, the Soviet leaders, quite understandably, felt compelled to turn their attention to ensuring that their country would not be embroiled in the conflict. In particular they were not to be manoeuvred into a position where they would be facing Germany alone, with the western democracies standing by watching the two protagonists tear each other to pieces. They had made it clear long before that they were prepared to sign pacts of non-aggression – not 'mutual assistance'- with any nation without qualifications, and, indeed, had done so with France, Czechoslovakia and other countries. However, no-one had considered their signing such a pact with Germany, and it was clear that they did so as a last resort, considering it necessary for the defence of the Soviet Union only after the failure of their attempt to built a peace pact.

Nevertheless, it came as a great shock. For the British and French governments it was catastrophic for it marked the total failure of appeasement. It now presented them with the threat that a Germany which they had re-armed and strengthened was not going to turn against the Soviet Union, but might even turn on them, a possibility Stalin had warned about at the Eighteenth Congress of the C.P.S.U. the year before.

For communists and socialists, the shock was just as bad. For years we had led the fight against fascism and had looked upon Hitler and Mussolini as the greatest threat to humanity. The Soviet Union had been the main force, the only nation, that had stood up against the fascists – in the Spanish Civil War, the invasion of Abyssinia, and the onslaughts against Austria and Czechoslovakia. It seemed inconceivable that they could ever sign a pact with Hitler, the man who had so brutally destroyed the German working-class movement and tortured and killed many thousands of our comrades.

Yet, after a period of intense discussion and a great deal of heart-searching most of us recognised the bitter logic of the step the Soviet Union had taken. The prime responsibility of the Soviet leaders was to defend and preserve their country. The greatest threat to it was from German aggression, tacitly supported by Britain and France. They had tried hard to minimise this threat by proposing an anti-fascist alliance, but this had failed. It left open only one option, however unsavoury: to make terms with the likely aggressor, hoping that this would postpone the Soviet Union becoming embroiled in a war, which it was, in any case, ill-prepared for. It would give it time to prepare, for there were no illusions, as Lenin had warned, that sooner or later any war involving the major capitalist powers would ultimately involve the Soviet Union.

Of course, a major factor in determining our attitude was the record of the Soviet Union in the fight against fascism. Call it faith in the Soviet Union if you like, but it was a faith based on fact and experience. Nor was it only Communists who accepted the Pact as an unfortunate necessity, but a wide strand of left and progressive opinion in this country.

Having said that, I must say that it was a bitter pill to see photographs of Stalin shaking hands with Ribbentrop and the declarations of friendship between the Soviet and German leaders. We excused it on the

123

grounds of diplomatic necessity. Nor were we aware, of course, of the secret parts of the agreement, under which the Soviet Government handed back to the Nazis some German Communists who were in prison in the Soviet Union. This only came to light twenty years later, and I am sure it would have appalled us had we known about it.

It was recognition of the failure of their policy to turn Hitler towards the Soviet Union that led Chamberlain and Daladier to change their policy. The Nazis had occupied the Rhineland and nothing was done; their invasion of Austria had met with no response; the Munich Agreement had been torn up and the Czechs left to fight aggression alone; there had been connivance to help the fascists conquer Spain. But suddenly, for the British and French appeasers, it became a matter of principle to go to the aid of an invaded country. And ironically, unlike the other countries that had been swallowed up, Poland was not even a democracy.

We heard Chamberlain's mournful voice announcing that Britain was at war with Germany over the factory loudspeaker system. The atmosphere was subdued. The announcement was not, of course, unexpected, but many people had a sneaking, and quite understandable, feeling that there might be a repetition of Munich – a last-minute climb-down. As it turned out, this was an altogether different ball game.

It faced Communists and all progressives with a dilemma. What now should be our attitude towards the Chamberlain government and to the war – of course, for the wiseacres today who pontificate from a comfortable vantage point half a century away from the events, there is no problem. With the benefit of hindsight they lecture us on "where we went wrong." Believe me, it was far from easy for us who lived through those days.

We had been fighting fascism all our lives and our natural instincts were to give every support to a war against its worst manifestation. Yet, the Tory government had connived in building Hitler, was paranoiac in its hatred of the Soviet Union and socialism, and had proved time and time again that it could not be trusted. How could we back such a reactionary and treacherous government?

On the Friday night before war was declared I had to face up to this question at a meeting of the Southampton Young Communist League. Being the Party branch representative in the League, I was naturally asked what our policy should be. My reply was that we should support the war effort against fascism, but at the same time conduct a political campaign to bring down the Chamberlain government. And this was, in fact, the policy adopted by the Communist Party. The next day, its Central Committee issued a manifesto:

You are now being called upon to take part in the most cruel war in the history of the world. One that should never have taken place. One that could have been avoided . . . had we had a People's Government in Britain . . . we are in support of all necessary measures to secure the victory of democracy over fascism. But fascism will not be defeated by the Chamberlain Government.

This line became known as the "war on two fronts." Within a few days, 50,000 copies of a pamphlet by Harry Pollitt, "How to Win the War," were on sale.

But we all had doubts, and there were heated discussions, not only in the Party, but also among many socialists outside. We were only too aware of the treacherous character of the government and were not convinced of its sincerity. We were strongly suspicious that we were being tricked. It seemed obvious that it had declared war on Hitler because he was no longer seen as an anti-Soviet tool. The idea of Chamberlain waging a "just" war for democracy and freedom seemed utterly absurd, both in the light of his record and because of the way the millions of subject peoples in the colonial countries were being oppressed. Even before the war started, Daladier had already banned the French Communist Party, and we now know that this was considered in Britain. Then there was the somewhat unrealistic nature of the alternative: to bring down a government firmly entrenched with a huge majority of two hundred and seventy eight and to replace it with a "people's government," especially in a war situation when there were strong emotional and patriotic feelings for national unity behind the nation's "leaders." It needs to be said, though, that there was little jingoism and nothing like the atmosphere that prevailed in 1914.

I make these points to counter the lie so often stated that the "change of line" by communists in the first few weeks of the war was a servile acceptance of Soviet policy. It was not remotely like that. When the Comintern condemned the war as an "imperialist and unjust war . . . not a war against fascism" it was in line with what many British communists were thinking and what we were all arguing about. Since the downfall of the Soviet Union, the verbatim records of the meetings of the Central Committee of the C.P.G.B. have been published in a book entitled *About Turn* and they disclose the heated debate that went on in the Committee. But although we members of the Party didn't know until later the Comintern position and the arguments discussed by the C.C., there was not a political position expressed in the Committee that we didn't think of and debate among ourselves.

This must be stated because in the introduction to *About Turn*, Monty Johnstone argues that the Party accepted the change of line because "the membership did not hear the opposing arguments advanced in the Central Committee discussions." What nonsense this is. We were not morons. We were quite capable of analysing the situation ourselves. In the complex situation that we all had to grapple with, I find obnoxious the attempt now being made to divide the Party, including the E.C., into "goodies" and "baddies," with Palme Dutt characterised as the chief villain. This is an unjust and grossly over-simplified approach to the reality.

True, the Comintern statement tipped the balance against supporting the war, and gave support to the expressed views of Dutt and other members of the Central Committee. But in the October issue of *Labour Monthly*, not included among Johnstone's many quotations, Dutt clearly expressed the complex nature of the problem confronting us all . . . the basic character of imperialist conflict for the redivision of the world appears intermingled with other factors, with questions of national liberation and with the question of the democratic struggle against fascism in a tangled knot which requires the most careful unravelling.

On 2nd October the Central Committee accepted the Comintern analysis (the Comintern itself did not make any public statement until November). Five days later a new manifesto was issued stating that the war "is not a war for the liberation of small nations. It is not a war for the defence of peace against aggression . . . the British and French ruling- class are seeking to use the anti-fascist sentiments of the people for their own imperialist aims." That this line was generally acceptable among communists and many on the left is indicated by the fact that membership of the Communist Party, which had increased from 6,500 in February 1935 to 18,000 in August 1939 went up to nearly 20,000 by the following March. A measure of some popular support was the fact that daily sales of the *Daily Worker* were 15,000 a day higher at the end of 1939 than at the beginning.

Labour Monthly circulation increased from 7,000 a month at the start of the war to 14,700 in March 1940 and 20,000 by the end of the year, even with the loss of its substantial overseas circulation. And in March 1940, an anti-war candidate in a bye-election received a surprising 6,000 votes. Even the Labour Party was forced to recognise the strength of anti-war opinion within its ranks. It published a pamphlet, "Is This An Imperialist War?" by EC member, Harold Laski. After explaining the official attitude, Laski goes on to say "But it would be wrong to deny that a large number of Labour Parties contain members who do not share this view. To them the present war is simply, like the last, another "imperialist war." He then goes on to concede that there is some truth in this, but that "fascist imperialism is imperialism of a new type."

14. THE WAR YEARS IN SOUTHAMPTON

The months that followed the outbreak of war seemed to confirm all that we had said. It was the period of the "Phoney War," when, although there was a great deal of vituperation and activity, there was no sign of any move to take on the enemy. A blackout was immediately imposed and more children from cities were evacuated to safer areas (some had already gone). Everyone had to carry respirators, and Identity Cards were issued and had to be produced on the demand of almost anyone in uniform: police, soldiers, civil defence workers, etc. Often buses were stopped and the I.D.'s of every passenger checked. Unlike the First World War, conscription was imposed from the start, and the number of uniformed men and women on the streets increased rapidly.

But there were other changes, not quite so acceptable. Prices soared and profiteering was rife; the rationing of essential foods was not introduced until the beginning of 1940. An onslaught was made against working conditions and workers' rights. Civil liberties were severely curtailed, and in place of debates and legislation, Parliament handed over to the government the right to govern by decree, by the issuing of Orders in Council. Using this procedure, important sections of the Factory Acts and safety regulations were arbitrarily suspended. Essential Works Orders were enforced which among other things introduced 'direction of labour' severely restricting the right of workers to change their jobs, and making "persistent" lateness, absenteeism, strikes, refusal to work overtime and virtually anything that could be construed as workers interrupting production, offences subject to prosecution. Indeed, the trend towards fascism in Britain, already noticeable in the pre-war policy of the Chamberlain government, became even more marked.

127

Employers had a bonanza, not only in the power it gave them over their workforce, but also in the no-risk profits they could now make. The government introduced an incredible "cost-plus" system, whereby firms were guaranteed profits amounting to a percentage of total costs – a bonus for inefficiency!

And yet there was no sign of Britain taking on the Nazis. As William Gallacher wrote in a pamphlet that sold 32,000 copies, "all is quiet – except on the home front." No wonder that anti-war feeling in the labour movement grew. By the end of 1939, eighty four Labour Party organisations, twenty four trades councils, ninety seven trade union and thirty one Co-operative bodies had passed anti-war resolutions. In February 1940, a conference called by Labour Monthly attracted eight hundred and seventy eight delegates representing three hundred and seventy nine organisations, and passed a resolution that "this war does not serve and cannot be made to serve, any interest or aspiration of the people." The TUC, on the instigation of right-wing leader, Ernest Bevin, took action against Glasgow, Edinburgh, Aberdeen, Dundee and twenty English trades councils for their anti-war attitude.

Then, a development took place that galvanised the government into action – but not against the Nazis. Following the rapid advance of the German army and the collapse of the Polish government, the Soviet Union had occupied Polish territory bordering on its own frontiers. Leningrad, the second largest city of the Soviet Union, was only twenty miles from the Finnish border and the heavily armed "Mannerheim Line" (a defensive line built by General Mannerheim, the pro-Nazi Finnish chief military commander who had suppressed a revolutionary uprising in 1918, slaughtered 15,000 men, women and children, and taken part in the war of intervention against Russia). It was, in fact, possible to bombard Leningrad from within Finnish territory. The Soviet Government regarded this as a potential threat to Leningrad and Russia's northern sea route in the event of the war spreading to the Baltic states. It proposed that the border be moved back a little, and in exchange offered Finland extensive territories further north. The Finns refused and, after a border incident, Russia invaded Finland on 30th November 1939. It is debatable whether they were justified in taking such drastic action, especially as there were many moderate Finns who supported a compromise; but in view of Mannerheim's record and Finland's subsequent role as an ally of Germany, they clearly had every reason to be worried.

The immediate reaction of the Chamberlain government seemed to bear out all that Communists had been saying about its real motives, that it was anti-Soviet rather than anti-Nazi. For three months there had been no sign of it wanting to take on the fascists and the British Expeditionary Force in France stood idle. Now, suddenly, there was frantic activity. Although shortage of arms was the reason advanced for not fighting the Germans, miraculously they suddenly materialised to fight the Russians, planes, heavy guns, bombs and military equipment of all sorts were dispatched to Finland. A joint British-French expeditionary force of 100,000, set up to fight on the western front, was quickly assembled to fight the Russians, but was delayed from going to Finland by the refusal of the Swedish and Norwegian governments to allow it passage through their waters. An appeal was made for volunteers to fight the Russians and a recruiting centre was set up in London with a British major placed in charge of the volunteers. Incredibly, discussions started with the two fascist dictators, Mussolini (Italy had not yet come into the war) and Franco of Spain, with the aim of co-operation. However, on 12th March, the very day that France and Britain had chosen for direct intervention, the war in Finland ended.

The media conducted a violent campaign of hate against the Soviet Union, far more virulent than anything it directed against the Nazis. In contrast with its policy of "non-intervention" when the Spanish Republic was being destroyed, the right-wing Labour Party leadership now called for international aid to be sent to Finland. It expelled the famous barrister M.P., D. N. Pritt, for his opposition to Labour Party policy on the Finnish war.

The hysteria generated did result in an increase in hostility towards Communists – more than the party's anti-war policy had provoked. Nevertheless at the height of the Soviet-Finnish war, Harry Pollitt received almost 1,000 votes when he stood as Communist candidate in a parliamentary by-election in Silvertown.

Beginning with the German invasion of Norway and Denmark in April 1940, then the rapid capture of Belgium and the Netherlands, followed by the fall of France, the "Phoney War" ended and the real war began in earnest, and with it the realisation in Britain of what total war meant. In May, Churchill became Prime Minister. It is worth noting in these days when every Tory who lived through these events swears with hand on heart that he never supported Chamberlain, that in the crucial vote of confidence leading to his resignation, not only did he win, albeit by a small majority, but the majority of Tory M.P.'s voted for him to remain Prime Minister.

Understandably, as the war began to bite with the start of the bombings and the mounting casualties, matters became more difficult for Communists, but still not as much as some would have expected. This was because the Party, while opposing the war politically, maintained its close links with ordinary people and campaigned on their behalf. For example, on civil defence. Even before the war, the government was acting on the assumption that the main threat to civilians would be poison gas, so respirators were issued to everyone and householders were instructed to make one room of their house gas-proof: a measure that was absurdly impractical for most families. But the Party and the left, bearing in mind the experiences of the Spanish Civil War, argued that the main danger would not be from gas, but from mass bombing. The famous scientist, J. B. S. Haldane, who worked closely with the Communist Party and wrote regularly for the *Daily Worker* (he later served on its Editorial Board), published a popular Left Book Club choice, *The Defence of the Public Against Aerial Attack*, followed by a high-selling booklet based on it. Everywhere, we campaigned for deep air-raid shelters to be built, and in London the Party led a highly successful campaign – against determined government and police opposition – for the opening of the London Underground stations as air-raid shelters. *The Southern Daily Echo* published a long letter of mine putting the case for deep shelters in Southampton, and the District Committee of the Party produced a leaflet calling for shelters to be built in the danger zones of Portsmouth and Southampton. It exposed plans to evacuate 30,000 children from these cities to the Isle of Wight, Bournemouth and Poole – places still in the direct flight path of enemy planes heading for the southern ports. It demanded that the children be sent to safe areas well away from the coast, that special camps be built for them and that the country houses of the rich be commandeered to house evacuees.

The Party also campaigned against war profiteering and rocketing prices, and defended the rights of workers in the factories. Most workers recognised that although we were against the war, we had an honourable record of opposition to fascism and were not in any way pro-German, although some of the gutter press and right-wing Tory and Labour politicians did try to use this smear. Added to this was the fact that a great many individual Communists in the trade unions and workplaces were respected and trusted because of their record in fighting on behalf of their members and fellow-workers. For all these reasons, public attitudes to the Communist Party were ambivalent. Most people opposed our anti-war policy, yet there was wide recognition, particularly in the labour movement and the workplaces, that our position was not a defeatist or negative one and that our main concern was – as it always had been – defending the interests of the working class.

It was recognition of the fact that workers believed this that stopped the Government from banning the Party. And in a letter to Regional Commissioners, the Home Secretary admitted that there was no evidence of organised attempts by the Party to slow down production or industry.

The main demand of the Party was for a People's Government, and it aimed to make this the basis for the development of a broad, popular movement. Five hundred prominent national and local men and women, mainly from the labour movement, signed an appeal calling for a "People's Convention" to be held on 12th January 1941 in the Manchester Free Trade Hall. Three weeks before the Convention met, the Free Trade Hall was destroyed and the conference was moved to London. According to its Chairman, Harry Adams, a highly respected builders' trade union leader, it "surpassed all expectations:" 2,234 delegates attended, including, incidentally, Indira Gandhi and Krishna Menon, who were to become India's Prime Minister and Foreign Minister. It called for:

A people's Government, truly representative of the whole people and able to inspire the confidence of the working people of the world. A people's peace that gets rid of the causes of war.

The Aircraft Shop Stewards National Council grew in strength during this period, and I continued to write regularly for *The New Propeller*. Its circulation reached 31,000 by the end of 1939, rising to 45,000 during the next few months, being sold in one hundred and fifty factories including the largest and most important. In November 1939 I attended a national meeting of shop stewards, called by the Council, at which reports were given from all over the country of the unrest arising from the arbitrary way in which employers were using the situation to undermine safety standards, enforce overtime and attack long-standing agreements on working conditions. Soon after this conference, it was decided to broaden the movement, and the council became the

Engineering and Allied Trades Shop Stewards National Council. It was a period of intense political activity, with *Daily Worker* sales drives, leaflet distribution and meetings – including the regular Sunday pitch on Southampton Common. The Southampton branch of the Communist Party now had over sixty members, and the number was slowly increasing. It had an office and, for a time, a full-time secretary. But the leading figure was the Hants and Dorset District Secretary, Jack Dunman. An Oxford graduate, Jack had for some years been editor of the *Country Standard*. Somewhat reserved, he had a keen political brain and was always ready to help the rest of us, qualities I only fully appreciated in later years when I got to know him quite well.

On May Day we organised a very successful march through Southampton, probably the first May Day march in the city's history. I was a marshal, and between one and two hundred took part. We expected some opposition, but I noted in my diary that there was, in fact, very little. There were some screams of abuse from a few bystanders, but these were cancelled out by the surprising number of people – including servicemen – who clapped us.

George and Arthur had now joined the Communist Party, as had our younger brother, Emrys, in Tredegar. Subsequently Bert was also to join, so that five of the six of us would be members. George had been threatened with expulsion from the Labour Party because of his anti-war views and the fact that he took part in a Communist-led demonstration. In a letter to me he took exception to reports in the national press that students had thrown rotten eggs at the demonstrators; they were not rotten, he wrote, because he had taken some home and had them for breakfast! I don't want to give the impression that political activity was all that easy in the first years of the war. It wasn't. But most of our difficulties arose from harassment by the police and the authorities rather than from public reactions. There was a "cover-all" offence of "spreading alarm and despondency," which was often used against those who publicly criticised the government. A friend of mine was arrested for trying to collect signatures to a petition demanding deep shelters. It was not the most tactful place or time, for it was in a shelter during an air-raid, and he was explaining how inadequate the shelter was!

More often than not, however, it was used quite blatantly to stifle criticism. Jack Dunman and the Party branch secretary were arrested while speaking outside a factory. But the most bizarre incident concerned Fred Ward at Folds. It was in June 1940, when, following

Dunkirk, the Germans had invaded France and entered Paris. The French government resigned and a new government was formed. This was being discussed by the blokes in a crowded toilet, and in answer to a question, Fred expressed his belief that the new government was one of capitulation, which proved to be the case. A chargehand reported what he had said, and a couple of hours later two policemen arrived and rather dramatically escorted Fred out of the factory. After spending three days in jail he was then charged with "holding an illegal assembly in a protected area." He was fined, sacked from his job and dismissed from his voluntary Air Raid Precautions responsibility.

It was about this time that the bombings started in earnest. Netley was about three miles from Southampton, and in our innocence we began by treating the first raid on the city as a spectacle that we watched from our garden. As it hotted up, however, we all felt somewhat scared and spent most of the night spread over the kitchen floor. It was only the next morning when we picked up pieces of anti-aircraft shrapnel from around where we had been standing, and heard of the destruction the bombers had wrought, that the grim reality of air bombardment was brought home to us. One of the first factories to be hit was Vickers Supermarine, where the Spitfires were made. As well as being a prime target, it was also an easy one for the Luftwaffe, for the pilots knew it intimately. Before the war many of them had often visited the factory as honoured guests of Vickers!

Thereafter, air raids became routine, and we spent many sleepless hours at night down the shelters. Usually, during the day we ignored the sirens and the German bombers flying high overhead, until it became clear that our area might be the target.

A few months before I had changed my job. Matters at Cunliffe-Owens had come to a head when the firm insisted that everyone wear the firm's overalls with a big "S" (for Sikorsky) on the back. To add insult to injury, the management proposed making a weekly deduction from our wages to pay for the overalls and for their cleaning. This move was thwarted when I pointed out that it was a violation of the Truck Acts, which declare it unlawful for deductions to be made from pay without the written consent of the employee. After taking legal advice, the firm accepted this; but a week or so later they counter-attacked, sacking everyone, but agreeing to immediate re-employment on condition that a consent form was signed. By this time I had had enough and refused to sign. As it happened, at that very moment the Manpower Board was

133

hastily getting together some skilled workers for a special job at Air Service Training at Hamble, and I was directed there.

A.S.T. had been a private training college for potential pilots, drawn largely from ruling circles in the colonial countries; but it had been taken over by the Air Ministry to repair and service Spitfires damaged in the air conflict. It was hard work but extremely interesting and absorbing. Planes would come in straight from action, and after any mess (sometimes including blood) had been cleaned up, we had to repair them. We had to improvise a great deal, not having the machines and sophisticated tools of a factory, and I became an expert in repairing one particularly difficult part of the Rolls Royce Merlin Engine, for which I was later commended by an R.A.F. boffin. We worked literally around the clock, often snatching a few hours sleep curled up underneath the workbench. It was arduous, but quite exhilarating. We were, of course, a prime target for German attacks. One incident I remember was during our midday break when we were sitting on the grass by the side of the runway eating our sandwiches. A low-flying plane suddenly appeared out of the clouds, roaring towards us, and we realised abruptly that it was an enemy bomber. I have never seen men move so fast. One bomb hit the runway, but another landed on a nearby school. Thankfully, there were no pupils in it and no-one was hurt. My old factory, Cunliffe Owen, received a direct hit; sixty nine were killed and one hundred injured.

As the bombings increased in frequency and intensity, rather belatedly the powers-that-be were forced to recognise the stupidity of aircraft production being concentrated so much in the south of England. Production became more dispersed, and I was given the opportunity of moving to Westland Aircraft at Yeovil, or to South Wales. My choice was obvious. So it was that at the end of 1940 I left Southampton to return to my native heath. It was not without a feeling of sadness, for I had made many good friends, met a great number of interesting people and had many fascinating experiences during the politically eventful four years I had lived and worked beside Southampton Waters.

Self portrait,May 1937
Note the Labour League of
Youth badge

Aero engineer!   Hamble aerodrome, May 1937

Recruit

Communist Party Demonstration, Southampton 1940
(Fred is on the left wearing a marshall's armband)

Anticipating "demob"

The monastery of Monte Cassino after the battle.
Photo taken by Fred, with Brownie box camera

Fred and Kath when young

Fred, Kath, father, Gwyneth, mother and Bronwen

Fred and Kath's
firstborn, Glyn

At the Lenin collective farm.
Fred and Kath second and third from the left.
James Klugman second from the right.

Notts miner's leader,
Communist Joe Whelan, who
died tragically young

On the campaign trail

The Party Offices, 65 Castle Boulevarde, Nottingham, June 1969

Fred and Kath on a delegation in Yalta

Public forum on "Matters of Social Concern" Mansfield, June 1969
Dennis Concannon M.P., Rev. R.T. Warburton (Rural Dean of Mansfield)
Rev. K.G. Greet (Methodists Citizens Department)
Fred Westacott (prospective Communist Candidate for Mansfield)

Film Maker

Win Clark with Jock Kane
Guests of honour at Communist Party
Notts and Derbys Coalfield Area annual
dinner

At Bronwen's wedding

George Johannes, with Fred outside the Derbyshire Miners Area Council Offices, before giving the 18th Kath Westacott Memorial Lecture, 1993

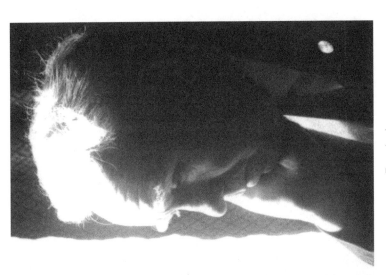

Pensive!

Young Campaigner:
Grandson at the Greenham Common Peace Camp

Grandpa with family on holiday at Dolgellau - "Hengwrt".
Bronwen and Ruth; Gwyneth; Roger; Alex; Lee
Joanne; Fred; Amy; Sophie; Vicky and Emily; Gareth; Emrys

Eightieth Birthday Party
With Tony Benn and Barry Johnson

Eightieth Birthday Party
Ida Hackett and Barry Johnson

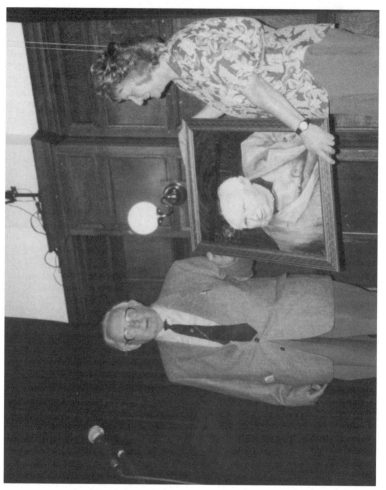

Eightieth Birthday Party

Shirley Clark presenting her portrait to Fred

Conference delegate

Shirley Clark's portrait of Fred

With Bas Barker and miners supporters, Armthorpe 1984

North Derbys delegates
at Pensioner's Parliament, Blackpool 1996

The Pensioners Movement:
Chesterfield pensioners meet up with colleagues from
Liverpool and Glasgow at Wortley Hall, July 1992

At Chesterfield Communist Party stall May Day

At home, April 1995

CHAPTER IV

1940-1943: RETURN TO WALES

15. THE SHOP STEWARDS' MOVEMENT

The Manpower Officer instructed me to report to Ludlows (Welsh Metal Industries) at Caerphilly. This suited me fine, for Caerphilly was only twenty miles from Tredegar and not far from Cardiff. However, I was only there a few months before I was transferred to Helliwells, a Birmingham-based aircraft sub-contracting firm that had a large factory on the big Treforest Trading Estate, near Pontypridd. Even so, in the short time at Ludlows I was involved in a spot of bother when the tool-room workers went on a "go-slow" to get rid of a particularly obnoxious supervisor.

I was fortunate enough to get first-rate 'digs' with an all-female family, a mother and her three teenage daughters. They were neighbours of a party member who told me afterwards that they had decided to take in a lodger because they felt safer 'having a man about the house.' They certainly were determined to keep me, for they looked after me well. Apart from the excellent meals, a marked attraction for me was that I had a private sitting room, which eventually I also used as an office. The back of the house overlooked the splendid Caerphilly Castle, one of the largest in Europe, at that time neglected, but now a well-kept tourist attraction.

There was a good Party branch in Caerphilly and it boasted a Communist councillor, Jack Roberts, a miner who had fought in Spain, and a popular local figure affectionately known to everyone as "Jack Russia." I soon became active in the Party branch and in the union.

Helliwells was a union firm, and as one of its specialities was making jigs and press tools, the toolroom was comparatively large, with over sixty workers. After being there a few weeks I was elected toolroom shop steward and a member of the works committee. The Convenor, Dan Jones, subsequently became a Labour M.P.

On the 21st of January 1941, Home Secretary Herbert Morrison, banned the *Daily Worker* and Frank Pitcairn's (Claude Cockburn) newssheet, *The Week*. The Cabinet had been discussing this for some time but held back taking action because it would be seen as an attack on free speech, and, also, because they could find no evidence whatsoever of any Communist Party in any country supporting or helping the fascists (this was disclosed years later, when the Cabinet Papers of the period were made public). Nye Bevan forced a debate on the ban in the House of Commons, but to no avail. The great Irish dramatist, Sean O'Casey, who was a member of the Editorial Board of the *Daily Worker*, caustically commented on the "harrowing English, known only to the chosen few" which the Home Office used, and concluded that "out of the cloudy gathering of words shoots out the order that the chosen ones are not to be criticised."

It was clear that there was the possibility of the Party being driven underground. In the first few weeks of the war, preparations had been made for this; after all, the French Party had been banned right at the start, when it was still supporting the war. Membership lists, typewriters and duplicators were dispersed to the houses of lesser-known or undercover members, and "shadow" committees set up which would take over if the members of the existing committees were arrested. We were told not to put anything that could identify people in our diaries or wallets, and to cut out any names and addresses on personal letters we might want to keep. Now the threat of illegality seemed to be very real again.

Not having the *Daily Worker* was a severe handicap, but we made up for it by driving all the harder to sell pamphlets and *Labour Monthly*. Of course, the campaign to get the ban lifted started immediately and won wide support, not only in the labour movement, but also among progressives who were uneasy that in a war which was supposed to be fought to preserve free speech, political criticism was forbidden.

One morning in June 1941, during a visit to Tredegar, I was lying in bed in that drugged frontier between sleep and consciousness when the peacefulness of the moment was rudely shattered:

"You had better come down. You've got a problem on your hands!" It was my father shouting up the stairs. "Germany has invaded Russia!"

This is how I first heard the historic news that changed the character of the war and almost certainly decided its outcome. It came as a complete surprise, yet it shouldn't have done. We had always believed that sooner or later the Soviet Union would become involved; the only questions were when and how. Communists have often been accused of suddenly changing their line when it happened, but this is another over-simplification. As Dutt had said at the start of the war, its exact character was complex. Although mainly a struggle between two groups of powerful imperialist nations, within this was the struggle for liberation and independence, on the part of the peoples of most of the countries invaded. And this factor increased in importance as more and more countries were overrun by the Nazis. The invasion of the Soviet Union brought two hundred and fifty million people into the liberation struggle.

Secondly, there was an obvious shift in the standpoint of the dominant sections of the British ruling class. They had certainly changed their line. At the start of the war, although the need to defend Britain's imperialist position from the challenge of Germany was uppermost, anti-Sovietism came a close second. Switching the war to one against the Soviet Union was never very far from the top of the agenda and, indeed, was openly advocated by some leading Tories. Churchill becoming Prime Minister, and the formation of a coalition government which included the Labour Party, represented a significant change of emphasis. It reflected a strengthening of those forces determined to win the war and defend Britain and the Empire at all costs. Although their hatred of communism never changed, Churchill and those around him were not obsessed, as were Chamberlain and the appeasers, with destroying the Soviet Union – at least not at that time.

Churchill's historic speech on the day following the invasion, in which he declared full support to the Soviet Union in the fight against fascism, reflected this decisive break with Munichite policies and was a rebuff to those Tories who hoped to see Germany and the Soviet Union tear themselves apart while Britain looked on. It must be said that we communists did not appreciate the full significance of the changes that had taken place after Chamberlain's removal. Although in practice we concentrated mainly on defending the day-to-day interest of the workers in a war situation, so far as the war itself was concerned we maintained our political opposition to it.

The changed character of the war clearly demanded a re-examination of our policy. Of decisive importance for us was the fact that the only country where the workers were in control was now fighting for its very existence. If it were destroyed it would be a crippling setback to the world struggle for socialism. I do not think there is any reason to be apologetic about this, as were some so-called communists in later years.

137

As the achievement of socialism was our primary objective, there was only one logical attitude we could take up. So we now threw our whole weight behind the task of defeating the fascist powers.

It is difficult today for those who did not live through the experience to imagine the electrifying effect the involvement of the Soviet Union had on the people of this country. While the majority had, from the start, clearly supported the war, some demoralisation had set in owing to the military setbacks our forces had experienced; and among the more politically aware, there was an undercurrent of distrust over the fact that there were still people with Munichite associations in responsible positions. There was widespread criticism of the inequalities and bungling that were commonplace, and profound anger and cynicism at the profiteering which everyone knew was going on. While petty local black-marketing was in practice accepted, and with a degree of good humour, people were outraged at the stories of black market operations on a large scale.

With the Russians on our side, the atmosphere changed. Britain was no longer alone; we now had a powerful ally. In itself, this would have been sufficient to raise the spirits of the British people. Yet it only partially explains the tremendous uplift that took place. In my opinion, the surge of emotion that occurred was primarily because there was a feeling that we now had on our side an ally that would not compromise and alongside whom we could defeat Hitler. Despite twenty years of anti-Soviet propaganda and an acceptance of much of it, there was still an instinctive feeling among many workers that the Soviet Union was different from other countries, that it had no capitalists, no profiteers, and workers were at least trying to run things themselves. How else can one explain the remarkable transformation in industry and the increased enthusiasm for the war effort that took place almost overnight – Churchill was to complain that it was easier to get workers to produce arms going to Russia than for Britain. "Tanks for Joe!" "Arms for Joe!" "Joe for King!" – were popular slogans chalked up in the factories and on railway trucks. And this feeling grew, rather than weakened, as the German advance into Russia continued.

Significant, too, was the growing demand for workers' participation in management and production. Already, the government had been forced to take over the famous Shorts Aircraft Company because of management inefficiency, and the management of the mines had to be taken out of the hands of the notoriously backward and avaricious private owners. Engineering employers, in particular, jealously guarded their "right to manage" without interference from outside. The idea grew of Joint Production Committees of workers and management in every workplace. Helliwells was one of the first factories in Britain to set up a J.P.C., and the Parliamentary Secretary for the Ministry of Aircraft Production came down to start it off.

I was on the Committee from the first, and at our weekly meetings we soon put the management on the defensive. We would sometimes be up all night trying to break down its obduracy, for there was great resentment among most bosses at what they saw as our trespassing on their territory. The infamous 'cost-plus' system still operated, which meant that employers had no incentive for efficiency. They could hardly care less: if workers or machines stood idle for want of material or parts, the firm still made a profit – indeed, the greater the costs the higher the profit. There was one occasion when an entire shop was on 'waiting time' for days because of the lack of a particular size bolt. The workers' representatives on the JPC insisted that cars be sent to Cardiff to scour the ironmonger shops for these bolts – an exercise which was highly successful.

This atmosphere did not mean that workers were docile and easily willing to give up hard-won rights. Significant concessions had been made almost from the start of the war, such as agreeing to dilution – unskilled and semi-skilled workers, particularly women, being quickly trained to do many skilled jobs – and accepting some relaxation of safety laws. Probably the biggest transformation was in the toolroom where the acute shortage of toolmakers resulted in drastic technical changes that were to become permanent. The traditional toolmaker not only designed the tool, but constructed it entirely. He did everything from start to finish, the fitting, turning, milling, grinding, and often proudly gave the finished tool a decorative finish. He could not and would not be hurried, and this was accepted because production depended on having accurate press tools and jigs. Consequently, toolmakers were not on piecework, but usually had a bonus based on that of production workers. The big expansion of war industries and the need for speed meant that there were not enough toolmakers to meet the demand. This was partly overcome by breaking down the job through a division of labour. Thus we had skilled fitters becoming toolroom fitters, skilled lathe operators doing the turning, etc. It was no longer necessary to have one person who could do everything. Most controversial was the introduction of tool designers, draughtsmen with no practical experiences of toolmaking. The old adage that an ounce of practice is worth a pound of theory proved so often to

139

be right, and we took malicious delight in taking some of the drawings to the Production Committee and pointing how stupid or impractical they were. Yet even the proudest of the old toolmakers reluctantly had to accept that the changes were necessary in order to win the war.

Of course, in every factory, grievances over particular issues sometimes reached boiling point, often due to the arrogance or insensitivity of management. One such incident landed me in court. A new foreman was appointed for the toolroom, an outside man with no great knowledge of toolmaking, but with an inflated sense of his own importance. He soon made himself thoroughly unpopular, and matters came to a head when he recommended to the manager that two of the older workers be punished for swearing at him. At an angry meeting of the workers there was a call for strike action, but it was at a time when the war was going badly, so I proposed that we start by simply restricting our action to a ban on overtime. This was agreed to. A few days later I received a summons to appear in court in Caerphilly to answer three charges of contravening the Essential Works Orders by refusing to work overtime on two occasions and of not having been at work one morning. The Manpower Officer was made to look a fool regarding the last charge when I produced an order from him instructing me to be at his office on the morning in question; and I was, in fact, having a discussion with him at the time of the alleged offence. The convenor, Dan Jones, put the obvious point to the magistrates that I was being charged because I was the shop steward, but his eloquent appeal didn't stop the worthy Labour dignitaries on the bench fining me £6.

The national shop stewards' organisation was thriving, and after discussions within its leadership and with the Party in South Wales it was agreed to set up a Welsh section of the movement. The main reason for this was the rapid growth of war production engineering in Wales. It was decided that I convene a meeting of representatives of all factories in South Wales. The meeting was an outstanding success, with works committees of all factories of any importance, old and new, being represented. It was unanimously decided to form a Welsh section. A committee was elected and I was chosen as Secretary.

Our movement soon established itself, exchanging information and co-ordinating efforts in dozens of factories. There were three main issues we took up: union recognition and organisation; increasing war production; and defending the conditions and rights of workers.

Despite the fact that the important contribution the trade unions were

140

making in the fight to win the war was now officially recognised, there were still firms which held out against recognition. Chief among these was British Overseas Airways which employed about 1,500 at Treforest. They refused even to talk to the union. As it was next to Helliwells, I was strategically placed to help organise union propaganda efforts and to contact workers. When we had recruited about eighty per cent of the workforce into the union, it was decided to take direct action. Wal Hannington, who had moved from organising the unemployed to become a national organiser of the A.E.U., came down, and soon demonstrated that his flair for doing things dramatically, but effectively, had not left him. A mass meeting of B.O.A. workers was called outside the factory, and after a rousing speech Wally called on the workers to follow him. They marched into the factory, past the security men, up to the manager's office. Wally went in, plunked himself in a chair opposite the manager and said, "Right, now we are going to talk!" Despite blusters and threats, talk they did, and it was not long afterwards that B.O.A. capitulated and recognised the union. We were successful in increasing union membership and winning recognition in a number of other factories.

The war had entered a dangerous new phase, with the Germans continuing their advance towards Moscow and the Volga, and with tanks, planes and guns being desperately needed for our own forces and for our allies. The United States and Japan had come into the war and Singapore had fallen. A powerful campaign was underway in Britain for the western allies to open a second front in Europe. The absence of such a front meant that the Nazis were free to concentrate over three-quarters of their military might on their Eastern Front. The danger seemed obvious to us: the defeat of the Soviet Union would put the other allies in a dangerously weak position and could lose us the war.

In this situation, increasing war production was a paramount preoccupation of our Welsh Shop Stewards Council. In February 1942, I organised a shop stewards' conference in Cardiff on behalf of our Council. Ninety three delegates attended, from aircraft, engineering, munition, steel and ship-repair factories employing a total of 90,000 workers. The reports of the delegates confirmed what we already knew – that it was the organised workers who were leading the fight for increased production, often in the teeth of open hostility by managements. Joint Production Committees were not compulsory, and some firms opposed setting them up. Lucas's, employing 5,000 workers in their Cwmbran factory, was one, and the reason was obvious when it was

141

disclosed that forty per cent of what was produced was scrapped, and that girls and women were falling asleep on the job because they had to get up at 4.30 every morning to get to work on time – such was the state of the firm's transport system.

16. LIVING CONDITIONS IN WARTIME BRITAIN

What was it like living and working under wartime conditions. Later generations have gleaned an inkling from films and T.V. documentaries. But it is only a pale shadow of reality, and reality is always much fuller and richer than portrayals and accounts can possibly convey. What was amazing was the adaptability of people, how quickly everyone accepted the bizarre, almost surreal way of life. The blackout was an example. On overcast nights, especially in the winter, when darkness was total and one literally could not see past one's nose, we groped around more help-less than moles in their underground passages, for moles can only go one way and have senses other than sight to guide them. We learned to cope very well in familiar surroundings, but in strange places instinct had to take the place of knowledge, which it did not always do successfully. One dark night I was hurrying to a meeting when my head collided with a telegraph pole, producing lights that broke all blackout regulations and leaving me totally confused for quite a while! Seeing to the blackout curtains at dusk soon became routine, and the Air-Raid Warden's cry, "Put that light out," if a chink was showing, became as familiar as the postman's knock.

Stringent petrol rationing restricted private motoring and meant that most vehicles on the road belonged to drivers who had extra fuel because of the jobs they were doing. Most road transport consisted of buses or military vehicles. The scale of the operation required to take a large part of the adult population from every town and village to the widely dis-persed factories necessitated armadas of buses. A common quip was that they all seemed to be going to the same place – "Relief" (the word on the destination boards when vehicles were forbidden to use place names in case it would give information to the enemy). In the same quirky vein of humour, it would be said that the most bombed place in Britain was "Random," because the standard formula used on the news every day was: "Last night enemy planes dropped bombs at random."

Travelling by train was arduous and sometimes adventurous. Timetables were usually chaotic, and main line trains, when they came, were usually packed solid, with passengers – most in uniform – standing in the compartments, in the corridors and pressed tightly against the doors. On some occasions when I was in uniform, the only way I managed to get on my train was head-first through a window, helped by fellow – "squaddies" inside. Of course, travelling at night was more boring because it wasn't possible to read by the tiny glow of light allowed.

Although there was plenty of grumbling, rationing was quickly accepted as a way of life. Most people recognised it as being necessary and fair – which in general it was so far as most people were concerned. Of course, there were anomalies. If the butcher managed to get an extra supply of offal or sausages off the ration, he could keep them "under the counter" for his friends or favoured customers. There was the queuing when word got round that a shop had acquired something in short supply. And there were always one or two local "wide boys" who could sometimes lay their hands on that odd bottle of whisky or pair of silk stockings for special occasions. This local black market was tiny in relation to the official system of distribution, and was tolerated good-humouredly – and used – by most people.

However, it was a different story when it came to the rich. As is usually the case, there was one law for the masses and another for them. They – or their friends – had their own farms. They also had extensive resources, knew the right people and could eat out at expensive restaurants where meals were not rationed. They had jobs in the massive war bureaucracy or could contrive in other ways to get extra petrol for their large cars. There was smouldering indignation at the luxury goods still available to those who could afford to buy them.

Food rations were adequate but boring, and consisted primarily of what could be produced in this country. This meant that fruit from overseas was in very short supply: no bananas were imported at all, and oranges were few. Rations varied according to the work you did; workers in heavy industry or on the land, for instance, had a greater quantity of cheese. The government launched a "dig for victory" campaign, encouraging people to have allotments to grow their own vegetables. We had to get used to new tastes, like whale meat. When American "lease-lend" started, and particularly when the U.S. came into the war and its soldiers were in Britain, there was some improvement, and we were introduced to the delight of "Spam." The Ministry of Food had regular spots on the wireless and issued a stream of leaflets on how to make the best of what was available – my favourite is a pamphlet I still cherish entitled "Enjoy

Potatoes in Eighty-One Ways"! Special provisions were made for babies and young children and free vitamin drinks and capsules issued to them, which meant that children in the depressed areas were actually healthier than they had been in peacetime.

What helped us cope with the rationing was eating in the factory or pit canteen. There was also the brilliant idea of the "British Restaurants." These were public canteens run by local councils in association with the Ministry of Food. The idea behind them was that it was cheaper to prepare food in bulk, and these public canteens also gave the authorities some control over people's nutrition. They were so popular that they continued – and remained popular – for some time after the war. It was a great pity when, in response to pressure from the Tories and restaurant interests, they were closed down.

After the first year of the war, during which we didn't know what to expect, air-raid warnings were largely ignored except in obvious target places like London and some of the other cities. The sirens would sound if enemy planes entered the civil defence area, but we soon learned to look out for them or listen for the familiar beat of their engines as they passed overhead, usually bound for a target elsewhere. Occasionally people were caught out, when pilots jettisoned their remaining bombs randomly before returning to Germany. This happened when I was home one night in Caerphilly. We heard the whistle of a bomb dropping – the whistle indicated it was going to land near us – but fortunately no-one was hurt. The banshee wail of the air-raid siren still produces an unpleasant reflex reaction whenever I hear it in old war films.

When at work, although anyone could go to a shelter when the warning sounded, very few did. It became a point of honour not to allow the enemy to disrupt production. Even when the sky was lit up with bombs dropping on Cardiff (which was only a few miles away) or Newport or Bristol, we would go out to look at the spectacle, and then get back to work. My brother George, who worked at Vickers, Weybridge, told how most workers continued working even when bombs were dropping all around, and how one night a row of bullet-holes appeared on his bench in front of him.

How about the spirit of camaraderie which existed during those war years and of which much has been made? A recent book has sought to debunk it, claiming that "the spirit of the war years" is a myth. Of course, the author wasn't around at the time. If he had been, he would not have been so cocksure. Even allowing for some romanticising with the passing of years, I have no doubt whatever that there was a different spirit, a more co-operative and caring feeling arising from the character of the war and the fact that the whole community was facing the same enemy and similar problems. It was most dramatically demonstrated during the blitzes, in the selflessness and risks taken to help bombed neighbours; but something of the same spirit existed everywhere and developed naturally. A major factor was that there were no sharp divisions; the community meant much more than it did in peace time, and the individual was so obviously part of a co-operative enterprise. There was also the fact that, unlike the First World War, civilians were in the front line: if not to the same extent as the armed forces, enough to feel that they were direct participants. There was a natural instinct to keep together.

This doesn't mean, however, that all was sweetness and light. Of course it wasn't. Since people are only human, there were differences and divisions; some acted cynically, and many resented the hardships and the sacrifices they were called upon to make. But such attitudes were overshadowed by the powerful feeling of unity in struggle, which was general.

This feeling was particularly strong after the fall of France, when Britain stood alone and faced the possibility of invasion. True, mixed with it was an element of fear, of not knowing what would happen if the Germans really did take over. I was in Southampton at the beginning of this period, and understandably it was more marked there, an atmosphere of waiting for something to happen, for the first Nazi parachutists or landing parties to arrive. Road signs were taken down and no shop was allowed to display any name or sign indicating the place. The idea was to confuse the enemy. It certainly confused me and my mates one weekend. We had cadged enough petrol to drive to South Wales, and got lost on Salisbury Plain during the night. We had to wait until the morning before we were able to discover where we were.

Like all effective propaganda, war propaganda did not create basic attitudes, but reinforced feelings that already existed. The crude presentations of the Chamberlain period were replaced by the highly sophisticated propaganda of the Churchill years. Whatever criticisms can be levelled at Churchill – who was, after all, a lifelong opponent of socialism and the working class – one has to admit that he was a superb propagandist, a master at the art of reading the mood of the people and building on it (although in this he was not infallible, as 1945 was later to show). When, on taking office he said, "I have nothing to offer but

145

blood, toil, tears and sweat . . . he simply expressed what everyone knew. Theatrical though it might appear, it was a refreshing change from the cover-up stories and exhortations that everyone had become completely cynical about. The impression deliberately created was that here was a leader who was frank and truthful, someone who could be trusted not to shelter behind meaningless platitudes. Similarly, when everyone was elated at the news of the victory at El Alamein, Churchill cautioned, "This is not the end, it isn't even the beginning of the end, but it may be the end of the beginning." And with invasion seeming imminent, there was no glossing over the situation. When he spoke on the radio and said, "We shall fight on the beaches, we shall fight on the landing grounds; we shall fight in the fields and in the streets; we shall fight in the hills; we shall never surrender!" he expressed what so many wanted to hear, and by doing so he strengthened the determination to resist.

Having been a propagandist myself, I can appreciate the speeches of Churchill; and as Lenin once said concerning Lloyd George, we should never be averse to learning from our class enemies. Liberal leader, Sir Richard Acland, in an analysis of Churchill's speeches, made the point that they were extremely well-prepared. Hours would be spent on a single phrase – usually those phrases that have proved to be the most memorable.

Another superb example of propaganda was the "Postscript" talks on the radio after the evening news. Particularly effective were those delivered by J. B. Priestley and the American journalist, Quentin Reynolds. Again, they were carefully scripted and had a vast audience. Visual propaganda also improved and used humour instead of dry exhortations. The most memorable, perhaps, were the Fougasse cartoons, such as those centred around the slogan "Careless Talk Costs Lives," these were seen everywhere, particularly on buses and in factories.

17. VICTIMISATION

Being a Communist perhaps made me more sensitive to the atmosphere of comradeship that existed. It was a strange experience to be in step with everyone else – indeed, to be respected more precisely because one was a Communist. We were identified with the Soviet Union and the Red Army, and the epic struggle taking place on the 2,000-mile front stretching from Leningrad to the Crimea. It was a time of great solidarity meetings, when Communists spoke along with Labour, Liberal and Tory politicians; and bishops, businessmen and trade unionists rubbed shoulders with each other on the same platform. There was the occasion when a crack Soviet sniper, Lyudmila Pavlichenko, visited Cardiff. The station platforms were filled to capacity by the waiting crowd, with the Lord Mayor and prominent people from all walks of life in the city making up a welcoming committee. As the train steamed into the station, engine draped with red flags, a mighty roar went up. But what completed the picture, from my point of view, was the sight of the engine fireman, who, by a happy stroke of luck, happened to be an active Party member in Cardiff, leaning out of his cab giving the clenched fist salute.

Of course, I became active in the local Party branch in Caerphilly. After a few months, I was elected secretary and soon afterwards was elected to the Party's Welsh Committee. This is when I first met Will Paynter, who used to pick me up on his way to the Committee meetings. I am afraid I was a bit diffident in taking part in discussions with powerful labour movement figures who were known not just in Wales but throughout Britain: Arthur Horner, Idris Cox, Will Paynter, Len Jeffries, Edgar Evans and a host of others. Often, Harry Pollitt or Palme Dutt would attend, for South Wales was one of the strongest areas of Communist influence, with a wealth of experience arising from its magnificent history of struggle.

With the rapid growth in Party membership, it was decided to set up an East Glamorgan Sub-District, and I was made its Secretary with Will Paynter as Chairman. Will, or Bill as he was more often called, was a full-time miners' agent and was based on Bargoed, further up the Rhymney Valley. His wife had recently died, leaving him to bring up a young family of girls. He was widely respected, having fought in Spain and having been a leader of the unemployed movement of the 1930's. After the war he was to succeed Arthur Horner as General Secretary of the National Union of Mineworkers. (When he retired he wrote a short but very interesting autobiography, called *My Generation*). We used to meet at his house, although on one very warm Sunday afternoon we decided to hold our meeting sitting on the grass in a nearby park. It was not a success, for we did not reckon with the local popularity of Bill. We had hardly started the meeting when individuals who knew him and were taking a stroll came and joined in. In a short while the committee had doubled in size!

Towards the end of 1941 the German army had advanced to within sixty miles of Moscow and the fall of Russia's capital city seemed imminent. It was a distressing, nerve-racking period, and we listened to the

147

wireless hourly for the latest news. It was a Friday, and I thought the least we should do was to hold a public meeting as quickly as possible, if only to wear off some of the frustration we were all feeling at our help-lessness. I was on the afternoon shift, but I got hold of a piece of paper and retired to the "reading room" (our euphemism for the toilet). There, I drafted a leaflet calling a public meeting in Caerphilly Park for Sunday. It was headed – "MEN AND WOMEN OF CAERPHILLY. MOSCOW IS IN DANGER," and went on: "The war machine of the Nazi beasts, regardless of cost in human life, is forcing its way towards the Soviet capital. The Red Army is resisting with a heroism unsurpassed in human history, but faced with the armed resources of the entire continent it has been forced to fall back. The battle for Moscow is the battle for the world."

It then called for telegrams and letters to the Prime Minister demand-ing the opening of a Second Front in Europe, and urging no let-up in the fight to increase the production of coal and armaments. It ended: "COMRADES! CITIZENS! The heroic defenders of Leningrad, Odessa, Kharkov and Moscow are giving their lives so that we may live. We must help them all we can. WE MUST NOT FAIL."

I have quoted the leaflet to give some idea of how moved we were by the situation – and the sort of language we used, which was quite accept-able then, though it might not be today. "Comrades" became quite a fashionable word.

On the way home late that night I dropped the draft through the letter-box of a local printer, appealing to him to rush out a few thousand right away. This he did, and we spent Saturday giving them out. We had no permission to use the park, but no-one objected and we had a first-rate meeting.

The battle for Moscow is now history. For the first time since the war began the Nazis were repulsed on a major front, but at an enormous price in Soviet dead. Field Marshall Timoshenko launched an all-out attack on the German forces, forcing them to retreat further. This defeat presaged the decisive rout of the German 6th Army at Stalingrad ten months later, a defeat which proved to be the turning point of the war. Following the attack on Pearl Harbour by the Japanese, the United States had entered the war, and in October 1942 Rommel's Afrika Corps was defeated at El Alamein. So 1942 was a difficult but exhilarating year, for after fac-ing defeat and the grim prospect of invasion, we now scented victory.

It was a period of non-stop activity – political and trade union as well as on the job. When I was working nights I often never bothered to go to bed. One of the problems of Party organisation was that members were all on different shifts in various pits and factories, making branch meetings difficult. This was one of the reasons the formation of factory branches became so necessary. Another reason was the need to develop political work where it could make the biggest impact – at the point of production. We formed a Party branch at Helliwells and met in the canteen between shifts.

In September we had a great boost: the fight to get the ban on the *Daily Worker* lifted succeeded. This was the result of tremendous pressure, including a resolution at the Labour Party Conference. Immediately, selling the paper was a priority task. In the factory, we did it quite openly, and it was great to see copies of the paper on benches all over the factory (as well as in the toilet). Every week in the toolroom we raffled a political book to raise money for the branch – again, quite openly – and hammer and sickle badges were very popular.

It was during this period that I first met Betty Ambatielos. At that time her name was Bartlett and she was a young teacher from Yorkshire who had come to teach at a school in the village of Cefn Forest, near Blackwood. She took part in some of our activities in Caerphilly. One Sunday, we were faced with the predicament of having a good audience at an open-air meeting we had organised, but no speaker. Some mishap had prevented him attending. I didn't regard myself then as much of a public speaker and the other comrades were far too timid to venture getting up on the platform. And the audience was waiting. It was left to me and Betty. "You've got to speak," I said. She was horrified. "I can't do it," she said, "I've never spoken in public before." But speak she did, and the meeting was carried through successfully.

I relate this anecdote partly because Betty became one of the most effective public speakers the Communist Party produced, but also because of her subsequent political career. She became Cardiff organiser of the Party, when she met and married Tony Ambatielos, the 28-year-old General Secretary of the Federation of Greek Maritime Unions, which during the war was based in Cardiff. Tony was also a Communist. Betty served for a time on the Executive Committee of the Party, but when the war ended she joined Tony in Greece.

With the swing to reaction in Greece, Tony was imprisoned for eighteen years, most of the time on a notorious penal island. During those years, Betty tirelessly campaigned for his release and that of his fellow political

149

prisoners. With the return of democracy, and his freedom, Tony became a Communist M.P. However, I have a particularly personal reason for being grateful to Betty, which I shall mention later.

In May I was faced with a big dilemma. The Manpower Inspector declared that because of the general shortage of toolmakers six men were to be transferred from Helliwells to other factories where they were more urgently needed. We couldn't object to this, but we did object to some of the names on the list, which included married men with families for whom it would have been a hardship to move away from home. I discussed it with the Inspector and he agreed to amend the proposals. He also agreed that the transfers be to other factories in South Wales. A few days later we received the new list . . . and I was on it. The works committee was up in arms and proposed that we reject my inclusion on the grounds that I was a leading shop steward and my leaving would weaken trade union organisation in the factory. I stood out against this, arguing that we had agreed to the transfers because it was consistent with our line of doing all we could to help the war effort, and that we ourselves had made the stipulation that single men should be considered first. I felt it would be wrong for me to claim special exemption, particularly as the union was quite strong in the factory. In any case, still being in South Wales meant that I would be able to continue carrying out my job as Secretary of the Welsh Shop Stewards Council as well as my other political commitments.

Maybe I was too naïve, for it transpired that the Manpower Board had other plans. Five out of the six on the list were sent to jobs within five miles of Treforest. There was one exception . . ! I was told to report to a small firm in the village of Llanberis, at the foot of Snowdon, in North Wales. There could hardly have been a more effective way of taking me out of activity; I knew something of what Russian political activists must have felt when they were exiled to Siberia. It confirmed what some of the stewards had warned about – that we were walking into a trap.

Still, maddening though it was, I couldn't refuse to go. So, I packed my trappings and took the train to Colwyn Bay, where I reported to the North Wales Manpower Inspector. He was most disconcerted and apologetic, and disclaimed having made any request for a toolmaker. The firm said it only wanted fitters. Moreover, officials at the Labour Exchange maintained that they had told the Ministry of Labour that they couldn't find accommodation for any more workers in the area because the Ministry of Food and other government concerns had moved there. That it really was an acute problem was soon demonstrated. For three days the Labour Exchanges of Colwyn Bay, Llandudno and Conway combined their efforts to find a place for me to stay – even putting someone specifically on the job. The Billeting Officer and even the police were roped in. All to no avail. In the meantime I stayed in a hotel. Not without a sigh of relief on the part of the Manpower Inspector – as well as myself – he ordered me to return to South Wales.

I immediately sent a detailed account to the A.E.U. Llantrisant District Secretary, Dai Harry, who was attending the meeting of the union's National Committee at Blackpool. By a fortunate chance, the union had just conducted an inquiry into the misuse of manpower and the inefficiencies of the Ministry of Labour. The union's president, Jack Tanner, seized upon my report, which was discussed by the Executive Committee. It was just what they were looking for, and Tanner personally raised it with Ernest Bevin, the Minister of Labour. I did not hear the whole story until later, but I did wonder at the alacrity with which the Ministry's South Wales Regional Director acted. It surprised me when, instead of having to deal with one of his underlings, I received a phone call asking me to go and see him in Cardiff; it surprised me even more when he apologised and agreed, without a murmur, to pay not only all my expenses, but also loss of wages from the time I left Helliwells.

I was now directed to work at John Curran's in Cardiff, an old established general engineering firm, part of the Curran combine. Although it was organised and there was a full-time A.E.U. representative covering the combine, there was no shop stewards committee, and there was general cynicism regarding the representative, Bill Davies, who was regarded by everyone as being a stooge of the management. He and John Curran were fellow Masons. There was a Joint Production Committee, but its role was severely limited. However, there was a very good Party branch, led by Harry Hitchings, a fine comrade who played a prominent part in many working-class struggles in post-war years.

Harry and myself, together with the Party comrades and other militants, worked hard to get an effective union organisation and J.P.C. established. But just when we were on the point of succeeding, the management struck back: they sacked about thirty workers, among them almost every Party member and militant, including the one progressive member of the management staff. (The Essential Works Orders allowed employers to sack workers but didn't allow workers to sack themselves by leaving). The immediate reaction of the rest of the workers was to

151

strike. To prevent this, Harry and I immediately went to the Cardiff Party office and, with the help of Betty Bartlett (who was now the Party's Cardiff Organiser), duplicated a leaflet urging the workers to take up the issue through their unions and with the management.

What came after revealed a sordid conspiracy, involving John Curran himself, Robert Armstrong (a National Organiser of the A.E.U.), Bill Davies and local officers of the Ministry of Labour. Armstrong was in Wales because of the death of the Divisional Organiser. As a result of actions we took in our defence, Harry Hitchings, a Londoner called Grey, and myself were hauled before the right-wing dominated District Committee of the A.E.U. and accused of "acting against the interests of the union." I was fined three pounds and the others two pounds. The specific charges were:

1. Being responsible for submitting to the *Daily Worker* an article likely to create a false impression with the general public as to the action taken by our Divisional Organiser over dismissals at Messrs John Curran & Co.

2. Causing to be issued a leaflet which was not true to fact and was likely to prejudice the amicable relationship between Messrs John Curran & Co. and the A.E.U.

3. Assisting in organising a mass meeting of the workers at John Curran & Co. without first consulting the local A.E.U. officials.

There were many protests from A.E.U. branches, including our own, and we appealed to the Executive Committee. In my appeal, I broadened the issue to include the dubious activities of Armstrong, an avowed trotskyist, in South Wales. The full story is best told in extracts from the letter I sent to the union's Executive Committee:

In April I started work as a toolmaker at John Curran & Co., Cardiff. My experiences as a shop steward in other factories and as an active member of several years standing of the A.E.U., enabled me to see that all was not well with union organisation at this factory.

There were no shop stewards and only two union representatives on a committee covering all the firms composing the Curran Combine. With their full support and that of the full-time A.E.U representative covering the combine, I proposed that a steward be elected for each department of the factory. This was unanimously approved at a factory meeting of A.E.U. members, and submitted to the Cardiff District Committee for its approval. This was given and a convenor appointed for John Curran, in accordance with rule. The Convenor was one of the

Combine committee-men, Brother Hitchings.

A Joint Production Committee (called a Joint Advisory Committee) had already been set up in John Currans, with Bro. Hitchings as Vice-Chairman. This Committee had brought about some improvement in production and welfare conditions, but it soon became apparent that the prevailing chaotic conditions, bad organisation and chronic 'idle time' could be altered only by a radical alteration in the system of management. After several months of trying to improve the situation, the workers' representatives on the J.P.C. and the shop stewards committee decided to compile a statement on the bad state of affairs, for submission, in accordance with the recognised procedure, through the District Committee of our union to the Regional Production Committee. It was decided to submit this to the full meeting of the J.P.C. the following day and afterwards to a factory meeting.

Five minutes before the J.P.C. was due to meet, the Convenor (Brother Hitchings) and the J.P.C. Secretary (Brother Grey) were given their cards and the meeting was cancelled by the management. The full-time A.E.U. representative was immediately informed, but the next morning I was given my cards, along with other workers. The reason given was 'redundancy' and we were all given a week's pay in lieu of notice. Brothers Hitchings, Grey and myself insisted on reporting for work every morning until our notice expired, but we were not allowed on the premises.

One of those dismissed was a member of the administrative staff, who told us he was calling a meeting of certain staff members and dismissed workers for the following day. We told him that we could have nothing to do with the meeting unless our union approved.

On the Monday morning Brothers Hitchings, Grey and myself called at the District Office of the A.E.U. and informed Brother Armstrong and Brother Rosser of the events of the weekend. Instead of meeting with the sympathetic hearing we expected from our officials, we (and myself in particular) were subjected to a torrent of abuse from Armstrong, who said that he "didn't care a bugger about production or production committees." On being reminded of the official policy of our union he launched into a long attack against our Executive Committee, and after stating that it was "the worst Executive Council the A.E.U. has ever had," he went on to tell us that the agreement regarding J.P.C.'s was not constitutional and had not been approved by the National Committee. He then made a somewhat incoherent political attack on myself and challenged me to a debate on the present war. I refused to discuss political issues with him at that moment, and insisted on him dealing with the question of our dismissals. He then told us that he was not concerned how many of us were dismissed.

On reporting to the factory that afternoon we were informed that there was to be a meeting of the J.P.C. that evening, and as the notices of the workers' representatives had not expired, they insisted on attending.

The next development was on Wednesday, when we were told by Mr John Curran himself that a number of the girls were to be given jobs in other Curran factories, but "Mr Armstrong had phoned and told him not to employ us three." When we later raised this with Armstrong, at first he was evasive, but then denied it.

By this time the dismissals had aroused great interest in Cardiff, and I was approached by a *Daily Worker* reporter for an account of what had happened. The report I gave him was factually correct and a restrained summary of what had happened. I mentioned Brother Armstrong's attitude to production because it was necessary to explain why nothing was being done by our union and because he stated that he didn't care who knew about his attitude. If anything, the report erred on the side of moderation and nothing was said about Armstrong's attitude to the Executive Council.

By the Friday, the dismissed workers were getting impatient that nothing was being done, and workers in the factory were threatening to strike, so we decided, as shop stewards, to issue a leaflet indicating the necessity for the workers in the factory to meet and discuss the issue, and also the need to discuss it at their trade union branch meetings. We urged them not to strike. These were distributed outside the factory. This leaflet was of a general character and made no appeal to members of any particular union, for the dismissed workers were members of several unions. It stressed that action should be taken through the union branches.

Subsequently, in a discussion with Brothers Rosser and Armstrong, we were asked to appear before the next District Committee meeting. No mention of a charge was made and we were under the impression that the purpose was to discuss the dismissals.

We attended the meeting and were astounded when we were charged with organising a meeting of A.E.U. members without the consent of the District Officers. Not only had we not organised the meeting referred to, but we had told Brothers Rosser and Armstrong who had, and that we were opposed to it.

I protested at the fact that we had not been given prior notice that we were to be charged, but nevertheless the Committee found against us. A lack of experience by members of the Committee of factory organisation and procedure (the majority are connected with ship-repair), and the irregular manner in which we were charged not giving us time to prepare our defence, are the main reasons for the decision. I appeal against the three charges on the following grounds:

1. The report to the *Daily Worker* was a true record of the situation. It was restrained and moderate, stating the facts of the dispute and the opinions of Brother Armstrong (which he has not renounced) that production is not our concern.

2. The leaflet issued was true to fact. It was an appeal to the workers to use the legal and constitutional procedures of getting their grievances righted through meetings and their unions.

3. I categorically deny having anything to do with the meeting organised by a member of the administrative staff. On the contrary, I opposed any meeting which had not the support of our union – and informed Brothers Rosser and Armstrong of this (although, in fact, there is nothing in our rules which stipulates that a shop stewards convenor cannot call a meeting of workers if thought necessary; prior permission of union officials is not required).

Now about the motives behind these charges. The individual directly concerned is Brother Armstrong. I maintain that the attitude of this official towards Brothers Hitchings, Grey and myself, when we first informed him of the dispute, is the key to why he pressed these charges. Since coming to South Wales he has earned a certain notoriety for his anti-war views, his support of strike action as a remedy for the smallest grievance, his attacks on the Executive Council and his fanatical opposition to the progressive win-the-war policy our union is pursuing in the factories. Before these charges were brought against us, several A.E.U. branches in this Division had protested to the Executive Council at the attitude and activities of Brother Armstrong. At British Overseas Airways, Treforest, he advocated strike action to force the management to recognise the union. This advice was rejected by the stewards and recognition won without losing a minute's work. The times he has advocated such action are too numerous to set down in full, and would certainly bear investigating by the Executive Council.

I am condemned for giving a report to the *Daily Worker*, yet Brother Armstrong only a few weeks ago gave a report to the anti-war "New

Leader" regarding the dispute at the Tredoman factory. A fact that is perturbing our members is how this paper is able to get hold of information regarding the internal affairs of our Union that it is difficult even for our members to obtain. In South Wales we have a pretty good idea. The best example of his attacks on the Executive Council is when he addressed mass meetings of workers at the Lucas factory, Merthyr Tydfil, and openly condemned the Executive Council. Shop stewards and Convenors from these and other factories are prepared to testify regarding Brother Armstrong's attitude before the Executive Council or any investigating committee it may set up. The charges against myself and my colleagues were motivated by Brother Armstrong's violent political opposition to myself, and the attempts we have made to get the production policy of our union accepted and operated in South Wales.

In conclusion, may I point out that although I am only twenty six years of age I have played an active part in our union's affairs for several years and have served it in a number of positions. I was Branch Chairman and Deputy District Committee member at twenty two and have been a shop steward at several factories. I have always aimed at strengthening our union and have never consciously acted against its interests or weakened it in any way. I can obtain testimonials of appreciation from numerous officials of our Society indicating the work I have done in the branches and the factories where I have been employed.

Lengthy though this statement was, it didn't tell the whole story. For example, when Hitchings, Grey and I reported at the factory gate one morning, instead of being barred entrance, we were invited in. We were told that old Mr John Curran, the owner of the firm, who hardly ever came to the factory, had put in an appearance and wanted to see us. We were shown into his office and he greeted us most affably. "I am sure," he said, "we can sort out this trouble in a way that's satisfactory to all of us." He then proceeded to tell us what that way was. Grey would be made manager of an overall-cleaning plant that would be created (he once worked in the clothing industry), whilst Harry and I would be made foremen in two of the engineering shops – on condition, of course, that we stopped the agitation. He was doing this, he assured us, even though Armstrong had told him not to employ us.

He seemed genuinely surprised when we told him what he could do with his offer. Bribery of this sort is, of course, a recourse often adopted by managements and, unfortunately, sometimes accepted.

There were at least two other occasions when I had been offered supervisory jobs, with the obvious intention of disarming me and at the same time producing cynicism among workers.

By the time our Appeals had gone through the procedure of being considered by the A.E.U. Executive Council, I was in the army. The Appeals were upheld in full, and the District Committee was instructed to annul the decisions and to repay the fines. The District Committee put all the blame on Armstrong. Years later I was told by George Crane, one of Armstrong's fellow National Organisers at the time, that the Appeal had caused quite a stir and that the E.C. had, in fact, investigated Armstrong's activities and condemned him. I understand he was either asked to resign or dismissed, but I have never confirmed this; certainly, his term as a full-time worker for the union did abruptly end. Predictably, the Ministry of Labour turned down our appeals against dismissal.

I have cause to remember the episode for another, very personal, reason. Among those of us dismissed was a most unlikely factory worker, let alone a revolutionary. Her name was Mary, although we called her "Bobbie," and she came from a middle-class Scarborough family. She had been a professional ballet dancer, but had volunteered to do factory work as her contribution to the war effort. About two years previously, Bobbie had joined the Communist Party and was active in the Party in Cardiff. She was a real "stunner," with the kind of beauty often associated with a ballerina – slim, a flawless peach complexion, a classical countenance and jet black hair swept back and parted in the middle. Bobbie and I became very close and I found her wonderful company. Obviously, we worked together politically, but she loved reading, particularly poetry, and we would often relax by reading from our favourite writers; we sometimes even exchanged our own poems. But her main characteristic was her bubbling vivacity. She enlivened any company she was in; indeed, when we visited Tredegar, not only did she endear herself to my mother, but she was the only person I knew who could bring Clarence out of his usual shell of silence when he was at home!

Bobbie could not go long without succumbing to the urge to do something different. In the middle of the Curran affair, after we had spent an arduous morning giving out leaflets, she dashed us down to Barry Island to spend almost the entire afternoon on the switch-back, making ourselves giddy and sick in the process. On another occasion, we went paddling in the sea late at night at Penarth.

This was the first of my only two meaningful love affairs. We seriously

considered getting married, but decided to postpone taking a final decision because the situation was too uncertain. However, our ways were
soon to part, Bobbie returning to Scarborough and me enlisting in the
army. I met and married Kath, and she married a Norwegian naval officer
who, after the war, became a junior minister in the Norwegian government. The last time we saw each other was about 1950 when, on a visit
home, she came to see Kath and me in Nottingham.

18. PROFESSIONAL REVOLUTIONARY

In view of the shortage of toolmakers I thought I would be quickly placed in
another factory, but, surprisingly, this didn't happen. I had to keep prodding
the Manpower Office, and found that even when they sent me somewhere,
the job would mysteriously disappear or have been filled by the time I
arrived. It soon became obvious that I had gained something of a reputation and was "blacklisted" by engineering employers in South Wales.
No firm wanted to be saddled with such a notorious trouble-maker.

Having no job, I was living at home. One morning a telegram arrived.
It was from Idris Cox and read, "Don't start work until you've phoned
me." Intrigued, I phoned right away, and was bowled over when Idris
proposed that I should work for the Communist Party. Such an idea had
never entered my head, but I felt extremely flattered at being asked to
join the, to me, high-powered group of professional revolutionaries
leading the Communist Party in Wales.

I went down to the District Office at St. Andrews Crescent, Cardiff,
and Idris explained what he had in mind. The District Committee had set
up a Labour Movement Department, to pay detailed attention to developments in the various sections of the movement and the party's role.
Mavis Llewellen, a Communist Councillor in the Rhondda, was responsible for local government (there were many Communist councillors in
South Wales), other comrades dealt with the Labour Party and the
Co-operative movement, and I was to be responsible for the trade union
field. Len Jefferies, the District Organiser, was in charge. Although I
wasn't very confident in this new and at first strange environment, I
found it absorbing. What was especially interesting was being involved
with industries other than engineering, particularly mining, and talking
to comrades like Arthur Horner, Will Paynter and Dai Dan Evans.

The comrades with whom I worked formed a talented and friendly
group. The District Secretary, Idris Cox, was a Welsh-speaking ex-miner
from Maesteg. Leaving school at twelve, he started work on the surface

of the local pit at thirteen, and went underground a year later. He had a strong sense of national identity and was probably the first British Marxist to argue that the national question was a vital issue, not only for Ireland, but also for socialists in Wales, Scotland and England. In subsequent years he served for a time as editor of the *Daily Worker* and for many years worked alongside Palme Dutt in the International Department of the party.

Len Jefferies had "done time" in Parkhurst high-security prison for "inciting disaffection" among members of the armed forces. He had helped produce a paper *The Soldier's Voice* and had been caught distributing it to soldiers at Newport Barracks, for which "crime" he was sentenced to three years' imprisonment. In his book, *Walls Have Mouths*, Wilfred Macartney tells the story of how Len's first Christmas in prison threw its system out of gear:

At Christmas men are allowed to receive Christmas cards. To Len from all over the world – from Shanghai, from California, from Harbin, from India and Canada, were sent hundreds of greetings from comrades. So many were they that the post office sent a separate bag with Len's Christmas cards. The Governor sent for Jefferies.

"Look here, you know you can't have all these cards."

"Why not, governor?"

"Oh, be reasonable; there are hundreds of them."

"Well, I've plenty of time in my cell to look at them."

"I can't let you have so many, but you can make a selection of those you wish to have in your cell for a limited period."

So Jefferies was withdrawn from labour, a table set in the schoolmaster's room, and old Len went serenely through all his revolutionary greetings. Now, it is a regulation that any card, letter, etc., coming for a prisoner must be initialled and dated by the schoolmaster, and to his great grief he had to date and initial hundreds of fiery greetings from reds in every part of the world.

When Len made his selection he asked the governor if he could reply to all of them – meaning him writing several hundred letters. Blandly, he told the governor it was merely a question of politeness and manners and he regretted keenly that his desire to be courteous to his well-wishers should disorganise the prison service. The governor eventually agreed – providing Len paid the postage!

Len helped me a great deal in those early days, and it was to him I would go to if I wasn't sure what to do, or if I needed advice. "An organ-

159

iser who makes himself indispensable has failed in his job," are words of wisdom I always tried to remember. The other comrade I worked well with was Edgar Evans, an ironmonger and a Communist councillor in Bedlinog. During the Taff Merthyr strike against company unionism, he was co-opted onto the local strike committee and was arrested, spending several months in Cardiff jail. He made union history when the Miners' Federation took on and paid for the defence of someone who was not one of its members.

I have already referred to Betty Bartlett, and there were several others. They were a great band of comrades and I have always been grateful for the privilege of working with them. Together with the clerical staff, there were enough of us to qualify for a canteen and special rations. Meal times were relaxing and often funny, especially when Len would relate some of his experiences or tell a story. It was at one meal time that Betty surprised most of us by announcing that she and Tony Ambatielos were to get married.

I confess that I felt a little intimidated by Idris Cox, the District Secretary, who appeared to me to be rather stern and not easily approachable (although when I knew him better in later years, I had to revise these first impressions). He was certainly in control and insisted on a disciplined attitude to work. Any slovenliness would quickly bring a reprimand, and unpunctuality was not tolerated without good reason. Promptly at nine o'clock every morning the entire staff of about twelve had to assemble. Idris would already have read most newspapers and would give a résumé of the day's news, then, after discussing it, we would all have to outline our programme for the day, and raise problems or points in connection with our responsibilities.

The number of full-time party workers reflected the rapid growth of the party after the Soviet Union came into the war. In two years the party membership trebled, reaching 60,000 in 1943. Something of the pace of recruitment can be gleaned from the fact that in the first three weeks of 1942, over 3,000 joined nationally, including two hundred in Wales. Wales made 1078 new members and the formation of one hundred new groups in the first three months of the year, and at the end of the "Ninety Day Campaign" from October to December the District Committee recorded "the serious failure of winning only seven hundred and thirty three new members during the campaign!"

It was an exhilarating experience to see people queuing up to join the party at big demonstrations. Those who joined have often been dubbed

"Red Army Recruits" – by our opponents – to belittle what was achieved, and by many Communists in later years to excuse the fact that the party was not able to retain most of them after the war. This over-simplifies what happened. It was quite understandable for men and women to be inspired by the struggle the Russian people were putting up, and to want to be identified with the party leading that struggle. So many had their eyes opened about the Soviet Union after years of lies and misrepresentation. And there were those who recognised for the first time the correctness of the pre-war policies of the British Communist Party, and appreciated the part it was playing in every aspect of life in war-time Britain.

It would, perhaps, have been idealistic to expect that all who joined during a particular high point of the struggle would remain in when the struggle subsided, and particularly after the commencement of the Cold War with its virulent anti-Communism. But a major reason so many left after the war lay with the party itself. We were just unable to cope with this new phenomenon.

Although we organised classes in Marxism – one hundred and fifty eight in Wales in three months – held discussion meetings, and issued printed material, we were so immersed in the crucial immediate struggle that we did not go deeply enough into what was needed to retain all the new members. Converts made on the basis of one issue, however deeply they feel about it, will not retain the motivation when the issue ceases to be crucial, unless, in the meantime, their political outlook has been broad-ened and deepened.

The main campaign during this period was for the opening of a second front in Europe. It seemed, not only to Communists but to a wide section of the British public, incomprehensible that the Red Army was being left to fight the bulk of the German army on the Eastern Front, while British, American and Allied forces were standing by doing noth-ing. The war in Italy is often pointed out as a face-saver, but this is put into perspective when one realises that more German troops took part in the single battle of Stalingrad than the total number of German and Italian troops involved in the entire North African and Italian campaigns. Documents published since the end of the war make it clear that it was not military considerations, but post-war political alignments that dictated the policy of Britain and America.

The governments of these countries were quite happy to see the Soviet Union shoulder almost the whole load of the struggle and

161

weaken itself, so long as it was doing the job of defeating Germany. There were huge demonstrations calling for the Second Front. At one I attended in London, over 100,000 were present – a remarkable response in war-time conditions.

On the industrial front, there was a growing feeling of frustration at the lack of equality of sacrifice. Employers continued to rake in vast profits, while workers were expected to give up hard-won rights, to forego safety standards and not to use the situation to win higher wages. One of the purposes of the Essential Works Orders was to control the supply of labour, and an important reason for this was to keep wages down. Under market conditions, with the demand for labour being so much greater than the supply, wages would have rocketed. As it was, alongside a desire to win the war, workers in many places were provoked beyond endurance to take action in defence of their conditions.

I have already mentioned the strike at the big Royal Ordnance Factory at Tredoman, near Aberdare, but the biggest problem was in mining. Coal was vital to the nation, which is why the Churchill Government had taken control of the industry out of the hands of the private coalowners (who nevertheless continued to draw fat profits). However, despite the importance of coal and the acute shortage of miners, wages of pit workers increased only slowly and fell further and further behind that of workers in engineering and other industries. The frustration of the miners was understandable. There were sporadic strikes – only a fraction of what took place in peace time, but serious, nevertheless.

One such strike involved a large number of pits in West Wales. The party was particularly worried about it because Communists participated in the leadership of it. Party General Secretary, Harry Pollitt, attended the District Committee meeting called to discuss it. It was a highly charged debate, and Harry was at his emotional best. He drew a graphic picture of the sacrifices the Russians were making and argued that the strikes were weakening the demand for a Second Front. He invoked party discipline and speaking directly to one of the strike leaders he said: "I have known you all the years I have been in the party and I greatly value your friendship, but if you continue to support this strike I, personally, will demand your expulsion. "Answering those who said that Churchill had never been a friend of the miners and had been responsible for sending troops into Tonypandy in 1911, he said: "Whatever Churchill did in the past or will do in the future, he will go down in history as one of the men who saved the world from fascism."

The strike was, in fact, soon over.

In 1943 the Communist Party decided to apply again for affiliation to the Labour Party. Except for the period 1928-29, this had been an aim since the Party was founded in 1920; it was possible because of the unique character of the Labour Party. Unlike continental Social Democratic Parties, the British Labour Party is a loose federation of organisations that includes trade unions, Co-operative bodies and socialist organisations. For example, the I.L.P., the Fabian Society and the Socialist League were all affiliates, maintaining their own organisation, policies and freedom of action providing they accepted the general aims of the Labour Party and did not put up candidates against official Labour candidates. The Communist Party could quite easily accept the aims, chief of which were to win a Labour majority in Parliament and establish a socialist Britain (the famous Clause Four).

In the years following its formation the Party regularly applied for affiliation. At that time, Communists could be members of the Labour Party as individuals, and even stand as Labour candidates in local and national elections. Indeed, the first Communist M.P.'s, Walton Newbold and Shapurji Saklatvala, were elected as Labour M.P.'s. But the right-wing leaders of the Labour Party, particularly Ramsey MacDonald and Phillip Snowden, fought hard and, by a very small majority, succeeded in forcing through a rule change barring Communists from being individual members. Every year, the Labour Conference debated a motion to accept Communist affiliation, and every year it was rejected. In 1928 the policy of the Communist Party changed. It was the beginning of the disastrous "New Line" period of extreme sectarianism, exemplified in its new programme, "Class Against Class," a period when the Labour Party was condemned as being an outright bourgeois organisation and its leaders stigmatised as "social-fascists."

In the early 1930's this line was abandoned. The former characterisation of the Labour Party was accepted as being incorrect, and the increasing danger of war and fascism made it imperative to build the greatest possible unity within the labour movement and among other progressive forces. The standing of the Party rose because of the role it played in the struggle of the unemployed, in the fight against fascism and in defence of Spain. Under these circumstances, immediately following the 1935 General Election, the Communist Party applied for affiliation. This was rejected by Labour's Executive, and a campaign was then started to win a majority at the Labour Party Conference. Despite having

163

the support of big unions like the Mineworkers Federation, the A.E.U. and A.S.L.E.F. and of prominent individuals on the left, affiliation was rejected, although it received 592,000 votes – over a quarter of the votes cast.

In 1943, the Party felt that its growing influence and the unity in action that existed in the workplaces and localities gave it a good chance of winning a majority, and a massive campaign was launched to win the support of the trade unions, local Labour Party organisations and individuals. With the ending of the Communist International (Comintern), one of the main arguments of the right-wing – that the Communist Party was part of an international organisation – was no longer valid. I was very much involved in this campaign, visiting and writing to Labour councillors and other personalities, and speaking at trade union and Labour Party branch meetings. It was particularly important to get a public pledge of support in writing from Nye Bevan, who had supported affiliation in 1936 and who was now recognised as the leader of the left in the Labour Party, and I was given the job of approaching him. This I did, and as a result he wrote to me:

I have always supported the affiliation of the Communist to the Labour Party, and shall continue to do so, although there is some doubt in my mind as to whether this is the best course to pursue in the present circumstances. It would appear that what should be done is for the representatives of the two parties to meet with a view to agreeing upon a line of concerted action so as to unify the full forces of labour. However, perhaps the only way we could bring this about is to press for affiliation. When the issue comes up before the Labour Party Conference this year, I hope to be able to support affiliation.

This was published in the *Daily Worker* and received a lot of national publicity.

Affiliation received the greatest support ever, both from trade unions and from local Labour Parties; but despite powerful appeals from Bevan and others, it was again rejected. Subsequently, at the 1946 Conference a decision was taken not to accept any further affiliations, a move obviously intended to stop any further discussion on Communist affiliation. Dennis Healey, in his autobiography, boasts that he initiated this move.

The continued growth of the Party necessitated more changes in Party organisation in Wales, and it was decided to make Monmouthshire a Sub-District, with me as the organiser. As I worked from home in Tredegar, and the job entailed a lot of field work, travelling around the towns and valleys of my own county, and visiting Party members in their homes, I enjoyed it very much. The warmth of the welcome always awaiting me from comrades and their families made up for the long hours of waiting in bus queues. The first greeting was usually, "Pull up a chair and have something to eat" – and eat I had to whether I wanted a meal or not. Among comrades who had been in the Party some time, this was probably a reflection of the situation before the war when full-time Party organisers were lucky to get any income at all. The story was told that when veteran Scottish Communist, Bob Stewart, was sent to work in Caerphilly for a short while, he was kept going by doing the round of Party members, eating at a different house each day.

It was a new experience, too, visiting pit branches and groups and being expected to help sort out the often quite difficult problems arising in the pits, which sometimes meant being taken to discuss matters with non-communist members of the union committee. This arose naturally out of the special respect South Wales miners had for the Communist Party, a respect going back to the 1920's and 1930's and rooted in the kind of experiences so vividly portrayed by Lewis Jones in his two novels *Cwmardy* and *We Live*. Lewis had been a Communist County Councillor in the Rhondda and died in 1939 while doing a hectic round of meetings in support of Spain. It was my first direct involvement with mining, and the start of a special commitment that has remained with me to this day.

We had a new and fast-growing branch in the big R.O.F. at Glascoed near Pontypool. The dramatist André van-Gesygen was doing war work there and was a member. A few of the management staff had joined the Party, and this produced a minor problem which was indicative of the new situation. At the well-attended branch meetings, some of our newer members would be deferential to these comrades, even calling them "Sir" in discussions, as if they were still in a factory situation. I had to make it clear that within the Party all distinctions of authority disappeared outside the workplace, that all comrades were equal and must be treated as such. On one occasion, the branch organised an open evening meeting in the works canteen, publicising it throughout the factory. I was the speaker, and we had a really good audience. Then, just as the chairman had introduced me, there was a power failure, a black-out. I managed to get through my speech without notes in total darkness, and when question-time came, it was eerie having to respond to disembodied voices coming out of the blackness. When the lights came on at the very end of the meeting I fully expected to find most of the audience gone, but, surprisingly, there they still were – and most of them awake!

CHAPTER V

1943-1946: IN THE ARMY

19. ENLISTMENT AND MEETING KATH

At the beginning of 1943 I received a phone call from one of the officials in the offices of the Manpower Board in Cardiff who I had known quite well during my shop steward days. He was quite a decent bloke and more progressive than his colleagues. He tipped me off, unofficially, that I would soon be called up unless I went back into industry, toolmaking being a reserved occupation which normally exempted one from military service. Maybe I was a romantic, but it seemed to me that this would be an unprincipled thing to do, putting personal inclinations before the needs of the struggle against fascism.

Consequently, I was put down as a volunteer and in a week or so I received instructions to go for a medical examination, which I passed A1. I expressed a preference for the R.A.F., but this was turned down. The Royal Electrical and Mechanical Engineers (R.E.M.E.) had recently been formed and it badly needed skilled engineering workers. So it was that soon afterwards I received my calling-up papers for the army. As for so many others, the moment the postman dropped that inoffensive look-ing buff O.H.M.S. envelope through the letter-box marked the start of a phase that was bound to alter drastically my entire life. For the next four years there was an addition to my name that I would never be allowed to forget – Army Number 14574600.

All enlisted men had first to receive basic military training, so I was ordered to report to the Primary Training Centre at Ruskin Park, Sheffield on 1st April. It was a wet, dismal day when I arrived in Sheffield, and the city looked grey and uninviting. (I have since come to know it quite well, but whenever I visit it, I still have a lingering feeling in my bones of the desolation felt at that first encounter). The morale of the motley batch of miserable erstwhile civilians from all over Britain who gathered outside the station was not improved by the unsympathetic, shouting sergeants who met us and shepherded us to our venue. We were marshalled into a small hall and were soon joined by an arrogant, regular-army Captain, complete with waxed moustache and a swagger-stick which he slowly slapped against his thigh as he contemptuously surveyed us in silence for a few minutes. "Are there any pacifists here?" were the first words he barked out, and in a tone that boded ill for any who dared to admit it. Disappointed that there were none – or none that had the temerity to stick their necks out – he then proceeded to console himself by reducing our morale even further. "The six weeks you'll spend here," he said, "will be hell, wherever you go, whatever action you'll see in this war, it will be nothing compared with what I'm going to put you through, it will be an experience you'll never forget!" he concluded with smug, sadistic satisfaction.

How right he was – at least so far as I was concerned! The army called it "the hardening process." From dawn to evening we were at it: square-bashing; route-marching through mud and rain; sometimes trotting in full kit, with heavily loaded back-packs, steel helmets, and with the weighty Lee-Enfield 303 rifle hanging from our shoulders. Some days wearing heavy great-coats; being bullied into doing feats of gymnastics and endurance on assault courses that up to then we would have considered utterly impossible; occasionally spending days in damp clothes. As well as training us for what could become reality, it was supposed to prove to us that when we thought we had reached the limit of endurance, there was always a reserve of energy left to call upon.

Foot-slogging on long route-marches gave me my first sight of the Peak District, which later I came to love; but then we had neither the time nor the inclination to admire the scenery very much. When we were square-bashing in Ruskin Park, civilians, seeing the condition we were in and how we were being treated, would shout insults at the N.C.O. One particularly sadistic sergeant used to enjoy marching us up to a brick wall and then screaming, "Who told you to stop?" when we could go no further.

The only respite from physical exertion was the talks and lectures. Army instructions assumed that everyone was a moron and knew absolutely nothing, so the lecture on the rifle would begin with the sergeant pointing to a rifle and saying. "This is a rifle," and then, "this is the barrel, this is the butt and this is the trigger" – a procedure gently satirised by Henry Reed in his poem, "The Naming of Parts."

Yet, hard though the training was, towards the end one extracted a strange kind of satisfaction from it all. I was certainly fitter than I had ever been. Apart from the drill, the discipline and the monotonous routines, I found much of the training I received at Sheffield and at subsequent postings interesting – such as learning how to fire a rifle, how to use different weapons and grenades, unarmed combat, battle tactics and the art of street fighting. And there was something else I discovered, which I found to be true wherever I went during my years in the army. It was the comradeship that was quickly established among men who were formerly complete strangers, coming from all parts of the country and with the most varied occupations, when thrown closely and continuously together and facing the same adversity. There was also the humour. In every group there was usually a joker who could produce a laugh out of the must humourless situation and thus help to make it bearable, leading me to believe that humour is perhaps an essential condition for human survival.

When the six weeks were up I was transferred to the R.E.M.E. at the Central Ordnance Depot, Old Dalby, near Melton Mowbray, where they were building the first RADAR experimental apparatus. It was heaven compared with Sheffield, and great to be back at something like my old job again, even under army conditions. There was still discipline and some military training, but the atmosphere was more relaxed and most of our day was spent in the workshops. However, the equipment and techniques were very primitive compared with factories I had worked in.

At Sheffield we had been billeted in requisitioned houses, but at Old Dalby we were in Nissen Huts, about twenty to a hut. I found some of my hut-mates extremely interesting. They were German and Austrian Jews who had managed to escape from the Nazis and had been drafted into the British Pioneer Corps. They were the labourers of the army, regarded as the lowest of the low, who did all the unskilled heavy work, such as digging trenches. They were mainly professional people, and two with whom I became friendly had both been Communist Party members, one in Berlin and the other in Vienna. The German comrade was still bitter at the indecisiveness of the leaders of the German Party when Hitler seized power. Seeing what was coming, he said, the Party had formed underground military units and had its own arms caches. When the Nazis burned down the Reichstag and falsely declared it to be the work of Communists, he and his comrades believed this was the moment, that the time had come for armed resistance. His unit gathered in a cellar, with arms, ready to take to the streets . . . but the call never came. As we now know, Torgler and some of the other leaders of the Party actually went to the police to prove they were not near the Reichstag – and were, of course, promptly arrested and subsequently tried. The Party's honour was at least partly saved by Dimitrov, who was tried alongside the others, but who – unlike them – refused an officially-appointed lawyer, defended himself and used the trial to make a devastating exposure of the Nazis.

The Austrian comrade, a lawyer, had a passion for Beethoven. He knew every symphony and composition, and I'm sure that if an instrument in an orchestra played one wrong note he would have detected it. We had no radio in our hut, but I remember one bitter wintry evening, hurrying from the N.A.A.F.I. and coming across a muffled-up Heinz, looking like a snowman and crouched outside the window of a building from which came the strains of a Beethoven symphony. When he came into the hut later, all he said was, "Ach, they left out part of the last movement."

I used to get hold of the *Daily Worker* whenever I could. I would pass it round, or read it conspicuously in the N.A.A.F.I, hoping to come across fellow readers. For a long time I didn't, which wasn't surprising because our R.E.M.E. unit was part of a very large Ordnance Depot and the N.A.A.F.I. we used covered just a small corner of it. One day I was overjoyed to see someone reading a Communist Party periodical: he turned out to be a Birmingham Party member, Eric Pearce, the brother of Bert Pearce who subsequently became a leading full-time worker for the Party in the Midlands and South Wales. It was great to have a fellow spirit with whom to discuss the political issues of the day.

We soon discovered that there were others who took the *Daily Worker*, and on one occasion the paper published a story about the state of the blankets used there, exposing the fact that they had not been changed for a year. It caused some annoyance to the top brass, who issued a denial (so someone in authority must also have been a reader). I was told privately by a sergeant-major that they thought I was responsible for the report, although nothing was said to me.

A short while afterwards, however, the Colonel came to inspect our workshop and singled me out to answer questions about how I liked the army. I didn't know then, but later got proof that a dossier with my infamous political record followed me around wherever I went. This explained the mystery of why, soon after I was posted to any unit, the commanding officer would, unusually and inexplicably, find a pretext to see me, obviously curious to identify this notorious character. Soldiers were not allowed to take part in political activity, but the more politically conscious among us found ways of circumventing this order, although, of course, we had to be discreet. I called at the Party District Office in Nottingham and learned that although there was no branch of the Party in Melton, there were one or two members. More by accident than design, I also discovered a number of comrades, government employees, who had been evacuated from London and were working as civilians at Old Dalby and other establishments in the area. As a result, we were able to form the first branch of the Communist Party in Melton. A problem was that the civil service comrades and myself could not do any open activity. However, we did hold regular discussion meetings and Marxist classes; and as far as we were able to, we did some surreptitious public work. I would leave leaflets around at Old Dalby and in bus shelters in the neighbourhood, and the other comrades would distribute leaflets door-to-door in the evenings. We even organised a public meeting, with a Melton comrade in the chair, of course. This is how I met Margaret Stanton, the secretary of the Leicester branch, who was the speaker and who has been a friend ever since.

In April 1944, I went home on leave, but I spent most of it idly wandering around my old haunts and feeling very bored as all my mates had been conscripted or were working away from Tredegar. Bert had been called up and had been posted to Burma in the Signals Corps while Emrys, who had opted to go into the R.A.F., was called up into the army and found himself working at his trade constructing a P.O.W. camp and aircraft runways in South-West Wales. He was later transferred to the R.A.F., but when the war ended he was released because of the acute shortage of building trade workers who were needed so urgently for reconstruction. George and Arthur were still in London, working in aircraft factories. Being at a loose end, I decided to go down to Cardiff and visit some of my old Party friends, one of whom was Betty Bartlett, who had now become city organiser. I arrived at the Party office just as she was leaving and walked along with her. "Where are you stationed?"she asked me. When I told her, she remarked "There's a comrade at our Party School who works at Newport but comes from Melton Mowbray. I'm going to the school now. If you like, I'll introduce you to her."

That's how I first met Kath Powell. She was secretary of the Newport branch of the Party and a lecturer at Newport Technical College. As luck would have it she was on holiday, and intended spending it mainly at

Melton. A week later we had our first 'date', outside a pub near the army camp, and we walked the seven miles to her home. She was small, had lovely, naturally wavy, dark hair (which remained such all her life), was reserved and modest, yet clearly very intelligent. While at Manchester University she had become Secretary of the University Socialist Society, and at nineteen had joined the Communist Party. She had acquired an interest in politics from her father, especially during the years of the Spanish Civil War. His name was Arthur; he was Welsh, a mines electrician from Monmouthshire. Her mother, Katherine Powell (née Lewey), had been a schoolteacher at an Aberbeeg school near where he worked. Kath's mother was proud of being a genuine Cockney, one of twelve children born to a middle-class family living in Tottenham Court Road – well within the sound of Bow Bells. She had been an active Suffragette and had met many of the leaders of the movement. Arthur and Katherine had gone through a very tough period soon after they were married, due to the shortage of work in South Wales, but eventually he was appointed civilian Garrison Engineer at the Old Dalby Depot, and the family moved to Melton Mowbray.

Soon after we began seeing each other, Kath invited me to spend Sunday at her home to meet her parents, but my hope of making a good first impression on her mother was dashed at that first meeting. Their living room had a highly polished mahogany floor, which she was very proud of. It was with sheer horror that I looked down after that first meal and saw that my army boots had gouged deep and long scratches in this paragon of a floor. Thereafter, she quietly always put a small mat in front of my chair.

By a stroke of luck I was able to partially redeem myself, at least in the eyes of her father. Although not active in party politics, he was a supporter of the Labour Party, had a good knowledge of its history and very much liked a good argument. His interest in politics turned out to be the means of raising my standing in his eyes. He asked me if I knew anything about the Sidney Street Siege. This was an event that took place in 1911, when police tried to evict three alleged anarchists, one of whom was known as "Peter the Painter," from a house in London's East End. According to the official account, they were armed, and in the ensuing affray three policemen were killed. Winston Churchill, who was Home Secretary, typically brought in army units and personally took charge of the operation. Thousands of rounds of ammunition were fired into the building, which caught fire and was burned down. In the ashes they

found the remains of only two bodies, and there has always been speculation over what happened to the third man. Of course, I knew this outline of the event, but, by a stroke of good fortune, I had recently read a
book dealing with it in detail, and the author expressed his belief that the
third man had gone to Australia. As it happened, before he was married
Arthur had spent some time in Australia and maintained that there he had
met a man who, after they had been buddies for some time, confessed to
being Peter the Painter. He had told this story often after returning to this
country, but no one would believe him. Now, at last, I had confirmed that
it had some substance and was not just a figment of his imagination!

I always got on well with him, not only because we were both Welsh
and from the same area, but because he enjoyed a good discussion. He
claimed that it was a member of his family who really invented the
Bessemer steel process. The story, which had become part of family
folklore, was that this forebear of his, who worked in the famous
Blaenavon iron works, was travelling up the valley by train from
Newport and started talking to the man sitting opposite. In the course of
the conversation he showed the man diagrams he had drawn of a process
for making steel by blowing air through pig iron. The man introduced
himself as Mr Henry Bessemer and said he was interested in steel production. He offered to buy the plans, and eventually a deal was struck
whereby he paid a sum equal to £100 for each of Powell's children –
quite a large amount in those days, especially in view of the size of
the family.

Kath's mother had the reputation of being a first-rate schoolteacher,
and although she could be just a bit of a snob, was not only a Liberal
politically, but liberal in outlook, always gentle and tolerant. I suspected
that she was most disappointed that her eldest daughter had become
entangled with a man with little prospects and outlandish politics,
especially after they had paid for her to go to university; but never once
did she give a hint of this to me. Kath was the oldest of their four daughters.

In the weeks that followed, Kath and I walked or cycled around the
Leicestershire countryside, and our discussions were almost all on serious topics like politics, science and literature. Our friendship deepened.
One day we were out walking near Melton and got caught in a sudden
rainstorm. We ran for shelter under a tree. I was first, and as she came
up, I impulsively caught hold of her and kissed her. That was how our
love affair started. Years later Kath confessed to me that she was somewhat overawed at walking out with a "professional revolutionary" who

had, as it seemed to her then, a wealth of experience and a seemingly encyclopaedic understanding of Marxism and working-class politics. I had to admit that I was equally apprehensive about going out with a girl who had been to a university and had gained an Honours Degree in history. It should be remembered that this was at a time when only a comparatively small number of people, and very few from working-class homes, went to a university, and when having a degree was so exceptional as to make local news. I was acutely self-conscious about my lack of any real formal education.

Many workers unjustifiably suffer from this sort of inferiority complex. In my case, it was finally laid to rest when, years later, as a Party organiser, I had a lot to do with students and university lecturers, and came to realise how limited and unsatisfactory purely academic knowledge is. In the quotation given earlier, James Klugman makes the same point when he relates how the brilliant but arrogant group of Cambridge students to which he belonged in the 1930's was humbled by the superior knowledge and understanding of life possessed by the hunger marchers whom they hosted.

For the next few months, the only times Kath and I met was when she visited Melton on holiday or I was on leave in Tredegar. Our lives seemed to be spent in walking and talking. When on leave, I would meet her in Newport after school and we would catch a bus to Caerleon, and wander around the countryside until quite late. Sadly, this was to last no more than a few months, for events decreed that we were to be separated for a time.

20. OVERSEAS POSTING

The R.E.M.E. had two kinds of officers. Regimental officers were usually regular army types, of somewhat limited intellect, whose job it was to maintain discipline and organise military training. Technical officers, however, were of a different calibre. They were not really soldiers, but civilian technicians and scientists in uniform, conscripted because of their specialist knowledge or experience. Even so, it was obvious that they were all drawn either from the universities or from the top levels of management.

One experience I had at Old Dalby demonstrated how far-sighted and shrewd some of them were. Highly skilled men among the "other ranks" were rare indeed, and two of us (the other one was an inventor in civilian life) were selected to experiment on two projects: making a device that could emulate the recoil action of a field gun, and building an engine crank-shaft grinding apparatus that would work effectively on a small trailer, an extremely difficult thing to do because of the lack of a firm base. In my innocence, I thought that the officers initiating these projects were motivated only by patriotism and zeal to win the war. A friendly subaltern shattered these illusions. He explained that every invention was registered, and that when the war was over financial awards would be made to those responsible. So it was the old, old story I've seen repeated often in civilian life: the workers do all the work, including the inventing and developing, but the smart boys at the top take the credit – and the reward. Yet, I must admit that I was glad to be singled out for special assignments. The production methods belonged to the last century, each component being laboriously produced by hand, and it was a revelation to the officers in charge when I showed them what a simple press-tool could do.

It was probably the thought of losing a skilled and innovative worker, rather than from any consideration for my welfare, that caused the Major under whom I worked to try hard to dissuade me from volunteering for overseas service. Although R.E.M.E. volunteers had been asked for, he assured me that he could keep me in this country for the rest of the war. Asking for volunteers seemed somewhat suspicious, for usually there was no choice; you were just posted overseas. It could mean that there was something special about this. Nevertheless, Eric Pierce and I decided to risk it, hoping that we would be taking part in the opening of the Second Front, which we felt could not be delayed much longer. For two years the Russians had been left to fight eighty per cent of the German Army on their own, sustaining appalling losses, despite repeated appeals from Stalin to the other Allies to relieve the pressure by launching a western offensive.

We now know that one of the motives in delaying the opening of the Second Front was the hope held by some leading circles in Britain and the U.S.A. that the Red Army would be so weakened as to undermine the Soviet Union's bargaining position when peace talks came. It so happened that they grossly miscalculated. After defeating the German Sixth Army at Stalingrad, the speed of the Russian advance made it imperative for Britain and America to quickly get in on the act. So, on 6th June 1944, the Second Front was started with the Normandy landings.

Eric succeeded in taking part in it, but to my chagrin I was posted to Italy. He rubbed salt in the wound later by writing me long letters giving a blow-by-blow account of his arrival in Normandy a few days after D-Day. During my embarkation leave, Kath and I were in London when the first V2 rocket landed. We heard the explosion, but the story put out was that a gasometer had blown up. My unit left Liverpool on 28th September 1944. We thought we were going to the Far East but we realised our destination when we were issued with Italian money en route along with our tropical kit. The sergeant major at the embarkation centre at Hucknall was a childhood hero of mine, the famous footballer Dixie Dean. He proved to be one of the nastiest N.C.O.'s I came across in the army. Thus are illusions shattered!

The ship we sailed in was one of the luxury Empress passenger liners, converted to a troop carrier. There was nothing luxurious about its new role. Every available inch of space, including some of the decks and the empty swimming pool, was occupied by bodies. We were put in holds well below the water line, making escape virtually impossible if we were hit – an indication, we cynically believed, of how low down the priority scale the R.E.M.E. was. We slept hundreds together, closely packed in hammocks.

One night, when we were still in the North Atlantic, I awoke with the feeling that something was amiss. It was the silence and the total darkness. All power had been switched off and I realised that the engines had stopped and the ship wasn't moving. Then there was a succession of explosions and after each explosion the ship trembled violently. We lay awake all night, and I'm sure that a good many prayers were said during those long waiting hours by those who believed in their efficacy – and by some who didn't. I experienced what it was like to be completely powerless in the face of imminent great danger, even death, for we would have been helpless if the ship had been torpedoed. We learned next day that a pack of U-boats had been stalking the convoy and that the explosions we heard were depth charges being dropped by our escorting destroyers.

After spending many days in our overcrowded troop ship, Naples was indeed a welcome sight when we arrived in the early hours of the morning. The wide sweep of the bay from Ischia to Sorrento dotted with dozens of small fishing boats, the white buildings of the city reflecting back the morning sun, Vesuvius standing guard with a wisp of smoke rising from it in a clear blue sky; this was truly a picture postcard vision. "See Naples and die" was the obvious saying that came to mind – although we all fervently hoped it wouldn't be true for any of us.

One of the first sights that greeted us when we anchored at the quayside was the large number of people begging; it shook me to see men fighting over scraps of food thrown to them from the ship. The impression of extreme poverty and hardship was confirmed as we marched through the streets and saw the ragged, bare-footed women and children living amidst the rubble of the severely bombed buildings.

We were transported to tents on the outskirts of the city below a bombed cemetery containing the remains of the famous tenor, Enrico Caruso. So began my two and a half years stay in Italy, a country I came to like very much despite the adverse circumstances.

21. NAPLES AND BAIA

Our stay at the camp was only a temporary stop until we were posted to permanent units. For this I was thankful, as the conditions were primitive and the sergeant major an eccentric six-foot-four regular army martinet, who loved throwing his weight about. "My name is Snow White," he barked at us on our first parade – a name he seemed inordinately proud of and which presumably had been given him because he liked to see everything, including his own equipment, painted white.

The first night under canvas was a disaster. The heavens opened and the rain poured down non-stop, so that by the morning the camp was under several inches of water. Most of our kit and clothes was drenched. When daylight came, we looked what we felt like: a miserable bunch of squaddies who fervently wished they had never left home! Fortunately the day soon became hot, but the camp was one big mud bath. Whoever had sited it could never have been in the Woodcraft Folk or the Scouts, for it was in a veritable water trap: a saucer with steep slopes around most of the perimeter. True, downpours such as we had experienced were very rare; indeed, I never experienced one as bad all the time I was in Italy. The area was surrounded by fig trees, so for the first time in my life I was able to gorge myself on figs in their natural state and not out of boxes!

My first impression of Naples didn't improve during the following week. One of my tent-mates and I decided to explore the part of the city that was within walking distance of the camp. Even though we expected to see bomb damage and poverty, the reality was far worse than I had imagined. It wasn't only the ruined buildings, but the people who occupied them; they looked so utterly depressed. More cheerful were the hordes of ragged, barefooted urchins who noisily followed us around,

begging for anything they thought they could get, but particularly cigarettes – which I soon learned were the universal currency – or offering
to take us to their "sisters" who "would give us a good time." Some of
the kids could only have been five or six.

On the way back to camp that evening, we were caught up in a shoot-
out. We were crossing a small piazza when there was shouting and a
fusillade of automatic fire right near us. The speed with which we threw
ourselves flat on the road would have gladdened the hearts of our primary
training instructors who had tried so hard to din this basic procedure into
our heads. We lay there as bullets flew over our heads, not daring to
move until well after the shooting had stopped. We learnt later that an
army unit had unearthed a band of fascists who had holed themselves up
in one of the buildings.

Painted slogans were everywhere, testimony to the political struggle
going on. "Viva Stalin," "Viva Togliatti," "Il Morte de Re" ("Death to
the King") seemed to be the most popular, although there were a few
"Viva il Duce" and other fascist graffiti.

During our stay at the transit camp we were given a briefing by the
Officer Commanding. He expressed utter contempt for what he called
"the Eye-ties." "You may have been told," he said, "that they are now
our "co-belligerents." Don't believe it; they are still our enemies. Have
nothing at all to do with them, and above all, don't fraternise" – advice
he didn't follow himself, being comfortably ensconced nearby in the
house of his Italian mistress.

Eventually I was posted to the Chemical and Metallurgical
Laboratory of the C.M.F. (Central Mediterranean Forces) at Baia, a fishing village on the Bay of Naples about eight miles to the west of the city.
The unit came directly under the Allied Forces Headquarters, situated at
Caserta, just north of Naples, but for regimental purposes it was part of
the 693 R.E.M.E. Base Manufacturing Workshop (B.M.W.) of the 1st
and 8th Armies. The British had seized what was left of the large
Ansaldo torpedo factory after the Germans had mined it. The R.E.M.E.
had restored some of the workshops and was running them with Italian
civilian labour. Our laboratory was away from the main buildings and
had a complement of about twelve men – often fewer – including three
officers and three N.C.O.'s.

I had hoped to be posted where the action was, and had, in fact, volunteered to serve in a L.A.D. (Light Aid Detachment), but nothing came
of it. Most people would have envied my good fortune. Not only had I

not been sent to a front-line unit, but the Chem and Met Lab was small, independent and interesting. The officers seemed to have a minimal interest in military procedures, and were simply scientists in uniform. Captain Parker, a metallurgist, had been a university professor and looked the part; in a somewhat untidy uniform he usually shuffled around with head down, deep in thought and appearing to be only half-conscious of what was going on around him. As a civilian he had invented a special method of case-hardening steel. Major Davies, the Officer Commanding, and Captain Rainbow were both chemists and university men. Rainbow had the useful distinction of being an authority on beer; he had been a lecturer on "industrial fermentation" in a department at Birmingham University financed by the brewing companies at nearby Burton-on-Trent. Our small workshop consisted of one each of the basic engineering machines plus a workshop, and it was attached to a well-equipped laboratory.

One purpose of the lab was to test the metals used in enemy armaments and detect the causes of faults in our own; another was to analyse the composition of substances used by the Germans. An example of the former was trying to discover why the breech block of a heavy field-gun had burst, killing the operator; an example of the latter was finding out what poison had been used in substances dropped from the air by the enemy. The main job of those of us in the workshop was to make test-pieces for the various metal-testing apparatus in the lab. This wasn't as straightforward as it sounds: not only had we to work to very fine limits of accuracy, but we could do nothing which altered the nature of the metal being tested, such as annealing it to make it softer. It took a great deal of hard work and ingenuity to cut out and machine test-pieces from a hardened steel breech-block. On the whole, I found the work very interesting; certainly not at all what I imagined I would be doing when I volunteered for overseas service.

Although, in the line of command the Chem and Met Lab came under Allied Forces H.Q., for most purposes outside of our work we were answerable to 693 B.M.W., so we couldn't escape guard duty and most of the "bull" all soldiers are burdened with. I was billeted nearby with the truck drivers of the Motor Transport Section. The billets had been the offices of the torpedo factory and there were at first about eight of us in one large room, although later the number doubled. From the balcony we had a fine view over the bay. The first thing I discovered was that if I wanted something comfortable on which to sleep I had to provide it myself, so there was no alternative but to wrap up in my two regulation blankets and curl up on the hard tiled floor inside my precariously perched mosquito net. I endured this for a few weeks, until I was able to make a bed with some canvas and a wooden frame acquired by bribing one of the Italian woodworkers.

When I got to know them, I found most of my room-mates a friendly lot. They were hardened veterans of the North African campaign and were always exchanging experiences and recounting tales that I found quite absorbing. Two or three of them had been in the battle of El Alamein. They were tough and noisy, but I soon realised that in many cases this was just a front to hide vulnerability and the ache of being away from their families, in most cases for four years. Some had not seen their children, born after they had been posted overseas. Most were known by nicknames:"Fishy" predictably came from Grimsby; "Taffy" was the other Welshman; "Darkie" was not black but deeply tanned from the North African sun; and "Jigger" Joynes was editor of our paper. There was a "Mac," a "Geordie" and, of course, the inevitable "Chalky White," and a few others whose names I cannot remember. Eric Stead and myself completed the complement. Except for the few of us who worked in the Lab, they were all truck drivers.

There was always plenty of argument and discussion going on, covering a surprisingly wide range of topics. There was a general militancy, and a few members of the unit were quite good politically; one had been a *Daily Worker* organiser. I soon became friendly with a lance-corporal who was beginning to take an interest in politics. Thin and slightly stooped, Eric had been an art student before his call-up, and he spent much of his leisure time drawing superb pictures of the locality. He had a wide knowledge of literature and poetry, but his pet theme was religion. He was an atheist, yet he knew the Bible and the Koran inside out. We would spend hours after lights-out discussing every field of knowledge, or I would listen to him describing his experiences in the North African Campaign, which he had been through from start to finish. There are some people who take part in epoch-making events, or travel to fantastic places with their minds and eyes shut. Not so Eric. He savoured every experience and tried to squeeze every ounce of knowledge from it.

My position in the billet was interesting. I was not a hard drinker like most of the lads; I didn't swear and my way of relaxing at weekends was not at all like theirs. Peculiarly, I was wrapped up in politics – and was

179

a Communist to boot. Yet I quickly became accepted as "one of the boys" in every respect. I can honestly say that although I knew some of them better than others, there was not one among them whom I disliked or who showed any unfriendliness towards me. Oddly enough, apart from Eric Stead, I got on best with the toughest, most belligerent and hardest-drinking members of our group. In time I came to be regarded as the fount of all wisdom, someone to whom they could come to resolve an argument or to discuss a problem. The role of Agony Aunt has always plagued me. I was expected to lend a sympathetic ear to the most personal problems arising out of letters from home. On one occasion, for example, a man who had been away from home for four years wanted me to write a letter to his wife telling her that he had fallen in love with a member of the A.T.S. stationed in Naples. Needless to say, I didn't agree. Another was worried stiff because his family was being evicted; on that I was able to give some advice and composed a letter to his M.P.

A refreshing change from my army life so far was the informality of the set-up and the small amount of regimentation. There were no parades, except when on guard duty, and after breakfast we simply went to our allotted tasks, on Sunday lying in as long as we liked. Kit inspection, or any other kind of inspection, was extremely rare, and two civilian women came in every day to keep the billets clean. We were simply left alone, apart from the Orderly Sergeant doing the rounds at lights-out, and then he often stayed for a cup of tea, which we brewed with the help of a petrol blow-lamp. It wasn't quite as relaxed at the main unit, but it is a fact that the Eighth Army was noted for its disregard of army conventions, particularly in dress. This idiosyncrasy has been immortalised by "Jon" in his Eighth Army cartoon characters, "The Two Types," showing two officers eccentrically clothed. This appeared regularly in the Eighth Army paper, *The Crusader*, and in the forces' paper, *The Union Jack*. We had to walk the two miles to the main unit for our meals, but we had our own small bar near our billets where we usually went in the evenings to imbibe the local vino, talk, play cards or listen to music.

Official Entertainment was usually variety programmes with our own talent, but there was the occasional E.N.S.A. concert, although these were usually in Naples. Singing, and listening to music on the Forces Radio, was an important part of army life. There was the traditional repertoire of bawdy army songs, sung with gusto on every occasion, but listening to popular topical songs on radio was also very popular. Many of today's generation pour scorn on the sentimentality and nostalgia of

180

those songs, but in doing so, they miss the social significance of them. In the same way that the songs of Bob Dylan reflected the mood of young people in the 1960's, Vera Lynn articulated the feelings and the yearnings of millions of men who were far from their homes and loved ones, and they offered hope. Both in the first and second world wars, the songs that were popular expressed the changing fortunes of the participants. Thus, the jingoistic songs of 1914 soon changed to the sad "There's a Long Long Trail A'winding" and "Keep the Home Fires Burning," as the prospect of immediate victory gave way to the horror of the trenches. The songs that were all the rage at the start of the Second World War were flamboyant and confident – "Run, Rabbit, Run," "We'll Hang Out the Washing on the Siegfried Line" etc. As the war progressed, they were replaced by the nostalgic songs associated with Vera Lynn – "When They Sound the Last All-Clear," "We'll Meet Again," "Wish Me Luck as You Wave Me Goodbye," "The White Cliffs of Dover" and the German song that became popular on both sides, "Lili Marlene."

Letters from home were the highlight of every week, although they tended to come in batches. I was extremely fortunate in having so many correspondents and was always faced with the problem of finding time to reply to them all. During the time I was abroad Kath and I each wrote one hundred and fifty letters to one another, and she kept me regularly supplied with the *Daily Worker* and pamphlets, as well as the occasional book; so I was well appraised of political developments at home. As she kept my letters to her, I have a very good personal reference library to augment and correct my memories, although, of course, there was a great deal of information which army censorship forbade me to mention at the time.

As Italian civilians did all the chores like spud-bashing, we didn't have to do the jobs all soldiers traditionally grumble about. But there was one unpopular task that couldn't be farmed out to civilians – guard duty. Night guard duty came round every few weeks and I grumbled about it as much anyone, although, in some ways I didn't mind. It was the usual two hours on, four hours off, and for one of the guard periods one of us would prowl around the extensive ruins of the factory. I usually found it quite soothing, slowly walking around under a starlit sky with one's own thoughts and listening to the fishermen singing on the bay. The songs seemed to be always sad, and the Moorish ancestry of many Southern Italians appeared to be reflected in the monotonic melodies. Every boat would have a light hanging under the water, presumably to attract the fish. Of course, the need for us to be alert at all times was always being stressed, for there were plenty of fascists still around and acts of terrorism were common. The other two hours were spent on sentry duty at the gateway, and one of the problems then was to be alert in case a conscientious duty officer crept up to test whether he would be challenged in the correct manner.

Baia has a long and interesting history, although this was not obvious from the frontage of old tenement buildings that ran parallel to the shore. However, behind the houses were the remains of Roman temples and thermae, uncared for and looking like part of the war damage, although still remarkably substantial. On a rocky promontory jutting out from the small bay was an old but solid castle, over-shadowing the caves where Nero was supposed to have murdered his mother. The town was originally part of the first and powerful Greek colony of Cumae, and got its name from Baios, a companion of Ulysses. It was the largest spa of ancient Italy, popular with Roman patricians, whose goings-on – according to early writers, including Cicero and Varro – were not always very edifying! Both Byron and Shelley had stayed there.

I found exploring the area fascinating. Not far away were the ruins of Cumae and the Grotto of the ancient Roman oracle, The Sybil. The Grotto and the extensive caverns connected to it were cut out of the rocks and were remarkably well-preserved; reputedly, they were still almost as Virgil once described them. Standing in the total silence and the half darkness of one of the chambers was quite eerie, and one could easily be transported back in time and imagine the Emperor Claudius coming to consult his favourite prophetess. The site was deserted and neglected; what security there might have been had disappeared because of the war, something common to most historic sites. A.M.G.O.T. (Allied Military Government of Occupied Territories) was only just beginning take charge of them and re-establish some kind of supervision.

Life soon settled down to a set routine. Although the army was very much a closed and self-contained community, there were plenty of opportunities for absorbing the local way of life. Fishing was one of the main occupations, and the small open sailing boats, with their two or three man crews, would go out each evening and return the next morning, to spread out on the beach their nightly catch for potential customers to inspect. There was a great variety of fish, most of which I couldn't recognise, although small octopuses were greatly in demand. It intrigued me to see quite large boats being made on the beach, from tree trunks to finished vessel, entirely by hand and without the use of even the smallest power tool. The trunk would be perched on high trestles and two men, one underneath and one on top, would cut planks with a two-handed saw, working down the length of the timber – an extremely slow and, it seemed to me, an excruciatingly arduous task, particularly in the heat of the day.

The main relaxation of the older men seemed to be sitting around talking, or else playing their kind of boules – bowls played on rough ground with heavy iron balls. The women appeared to keep indoors, and when they were out shopping they wore dark, often black, dresses with dark shawls over their heads. I never discovered whether this was normal or because so many of them were in mourning. There were not the hordes of ragazzi to be found in Naples, but the dark-skinned, bare-footed and half-naked youngsters in the locality ran around, either playing football with anything they could find, or catching basking lizards by encouraging them to put their heads into looped straws. Of course, they were always begging for anything they could get, and would gather around the entrance to our canteen hoping to collect some of the food we were throwing away. Although the army had its own hairdressers, I preferred to absorb the local atmosphere by going to the barber's shop in the village. It was not particularly clean, but it was usually full of men arguing – with their hands as well as their tongues – in typical Italian manner.

Most people showed no hostility and many were friendly, often even irritatingly servile; but some were obviously resentful of our presence. There was a youngster in one of our offices who was always quietly whistling the fascist anthem – until I let him know in no uncertain terms that I knew what the tune was. Things were not made easier by the attitude of many soldiers, who had a contempt for the "eye-ties" and showed it. It was a strange mixture of militancy on British political issues, and the typical imperialist arrogance of a conquering army. At the same time compassion often showed itself, particularly towards children. On one occasion a group of soldiers I happened to be with passed a bread shop where a number of kids were standing silently with noses pressed to the window, just looking at the cakes on the stand inside. One of the men took a collection and bought up all the cakes for the youngsters. Another incident I saw was when a barefooted woman with a small child was standing silently outside our canteen hoping for scraps of food. A passing soldier went in and returned with a supply of food and chocolate that must have used up his week's pay.

Italy was roasting under a heat-wave during that first year, and everywhere was brown, dry and dusty, but as we were billeted alongside the sea, we were able to spend a lot of time cooling off in the then crystal clear water of the bay, usually going for a swim before breakfast and after the evening meal. The main hazard was a particularly nasty variety of stinging jellyfish that sometimes floated in near the shore. The brown scorched earth, the shortage of the lush greenery we are so used to at home and the absence of song birds made me appreciate very much the nostalgia Browning felt when he wrote from Italy, "Home Thoughts From Abroad." Yet, there were compensations – such as the orange groves, where, for a few cigarettes, one could pick all that one needed, the vineyards weighed down by grapes, and the plentiful supply of other fruit.

Every Saturday, and sometimes on Sundays, we would pile into a truck and go into Naples. Being with the M.T. Section meant that there was never a shortage of vehicles to go anywhere, provided we had a pass. Naples was one of the main leave centres for troops in the C.M.F., so there were soldiers from all parts of Italy there. As the city had been liberated by the British, for once the amenities for British soldiers were better than for the Americans. With unusual imagination, and to rub in who were the victors, the luxurious royal palace of Victor Emmanuel (the king of Italy under the fascists) had been converted into a N.A.A.F.I. The imposing marble stairways led to ballrooms transformed into cafes, restaurants, concert halls, games and craft rooms, and there were plenty of other rooms in which to lounge around in comfortable chairs and talk, listen to music or read against the background of gilded ornamentation and oil paintings.

Naples did not live up to its picture-book image. True, there were imposing public buildings, piazzas and arcades, and the main street, the Via Roma, gave out a superficial impression of there being plenty to buy. But in the back-streets one saw the grim reality of squalor and poverty. The stench was appalling, and hordes of under-nourished kids seemed to be everywhere. These areas were out of bounds to us squaddies, but I was able to do some investigating while keeping a sharp lookout for Redcaps (the Military Police). One of the first actions of the Allies when Naples was liberated was to disinfect every house with D.D.T. – a massive operation but obviously necessary to prevent the spread of disease. Prostitution was, of course, rife, and, in accordance with the law of supply and demand, cheap. Everywhere were army warnings about V.D. and directions to the nearest "Pro (Prophylactic) Centre" for precautionary measures and tests. A massive problem was the army of homeless ragazzi, many of them war orphans and some badly deformed as a result of the bombings. At night, every doorway had its quota of kids sleeping rough. Occasionally, the authorities would round them up, and at one time Bacoli Castle at Baia was used as a shelter. We organised food and clothing for them, but what seemed just as welcome were the footballs we supplied. Maybe an augury of Italy's present football pre-eminence was the enthusiasm of those youngsters for the game, which they always played with bare feet.

I tried to convey something of the stark contrast between the idealised picture of Naples presented by poets and writers, and the grim reality I saw around me, in a poem I wrote at the time, which, although no great shakes as a poem, did express a little of the cynicism I felt:

SEE NAPLES AND DIE

Have you been to Naples,
And gazed enraptured from white-walled Vomero
Out o'er the sublime splendour spread before
From proud, smoke-capped Vesuvius to Capri –
    Yes, I have been to Naples,
    And walked the narrow streets, the stinking slums,
    Seen the child pimps, the prostitutes and beggars.
    Misery compounded by ravages of war.
Have you been to Naples,
And heard the murmuring music of the city,
Play to the moon-lit, white-tipped waves,
Dancing a tarantella in the ballroom of the bay.
    Yes, I have been to Naples,
    And heard the sad laughter of its children,
    Playing around the doors of our canteen,
    Rummaging the bins for scraps of food.
The whiteness of the lily on the pond,
Can hide the black water underneath.
The glorious music of the caged song-bird
Can drown the misery within its breast.
The lyric language of the entranced poet,
Can mask the truth it takes blunt words to tell.

For all that, Naples and the surrounding area was an interesting place

185

to be. After wandering around, or visiting one of the fine re-opened art galleries or museums, I liked to idle away an hour drinking vino or eating ice cream on Santa Lucia, looking across the bay to Sorrento, a place I visited for the first time when the M.O.T. lads were asked to act as escorts to a group of A.T.S. girls who had just come out from England, a duty which, for once, we were all too willing to carry out! Neapolitan songs, I discovered, were not a romantic invention. The style was unmistakable and could be heard everywhere. The words and music of local topical songs – many of them anti-fascist – were sold at street stalls and seemed to be popular. Although we were paid weekly in Lire, I soon had it confirmed that by far the best units of exchange were cigarettes, and as we received fifty free English fags every week this was extremely useful for non-smokers like myself.

During my stay in Italy I was able to see lots of places which in peacetime I had only dreamed of ever visiting. Several times a few of us took a boat to Capri, travelling around the island in a donkey-cart, climbing to the church of San Michele and swimming in the famous and lovely Blue Grotto. A sore point was that until the war was over, Capri was a U.S. rest camp and out of bounds to British troops. One odd incident was when Mac, myself and an American girl from Boston we had teamed up with, were invited to tea in the chateau of an obviously rich lady who turned out be a staunch fascist supporter. The three of us were revolted, despite the lovely meal and the delicate china.

One Sunday a small group of us spent a gruelling day climbing to the top of Vesuvius. The first half we were able to cover by truck, but the final, gruelling, 2,000 feet we had to ascend by foot. The climb got steeper and steeper, until we felt like flies on a wall, and the conditions worsened as the ground grew hotter and we became immersed in clouds smelling strongly of sulphur. At the summit we able to look down into the half-mile diameter crater from which sulphurous fumes belched up. They didn't rise steadily, but in gusts, as if a giant down below was smoking a huge pipe. The earth where we stood was hot, and a piece of paper could be set alight simply by poking it into a crack in the ground. Surely, this might have given Dante his idea of what the entrance to hell was like. "Tony," our Italian guide, assured us that it was quite safe because the volcano had erupted the year before and there wasn't likely to be another eruption for the next ten years. A few minutes with handkerchiefs around our noses was all we could stand. There is a similar phenomenon at Pozzuoli, a small town between Naples and Baia, where the earth's crust is so thin that one can look down into pits of boiling mud.

I visited Pompeii three or four times, spending the best part of a day there on each occasion. They were memorable experiences. The modern town of Pompeii is about fifteen miles from Naples alongside the then bomb-cratered autostrada leading to Salerno, so it wasn't difficult to hitch a lift from an army truck. The first sight that greeted us when we arrived were large slogans on the wall of a hospital next to the car park: "Viva Stalin" "Viva URSS." As usual we were surrounded by a host of people begging or selling anything else they thought they could unload on to us. They included nuns leading little children by the hand while begging for money for the "war orphans," and dirty travelling friars, straight out of Robin Hood, asking for alms. Near the ancient city we were surrounded by would-be guides, young and old. I decided to be my own guide.

I imagine it was an almost unique experience being able to wander around the wonderfully preserved and almost deserted Roman town, walk along the roads marked by chariot wheels, sit quietly in the gardens of the villas, or in the large amphitheatre and open-air theatre, absorbing the spirit of the place. It was strange seeing ancient election slogans on the walls and paintings in the houses, including some crude pornographic drawings on the walls of the brothel. Now, of course, the place is invariably crowded and visits are highly commercialised, with tourist parties being hurriedly herded around on conducted tours.

Being the land of opera, it was not surprising that Italy's second city possessed one of the finest opera houses in the country, the San Carlo. During the period when the war swept over southern Italy, the San Carlo had been closed, but it was re-opened under the control of the Allied military authorities and when duties allowed I would spend my Saturday evenings there. It is a truly magnificent theatre, and usually a group of us would club together and pay for one of the plush boxes that filled three sides of the imposing auditorium. I heard many singers who were to become household names after the war, such as Luigi Infantino, Toto Del Monte, Tito Gobi and Tito Ruffo. It was announced that Gigli was to sing, but there was such an outburst of revulsion that an alleged fascist collaborator should be invited – and not just in the Italian press, but also in letters to forces' newspapers – that the proposition was hastily dropped.

It was my first real experience of opera, and it enthralled me. The only tedious part was having to stand at the start while the orchestra went through full renderings of The Marseillaise, The Star Spangled Banner and God Save the King!

187

22. POLITICAL ACTIVITY IN THE ARMY

For anyone interested in the epoch-making changes taking place at the time, Italy was an exciting place to be in 1944. Fascism had been militarily defeated, but German troops had invaded the country and were putting up a stubborn resistance as they were forced back northwards. Politically, the country was in turmoil. Anti-fascist exiles were returning, including Palmiro Togliatti, the leader of the Italian Communist Party, (Partito Communista Italiano, or P.C.I.), who had escaped to the Soviet Union after Mussolini seized power in 1922, and Socialist leader, Pietro Nenni. Although the Allied military command was in effective control of the country, there was a tremendous mushrooming of Italian democratic organisations. There were over forty political parties – including the Party of the Permanent Opposition and the Party of the Partyless! It was already clear, however, that four main forces were emerging in the new democratic atmosphere: the Liberals (equivalent to our Tories), the Christian Democrats, the Socialists and the Communists. Of these, the Communists were by far the best organised. As I was to be given evidence of later, unlike Germany, the C.P. in Italy had maintained an underground organisation right through the years of fascism, and when the war started it had led the partisans in the armed struggle against the fascist regime. This struggle was conducted throughout Italy, but in the industrial north the partisans became so powerful that, to the consternation of Churchill, they won popular control over large areas. There was some bitterness over the fact that it was only after the partisans were in control of Turin and Milan that the Allies bombed these cities.

Newspapers appeared to be run by whichever party had first managed to get control of the buildings and presses. The main Naples newspaper, *La Voce* was produced jointly by the Communists and Socialists. The national P.C.I. paper, *Unita*, and the socialist *Avanti* were also on the streets again. Propaganda slogans and the symbols of the parties were painted wherever there was a space.

I regularly sent necessarily guarded reports and my interpretation of the situation to the *Daily Worker*, and I was gratified to receive a letter from J. R. Campbell stating that these were usually the first real accounts they had of what was happening in Italy.

But it wasn't only the political situation in Italy that was exhilarating; it was the militant feeling among British soldiers. Overwhelmingly they were anti-establishment and profoundly cynical of promises made by our politicians. There was strong opposition to Allied interference in Greece, where Britain was brutally ousting the liberation movement from political power. Indeed, at one officially organized current affairs discussion I attended, and to the annoyance of the "one-pipper" who was giving a talk entitled "Private Enterprise – or What?" there was a spontaneous demonstration of support for the Greek democrats when someone mentioned them in discussion.

Of course, political activity of any sort was strictly forbidden in the armed forces, and any breach was a punishable military offence. The War Office issued many directives emphasising this, and after the success of the Cairo Forces Parliament it became almost paranoiac about it. (A few of the party members now stationed here had taken part in the famous "Forces Parliament," a remarkable democratic development in Cairo, closed down by the authorities because they saw it as a vehicle for spreading left-wing propaganda in the army). The ban included having anything to do with Italian politics, including attending public demonstrations and meetings. These were always placed out of bounds, but I did contrive to stumble on Communist Party demonstrations, which were often held in one of Naples' biggest piazzas. What impressed me was how colourful they were. They didn't have posters with slogans such as we usually carry in Britain; instead, there was a waving sea of red flags. I was sometimes accompanied by a U.S. sergeant with whom I had become friendly: he was a member of the United States Communist Party and had been a full-time organiser of the teachers' union in New York. A few months later I was to envy him an experience arising from Togliatti visiting Naples to speak at a big rally at the San Carlo. Joe risked going along to it (I was on duty), and afterwards, with typical American boldness, contrived to meet Togliatti, who invited him to spend a weekend with him and his wife at their home in Rome the following weekend – probably to get an idea of what feelings were like in the Allied forces. Joe phoned me and asked me to go with him, but I had to explain that in the British army we just couldn't get extended leave at the drop of a hat, let alone permission to suddenly go gallivanting off to Rome. He told me afterwards that he had had a great time and had promised to keep in touch with the Togliattis.

A lot has been written about relations between the British and American troops. There was an ambivalent attitude. On a person-to-person basis relations were friendly and there was a genuine feeling of being allies. Yet, there wasn't the collective closeness there should (and perhaps could) have been. Of course, there was an element of envy on the

189

part of the British squaddie: G.I.'s were paid more and received better rations. But this envy was exacerbated by what was interpreted as the Yanks flashing their money about – particularly with the girls. The difference in national temperament didn't help; the average G.I. tended to be more extrovert than his British counterpart, and this was often interpreted as brashness and crudity. It was also a sensitive issue that while so many of our lads were overseas, Britain was occupied by American troops. This caused genuine concern among men who had been away from home for over four years and who heard stories, usually wildly exaggerated, about the behaviour of G.I.'s in Britain. Everyone knew the saying "the trouble with the Yanks is that they are overpaid, over-sexed and over here." The respective army commands did nothing to strengthen relations. It was a sore point that while G.I.'s were permitted to use our N.A.A.F.I.'s, including the Royal Palace (which many of them did), British soldiers were not allowed to use the equivalent American canteens.

Soon after I arrived at Baia, I found one small, but revealing, piece of evidence that even among the Germans, despite the ruthless suppression of Communist and other progressive ideas by the Nazis, these ideals had not been completely obliterated. One of the rooms of the building we occupied had been a billet for German troops when they had occupied the factory. We were clearing out the piles of debris and papers left behind by the Nazis, including some soldiers' personal possessions. These were handed in, presumably to be returned eventually to their owners. But, tucked away between the papers in one of the wallets was, of all things, a photograph of Ernst Thälmann. Thälmann had been one of the leaders of the German Communist Party and was incarcerated in Buchenwald Concentration Camp. Towards the end of the war, just before Allied troops reached the camp, the Nazis shot him. That unknown soldier had certainly been taking a risk – and a rather rash one. For all I knew he could already have been dead, but I fervently hoped that he lived and survived the war.

In my unit it was fairly well known that I was a Communist, and one day a girl who worked in the office at Baia, came up to me and, rather hesitatingly, and in broken but understandable English, asked me if this was true. She revealed that she was a member of the P.C.I. She spoke good English and told me that her father had been a P.C.I. member working underground during the fascist years.

Later she showed me a tattered exercise book containing the Communist Manifesto written out by hand, which they used to study in secret – at the risk of imprisonment or even death had they been caught. The popular support for the P.C.I. was demonstrated in the most unusual ways: during religious holidays, for example. There seemed to be a Saint's Day every other week; there would always be a procession; and in the procession, some red flags with the hammer and sickle could usually be seen. Incidentally, one of the biggest festivals I saw was at Pozzuoli, to "witness" the annual liquefying of the blood of Christ. Some congealed blood of Christ was supposed to be kept in a small container, and when excitement in the huge crowd was at its peak, the Cardinal held up the container and announced that it had liquefied. It was a con trick on a gigantic scale, and it was depressing to see so many taken in by it.

My main concern was to contact other C.P. members in the Naples area, something my American friend also wanted to do. The best method of doing this was to look out for anyone reading communist or similar literature. Soon this paid off. I saw someone poring over an old copy of the *Daily Worker*, and he turned out to be a Party member. He told me that there were others, and we arranged to meet one Sunday evening in the Royal Palace. What he hadn't revealed was that there was a well-organised group in existence which was meeting there at that moment. After being closely questioned by the group leader, I was allowed into the meeting and introduced to the others. Thereafter, I was a regular participant. Because of duties, postings, leave, etc., attendances obviously fluctuated widely both in numbers and in the comrades able to attend. Ten to twenty was the norm. We would discuss the situation in Italy and at home, exchange information about our own units and discuss what we could do to spread the word – particularly by distributing what copies of the *Daily Worker* we could get hold of and writing to the forces papers. We also ran a class on Marxism. Lounging in easy chairs in one of the small rooms lit by cut-glass chandeliers, with thick carpets on the floor and walls bedecked with oil paintings – surely this must be the must luxurious venue ever for Communist branch meetings and a far cry from the darkened cellars or smoke-filled rooms communists are conventionally supposed to prefer.

On one occasion the Palestinian communists, who had their own organisation, asked us to supply a speaker for one of their meetings. It was agreed that I should go along, and Joe went with me. We were somewhat taken aback when, instead of the few comrades we expected, there was what looked like a public meeting – about one hundred officers and

191

other ranks, largely Jewish. Joe didn't stay; he said it was far too risky; but I decided to go ahead. It was a noisy and argumentative gathering, but everything passed off alright – at least there were no repercussions for me.

Although there were no other C.P. members in my unit, there were some kindred spirits. Eric, I have already mentioned; another was "Jigger" Joynes, the editor of 693 paper, *The Chronicle*, and McNaughton, whom Kath chanced to meet after the war and who by then had joined the Party. We, and others who could be roped in, would often have political discussions based on Dutt's *"Notes of the Month"* in *Labour Monthly* or one of the pamphlets Kath kept me regularly supplied with. We usually considered ways in which *The Chronicle* could be used to spread progressive ideas, and how we could circumvent the ban on political articles.

A feature of army life during the Second World War was the compulsory lectures and discussions on current affairs, run particularly in static units. Organising them was supposed to be the job of one of the top regimental officers, and the overall responsibility was that of the Army Education Corps and the Army Bureau of Current Affairs (A.B.C.A.), which also issued regular pamphlets and guides, some of them quite good; one about the Soviet Union, "Portrait of an Ally," was written by a Communist, A. L. Lloyd. The purpose was to keep the troops appraised of the situation at home and in the world, and to discuss post-war problems. As the war drew near its end, these discussions became increasingly important and there was pressure on Unit Commands to take them more seriously.

The Adjutant, a Major, who was in charge of education in 693 knew as much about current affairs as the man-in-the-moon, and was about as interested, as he was frank enough to admit. In the discussions, he had marked me out as being knowledgeable – and not backward in expressing myself. He also knew, of course, that I was involved with *The Chronicle* and had had a few letters about post-war Britain published in *The Union Jack*. He obviously thought I was qualified as someone to whom he could safely pass the buck. So towards the end of 1944 he sent for me. Would I be prepared to give some talks to the men on current affairs. Not revealing my enthusiasm for the idea I virtuously agreed to take on this extra burdensome duty. Thereupon he asked my Officer Commanding, the Major commanding the Chem and Met Lab, to release me for A.B.C.A. sessions, and permission was given. He was so relieved that he readily agreed that I should choose the subjects and the format of the discussions. In fact, from that moment he left me in almost complete charge of my A.B.C.A. talks.

There were two snags. The discussions were compulsory, which meant that most self-respecting soldiers ordered to attend had a reflex suspicion of them and welcomed them only because they meant a break from normal routine. And this attitude was reinforced by having had to listen to excruciatingly boring talks given by various highly reluctant junior officers dragooned into doing a job they were not the least interested in.

The first talk I gave was on "The Problems of Post-War Britain." A special effort had been made and there were about eighty there, but subsequent attendances fluctuated between twenty and fifty, made up of both conscripts and volunteers. My approach was a simple one: to have the minimum of formality, and to get the lads talking naturally about their lives and jobs in civvy street and what they expected when the war was over. The fact that I was not an officer, but one of them, helped enormously; and I was gratified that before long my meetings became the most popular of the admittedly few educational programmes taking place in the unit.

Soon afterwards I was ordered to go on a course at the Army School of Education in Perugia, to become officially qualified as an A.B.C.A. instructor. The journey to Rome in one of our trucks was easy, and at the transit centre I met up with a few others bound for the same destination. How we got to Perugia was left to us, so long as we arrived reasonably on time; in fact it took us three days. At the railway station we commandeered an empty van in a goods train going part of the way. The train meandered slowly through the countryside, with lengthy stops at odd places en route. Despite the fact that it was winter, the weather was glorious (though cold), and for much of the time we sat with legs dangling outside the open door of the van, looking at the spectacular views of the snow-capped Appenines and at the hilltop villages which are typical of that part of Italy. We lived on tins of corned beef and biscuits, and frequently stopped to brew up with boiling water from the engine. The last part of the journey was by road, in a small van. It was marked by only one memorable event. We were careering down a muddy road leading to a Bailey Bridge spanning the upper reaches of the Tiber, when our rendering of "Lili Marlene" was interrupted by the van veering off the road and stopping in the middle of the fast- moving river. With the help

193

of the grinning Italian sentries guarding the bridge, we hauled the van out and were able to continue the journey.

Perugia is a wonderful old town, the capital of Tuscany from where Lars Porsena led his armies to conquer Rome, only to be thwarted by Horatius, according to one of my favourite school poems. The streets were cobbled and narrow, with a distinct medieval flavour that was accentuated by the numerous bullock carts and the multitude of churches that always seemed to be ringing their bells. The Etruscan Arch, across one of the streets, built about 330 B.C., is supposed to be the oldest structure using a keystone – an invention that neither the Greeks nor the Romans had discovered.

The School of Education was in the old university and there must have been about two hundred students there from all Allied nationalities and from all branches of the services. Unlike me, most of the students had some formal academic qualifications, a good number having been teachers. Although most of them were officers and N.C.O.'s, it was made clear that rank was to be dispensed with during the course. The tutor of my group was a lecturer from Cardiff University, and the course was on modern history, with sessions on teaching methods and how to organise A.B.C.A. talks. He was a Catholic and not particularly progressive, but he was keenly interested in South Wales' Chartism.

After being there for a week, our group was given a special and interesting assignment. Fifteen miles from Perugia is Assisi, venerated for being the birthplace and home of St. Francis. We were instructed to write a guidebook of Assisi, for use by Allied and other visitors. It meant spending an enjoyable two days there, visiting the churches and shrines in the town and the surroundings, including, oddly enough, the well-preserved pagan Temple to Minerva. Like Perugia, Assisi is perched on a hill from which there is a wonderful view of the Umbrian plain, and the approach to the town is along the usual winding road. There had been several informal discussions about religion in the group, and the tutor knew I was an atheist. Maliciously, I believe, among the tasks he gave me was writing the life of St Francis! It was gratifying to see that even in this centre of religious mythology, Communists and Socialists were active. I witnessed an open-air meeting, called to rename a street after a patriot – a Communist – who had died in the resistance movement.

There was one highly-charged event during my stay at the School. At Yalta, Stalin, Churchill and Roosevelt were meeting to discuss the unconditional surrender of Germany, and the post-war national borders. In the Declaration issued when the talks were over it was revealed that the German provinces of Silesia were to be ceded to Poland, but that the part of Poland which had once been part of Russia was to be handed back to the Soviet Union. There was a large number of Poles at the school, members of General Anders' army and viciously anti-Soviet. They were furious. Because of the arguments going on it was decided to hold an all-college debate on the Crimea Conference.

The hall was packed, the atmosphere emotional and the debate heated, but it wasn't too difficult to pick out the Communists and other left-wingers – they had the best knowledge of the facts and the history, and were the most self-confident. Although no vote was taken, it was clear that the majority supported the Yalta Agreement, although by a much smaller margin than was the case in the army generally because of the considerable presence of Anders' Poles at the College.

At this time, the front line was about sixty miles to the north. The objective of the Allied armies was to get control of the River Po, which had been a famous key point in Garibaldi's Risorgimento campaign a hundred years earlier. But the onset of severe winter weather held up the offensive. On two occasions I was able to visit the front line, and, despite my attempts to be posted to a combatant unit, felt thankful that I wasn't among the lads bogged down in the mud and snow. They were eager to hear the latest news of the fighting in Europe, and were particularly elated by the advance of the Red Army into Germany.

The return to Naples was by train and truck, and proved to be as interesting as the trip out. We had to travel down one side of the Apennines, and the scenery was magnificent. Whenever we stopped for a brew-up, apparently in unoccupied and desolate country, sure enough, first children, and then adults would materialise from nowhere and gather around. We stopped at one remote village where a festival was taking place in the village square and were rewarded with the spectacle of the local girls dancing what we assumed was the tarantella in the way that it should be done. Dressed in simple but colourful dresses they inter-weaved in what was probably a prescribed and – so it seemed to us – intricate pattern. Starting slowly, the dance gradually became faster and faster until it was a dazzling swirl of dresses as the dancers spun around like tops.

Because of our dallying, the afternoon was coming to an end and we still hadn't left the mountains when we came to a notice:

195

BANDITS. Bandits are operating in this area. Army vehicles are forbidden to pass this point after 1700 hours.

The reason for the prohibition, of course, was the greater risk of travelling during darkness. We decided to ignore the warning, as the alternative would have meant going back at least to the nearest village. Needless to say, our driver put the pedal down and didn't stop until we seemed to be well out of the danger zone. Incidentally, the bandits were not necessarily Italians. Some of the more notorious were deserters from the Allied forces.

I was now an official A.B.C.A. instructor – not that it meant a great deal, because it didn't absolve me from my other duties except when there was a meeting. It did, however, mean a small pay increment. Our discussions were sometimes very lively, and one thing became very clear; the lads were not going to tolerate going back to the Britain of before the war. There was not a clear understanding of how things could be changed, but there was a determination that change there must be. Admiration for the Soviet Union and the Red Army was general, and a kind of feeling that the Soviet system did offer some sort of alternative to what we had in Britain. A lot of rubbish is talked about the standing of Churchill among the troops. He certainly wasn't especially popular in my unit. The men had a healthy cynicism about him and his motives; the 'V' sign he was always fond of giving was interpreted as meaning "two more years!" In order of precedence in the unpopularity table, Tory M.P. and arch-appeaser, Nancy Astor, was first because she had allegedly referred to troops in Italy as "D-Day Dodgers," Sir James Grigg, the War Minister, was second; and Churchill was probably third. By contrast, Stalin was greatly admired, as was, to a lesser extent, Roosevelt.

There was no interference whatsoever in my choice of subjects for discussion, although I usually covered myself by referring occasionally to the official guide, "The British Way and Purpose" and using the titles of one of the A.B.C.A. pamphlets available. On only one occasion did the Education Officer make a comment. One day a scribbled note from him was delivered to me with a gentle reprimand. "I hear that you discussed the monarchy at your lecture last week. Not a good idea. It's just not done, old chap!"

From what I heard after the war about people's experiences in other places, it was obvious that there were vast differences in the freedom of discussion allowed. So much depended on the Commanding Officer and his immediate superiors. I was surprised at the scope allowed me, because I had never hidden my views, and I was certain that the army authorities knew I had been a full-time worker for the Communist Party before being called up – something I was soon to have confirmed. The degree of toleration was probably due to the fact that 693 was a R.E.M.E. area workshop in which there was a high proportion of officers who were not professional soldiers, but former technicians and university men, whose general liberal approach affected the attitude of the Colonel and the regimental officers around him. In the Chem and Met Lab where I worked, I got on very well with the four officers, all of whom were scientists. Captain Rainbow used to borrow my *Labour Monthly* every month.

About this time I became Assistant Editor and subsequently Editor of *The Chronicle*, which came out about every three weeks and had a distribution between six hundred and eight hundred copies. At first it was printed on the somewhat primitive press of the factory, later, much more professionally, at C.M.F. Headquarters at Caserta, and finally by a local printer. Obviously, it could not be overtly party political, but it was possible to raise general political issues and to provoke discussion. What I found most revealing was that there was no dearth of material for publication from the lads of 693, whether it be short stories, articles or poems. There was a bloke called McGuiness, who acted and looked liked James Cagney, a tough guy who swaggered around and revelled in always being in trouble. He sidled up one day and handing me a scrap of paper: it was a poem he had written, quite a good one, but he insisted that on no account must I let on that he had written it; that would have stigmatised him as a sissy. It was just one indication of the talent that could be unleashed among ordinary people if only conventional taboos were lifted and abilities given full scope.

During my period as editor of *The Chronicle* I had occasionally to visit C.M.F. H.Q. Some time before there had been outrage among the troops in Italy at the reported remark by Nancy Astor that they were 'D-Day Dodgers,' and someone had written a song to the tune of Lili Marlene, called "The D-Day Dodgers." This was published in a forces newspaper and had become very popular. On one of my visits, a N.C.O. whom I knew gave me what he claimed was one of the original carbon copies of the typescript of the song. I still have it, and it's interesting to note how the original words have been changed by some singers over the passage of years.

197

In June 1944, the Second Front was opened with the Normandy landings. We now know that the governments of Britain and the U.S.A. were staggered by the rapid advance of the Red Army following the defeat of Von Paulus at Stalingrad. Alongside the desire for victory, there was also alarm that the Russians would occupy the whole of Germany. The race to Berlin was on.

Two days before "D-Day," Allied forces entered Rome, which, because of the Vatican and the city's cultural treasures, had been declared an Open City and was therefore not defended. One of the bloodiest battles in the advance to Rome, indeed of the Second World War, was fought at Cassino, about fifty miles from Naples. Some time afterwards, I visited the battlefield with a group of lads from the M.T. Section. The brother of one of them had been killed in the battle and he hoped to find where his brother was buried and to put up a new cross – which he had made in our workshop – on the grave. Amazingly, considering the vast numbers of graves there were, and so many unmarked, we found it. I photographed him by the side of his brother's grave. It was a most moving experience. The very first grave we came across had a soldier's name and number and the simple inscription "Erected by his Dad." Although construction of the Allied cemetery was well under way, there were many scattered graves of German soldiers, surmounted by rusting helmets.

Cassino, or rather the remains of it, was a sight that lives in my memory. The town itself had been razed to the ground by heavy bombardment and every ruined building had been fought for house by house in brutal hand-to-hand fighting. It was much more devastated than Pompeii, with only rubble remaining. The country around was pockmarked with craters and scattered with broken-down tanks and vehicles. It had been a quiet and picturesque market town alongside the River Rapido, near the head of the Liri valley. Dominating the valley was Monte Cassino, a 1,700-foot mountain, on the summit of which was the famous Benedictine monastery, founded in 529 A.D. by St Benedict himself. Cassino's misfortune was to be on one of the main roads to Rome. The day we were there it was suffocatingly hot, made worse by the reflection of the heat from the stones and concrete slabs that lay all around. Among the ruins were the whitened skeletons of German soldiers. My most abiding memory, however, was the silence, broken only by the occasional distant explosion as sappers disposed of another mine they had found on Monastery Hill, and, strangely, by the croaking of frogs in one of the pools amid the ruins.

Believing that the Germans occupied the monastery, the Allies destroyed it, first by a massive ground bombardment and then by Flying Fortresses dropping six hundred tons of bombs on it in one night – a highly controversial decision at the time and since. Certainly, the Germans occupied the heights, which gave them a commanding position over the valley along which our troops would have to advance. It was a perfect defensive position, and apparently the Russians were critical of the decision to storm it. When Churchill visited the place afterwards they named the road along the valley, Churchill Way, but it was more popularly known by those who had to fight their way along it as "the mad mile." It took four months, four battles and numerous assaults before Monte Cassino was scaled and what was left of the Monastery captured. The cost in human life was enormous, one estimate putting the number killed at more than 100,000.

We went by truck up the long, narrow and twisting road to the monastery, with our offside wheels often being literally inches from the unfenced edge of the steep drop below. Some of the monks showed us around what was left of the monastery, and their sullen looks and brusque manner spoke the hostility they felt – understandably under the circumstances. The photographs I took of the monastery with my battered and simple "Brownie" box camera are the best I've ever taken, even though in future years I had more expensive equipment and greater photographic knowledge.

23. PEACE, BUT NOT FREEDOM

As the end of the war crept nearer a new mood took over the lads in my unit. Civvy Street was no longer an abstraction, a nostalgic dream so indefinite as to seem unreal. It could now be discussed as an actual possibility. Those who had been overseas for a long time were excited at the prospect of being demobbed; yet, anticipation was mixed with apprehension at the thought of becoming civilians again after stultifying years in uniform. Some had jobs to go to, but others worried about finding work and the sort of work it would be.

On 20th April 1945 the Red Army entered Berlin. A week later Hitler committed suicide, and Mussolini was captured and executed by Italian partisans. On the 8th May the Germans surrendered and the war was over. During those weeks we thirsted for every scrap of news and clung on to every false rumour of peace. I was getting over a painfully poisoned hand, but this hadn't excused me from doing guard duty the night before, which meant being able to listen to most news bulletins on the forces radio throughout the night. The next day was very hot and at 3.00 o'clock in the afternoon I was sitting on an upturned rubbish bin taking a siesta in the shade outside the Lab when a workmate came up, "Pack up your kit," he said, "the war's over." "Another rumour," I replied. "five hundred lire it's true," said Sid. At that I began to take notice. At 4.30 I was to give an A.B.C.A. talk on "Work for All," but when all the lads had assembled, I said, "You've heard the news. I don't feel like talking and I'm pretty sure you don't feel like listening, so I suggest we scrap it!" – to which they agreed enthusiastically. As it happened, that evening 693 was opening a new canteen and we had all been storing up our beer rations for some time, so the event became a victory celebration in which beer flowed freely with vermouth, chartreuse and the local wine, and all inhibitions, whether of men or officers, disappeared. The next morning we were all totally immobilised with hangovers, but thankfully two days holiday had been announced, so everyone in my billet stayed long in bed exchanging groans. The next day I went for a long walk to the Bacoli in order to find the tomb of Agrippina, the mother of Nero. The village was gaily decorated with a mass of patchwork bedcoverings and a few red flags hanging from balconies, some with photographs of soldier members of the family pinned to them. I had to run a gauntlet of women shouting to me, "Finito guerra – Viva gli Inglese!"

In anticipation of V.E. Day, "Jigger" Joynes, Eric and I had prepared a special issue of *The Chronicle*. Eric designed the cover, which was based on a Welsh party pamphlet, "Wales in the New World," with the words from the Internationale, "Now the Last Fight Let Us Face" right across it, and an article by "Jigger" and me making the point that now the war was over we had another fight on our hands – building a new Britain. Before publication, every issue had to be submitted to the Adjutant of 693. This was usually just a rubber-stamp routine, although he had sometimes been critical of some issues because he thought "politics were being introduced." This time the Colonel himself sent for "Jigger" and me, and said he was puzzled about the cover of the paper, which the Adjutant had shown him. "What did it mean?" he asked. He didn't seem very convinced by our smarmy explanation, but he reluctantly passed it, though with a message from himself included. Oddly enough, he said nothing about the article.

Rather naïvely, perhaps, we hoped that when the war was over we would all soon be going home. Instead, there was a strong rumour that those of us who had not been overseas very long were to be shipped to the Far East. As for demobilisation, the government had decided that it was to be spread over a year and longer, depending on age and length of service. The main reason given was that occupation forces would be needed until peace was firmly established and stability assured; furthermore, demobilisation had to fit in with the transformation of industry from war to peace. This seemed reasonable. But the real purpose probably had more to do with avoiding any social unrest that might result from large numbers of determined men arriving home and demanding jobs or maintenance. There were some Tories who openly expressed their unease at the thought of millions of ex-servicemen, trained in the use of arms, determined on fundamental changes and with possibly subversive ideas, suddenly set at large in Britain!

The coming of peace brought big changes. The long-service men gradually left for home, and before each batch left we had a celebration and, filled with vino, beer and sentiment, vowed eternal oaths to maintain contact in Civvy Street – which hardly ever happened. Obviously, there was no longer a need for the lab, so we filled our time making cigarette lighters and other such mementoes to take home. Captain Rainbow started a chemistry class, and trips were organised to various places.

The decision to call a snap General Election on 5th July came as a surprise, for it was assumed that the coalition government would remain in office at least until after demobilisation and the restoration of some kind of normality in Britain. It was crystal clear that the Tories had taken an opportunist decision, hoping to trade on the supposed popularity of Churchill as the great leader who had led us to victory. Troops overseas were not as affected by this adulation as were the people at home, so another reason for the indecent haste might well have been that the Tories didn't want large numbers of servicemen let loose in Britain during the election campaign – far better to keep them isolated so as to minimise their influence.

For a political animal like myself it was extremely irksome not to be involved in the election campaign at home. I devoured every scrap of news that came out, and was fortunate that Kath was such a dedicated correspondent, giving me a blow-by-blow account of the fight and sending me press cuttings and plentiful supplies of the *Daily Worker*. These were passed around and widely read. The Union Jack devoted its pages to election news, but except when it published abridged versions of the

201

election manifestos of all the parties, including that of the Communist Party, it confined its coverage exclusively to the three main parties – although I did manage to get a letter published. There was one short item stating that a Captain W. Alexander was going home on leave to stand as a Communist candidate in Coventry. This was Bill Alexander, who had fought in Spain, and who in subsequent years was to become Assistant General Secretary of the Party.

Campaigning in the army was somewhat frustrating not only because of the ban on party political propaganda from any other source other than the controlled army newspapers, but because in the unit there was no one to campaign against! A straw poll of 'other ranks' in my unit revealed almost one hundred per cent support for Labour. Among the officers in 693 there was a sharp division; the regimental career soldiers seemed to be mainly Tory or apolitical, but the majority of technical officers – scientists, technicians and the other mainly university people who were not soldiers but civilians in uniform – were Labour, with some Liberals and a few supporting Commonwealth. The Communist Party had one supporter among the officers in my unit. Of course, there was plenty of discussion and, despite the ban, "Vote Labour" was chalked everywhere. Someone pinned an election poem to the notice board, and above the canteen door was a chalked hammer and sickle, with "Vote for Joe" (i.e. Stalin) above it. Very noticeably, during the period leading up to the election I was not asked to give a single A.B.C.A. talk. However, this did not prevent us discussing the election at length in the canteen and the billet. What was interesting was how much sharper these discussions were as the realisation grew that we were not now dealing with abstract, hypothetical questions, but with matters of immediate concrete importance, matters that could actually become reality if a Labour government was elected.

It is difficult to convey the intense feeling there was among ordinary squaddies, the determination that there was to be no return to pre-war conditions. The war was not just against fascism. It was a war against the conditions that had spawned fascism, the world of mass unemployment, depressed areas, homelessness, cruel poverty and extreme class divisions. The character of the war, and the experience of living, working and fighting together had brought about a subtle, but profound change in the outlook of large numbers of servicemen, and until 1945 few recognised its political nature.

This is why some of us could not understand the doubt there was back home about whether Labour could win. It transpired that the overseas forces were politically well in advance of the home voters. When Kath told me in March that the Communist Party was putting forward the idea of a post-war coalition government, including Tories, I was amazed, as were most of the comrades in our Naples group. We could see the point of trying to maintain a broad unity to tackle some of the problems of post-war Britain, but it had to be a unity around the progressive policies of a Labour government. Indeed, most hoped, maybe idealistically, that the post-war years would see the beginnings of laying the basis for socialism in Britain, and we couldn't see any Tories or Liberals, however "progressive," agreeing to that. But such was the persistence of the signals we were receiving from home that we began to doubt the evidence of our own senses, to believe that our optimism was not justified and simply reflected the limited abnormal situation in which we lived. Maybe there was little chance of Labour winning a majority. We were also very much concerned at the number of men who were not on the armed forces register of voters. Registration was not automatic, but had to be applied for.

Waiting for the results of the election to reach us was torture. I was working in the laboratory, and at hourly intervals the Officer Commanding, Major Parker, who was listening to the radio, came rushing into the workshop and up to me with the latest results. Came the moment when, excited as a child, he burst in, shouting out, "We are winning, we are winning!" I was anxious to know how many Communists had been elected, and was relieved later to hear that Gallacher and Piratin had been elected, but bitterly disappointed that Harry Pollitt had failed to win Rhondda East by the narrowest of margins.

Just as hard to take was the fact that it was the postal vote of servicemen that did it. It was understandable when one realised that men and women in the armed forces pinned all their hopes on the election of a Labour government, and that the Communist case never reached the vast majority of them.

When the final result was announced, a mighty cheer went up in the canteen, and I heard later that even at Allied H.Q. at Caserta there was a discreet outburst of applause. Our Colonel was furious, as was the new Adjutant, formerly a South African civil servant. He came up to me in the Lab the next day. "Well, Westacott," he said, "you've done it. But why are you working?" "Surely you don't need to work now there's a Labour government." Me: "All the more reason for us to work harder sir, we are working for ourselves now for a change." He: "Britain is starting to

203

go downhill, ignoring the accumulated experience of history."
Incidentally, what I said was literally true: at the time I was making
cigarette lighters for the officer Commanding and myself!

24. ROME – AND MEETING THE POPE

Although, like everyone else, I wanted to get home quickly, I was also
hoping that before doing so I would have the opportunity of visiting
Rome. It wasn't easy, for it was the main leave centre for all Allied
troops throughout Italy, and we were last on the list being already
stationed near the next main centre, Naples. However, with the war over,
my chance did come and I was granted almost two week's leave there. It
was a truly memorable fortnight. My mate and I visited everything that
tourists are supposed to visit – the Coliseum, the Forum, the Capitol, the
Baths of Caracalla, the Pantheon, numerous churches, the Catacombs,
and, of course, the Vatican and the wonderful Sistine Chapel, with the
frescos of Michelangelo. What impressed me most were the Catacombs,
outside the city on the Appian Way – miles of narrow underground caverns containing the remains of early Christians, some exposed, and
seemingly full of the original atmosphere; the Pantheon, once a pagan
temple and perfectly preserved; and a statue of Moses by Michelangelo
in the Basilica of St Paul. Of course, half of Italy seems to have been
designed by Michelangelo. It was Mark Twain who once wrote on a visit
to Rome that he was fed up with Michelangelo and was pleased one day
to hear that he was dead! Squaddies echoed this: whenever they saw anything unusual, be it an old car, unusual graffiti or an odd building, the
usual remark was, "Michelangelo did that!"

On the second day of our leave we became friendly with two girls,
one of whom turned out to a member of the Socialist Party. They acted
as our guides, and in the evening we would sit in one of the parks while
they tried to teach us anti-fascist songs. We went to the Metropolitan
Opera House and saw The Damnation of Faust, and saw another opera –
I believe it was Tosca – in the magnificent open-air setting of the Baths
of Caracalla.

We sometimes had a meal at a N.A.A.F.I., in the very room where the
Fascist Grand Council used to meet, and it was satisfying to stand on the
balcony of the Palazzo Venezia from where I had so often seen on film
Mussolini haranguing the crowd in the piazza below. Because of its
status as an Open City, Rome had been protected from bombing or military action from both sides. It was strange to see no bomb damage, and

to see the main streets ablaze with lights at night, with shops and lights undamaged. As in Naples, prostitution flourished and the black market was more extensive because there were more things to sell.

I spent some time in St. Peter's and looking at the paintings, and treasures in gold and precious stones displayed in the Vatican. It seemed to me indecent that so much wealth should be on show when so many people in Catholic countries were starving. Indeed, poor though they were, many of them contributed to this wealth.

The most bizarre incident of my visit to Rome was meeting the Pope. It happened like this. Pope Pius XII – a reactionary Pontiff, who had supported fascism and only grudgingly accepted the Allied victory – was installed in the Vatican. Probably in order to retrieve his good name and accommodate himself with the victorious powers, he made a show of welcoming them. One of the things he did was to grant occasional audiences to small groups of Roman Catholic officers and 'other ranks'. A mate of mine in the R.A.O.C. in Naples was a Catholic and a Communist sympathiser from Liverpool who had not long come over, but whom I had known in England. Some time before, he had visited me, beside himself with excitement; he had been drawn to be one of a party of about ten who were to meet the Pope. I congratulated him and thought no more about it.

As it happened, the date fixed for the audience was when I was in Rome and I bumped into Kelly at the Alexander Club (the main N.A.A.F.I. in the city). The following day he sought me out. Apparently, one of the party had dropped out because of a sudden illness. Of course, they could easily fill his place, but Kelly, either from a bizarre sense of humour or because he genuinely thought I would like the experience, had put my name down – and it had been accepted. "But I'm not a Catholic," I protested. "No-one will know," he said, "and you might even learn something. " What happened is best described in the account I sent to Kath:

We were taken to the Vatican Palace past a few picturesque Swiss Guards, along a lengthy corridor with wonderful tapestries hanging along both sides, up in a lift, past more guards, across a lawn, up a marble stairway, along another corridor, at the end of which were more guards in more gaudy costumes (jackets with puffed sleeves, wide breeches and queer cockade hats – colour of jacket and breeches, yellow with black longitudinal stripes) and strange imitation battle-axes, and were then shown into the Pope's reception room.

It was a very large, depressing sort of room, with walls and ceilings

205

highly decorated in the typical Italian style. At one end was a raised plat-form on which there was a throne. In front of the platform a Swiss Guard marched backwards and forwards with his 'battle axe' over his shoulder.

We waited for about half-an-hour, then there was the sound of orders being shouted outside the room. The guard halted and faced us, a door at the side of the platform opened, and the Pope appeared, accompanied by the Papal Secretary and an officer of the guard. He made short speeches in English, French, Polish and Italian (the French and Italian were irrel-evant as the group consisted of British, American and two Poles – but it was probably a set procedure). He then blessed everyone and approached each of us individually. He put his hands on my shoulder and blessed me, my family and dear friends (so presumably you are included). Much as I would like to, it was hardly the place to tackle him on his reactionary policy of bolstering up the falling ruins of fascism.

The day before I met the Pope, my mate and I had an interesting meeting with an Austrian Jesuit priest. We were sitting in St Peter's, when he came and sat with us. As he had spent six years in the U.S.A. his English was very good and we had a long and interesting conversation, during which he seemed anxious to cut the Pope down to size. There were mis-conceptions, he said, about his supposed infallibility: it was strictly lim-ited to a narrow field of dogma and he also acknowledged that previous Popes, and the Church itself, had often made grave mistakes and acted badly. I gained the impression that he had fallen out with his boss!

An interesting outcome of our acquaintance was that he took us on a long tour of the Vatican, showing us things that he assured us were not normally shown to visitors. As he was a believer in what is now called ecumenicalism, he no doubt thought that we would return to Britain and at least work for greater unity between the Protestant and Catholic Churches. Oddly enough, although I said at the start that I was an atheist, he seemed to dismiss this as being synonymous with being a Protestant.

Most Catholic priests I have met, particularly Jesuits, have been sur-prisingly tolerant compared with the priests of other denominations. There was one occasion when there was a big regimental church parade. Normally, I went along with the crowd and attended church service, for at least it was a rest and I enjoy hymn singing; and although attendance was voluntary, if you didn't attend you would be put on spud-bashing or some other chore. However, probably out of cussedness, on this occasion I decided to stand firm. The sergeant major shouted out, "Church of England to the left!" "Catholics to the right!" and went through the other denominations. At the end, I was left standing forlornly on my own. A Catholic padre came up to me: "What are you, laddie?" "I'm an atheist, sir." A slight pause, and then he grinned. "If the truth be known," he said, "had they the courage of their convictions, quite a lot of these would be standing here with you!"

I remember James Klugman, who played a leading part in the Christian-Marxist dialogue of the 1960's making the same point to me. A favourite commitment of his was to spend a few days each year, by invitation, at a Jesuit College near Derby. He said that some of them would have joined the party if they hadn't thought it inexpedient for them to do so.

On the last day of my leave I was taken ill and rushed to hospital with suspected malaria. It turned out to be only a bad case of tonsillitis, but I was nevertheless kept in for a week.

25. A MYSTERY SOLVED

Back at the ranch things were changing rapidly. There was obviously no need for a Chemical and Metallurgical Laboratory. The Staff Sergeant in charge of the office was demobbed and I took over his job. Major Rainbow became Officer Commanding and the first thing he did was to promote me, first to lance-corporal and then rapidly to corporal. One day he told me he was going into Naples, and after he had gone I went into his room to collect some papers. On his desk was a folder, marked "TOP SECRET" – which, of course, I immediately had a peek at. It contained two letters. The first was headed SECRET, and repeated "SECRET AND CONFIDENTIAL. ALLIED FORCES HEADQUARTERS (underlined in red). Office of the Assistant Chief of Staff G.2. From Lt. Colonel G. Eyres-Monsell." It was addressed to my former Officer Comanding, Major Davies:

I am writing to you regarding 14574600 Cfn WESTACOTT F. C., who is, I understand, under your command at the present time. This man has been known to the security authorities in London as a branch official of the Communist Party. For some time he also acted as a paid organiser of the Party. Since joining the army he was closely watched for a time, with satisfactory results and the authorities in London do not consider it necessary to re-open the matter. In view of his present location they are anxious to know whether he comes into contact with secret information to which it is undesirable he should have access and I shall be glad if you will let me know on what type of work he is employed.

It was signed G. Eyres Monsell.

207

One sensed some irritation in Davies's reply. He said that of course no man under his command had access to secret information. As for me, although I had "a tendency to discuss politics," he was bound to say that my behaviour had always been exemplary. I had been sent to the Army School of Education and he had received a good report of my work there. It wasn't a bad reply, considering that Davies was probably the only Tory Officer Commanding the Chem and Met Lab had. A revealing insight into the bias of the higher authorities was that at the time in question we had a corporal with us who admitted to having been a prominent member of Mosley's Blackshirts, but there was no enquiry about him. After the war, Eyres-Monsell became a leading Tory M.P.

This incident confirmed what I had already surmised. It explained why, a few weeks after I was moved to a unit, the Colonel would find some pretext to see me – something that was highly unusual, for Colonels don't usually fraternise with mere privates. My record was obviously following me around. It also explained why I had not been promoted earlier, although I was obviously well in line. It was only when Rainbow, who seemed to be a left-winger, became Officer Commanding, that I received any stripes. This didn't worry me, but promotion was acceptable when it came because it meant an increase in my demob gratuity. Although it might seem contradictory to outsiders that someone with such a "perfidious" record should be accepted, even encouraged, to take part in army education, this only arises from ignorance of the British army and how it was organised. It was (and probably still is) a vast bureaucratic structure, with a multitude of different sections working in their own sweet way and often ignorant of what is happening to other sections even on their doorstep. Thus, although the officer in command of the Chem and Met Lab was informed of my record, probably the command of 693 wasn't.

Xmas 1945 was horribly depressing. Almost all my friends had been demobbed, and they had been replaced by a different breed of regular army soldier who seemed to have nothing in common with us conscripts who had been overseas for some time. Now the war was over there was no longer any motivation to sustain us and make our presence overseas justifiable and bearable; and for me there was the knowledge that back home a big family gathering was taking place, with my brother Bert demobbed from India and George introducing his fiancée to the family. However, a few days later, depression gave way to elation with the news that I was granted twenty eight days leave in the U.K., and on 4th January a Lancaster Bomber transported me from Naples to Norwich. It had been stripped of all internal fittings, there was no heating and we simply lay in our great coats on the bare fuselage; for four hours we endured cold such as I had never experienced before nor ever want to again. Still, it was well worth it for what was at the end.

I spent the leave in Tredegar and Melton, and did two meetings about the situation in Italy. The return journey took five days and nights and most of that time we travelled in an unheated and overcrowded train, with the windows half boarded up, sitting bolt upright on hard seats. The only compensations were that we passed through the wonderful Swiss scenery and spent two days in Milan, another city I had hoped to visit before leaving Italy.

With the war over, the current affairs content of army education diminished, and the emphasis changed to formal courses on academic subjects, as laid down in a definitive handbook and conducted by full-time lecturers of the Army Education Corps. Formation Colleges were set up for this purpose and those taking part had to go to these centres. However, I was asked to give a course on Modern European History, and to speak to about fifty men on the situation in Italy, but my job as an A.B.C.A. lecturer was restricted to infrequent sessions.

The time came when Major Rainbow and I were the only two left of the Chem and Met Lab. We spent a few days filling in countless forms and gathering together all the files and papers from the offices to burn. Then, over a big bonfire in the yard, we shook hands and he said, "I'll see you when I rejoin the Party," but regrettably, we never did meet again. Some time before, we had had a long chat in which he told me that he had in fact been a Party member. He had graduated with Professor George Thomson, a famous classical scholar, and was a friend of the historian, Roy Pascal – both of whom were Communist Party members.

I felt sad at seeing the Chem and Met Lab pass into official history, having been in it almost from the start, and because its character and size meant that a close, friendly relationship had developed between everyone in it, officers and men. This was in marked contrast with my next posting, to 693 itself, which was large, regimented and impersonal. Probably thinking he was doing me a good turn, Rainbow had given me a testimonial lauding my clerical and organisational abilities, with the result that I was made Chief Clerk of the M.T. Section, responsible for the disposition of about twenty vehicles and their drivers. The vehicles were mainly Dodge trucks, but there were also a few Jeeps and small vans. Under me were two military clerks, one Italian clerk, two Italian girl typists and an office boy. Apparently, a request for posting me to another unit had come through from HQ, and had been returned marked "Indispensable"!

It meant leaving my comfortable billets at Baia and moving to a cold, almost empty and very large room in a building a mile away. Although I was annoyed at the time, it turned out not to be too bad because most of the drivers I knew were still there. They were delighted, because now they had a friendly N.C.O. in a position of authority, someone who had no compunction about arranging the driving rosters to suit their convenience, who didn't see them simply as numbers to be juggled around and who was prepared to manipulate the officer who was supposed to be in charge. This wasn't too difficult, because so long as everything ran smoothly he was quite prepared to leave well alone – an attitude I found very common. We had quite a democratic set-up. The drivers would sort out among themselves who was to do what and I would try as far as possible to make up the roster to fit in with wishes. If a run to Rome were needed, they would agree which of them would do it and which vehicle to take. If some had personal reasons for wanting to go to Naples, I would make out an order for a truck and a driver and, if need be, make out day-leave passes. When the officer called in, and calling in was just what he did, I would present him with a bundle of papers – the passes, the movement orders, and my replies to any letters received – and he would sign them automatically, often without even sitting down – just perusing the letters and replies.

I still had several Italian friends locally in the P.C.I., and within the limitations of language they would explain to me the Italian political scene. Local elections were about to take place and a massive campaign was underway. They invited me to a joint P.C.I.-Socialist election conference, but, of course, I had to decline. The ban on soldiers having anything to do with Italian politics had, in fact, became strengthened because of the strained relations that had developed between the growing democratic forces and the Allied occupying powers. However, when invited to attend a closed meeting of the local P.C.I., I thought it was an experience not be missed. There was an additional risk arising from the fact that many of the P.C.I. members worked in the 693 factory, and news of my attendance at one of their meetings could easily get to the ears of an unsympathetic R.E.M.E. officer.

They particularly wanted me to meet the Area Secretary of the Party,

210

a man they called "de boss". So one Sunday I met two comrades and they took me to the meeting place in a tenement building in the nearby town of Ansaldo. What followed is best described in a letter to Kath, posted in England by a mate going on leave because I was sceptical of official assurances that army censorship had ended:

As soon as I arrived I was ushered into a small room and was instantly welcomed by clenched fists from a dozen obvious proletarians seated around a large table strewn with books in the best St Andrews Crescent (the Welsh Party Offices) manner. I was put in the seat of honour next to the chairman – who was the double of Stalin in every detail. Whether he was made chairman because of this fortunate likeness I cannot say, but it certainly seemed likely, for of the attributes of a chairman he was singularly lacking. Not a word did he say all the time I was there. Be the discussion calm or heated, he just sat there like a rock, imperturbable, unmoved and apparently unaffected by the stormy waves of debate raging around him.

Most of the comrades were in overalls and had obviously came straight from work. Most were middle-aged or old, although there were some youngsters. I had asked that they try and provide an interpreter, and as soon as I arrived they sent for a twenty-one year old girl who was one of the most enthusiastic of the young members. Her English was not very good, but it was better than my Italian. Her name was Emma and she had joined the Party two years before although she admitted that she lacked the knowledge of Marxism a member of her standing should have.

In the middle of a very heated argument in which everyone in the room seemed to be participating, "de boss" himself entered. Instantly, there was silence; all stood up and gave the clenched fist salute; the Secretary gravely returned it, then reached across the table to shake hands with me. By this time the room had filled – there must have been about forty present, some standing in the corridor, and the atmosphere was getting somewhat thick. On the Secretary's suggestion we all moved to a larger room. It was enriched by having a piano, and on the walls were pictures of Marx, Engels, Stalin, Togliatti, Matteotti and others I could not recognise. The Xmas decorations were still up, with delightful little hammer and sickles and red stars hanging from them.

When everyone had assembled the Secretary made a long and impassioned statement connected with my being there, but as I couldn't make sense of it I simply tried to look profound and waited for my faithful Emma, who was seated besides me, to translate. All she told me, however, was that the comrades welcomed me there, for it indicated the international character of our party, and he hoped I would visit them often. I would always be welcome. In reply, I thanked him and told them how proud I was to meet comrades so enthusiastic. Whatever part of the world we lived in, our fight was the same. I asked them not to judge all English people by the reactionary ones they might have met or heard of. This was as wrong as English people judging the new Italy by the representatives of the old. I am certain all this was too complicated for Emma to translate, but whatever she said, it was greeted with great applause. Comrades then asked me questions about the situation in Britain. Here are a few –

"Is the Labour Party a socialist party?"

"If it is, why isn't its policy international?"

"Why hasn't the Labour government's policy to Italy changed?"

"Why are British troops so conservative and anti-Italian?"

There followed a long discussion on policy matters, with particular reference to the problems of building a mass party. Some of the comrades were strongly opposed to allowing everyone to join, especially ex-Fascist Party members. They argued that whereas in the old days people were fascist because it paid them to be so, now many are Communists, because it is the popular thing to do. A youngster of about nineteen replied very forcibly. He said that he and his generation had known no politics but fascist politics. Should they now be penalised because they see the new road before them and wanted to lead the way along it.

Halfway through the meeting Stalin II had a brilliant idea. He mysteriously disappeared, but materialised a few minutes later with a flask of red wine, which he silently put in front of me. The Secretary ceremoniously filled a glass and handed it to me. Thereafter, he and I drank alternate tumblers full, while the other comrades, who were doing most of the talking, dryly looked on.

At last the discussion waned and someone suggested music. Thereupon, a comrade sat at the piano and struck up "Bandiera Rossa." Oh, my Kath! – you should have heard those children of Garibaldi sing their great battle hymn. I cannot convey to you a tiny fraction of the fervour and enthusiasm they put into the words, as they sang it with clenched fists and eyes ablaze. The Vicar of God, in his Roman palace, must have shuddered, and ordered God himself to put another padlock on the Golden Gates!

They then sang the Internationale and several Italian working class songs – and as an anti-climax danced to the latest American hit tunes, but not before I had refused to sing the "Red Flag." Then, before leaving, I had to shake hands all round. The enthusiasm and spirit of these Italian comrades impressed me very much. They have the fire of pioneers and the fervour that brooks no obstacles. Their almost child-like love of melodramatic poses, like constantly giving the clenched fist salute, and the over-demonstrative respect paid to their leaders is, I suppose, a reflection of twenty years of fascism and natural in a new mass movement, the membership of which is so far largely politically immature. I was told they held meetings every week, occasionally twice a week.

One feature of life that became increasingly irksome as the strength of the unit diminished, was that the shortage of N.C.O.'s meant having to do guard duty more frequently. But by far the most unpleasant change resulted from the influx of regular army officers from Britain to replace those who had been demobbed. Most of these newcomers had never been overseas and came straight out of college. Our new colonel had been the commandant of a prisoner-of-war camp in Britain and brought his ideas on discipline with him. He began making himself a nuisance from the first day, and soon he had started ceremonial parades, guard parades, weekly kit-inspections and the accompanying polishing and blancoing of equipment – procedures we had forgotten all about. We had to salute officers at all times, even when they passed in a car. In Naples, the new brand of military policeman would pull a squaddie up if a tunic button was unfastened, if his shirt-sleeves were rolled up after dusk (forbidden because of the danger of malaria mosquito bites), or if he wasn't wearing a cap or not wearing one straight. It was obvious that a determined effort was being made to stamp out the informal atmosphere that had to some extent developed, particularly in the 8th Army, during the years when the need to defeat the enemy was seen to be more important than 'bull' and appearance. There was also bitterness at the increasing disparity between the life enjoyed by officers and that of the men. This seething resentment at the new regime, particularly as we were all waiting to be demobbed, led to the men at one of the biggest R.E.ME. depots in Italy refusing to go on parade one morning. Although they got in touch with several M.P's, the supposed ringleader was arrested and the men confined to barracks. Appropriate to the new regime was the 693 factory going over to producing truncheons for the Carabiniere in preparation for the coming general election!

213

As I've mentioned, the main workshops of 693 B.M.W. were staffed by Italian civilian workers, with R.E.M.E. personnel supervising. There had been unrest over conditions for some time: the remark was commonly made, "we were better off under the Germans." It wasn't only wages, but also the discipline imposed. There was understandable resentment at the fact that a private soldier could impose a fine, sometimes amounting to a day's pay, without there being any right of appeal. It reached the point when the workers in our factory and others in the area went on strike. How much it was fermented by fascists it was difficult to say, but there wasn't any doubt that the workers had genuine grievances and my natural inclination was to support them. It certainly put me in a serious predicament. Every day, army trucks with military escorts were sent out to the surrounding villages to recruit blacklegs, and there came the moment I dreaded when my name was on the list detailed for this job – no less dirty because the P.C.I. opposed the strike. Of course there was no way I could get out of it, for to disobey an order, especially in wartime, is a serious military offence. To my relief, the strike ended before my turn came up.

There was a feature of the strike that revealed one consequence of twenty years under fascism. Understandably, the workers were quite unfamiliar with the legal forms of struggle we are so accustomed to. Having stopped work, they were not sure how to proceed, for there was no trade union or factory organisation. I managed surreptitiously to get together a few of the activists and suggested that their next step should be to form a strike committee and formulate demands – something we take for granted, but which didn't seem so obvious to them. It reminded me of the saying allegedly once prevalent on the Continent that when three British workers get together the first thing they do is form a committee! Needless to say, it didn't take long before the Italian trade union movement could teach us a thing or two.

Towards the end of 1945 the political situation in Italy had sharpened. The Allies obviously wanted to postpone elections to a Constituent Assembly for as long as possible, and right-wing forces were warning of an imminent communist plot and openly calling for intervention à la Greece to prevent a progressive government being elected. There were massive communist-socialist demonstrations, and every available wall-space was covered with political slogans and massive hammer and sickle motifs painted with stencils. Main slogans were: "Bread, Work, Freedom;" "Fascism has given us hunger, misery and unemployment. A democratic Italy will give us bread, happiness and work;" "Death to the House of Savoy;" "Let Italians Govern Italy" – aimed at the occupying powers and their governing body, A.M.G.O.T. I attended one of the biggest demonstrations, with national speakers, and when it was dispersing an Italian Party member who I knew spied me and called me up to the platform, ostensibly so that I could take photographs, but really to introduce me to some of the speakers.

The situation was finely balanced. Some years after the war I took part in a debate with a leading Trotskyist at Nottingham University, and as an example of the iniquities of communists, he put forward a popular Trotskyist line that the P.C.I. should have seized power. How naïve can one be! Italy was occupied by a powerful military force which had just defeated Germany, and was ready and quite willing to intervene on the side of reaction, as it had done in Greece; except for parts of the north the partisans were not highly organised; after over twenty years of fascism the working class was only just beginning to build its organisations, even trade unions; and although fascism had been defeated, its ideas, and the reactionary ideas of the Vatican, still influenced large numbers of people. It was obvious to those of us who were there, that the prime need was to unify the genuinely anti-fascist, progressive forces in order to achieve full political independence. I relate this, because it is a classic example of the wishful thinking of so many Trotskyists and their disregard of concrete facts that do not fit in with their theory.

During 1945, most Communist Parties in the democratic countries were beginning to face severe ideological problems arising from their efforts to work out a correct perspective for the post-war years. The line that prevailed was that it was possible and necessary to continue the national unity built during the war into the period of peace, especially the years of reconstruction. Whilst the class struggle would still exist, it was of secondary importance to the need to preserve this unity, which implied some measure of class cooperation in rebuilding society. Internationally, the alliance with the Soviet Union could and should be continued and strengthened.

This attitude was expressed in its extreme form by Earl Browder, the general secretary of the Communist Party of the United States, who, as far back as December 1943, had questioned whether Communist Parties were still needed. He used as the basis for his argument the fact that the Teheran Conference of the heads of the Allied powers envisaged their unity and cooperation extending into the years of peace. He maintained

215

that as socialism now appeared to be a very distant objective, there was no point in having a party with revolution and socialism as its aim, and that Communists should work through existing parties to help make "the system of free enterprise" work, but with regard to the conditions of the working class. He developed his argument in subsequent speeches and articles. On 20th May 1944, the Congress of the C.P.U.S.A. passed a resolution dissolving itself and creating a Communist Political Association. The main opposition within the Central Committee of the Party came from its president, William Z. Foster, but even he did not oppose the decision at the Party Congress.

There was surprise and some disagreement among communists in other countries, but only the South African and Australian Communist Parties publicly condemned the line. A few South American parties, including Cuba and Colombia, supported it. Then, in April 1945, Jacques Duclos, a highly respected leader of the French Communist Party who had been a leading figure in the Comintern, published an article in Cahiers du Communisme, critically analysing Browder's line and concluding by sharply condemning it and the dissolution of the C.P.U.S.A. One of his arguments was that Browder was confusing diplomatic agreements between states, which, at that time were essential and positive, with class compromise within countries. After the war, the class struggle would continue, and hence there would be need for a Marxist-Leninist party to give leadership to it. It was nonsense to envisage, as Browder did, Pierpont-Morgan, the powerful American financier, subjugating his own profit-oriented interests and being prepared to work alongside Communists for the common good of the people. On July 26th, at an emergency conference, the C.P.U.S.A. was reconstituted and the previous line condemned as "opportunist errors."

Browderism, as it came to be called, was not supported by British Communists, although there was no forthright public condemnation of it. And there were elements within the party that did support it, probably the most important being the Midlands District Committee, which called on the C.P.G.B. to follow the American line. However, the thinking behind Browderism was reflected in some of the decisions taken by the C.P.G.B. Advocating the continuation of a coalition government after the war ended, was one such example. Another was the hasty decision to downgrade the importance of the Party's Industrial Department and shift the emphasis of organisation from workplace to area branches. During the war, powerful workplace branches had been built, correctly reflecting the importance the party attached to industry; but the new shift seemed to reflect the fact that now it regarded local activity in the streets, among tenants, and in the electoral field to be almost all-important. It was argued that the party still supported workplace branches, but the re-organisation of industry and the corresponding dispersal of workers meant that many of the workplace branches ceased to be viable. However, it was obvious that there was more to it than that, that the change of emphasis was based on a changed political attitude. A third example of Browderist thinking was the Party's continued support for workplace Production Committees even though the situation that made them necessary had changed. It was only when workers increasingly opposed them, and when the miners at a Yorkshire pit actually went on strike against their committee, that the line was changed. Afterwards, Arthur Horner was to say that it was an example of the workers being ahead of the Party.

Perhaps I can be excused for feeling a little smug, but I do have incontrovertible documentary evidence in the letters written during that time, of my opposition to Browderism and to the above changes in the line of the C.P.G.B. Indeed, in relation to Browder, I argued that the British Party had to accept some responsibility because we were closer to the C.P.U.S.A. than most other parties. A further point which I expressed then (and have always maintained) is that while British Marxists have paid a lot of attention to the influence of bourgeois democracy on the Labour Party and the general labour movement, we have neglected to study its influence on Marxism and Marxists. Alas, in recent years this neglect has proved to be catastrophic.

In the light of what has happened in recent years – the fact that social-ism seems further away in the main capitalist countries than was then envisaged – is there any substance in what Browder was saying – I do not think so. The fact that history has taken a certain turn which seems, however tenuously, to lend some substance to one of his ideas – of socialism not being on the agenda – does not mean that this was inevitable. To believe so is to adopt a gross fatalism that denies the pos-sibility of history taking different paths according to the interaction of very many forces, including the class struggle. Moreover, the main premise on which his analysis was based, that western capitalist govern-ments would be prepared to continue friendly and co-operative relations with the Soviet Union was soon to be shattered.

The war-time alliance had been based on the overall common need to defeat the fascist powers; but from the start, behind the public demonstrations of unity, Britain and America were haunted by the spectre of a strong Soviet Union coming out of the war. This had been the prime reason for delaying the second front. It was why British imperialism was determined not to allow Greece, with its strategically important position at the end of the Mediterranean, to have a government sympathetic to the Soviet Union. It was why the United States, which had suffered no invasion and whose industries had not been hit but, on the contrary, had grown stronger, had refused economic aid without strings to the Soviet Union.

It didn't take long for the covert anti-Sovietism to come out in the open. On 5th March 1946, only ten months after the war had ended, Churchill made his notorious speech at Fulton University, declaring that "an iron curtain has come down across Europe" and calling for united action against the Soviet Union and Communism. It was the start of the Cold War.

This new attitude was quickly injected into the army. It was reflected in a big way in the army newspapers and in the education programmes. In April, the head of the Russian Department of Birmingham University was brought over to lecture the troops on "Soviet Socialism," and 693 was one of the units he visited. About sixty per cent of the manpower – all who were not on duty or working – were ordered to attend. The lecture was every bit as bad as I feared. It was a blatant exercise aimed at undermining the friendly feelings so many soldiers had for the Soviet Union arising from the Red Army's record in defeating fascism. It was hoped that having an academic who was supposed to be an authority on the subject would have a big influence. It ended with an argument between him and me.

In Britain, local elections were to take place on 1st April, and the Tredegar Branch of the Party asked me to stand as a Communist candidate for the Sirhowy Ward of the Urban District Council "in absentia." This was permitted, although, unfortunately, it didn't qualify me for special leave, which only applied to parliamentary candidates. I stood along with Dai Maggs, the branch secretary, and a stalwart of the local labour movement. Emrys was our agent and a good campaign was waged, including Will Paynter doing a meeting. Our opponents made great use of the fact that even if I were elected, it would be some time before I could actually sit as a councillor. Of course, we never expected to get elected in what was an entrenched Labour area, but eleven per cent of the votes cast was quite good and just above the national average Communist vote. My standing in the election aroused a great deal of interest in the unit, and the election address was widely distributed and discussed.

A few weeks later it was announced that 693 was to disband, so once again I was involved in winding up the unit – I was becoming quite an expert at the job! My goodbye to Naples was made in good style: I was caught up in a near-riot on my last visit. A few days before, the P.C.I. offices had been attacked by fascists, with the armed police, the Carabiniere, looking on. When the comrades started fighting back, eight were arrested – but no fascists. There was a very tense atmosphere, and the centre of the city was being patrolled by squads of Carabiniere with fixed bayonets. A crowd was gathering in one of the piazzas and the Carabiniere fired several rounds of shots in the air. Outside the Town Hall, I found myself caught between a line of forty steel-helmeted, fully-armed Italian soldiers and about one hundred Carabiniere. There was nothing for it but walk slowly through their ranks, hoping my uniform would give some protection. Apparently, there was an additional reason for the large crowd that had gathered, apart from the protest against fascist provocations; it was a demonstration of unemployed ex-service-men who were demanding that the Town Council receive a deputation.

26. TRIESTE

The day before we disbanded we clubbed together to pay for a really slap-up meal and followed it in the evening with the mother of all booze-ups. All the drinks in the place were gathered together and we proceeded methodically to get rid of them. Fortunately, most of us were not leaving until the following afternoon, so we had time to get over the hangovers. My orders were to report to a transit centre at Treviso, near Venice, without being told my ultimate destination. A very special problem for me was the respectable personal library built up over two years – mainly books sent by Kath – which had to accompany me or be destroyed. I decided to take most with me, so several kit bags were purloined and stuffed with them. As the environs of Naples slowly drifted past the train I must confess to feeling a little sad, for it had become something of a "home town" where I had made many friends.

The journey took several days and nights, travelling via Bologna, Padua and Verona, and I was able to see something of the places we passed through on the way. Every town and village had a "Casa del

219

Populo" – "House of the People," formally the headquarters of the local liberation movement, but now serving as the meeting place for a local council. Usually, there was a red flag over the door and a red-draped board on the wall outside with the names of all the partisans who had died fighting fascism. Although I was at Treviso for two days, I was on duty most of the time, so, unfortunately, there was no opportunity to visit Venice. A few of us then left for a dispersal centre in Trieste.

That we were in a sensitive area soon became clear. At periodic road blocks civilian vehicles were being stopped and searched. Soon after passing a large road sign declaring in English, Italian and Serbo-Croat that we had entered the Province of Venezia Giulia, we came to a village, and above almost every door was pasted a red flag with a hammer and sickle in the centre. After crossing the Isonzo River, the old border between Italy and Austria, the political views of the inhabitants became even more pronounced. Walls, fences, houses, roads – everything that could be used to write on – were covered with slogans and symbols. Although they were in Italian they were all pro-Yugoslavian. The name of Tito figured very much, and for a mile along the road on which we were travelling, every fence-post had his name painted on it. His photograph gazed at us from many windows and from walls, sometimes with his Second-in-Command, Kardelj. Taking up the entire gable-end of one house was a huge painted slogan "Siamo Italiani ma Vogliamo Tito" – "We are Italians, but we want Tito."

Eventually I was posted to the 169 Infantry Base Workshop, at a village called Gradisca de Isonzo, near Gorizia and the disputed border between Yugoslavia and Italy. It was the R.E.M.E. unit for the infantry divisions in the region, and I was put in the Fifty-Sixth London Division, usually called the "Black Cat" division because of the shoulder emblem we had to wear. On arrival we were immediately told that we were in a politically sensitive area and that on no account must we talk politics to any civilian, or attend any political gathering. This warning was repeated every few days.

The reason for this sensitivity was that the future of Venezia Giulia and Trieste was a flashpoint in the high-level talks going on between the Allied powers. At a conference in Paris, the foreign ministers were dead-locked; Molotov was adamant that the area should become part of Yugoslavia; British Foreign Minister Bevin, supported by France and the USA, was equally determined that it should go to Italy. Although the arguments conducted publicly were mainly around ethnic and geographic points, this was a thin camouflage to hide the real reason – access to the Mediterranean and the Middle East. With the defeat of Italy, British imperialism was determined to re-establish its hegemony over the region, and particularly to prevent the Soviet Union and the socialist countries having more than limited access to it. This was the prime reason for British intervention in Greece. They were the first skirmishes of the Cold War.

Although Yugoslavia bordered the Adriatic, at that time it had no major port, and Trieste was such a port, as well as being a large and prosperous city. As I explained in an article I sent to the *Daily Worker* – which was published, though edited – the arguments on geographical or ethnic grounds were finely balanced; whereas the city was undeniably mainly Italian, most of the hinterland was Yugoslav, and there was strong evidence that Trieste had been artificially "Italianised" over a long period.

The entire region was a hotbed of political activity and the position of Communists was confusing to say the least. There were no less than three Communist parties in the region. The P.C.I. strongly maintained that Trieste should be part of Italy, one of its main election slogans being, "Long Live Italian Trieste in a Democratic Italy." However, Venezie Giulian members of the P.C.I., who insisted on pursuing their line of an independent region, were expelled from the Party and formed the Communist Party of Venezia Giulia. Unfortunately, there was already a Communist Party with that name in existence, closely associated with the Yugoslavian Party which was advocating the region becoming part of Yugoslavia. Each party had its own newspaper and used the hammer and sickle. As I wrote to Kath: "You say you have problems in Britain!" Jacques Duclos wrote an article in Cahiers du Communisme criticising the line of the P.C.I. This episode is interesting because it demonstrates that sharp differences between Communist Parties are not a peculiarity of recent years.

The Italian General Election took place soon after we arrived and although the region was not directly involved, all troops were confined to barracks; and for several days before the election, we were forbidden to cross the border into Italy proper – to visit Udine, for example. The P.C.I. received 4½ million votes, 18% of the total. Just before polling day the Vatican threatened reprisals, including excommunication for any Catholic voting Communist. Not surprisingly, the Christian Democrats won the most seats, but with no overall majority. A coalition government was formed in which Togliatti was Minister of Justice. The vote against retaining the monarchy was quite decisive.

Compared with the south, northern Italy is like another country. It was a welcome change to see fields, trees and hedges and to hear song-birds again – very similar to Britain and totally different from the dry, semi-tropical environment of Campania. The houses were more familiar, with sloping roofs; everything looked so clean and tidy. The people also were different; they seemed more independent. Italy was probably more sharply divided between the industrial regions – the northern half – and the economically backward southern regions than any other European country. This was reflected politically, for whereas the left, including the Communist Party, drew its main strength from the northern working class, the right-wing parties and the royalists were strongest in Sicily and the south. Rome was in the middle. The attitude of northern Italians to their southern brothers and sisters was often contemptuous, considering them "backward" and "uncultured." The P.C.I. were paying a great deal of attention to the south, for it rightly saw that to become a national party it had to win over Sicilians and Campanians and develop a more geo-graphically balanced economy.

Gradisca was a delightful, quiet, and clean small town, with the houses grouped on three sides of the market square. On the other side was a field leading down to the Isonzo river, a favourite venue for children to play and paddle. The most prominent building in the square was the "Casa del Populo," and, as usual, there were a number of cafes with tables outside always occupied by men basking in the sun, drinking and arguing pas-sionately with mouths and hands; but there were never any women. Hammer and sickle badges were worn by a good proportion of them, and I was sorely tempted to introduce myself, but realised that it would be quite foolhardy to do so. The town really came to life, however, after dusk, when seemingly the entire population, now including the women, came out of their houses to walk around in the cool of the evening or sit drinking vino. Hundreds of fairy lights were everywhere, and orchestras played in the two small open-air dance floors while youngsters either danced or flirted on the benches in the park. I found the most attractive quality of the Italian character was the ability to be cheerful and appar-ently carefree in the most difficult circumstances.

Within limits I was able to explore some of the country around, although we were warned not to go far from the unit unless in organised groups. Walking along a lane one Sunday morning, I heard the sound of "Bandiera Rossa" being sung with gusto, and soon I came across a farm cart gaily decorated with red streamers and overloaded with men, women and children – goodness know how the poor horse was able to move. Apparently, it was a local Communist football team going to play an away match. On weekends, we sometimes visited Udine and the sea-side resort of Grado, and fortunately, for a number of reasons connected with my job, I was able to spend quite a lot of time in Trieste.

When I arrived at the unit, I was seen by the Commanding Officer, a Major, and the first question he asked was, "Do you play cricket?" He was a cricket fanatic and cared about little else. He could remember facts and figures about the game going back to its origins, and was proud of his prowess at answering questions. He would have made a better "memory man" on the stage than an officer of an infantry division. The Medical Officer was another odd-bod. He didn't seem to know much about medicine, but was an enthusiastic collector of insects. His quarters and medical room were full of specimens, and a sure way of getting an "excused duties" note was to take him a good specimen of a beetle or butterfly. A repugnant set-up was that Corporals were separated from the men by having separate billets and their own mess. In most units this only applied to Sergeants. Most hadn't long come out from Britain and I didn't find them a very endearing lot; their racist, anti-Yugoslav attitude nauseated me.

Although, when I arrived, there was a Staff-Sergeant in charge of the office, he was soon de-mobbed and I was put in charge. The Commanding Officer offered to promote me to Sergeant, but only on condition that I postpone my de-mob for a few months – ostensibly to ensure that there would be time for the new rank to be substantiated, but really, I suspected, because he wanted to make certain that I would be there for the life of the unit. Needless to say, I declined the offer. As well as dealing with the usual daily pile of bureaucratic correspondence, company orders, passes, leave and demob arrangements, I was responsible for working out the pay and insurance for about one hundred civilian and army personnel, supposedly under the Adjutant, Captain Martin. I had several military and civilian clerks working under me, but it was still very hard work. Like the other officers, Captain Martin was a profes-sional soldier and an eccentric, but I got on with him quite well because he didn't use his rank and had made friends with several ordinary local Italian families. He was always looking for the odd and bizarre and one day insisted on taking me to the home of an Italian friend of his to see a plant which seemed to have nerves. If one leaf was touched, the hundreds of other leaves on the plant would immediately close-up.

By a stroke of luck I was sent to Trieste on an administrative course for about a fortnight, so I was able to have a good look at the city. Unfortunately, the heat was stifling, hotter even than Naples, so it was painful to walk far. Evenings were a relief, and because the power stations had not been damaged, Trieste was ablaze with light. Most exciting, however, were some other lights outside of the city. I had climbed to the old castle, from where one had a panoramic view of the mountains semi-circling the town to the north – those mountains which, not long before, had been the home of Yugoslav Partisans. And in the foothills all around were luminous red stars, hammer and sickles and the word "Tito." It was obvious that each sign must have covered hundreds of feet. Then I realised from their flickering what they were: ditches dug out of the ground and filled with bracken, wood, oil and other combustible material which were set alight and kept burning each night by the Yugoslavs.

There was an occasion when the political situation suddenly sharpened. For two days, troops were confined to barracks, but I had to go into Trieste on business and immediately sensed the tenseness in the air. Some streets were cordoned off, and the others were crowded with people and gangs of youths marching around. It transpired that fascists and their supporters had set fire to the Italo-Yugoslav Anti-Fascist Committee building, and had then proceeded to wreck one of the Communist Party headquarters. In the ensuing fighting some people were injured. The response of the democratic organisations was to call a general strike in Viezza-Giulia. It was complete. Nothing opened, not even the cafes and ice-cream kiosks, and no trains or buses moved. When I went into Gradisca on the evening of the third day of the strike, there were red flags everywhere, and a group of youths with red scarves and shirts was sitting on the green singing revolutionary songs. The next day they toured the surrounding villages singing the Internationale, Bandiera Rossa and other songs. A demonstration of 11,000 in Malfalcone demanded the incorporation of Trieste into a "free territory."

In the midst of all this, the Major called me into his office one day and I could see at once that he was really worried. "I've a problem, Corporal," he said, "The War Office has instructed all Officers Commanding' in the region to call their men together and explain to them what the political situation here is all about. Frankly, I know very little about it. You know all about current affairs, so can you brief me on what to say?" I was sorely tempted to be as partial as I felt, but instead I tried to give an objective account of the situation, leaning as far as I dared to the Yugoslav side. In fact, and probably because it was discovered that no officer was up to the task, a duplicated statement was issued by the regional HQ explaining the situation. It wasn't bad, and it was read out at a special parade of officers and men, but what a reflection on the way the army was run and the intelligence of those who were responsible for the lives of those they commanded.

At one session of the Paris Conference, Molotov made a serious accusation. He said that not only were American planes flying over Yugoslav territory, trying to provoke incidents, but British troops were being moved into new positions nearer the frontier. These charges were indignantly denied by Bevin, but those of us who were there knew he was lying through his teeth. We often saw planes going towards the Yugoslav border, and we had more direct evidence of troop movements. We were only about six miles from the border, and days before Molotov made his statement, infantry groups moved forward. For several nights we were ordered to sleep fully-clothed and be prepared to move at a moment's notice.

Soon afterwards, I could very well have become involved in an international incident myself. Major Martin and I had taken a Morris Utility to go into Trieste to draw cash from the bank to pay wages. Instead of taking the normal direct road he decided to take a picturesque route along the narrow country roads to the east of us. The result was that we got lost and in time found ourselves in the foothills of the mountains. It was obvious to me that we had crossed the border and were in Yugoslavia, a belief strengthened by the obvious Slav appearance of the peasants we passed. In time Martin admitted to being seriously worried – although I was looking forward to being captured by Partisans! We retraced our route and eventually found a major road, and just along it a military-manned border post. On checking the map afterwards we found that we had penetrated several miles beyond the border.

At the beginning of September I went on a fortnight's leave, travelling by train both ways. Soon afterwards, the Paris Conference agreed that Trieste and the immediate area around should be constituted a "free territory" for the time being, but that the rest of Venezia Giulia should become part of Italy – a decision that provoked huge demonstrations of protest in Gorizia and Malfalcone. Settlement meant that there was no longer need for a large Allied force in the area, including 167 IBW, so

225

once again I found myself involved in winding up a unit. This time, because there weren't many of us left and we had no larger resources to draw on, we were faced with a new, typically army, problem. It is laid down in army regulations that when a unit disbands it has to hand over exactly what it had at the beginning, or give good reasons for the discrepancy. In the previous experiences this wasn't too difficult; we simply "borrowed" equipment and materials from nearby units. We couldn't do that now, and what made it doubly difficult was that the things that were missing included a Dodge truck, a Jeep and several spare wheels (probably stolen or sold). The result was that we had to visit one or two army vehicle dumps and persuade the people in charge to let us have similar vehicles, however broken-down and even though it meant having to tow them back to the unit. It was a simple matter to paint new identification marks on them.

One day the Commanding Officer called me into his office and asked how quickly I could complete the disbandment. He said that I and the others left could proceed on demob leave as soon as the job was finished. With such an incentive before us, I said, "By tomorrow." We went hell-for-leather, working all night, disposing of equipment, tabulating and packing all documents and completing all forms. I had to conclude documents about a courts martial case and the repatriation of a Pole to Poland. The Major did nothing, but the moment came when the handful of us left could stand on the deserted site and survey the scene for the last time, a moment made more desolate by the cutting cold of the Boro wind, common at that time of the year.

What a wonderful feeling it was to be on a truck slowly moving along the winding mountain road through the Trevisian pass into Austria. Our destination was the "El Alamein" demob centre at Villach. It wasn't long before I understood why it had been dubbed the "British Belsen." It was a chaotic city of tents and Nissen huts scattered higgledy-piggledy over a vast area of mud. There was little organisation, the food was bad and conditions abominable, but eventually this was all left behind. The great moment came when, at Aldershot, on Sunday, 17th November 1946, I was handed a Post Office Saving Book with my gratuity and a cardboard box containing a standard de-mob suit. A civilian again.

Reading these memoirs it might appear that my life consisted only of interesting experiences, but, of course, they make up only a small part of the story. Three-and-a-half years, totally separated from family, friends and familiar surroundings, is a big chunk out of life when one is young

– years that can never adequately be made up. However interesting a particular experience might be, the yearning to be home was continuous and shared by everyone. If we had been given the choice there wasn't one of us who wouldn't have taken the next plane home. And the episodes and incidents I have recounted are those worth relating. But nine-tenths of army life, of course, is mindlessly dull and not worth recalling. There are parallels with being in prison: the isolation; the stifling of individuality; being ordered about; and being discouraged from thinking for oneself. Until the war ended there was the uncertainty about where we would be next week, for we had no control over the decisions others would take for us. Of course, it was great to feel that we were making history, but even though I was glad to be playing such an active part in defeating fascism, I missed very much the political struggle taking place in Britain in which I had always been so involved.

Now with it all safely behind me and with the benefit of hindsight, I can see that it had its positive side. I am conscious of what was gained from the years spent in Italy: seeing new places, having fantastic and unique experiences, and the companionship of wonderful people. And I very much appreciate that my war was, through no choice of my own, much easier than it was for many others. It was also my good fortune to have so many loyal correspondents, particularly Kath, who not only kept me continuously supplied with papers and books, but also over the entire period kept me in touch with home and bolstered my spirits. Our letters to one another are, for me, a permanent memorial of her.

CHAPTER VI

1946-1951: TIME OF HOPE –
AND DISILLUSIONMENT

27. RETURN TO CIVVY STREET

On the journey from Paddington to Newport it was not possible to savour to the full the reality that my war was finally over, for the train still seemed to be occupied by a surprising number of men wearing the all-too-familiar uniform. The metamorphosis was clearer on the final leg from Newport up the valley. As the bus leisurely crawled its way through the old familiar places with their mixture of Welsh and English names – Risca, Ynyddu, Cwmfelinfach, Pontllanfraith, Blackwood, Hollybush – past the pits whose names I had learned during childhood – Nine Mile Point, Pochin, Wyllie, Markham, Ty Trist, and their accompanying slag tips – everything and everybody appeared delightfully normal, almost as if the war had never taken place. Then into the Circle, still guarded by the Town Clock, another short journey in Charlie Hill's old bone-shaker of a bus, to Nantybwch and home at last.

Not even those who hold Tredegar in the highest esteem can claim it to be a beauty spot. Despite its fortunate position at the head of a valley, the proximity of unspoiled moorland to the north and Bedwellty Park, it isn't the first place that comes to mind when considering where to take the family for the annual summer holiday. Its attraction to those of us who were born and brought up there is similar to the affection one has for a familiar old woollen jumper: well-worn and shabby it might be, but one feels comfortable living in it. Even the steadily falling rain seemed appropriate to the occasion, and quite pleasant after the dryness of Italy – although a few days of it was quite enough.

Yet, it didn't take long to realise that the unchanged physical aspect of the town was deceptive. The people had changed. The break-up of the community resulting from the war, the absence of unemployment, the new status of the miners, relative economic security – all this combined with the broader and more sophisticated outlook arising from the experiences of those who had served in the armed forces or worked in the munitions factories to bring about a subtle transformation. The camaraderie in struggle, born of poverty and desperation, had all but disappeared. It was with some reluctance, and despite a strong feeling of nostalgia and of loss, that I had to accept the transformation that had taken place.

And there was something else that was new, something totally different from the Tredegar I once had known. It was a new confidence, an atmosphere of hope and anticipation. When, in 1945, the three hundred and ninety three newly elected Labour and two Communist M.P.'s assembled for the opening session of Parliament and – to the consternation of the King, as was revealed later – marked that historic occasion by singing "The Red Flag" in the hallowed Chamber of the House of Commons, they seemed to be heralding the new dawn that we all had worked for and which so many believed had at last arrived. Faith in the Labour Government was strong and seemed justified by its first year of power. It brought in Beveridge's National Insurance Scheme with its declared purpose of ensuring financial security for everyone "from the cradle to the grave." The hated means test had been abolished, and never again would there be a need to organise hunger marches. Aneurin Bevan had started the discussions that were to bring in legislation establishing the National Health Service, and a programme of nationalisation was well underway, including that great dream of generations of miners – the nationalisation of the coal mining industry. I was told of the rejoicing and even the tears shed on Vesting Day, that first day of 1947 when the mines passed out of the hands of the hated private coalowners and, with due ceremony at every pit, declared to be in the hands of the nation. So although times were still hard, with rationing, shortages, homelessness and unemployment, these were seen to be the consequences of war and problems of the transition to a new society. The dream was becoming a reality. Only Communists and some others on the left sounded a discordant note, welcoming the progressive changes but warning that the rejoicing was a bit premature.

It took me some time to settle in to the unaccustomed routine, basking in aimlessness, doing what one wanted to, visiting old friends and places, and catching up on the news. Bert and Emrys were now home and working at their trade as bricklayers. All my old mates were working,

229

but many were dispersed in jobs away from Tredegar. Cyril had been demobbed and was employed at the thriving Ebbw Vale steel works. Gordon, now a fully-fledged toolmaker, was at the Hoover works at Merthyr Tydfil, while Doug had moved to Weston-Super-Mare. The party branch was still active and both Emrys and Bert were members, but the Socialist League had been disbanded. I had a long chat with Oliver Jones who had written to me several times when I was in Italy; he was still active in the Labour Party, but becoming more involved in local history. On visiting the Party offices in Cardiff it was obvious to me that there was little chance of returning to my old job as a party organiser. With the ending of the war, Party membership had slumped, and with it, income. Only three full-time comrades were left of the dozen or so who had formed that close, enthusiastic, cheerful and confident band of 1943 and 1944. In any case, my future plans were by no means clear as yet, and were very much bound up with those of Kath.

The novelty of freedom and having no responsibilities soon dissipated and gave way to restlessness and dissatisfaction. My army pal, Eric Pearce, was also demobbed, after going through France from Normandy. I spent a week with him in Birmingham and attended the Congress of the Party's Midlands District (then going through a crisis). We decided we wanted to work in the Soviet Union for a year or so, but our hopes were dashed by a polite reply from the Soviet Embassy explaining that they had a few post-war problems to sort out before being in a position to accept our valuable help. Soon afterwards, I arranged to meet Kath in London at a women's equal pay conference: she was a delegate from the East Midlands District Committee of the Party, of which she was now a member. It was a notable weekend in another way, because it was on the train back to Leicester that she agreed to marry me. So the short period of uncertainty came to an end – and in the best possible manner.

Kath was now teaching in Leicester and I had decided to join her. My stay was intended to be temporary, but fate was to decree otherwise. In any case, however long I was to be there, a job was essential, for the army de-mob gratuity of fifty-three pounds didn't last long. As there were plenty of engineering factories in and around the city, it wasn't too difficult to find work, and I soon found myself on the factory floor once again, at the old established British United Shoe Machinery Company. My first impression of the toolroom was not good. In aircraft factories, toolmakers were the skilled aristocracy of the shop floor, the "proud mechanics" of the industry, and their awareness of the key position they occupied in it was reflected in their militancy and independent attitude. This was very far from being the case at British United. Never had I worked with such a miserable, spineless lot of workers. They were every bit as skilled as any toolmakers I had known, but this wasn't reflected in their obsequious attitude to the management, even to the foremen. It may have been a consequence of the paternalism of the firm, although I found a similar attitude at the next firm I worked for in the city. This lack of militancy was probably one of the reasons wages were lower than elsewhere, although another reason was that family incomes were higher due to the fact that so many women worked in hosiery and footwear. Leicester had not been hit as hard as most parts of the country by the prewar slump; indeed, in the 1930's it had the reputation of being the most prosperous city in Europe.

As it happened, I was only at British United for three weeks when the great 1947 freeze-up ground the entire country to a halt. It was the coldest February ever. There wasn't enough coal, and what there was couldn't be transported to the power stations because the rail system was almost immobilised and the roads were sheets of ice. With power cuts and no fuel we shivered in the bitter cold, indoors as well as outside. But the most serious consequence was a general shutdown of industry. As there was no knowing how long the crisis would last, most employers sacked their workers so as not to pay national insurance contributions, promising to re-employ them when the crisis was over. Typically, the main concern of many of the workers at British United seemed to be about whether they would lose the watches presented to them by a generous management on retirement, a condition being an unbroken employment record with the firm for twenty years – a disincentive against them ever taking strike action. They were relieved when a generous employer assured them that their watches were safe.

I couldn't stomach going back to such a miserable place, so when industry began to roll again I started work at Imperial Typewriters, only to find that although the work was more interesting, there was only a little improvement in the attitude of most of the workers. After a few months, I made another change, moving to B.T.H. which made machinery for making light bulbs and was a union factory with good militant shop stewards.

The Communist Party in Leicester was well organised and active, with almost two hundred members. There were three area branches and a University Staff Branch, with a dedicated band of comrades in the

231

leadership: Margaret and Mick Stanton, Harry Brown, John Wynne, Sid and Sadie Page, Johnny Rice, Harry Thompson, Albert and Edna Gillson, Sid Besborough, Harry Packer and others whose names I have forgotten. I had "digs" in the home of Margaret and John Wynne. Margaret was a teacher and John was a lecturer on agriculture at Loughborough College. It was very pleasant living with them, for not only were we kindred spirits who loved friendly arguments, but there was an easy domestic atmosphere and no restrictions. The branch did an impressive amount of public work in a variety of fields. Margaret Stanton was quite well-known locally and had helped to build a powerful tenants' association on the New Parks Estate where she lived. Every Saturday, Harry Packer manned a literature stall in the Market Place, and on Sunday evenings the branch organised an open-air public meeting. There was the usual *Daily Worker* or literature door-to-door sale over the weekend, and sometimes Bill Wilson, an enthusiastic agricultural worker, would browbeat some of us into selling *The Country Standard* in the Leicestershire villages, which was a useful and enjoyable way of spending a pleasant Sunday.

The most important task facing couples wanting to get married is usually finding a place to live, but in the immediate post-war period it was a problem of truly gigantic proportions. There had been no house building during the war; large numbers of homes had been destroyed by bombing; and there was a steep increase in the number of marriages after demobilisation. The government embarked on a scheme for building small, prefabricated bungalows that could be erected quickly, and it took powers to requisition any house standing empty. The pre-fabs were, in fact, quite well-designed, but they only touched the problem, and there was strong criticism of the fact that most large houses of the rich seemed to escape being requisitioned. My brother George, his wife Olive and their young daughter were living in the billiard room of a big unoccupied house at Shepperton. This one room had to make do as living room, bedroom and kitchen. Back in Tredegar, my friend Cyril had married Sylvia and they lived in a single room with a double bed against the wall and about two feet of space around two sides. Beginning in Scunthorpe and spreading throughout the country, a great squatting movement had developed at the end of 1946. Empty army and air force camps, and houses that had not been requisitioned were taken over by homeless ex-servicemen and their children. London Communists organised the Great Sunday Squat, taking over an empty block of flats in Kensington. At first, the

232

government had acquiesced, and Nye Bevan, the minister responsible for housing, authorised local authorities to connect the squats to water and power. But as direct action grew and property owners started fighting back, the government became alarmed. Although he was acting on Cabinet instructions, to the consternation of the workers involved and to many on the left, Bevan not only authorised the issuing of eviction orders against squatters, but also the cutting of water and power to force them out.

The situation had not changed when Kath and I started house hunting. Whenever we heard a rumour that rented accommodation was available, one of us, usually Kath, would speed to the place, always to find it was gone, or to join a long queue of would-be tenants. And there were always the contemptible landlords ready to take advantage of the desperation of the homeless. A favourite game was to ask for "key money," a lump sum paid in advance and additional to the rent. Sometimes prospective tenants were forced to compete with each other over the amount of the rent they were prepared to pay. One place I can remember visiting was a small single bedroom on the second floor of a house adjoining the Leicester Mercury printing works, with the use of a shared primitive kitchen in the basement. The noise and thudding of the machines rocked the building; and for this princely accommodation the landlord wanted five pounds a week rent (more than the weekly wage of many workers) and a year's rent paid in advance.

Then, by a remarkable stroke of luck, we landed on our feet. I was in a small newsagent shop when a young woman came in to put a card in the window advertising some furniture for sale. We got talking and she told me that she and her husband were moving to her mother's house. They occupied a top-floor flat rented from the couple who lived below them, and she said that if we were prepared to buy the furniture, she would put in a good word for Kath and I becoming the new tenants. Of course, I jumped at the proposition, and soon we took possession of three small rooms at 41 Saxby Street, not far from the city centre. This was where we lived the rest of the time we were in Leicester.

We were married in a dingy room which seemed not to have seen any paint since before the war, at Leicester Registry Office in Pocklington Walk on Saturday morning, 29th March 1947, my brother, Arthur, and Kath's parents being the only others present. The Registrar gabbled through the obligatory words, muttered "happy days," and opened the door for the next couple in line. Mr and Mrs Powell were probably disappointed that the first marriage in the family, and that of their eldest daughter of whom they were so proud, not only did not take place in a church, but lacked even a modest semblance of a ceremony. However, they made no show of their feelings and accepted that it was what Kath wanted. There was no honeymoon, due, we discovered later, to a mutual misunderstanding. Knowing Kath's contempt for convention, I didn't like to suggest that we take time off work and go away for a holiday. Apparently she thought the same about me. So we both lost out, and, to the surprise of my fellow workers, I was at work on Monday morning as usual.

Furniture was still rationed, but couples intending to get married had extra coupons and this enabled us to get a table with chairs, a sideboard and two small fireside chairs. Utility furniture was supposed to be basic, but although plain it was far superior to the self-assembled, veneered articles which are now the norm. I have always been good at any kind of handywork, so I searched the junk shops for damaged items made of wood, which I converted into things that we needed – notably book-shelves and cupboards. We covered most of the floor which large pieces of blue felt which Kath's mother had got hold of. Food rationing was still on, but we were well used to this and luckily were able to augment our rations with a steady extra supply of cheese from Bill and Freda Wilson. Being agricultural workers they had a generous ration of it – more than their needs – so they passed the remainder on to us.

28. ADVANCE – AND RETREAT
The magnitude of the problems facing the new Labour government can-not be disputed. They were problems unprecedented in character and scope. Industry had to be turned around, transformed from a wartime to a peacetime footing; there was a gigantic housing shortage; massive reconstruction of all parts of the economy was needed and work found for the millions of men and women being demobilised; the government was faced with a vast financial deficit, and trade with the rest of the world had to be re-established.

Yet, it is also true that Labour came to power in a most favourable sit-uation for any government seriously intent on transforming society and moving forward to socialism. It had a massive parliamentary majority and the wholehearted and enthusiastic support of the people. The work-ing class fervently wanted change, a desire that arose from having endured five years of war and with painful memories of what capitalism had been like prior to it. The wartime alliance with the Soviet Union meant that large numbers of people had had their eyes opened and now had a different attitude to socialism. Decades of media lies about the Soviet Union had been exposed, and the war had inevitably prompted the thought that a system that could stimulate such self-sacrifice by its people in its defence must have much to commend it. Moreover, over parts of Europe capitalism was in tatters, and new states opposed to it were emerging. The British capitalist class had been weakened by the war, and – particularly with its party having been so decisively rejected at the polls – not a little demoralised. In the climate of the times, it would have been very difficult for the United States, now the only really powerful capitalist state, to openly intervene the way Britain and other countries had done in Russia after the 1917 Revolution. Here, then, was a great opportunity for a genuinely socialist government.

Alas, this is what the Labour government certainly was not. This is not to decry the sincerity of those of its members who, without doubt, genuinely wanted to bring about changes that would improve the lot of working people and who, to varying degrees, regarded themselves as socialists. I make this point, because far too often deep political differences are personalised, and those holding strong views different from our own are stigmatised as unmitigated villains, rather than people who can be as sincere as we are, but with whose policies we maybe violently disagree. Sincerity is no guide to political correctness.

The socialism of members of the Labour government was not clearly defined or understood. Its approach was probably best described years later by Harold Wilson, when he defined socialism as "accepting social responsibility for matters that are of social concern" – a vague generalisation that can mean anything to anybody. The government as a whole lacked the ideological understanding, the perspective and the will to transform the system. To use a Marxist word, it was "reformist," which means that it wanted changes – but within the framework of existing society. Thus, better living conditions and social reforms were subordinate to and dependent upon the overriding need to preserve and make capitalism work more efficiently; indeed, they were seen as dependant on achieving this. Socialism, when it was invoked, was regarded simply as the nationalisation of some industries and better social services. The government was pragmatist, tackling issues and problems as they arose and not as part of a long-term plan. The continued existence of the Empire was taken as read, as was the special alliance with the U.S.A.

235

Changes there had to be; the pressures from below were too great to resist. This was recognised by all parties. After all, it was a Tory, R. A. Butler, who was the architect of the Education Act, and a Liberal, William Beveridge, who fathered the Welfare State. Capitalism well understands the need to make concessions when they are necessary for its survival. But the changed situation was reflected most of all by a new confidence among a growing number of people who had a genuine belief in a socialist future. While this was not fully expressed in "Let Us Face the Future," that election programme is still the finest the Labour Party has ever produced. When, today, we continually hear the chant, "the country cannot afford it," as an excuse for cutting the social services and state benefits, it is worth thinking back to those days when a Labour government, albeit under mass pressure, brought in far-reaching progressive reforms and made big increases in welfare benefits in an economic situation vastly worse than anything we have known since.

Whatever happened subsequently, the positive achievements of the first period of that government were historic, and our labour movement is right to remember them and hold them up as an example of what can be done. The National Insurance System and the National Health Service are monuments to what can be achieved even within a capitalist society: they lifted much of the burden of insecurity arising from the fear of having no income or of being ill and unable to afford treatment that had so oppressed working people for centuries. Indicative of the transformation was the fact that 40 million people, 98% of the population, put their names down on doctors' lists and over 18 thousand GP's out of 21 thousand joined the N.H.S. By January 1949, 3 million pairs of free spectacles had been issued and 2.2 million people were having dental treatment. The Tory press used these figure to accuse people of "cashing in" on the system, but in reality they showed how much the health of the people had been neglected. For who on earth would wear glasses or go to the dentist if they didn't need to! An indication of the deep-rooted popular basis of the reforms is the fact that almost half-a-century later, and despite the efforts of eight Tory governments, some of those reforms are still with us, and what are left are tenaciously defended.

However, the trades unions and the Labour Party were still firmly in the control of the right-wing. Ironically, the progressive advances, which were largely the consequence of mass pressure, strengthened the position of these leaders, who were not slow to claim all the credit. And this domination was soon to be reflected in the way "Let Us Face the Future" was interpreted. Collaboration with the employing class, not opposition to it, was the guiding principle – so aptly expressed by Herbert Morrison in his revealing statement, "I want to take every businessman by the hand and call him brother." The industries nationalised were those such as energy, transport and steel, which had been seriously run down through lack of investment, but which had to be efficient for capitalism as a whole to continue in existence. Years of bleeding these industries for immediate profits meant that there now had to be a massive injection of capital, which only the state could provide. Over-generous compensation was paid to the former private owners and the crippling interest on the loans needed to make these payments became a burden on the public and the workers in the industries for decades. The Boards set up to run the industries were composed mainly of businessmen devoted to capitalism. The Chairman of the Coal Board, for example, was Lord Hyndley, one of the most powerful of the former private coalowners. Eighty eight per cent of the members of the nationalised boards were representatives of the capitalist class. In 1949 Prime Minister Attlee boasted in the House of Commons that one hundred and thirty one "gentlemen" on the nationalised boards were "of a commercial character," sixty one were directors of private companies, twenty three were knights, nine were lords and three held the rank of Lt-General or above!

Despite this, most socialists welcomed nationalisation and saw it as an important advance. Given a genuine socialist government, it could have been a step towards full social ownership; but even in its distorted form there were possibilities of influencing by political means the way the nationalised industries were run.

The government's honeymoon period of reform lasted little more than a year. Lacking a bold and positive plan, the economy stumbled from one crisis to another. Retreat and cuts became the orders of the day. In September 1947, Sir Stafford Cripps, the Chancellor of the Exchequer, produced his "austerity plan," and this was followed by a wage-freeze which, although supported by right-wing trade union leaders, met with increased resistance – including industrial action – from the rank and file. In April 1949, 15,000 London dockers went on strike over a victimisation issue and, incredibly, the Labour government declared a State of Emergency and sent in troops to break the strike – which, predictably, immediately brought out dockers in other ports. It was a bitter blow to Labour supporters to see their government emulate Churchill's action against the miners of Tonypandy in 1911, and to do it so soon after

237

it had been elected with such enthusiasm and such hope.

Britain's economic crisis was acute, but not only (or even mainly) because of the problems of post-war reconstruction. In the decades before the war, British monopoly capitalism had steadily deteriorated compared with the U.S.A. and Germany. It was parasitic, living on vast tribute drawn from the colonies, with investment directed overseas to where huge profits could be made based on the low wages and the extreme exploitation of the peoples of the subject countries. Basic home industries were neglected and allowed to stagnate, as we saw during the 1920's and 1930's.

The war had been a heaven-sent opportunity for American capitalism to increase its supremacy. It had mercilessly taken advantage of the weakness of Britain, taking over much of its overseas capital investments and expanding into its trade preserves. Magnanimously, "Lend-Lease" was launched, a scheme whereby American industries supplied Britain with the essential goods and material it desperately needed – but only by building up a huge debt that had to be paid back after the war. Within four weeks of the election of the Labour government, the American President, Truman, without warning and contrary to all expectations, ended Lend-Lease, creating enormous problems for the new administration, especially as it meant having to start repayment. How far the U.S. was motivated by the desire to strengthen the shackles, or whether the real motivation was Truman's worry that Labour might start to introduce socialism, is a matter for conjecture. If it was the latter, it wasn't long before he was reassured!

As even *The Economist* later protested, Britain, having lost a quarter of its national wealth in the common struggle, by way of reward had to commit itself to paying £35 million a year for the next half century to those who had enriched themselves in the war – and to do it under humiliating conditions that opened up the British Empire to American penetration.

A few figures serve to give a dramatic idea of the extent of American expansion. By the end of the war, US capitalism controlled two-thirds of the productive capacity of the entire capitalist world and three-quarters of its investment capacity. Not having suffered the bombing and destruction suffered by its allies, its industries boomed. The productive power of its plants increased by fifty per cent and exports went up from thirteen and half per cent to thirty two and half per cent of the world total. The U.S.A became by far the strongest capitalist power, and it didn't hesitate to use its economic and political supremacy to compel other countries to conform to its will.

But with the coming of peace, US capitalism was faced with a big problem. It was quite prepared to use its dominant competitive position to amass greater profits, but it had to do this whilst at the same time preserving capitalism as a world system, this being essential for its own survival. Other countries had joined the Soviet Union in rejecting capitalism, and in some countries, notably France and Italy, the Communist parties were extremely powerful and were represented in government. The spectre threatening American capitalism was the collapse of European capitalism and the establishment of socialist states in the west. This was the incentive for the Marshall Plan providing for "economic co-operation" between the US and Europe. Ostensibly, it was a plan whereby the US would help the rehabilitation of European countries; but this help was only available if a comprehensive range of conditions was accepted. These included encouraging private enterprise, strengthening what we now call the market economy and cutting back social programmes.

The type of goods supplied was strictly controlled. Agricultural goods had to be purchased from the U.S., in many cases even if they could be obtained cheaper elsewhere – a way of dumping American surpluses. Wherever possible, other goods had to be bought from the US. Payment was to be made by cash or credit, or by the transfer of materials "required by the United States as a result of deficiencies in its own resources." Contrary to it being a generous gesture by the United States, the Marshall Plan, while giving aid for the rehabilitation of capitalism, tied Britain and the other participants closer to the US and in the long run increased the problems facing the Labour government. An important part of the "Plan" was to rebuild the shattered industries of Western Germany and the Ruhr, and to hand them back to Krupps and Thyssen and the other industrialists and financiers who had backed the Nazis.

Another reason for Britain's crisis was the determination of the government to hang on to the Empire. While proclaiming that imperialism was a thing of the past, it argued that Britain had a responsibility to the colonies and could not give them up until such time as the subject peoples "were fit to rule themselves." In fact, many of the "Labour-imperialists," as some on the left dubbed them, were every bit as bellicose and blimpish as the most die-hard Tories. Keeping hold of "the jolly old Empire" – Morrison again – was not because of a maternal attachment to it, or because it was in the interests of the native population. True, some clutched on to it as the one remaining symbol of Britain's past global supremacy; but more important was the fact that, weakened though it was, the Empire was still a source of great profits to British capitalists, as well as being seen as a counter-balance to the United States.

But the Empire was not as it had been. A totally new situation had developed. Men and women from the colonial countries had fought in a war supposed to have been in defence of freedom and democracy, and, not unreasonably, they assumed that this included their freedom and their independence. In all the colonial countries there was an intensification of the struggle for liberation and self-determination. Instead of welcoming this, the Labour government condemned it and shamefully adopted the same brutal methods as past governments to suppress it.

True, it claimed the credit for "giving" India its independence, but this independence was inevitable and could no longer be denied whichever government was in power. It was a freedom that the Indian people had won through years of bitter struggle. In fact, all that Labour had promised India, even in "Let Us Face the Future," was "responsible self-government" under the British flag, a formula that was immediately rejected by the Indian National Congress. And by imposing partition between India and Pakistan, they sowed the seeds of large-scale conflicts in the future.

What happened in Malaya is one of the most ignominious examples of the extent to which the Labour government was prepared to go to continue colonial rule. Britain had been humiliated by the ease and speed of the Japanese advance in 1941, particularly the subsequent collapse without a fight of the "impregnable" naval base of Singapore. After our forces had been driven out of the country, the Malayan liberation movement conducted a heroic three and half year struggle against the occupying armies of Japan.

When the war ended, the movement's leaders received lavish praise from the British government and were invited to take part in the victory parade in London. But, incredibly, Labour politicians, as well as Tories, believed that Malaya should, with some cosmetic changes, now revert to its former colonial status and that the rich rubber plantations and tin mines should be returned to the same whisky-swilling planters and mine-owners who had scuttled out in indecent haste when the Japanese advanced. The Malayan people thought differently, however. Having liberated themselves from the Japanese, they had no intention of meekly

240

giving up the freedom they had won at such a high cost; they demanded independence. Euphemistically calling it a "police operation," Britain's Labour government launched a large-scale offensive by land, sea and air to regain control. It involved the deployment of 70,000 troops, the destruction of villages, the banning of all trade unions and the imprisonment of 10,000 freedom fighters in the first year of hostilities. The Malayan patriots, who had been decorated by the British government and who had proudly marched down Whitehall, now became "bandits." Financially, the war was a crippling additional burden on the people of an already crisis-ridden Britain.

Using varying degrees of force, the Labour government took similar action against the independence movements in the other colonial countries.

Seizing the opportunities offered by the other changes taking place in Europe, a Labour government in Britain could have exerted a decisive influence on post-war world developments, helped in lifting the threat of war forever and made a powerful contribution to moving mankind towards a more humane society. Indeed, "Let us Face the Future," Labour's election programme, spoke of "a common bond with the working people of all countries, who had achieved new influence through the struggle against Nazi Germany," and it promised to "consolidate in peace the great war-time association of the British Commonwealth with the U.S.A. and the U.S.S.R."

Alas, it soon became clear that these declarations were empty rhetoric and that, as in domestic policy, the Labour government was to conform to capitalist policies – which, in the immediate post-war world, meant the policies decided upon by U.S. capitalism. When Attlee replaced Churchill at the Potsdam Conference, the conference which discussed the peace treaties and the possibilities for post-war Europe, James Byrnes, the US Secretary of State, was to remark that he could not discern the slightest difference in approach between the two. Churchill had said, "governments may change . . . yet on the main essentials of foreign policy we stand together." Attlee took with him the same advisers as Churchill – and boasted of it. If any change could be discerned it was that Ernest Bevin, Labour's Foreign Secretary, was less restrained in his virulent anti-Sovietism than his Tory predecessor. Indeed, Byrnes later wrote that the President and himself were worried that the intemperance of Bevin's language could be counter-productive. The seeds of the cold war, which were to grow into a Triffid-like monster threatening life on the planet for decades to come, had already been sown, and Labour, instead of destroying it at birth, played an important part in fertilising it.

On 6th August 1946 the Americans dropped the first atom bomb on Hiroshima, to be followed three days later with another one on Nagasaki. According to official historians, it was this that forced Japan to surrender. This is another example of the distortion of the facts for partisan purposes. The truth, as we were to learn later, is that the Japanese had already indicated to the Americans that they wanted to surrender. Why then were the bombs dropped? The eminent atomic scientist Professor P. M. S. Blackett (later Lord Blackett), who had contributed to producing the atom bomb, in his book, The Military and Political Consequences of Atomic Energy, gave his view: "We conclude that the dropping of the atom bombs was not so much the last military act of the second world war, as the first act of the cold diplomatic war against the Russians." Significantly, in violation of agreements about sharing scientific and technical information, the Soviet Union had been told nothing about the bomb, and even Britain was given only limited details.

In fact, the cold war was envisaged and planned some years before. It has been revealed by Harold Macmillan that as early as October 1942, Churchill submitted a memorandum to the Cabinet calling for an anti-Soviet bloc of European countries after the war; and in America, Roosevelt's Vice-President, Henry Wallace, has written that long before the war ended, he had been aware of powerful groups in the U.S. armed forces who were linked with important businessmen and looked on the Soviet Union as the enemy "in the next war . . . for which preparations had to be made." In March 1946, Churchill made his infamous speech at Fulton, calling for a "military alliance between Britain and the U.S." Three years later the North Atlantic Treaty Organisation (N.A.T.O.) was formed – a military pact that divided Europe and was quite obviously directed at the Soviet Union. The pretence that it was a neutral collective security pact was exposed when the Soviet Union's request to join was turned down.

The Warsaw Pact of the Soviet Union and its East European allies was formed as a counter-measure to N.A.T.O. I make these points because one of the distortions by official historians is that the Cold War was started by the Russians, either when the Communists came to power in Czechoslovakia or when the Warsaw Pact was formed. The facts speak otherwise.

There was complete agreement between the two main parties on foreign policy, and both Churchill and Attlee supported the Atlantic

Pact, the anti-Communist alliance between America and some of the main European capitalist nations. When Churchill made his infamous Fulton speech, Attlee refused to utter a word of dissent. There were, however, profound misgivings over government policy within the Labour Party. One hundred and five M.P.'s signed a motion condemning Churchill, and although the right was able to win a majority for the government at the Labour Party Conference, there was substantial opposition, which included the Chairman, Harold Laski, who called for a friendlier attitude towards Russia.

There is no doubt that the fight against Labour's reactionary foreign and colonial policies was constrained by the widespread desire to give full support to the government in its programme of progressive reforms at home. This was quite unscrupulously used by Arthur Deakin, Bevin's successor as leader of the Transport and General Workers Union (T.G.W.U.) and others, who met every threat of revolt with the warning, "Do you want to bring our government down and let the Tories reverse all that we have gained?"

The grovelling subservience of Attlee, Bevin and Labour's right-wing to the United States increased in the years that followed. An example of the depth to which they sank came to light decades later when it was disclosed that, without the knowledge of Parliament and with no discussion in the Cabinet, Attlee had made a secret agreement with Truman for permanent U.S. air bases to be set up in Britain. Parliament was told that the Americans were here temporarily and only for training purposes. Deceit was necessary because if the truth had been known there would probably have been a public outcry, and it is doubtful whether Atlee would have got the support of a majority of Labour M.P.'s.

The creation of the atom bomb (and later the H-bomb) injected a qualitatively new factor into international relations that henceforward was to dominate the struggle for peace. For the first time, it was possible for an aggressor to destroy cities and kill millions of people from afar and at one stroke. It was a monstrous scenario that was to haunt us over the remaining years of these memoirs. In June 1946 the Soviet Union put forward proposals to renounce the use, production, or stockpiling of atomic weapons and to destroy existing weapons.

This was turned down, and the Soviet Union thereupon set out to break the American monopoly. In 1947 it announced that it had done this, and less than two years later it tested its own atomic bombs. On both occasions, and many times in subsequent years, the Soviet Government

243

repeated its willingness to join with other nations that had nuclear weapons to renounce their use, stop all testing and destroy existing stocks.

29. LEICESTER

This was the political background to our immediate post-war activities. It is just an outline of some of the main facts, and much has been left out. It should also be borne in mind that it is how Marxists interpreted the situation at the time, for it was these contemporary attitudes that decided the precise nature of our activities then. However, looking back after fifty years, I believe our basic analysis stands up well to the judgement of history.

Those first few years of married life were among the happiest I can remember. Kath and I were together after a long period of separation; we had a comfortable flat in a city we both liked; we were members of an active party branch and with a band of grand comrades. And, surely, there is nothing nicer and more fulfilling than fighting for what you believe in with the one you love at your side.

Angry though we were with the betrayals by the Labour government, it didn't undermine our confidence in the future. When Kath asserted that it would be about twenty years before we would see the revolution here, I admonished her for her pessimism! After all, a new world had emerged from the war and although we realised that there were great obstacles to be overcome and battles to be fought, we couldn't see the march of progress being halted for very long, not even by the Americans and their allies in Britain. The pre-war imperialist encirclement and isolation of the Soviet Union had been destroyed, and more countries were now on the march to socialism, notably China. It was no longer "the socialist sixth of the world," but getting on towards being the "socialist third." In France and Italy, the Communist Parties had mass popular support; India seemed likely to take the socialist path; and throughout the colonial third of the world the oppressed peoples of the subject nations had found a new strength in their struggle to free themselves from their imperialist masters. And if there are some modern socialist historians who lack the imagination to transpose themselves to those days, and who shake their heads and murmur "tut tut" at our naïvety, I hope that many more will understand our optimism and appreciate that at the time it seemed we had every cause to be optimistic. "Bliss was it in that dawn to be alive, but to be young was very heaven!"

244

so Wordsworth remembered the French Revolution, and so we felt in those immediate post-war years.

I bought a new Raleigh bicycle, upright and heavy by today's standards, and we spent those weekends which were not filled with political activity meandering around Leicestershire, particularly exploring the area between Leicester and Melton and along the Vale of Belvoir, visiting old churches and ancient sites, and stopping on the way to picnic on sandwiches and tea. Usually, however, we had to be back by Sunday evening for a meeting. Whenever possible we would go to a concert or the theatre, and occasionally we'd travel to London to see the Sadlers Wells Ballet or a play. Life was full, varied – and, oh, so wonderful!

When I arrived in Leicester, some of the leading comrades were in the throes of a dispute with the District Committee about whether the three area branches in the city should combine into one. As so often happens, divisions that seem trivial with hindsight, at the time appear of world-shattering importance. In this matter, the argument became so heated that the Executive Committee sent down the Party's National Organiser, Peter Kerrigan, to sort out the matter. After spending a few days interviewing comrades, "Big Peter" delivered a judgement of Solomon: the arguments of both sides had virtue, therefore the existing branches should remain, but a Borough Committee should be elected to supervise them. A well-attended membership meeting elected me as Leicester's first Borough Secretary. Soon afterwards I was co-opted on to the Party's District Committee and eventually on to the Secretariat. In April 1948 I stood as Communist candidate in a bye-election in the Braunstone ward of the Leicester Borough Council.

There were two unforeseen consequences arising out of my standing in the election. In the same period I had been asked by the Workers' Educational Association (W.E.A.) to teach a class on industrial relations for the shop stewards at the Asfordby Ironworks, near Melton. *The Leicester Mercury* covered the election; this, and the fact that I was a W.E.A. tutor in Melton, was picked up by *The Melton Times*, which published a front-page story of the "red" who had infiltrated the W.E.A. and was contaminating the minds of local trade unionists. Kath's father, Arthur, was on the local W.E.A. committee, and he told me that it had caused consternation among its more respectable members, but the regional organiser in Nottingham, who appointed me, was quite firm that there must be no witch-hunt. However, the local committee insisted that one of its members attend each session of the class, ostensibly to help,

245

but really to make certain that I didn't inject subversive ideas into the minds of my students. At the next class, with the committee member present, I told the whole story to the shop stewards. They were furious, and wanted to continue the class without the W.E.A., with my fee being paid for by them, but I persuaded them that this was not a very good idea.

The other consequence was more serious, though it cannot be proved. Not long after the above incident, Arthur's job as Chief Garrison Engineer at the Old Dalby Depot, a job he had held throughout the war, was suddenly terminated. It was some time before he was due to retire, and no satisfactory explanation was given. He thought it was because he had protested to the War Office at the shocking waste of hundreds of new electric motors and other machines being buried because they were now "surplus to requirements." Maybe this was partly the reason, but Kath and I believed that it was more likely that the War Office had cottoned on to the fact that he had a well-known Communist as a son-in-law, something not to be tolerated in the cold war atmosphere that was developing.

The dedication and enthusiasm of the comrades in Leicester reflected our confidence in the future. We campaigned on everything, local, national and international. And though we were rejected as a party by the great majority of the people, our policies were widely accepted and our work met with a heartening response. The branch carried out a massive campaign on transport fares, and Kath put the party's case to the public enquiry. Meetings with national speakers were well attended – four hundred came to hear Harry Pollitt; three hundred and fifty attended a meeting at which Isobel Brown, one of the finest women orators the Party has ever produced, was the speaker; two hundred heard Palme Dutt and three hundred and fifty heard Phil Piratin. I chaired or spoke at all these meetings. The sale of the *Daily Worker* each weekend was in the hundreds, seven hundred were sold on May Day and on one weekend we topped the thousand. When Prime Minister Clement Attlee came to speak at the prestigious De Montfort Hall, we decided to do something about it. Our flat was not far away, so we arranged to have "runners" taking down what Attlee was saying and bringing the notes to the flat. There, with the help of "Comrade Gestetner," I was able to produce a statement replying to Attlee's speech and duplicate copies to give out to those who had been to hear him as they were leaving the meeting.

The most important industries in Leicester were hosiery, footwear and engineering, but engineering was largely geared to making machines for the first two. Hosiery and footwear overwhelmingly employed women, yet the relatively highly-paid skilled jobs were held by a small minority of men. This was reflected in the unions. Although women comprised over eighty per cent of the membership of the National Union of Hosiery Workers – most of them in Leicester – there was not a single woman on its National Executive. Kath was given responsibility for developing the party's work in the industry, working closely with the few comrades on the shop floor. However, she was conscious of the anomaly of a teacher with no workshop experience tackling such a job, so she decided to do something about it. She gave up teaching and started work as an unskilled machine operator at the Wolsey hosiery factory, at the same time, of course, joining the union. She was responsible for formulating the first Communist policy statement on the situation in the industry, and she wrote several articles both on policy and about her experiences. On one occasion she produced a statement exposing the profits made by Corahs, which produced the Marks and Spencer's "St Michael" brand of knitwear, and this was given out at meetings outside the factory. It obviously struck a tender spot with the firm, which, rather stupidly, attempted to reply in a statement distributed to employees with their pay packets. We gave the story to Walter Holmes, who was running the popular "Workers' Notebook" in the *Daily Worker*, and he devoted the whole of one of his articles to it, including our response. We used this for a sales effort outside the factory, and again the firm responded, but this time simply by issuing a statement.

Of course, I maintained my union activity and was in a lively branch where there were a few other communists, notably Albert Gillson, a devoted and hard-working comrade who was the branch's *Daily Worker* organiser. I was soon elected delegate to the trades council. Unlike today, most A.E.U. branches were well attended and there was plenty of discussion. A number of comrades in Leicester were in the A.E.U., and we worked closely with other militants in the union. The shop stewards' convenor at B.T.H. was a left-wing Labour Party member and we got on well together. The District Committee of the A.E.U. was not in the least progressive, and the District Secretary and President were both right-wingers; so we decided that something had to be done to change this situation. As it happened, the Presidency was up for election, and we decided to put forward a progressive candidate as a run-up to challenging the District Secretary when he came up for re-election the following year. It was decided that I should stand, even though I hadn't been in

247

Leicester very long (in contrast with the favourite for the job, Steve McTigue, a Leicester man who been president before). It was argued that I had become reasonably well-known in the union during the time I had been in the area and had a good record, and that the progressives had an effective organisation. At that time, although the ballot was secret, only those members who attended their branch meeting on the night could vote. With five candidates standing, I came second, not very far behind McTigue, so it had to go to a second ballot, which we were confident we could win.

However, it was not to be. Developments were taking place in the party which were to change our plans, and, indeed, again to alter the course of our lives. The East Midlands District Secretary of the Party was Bill Rowe, a fine comrade who had fought in Spain, and, largely as a consequence of this, had contracted a serious illness. Bill was forced by bad health to resign, and the local comrade whom the District Committee wanted to take his place, Les Ellis, declined the job. Thereupon, Party Centre (which is what we called our national H.Q.) proposed that the new District Secretary be Mick Jenkins, the Manchester Secretary of the Party, and this was agreed to by the District Committee. Unfortunately, at the same time, Harry Brown, the Party's District Organiser, was also ill and intimated that he, too, wanted to leave. On the advice of Party Centre, the District Secretariat asked me if I would consider working alongside Mick as District Organiser.

Mick came over one evening to tell us this, and it faced Kath and me with a dilemma. We were only just getting on our feet financially. Kath was not teaching at the time and hoped she would not have to go back to it, because, although a good teacher, it was not a job she particularly liked. She had a great love of and an aptitude for research work, particularly in the fields of history and politics, and hoped to make this her career. On my part, it meant abandoning the admittedly half-formed idea of a full-time career in my union. We were under no illusions that if I started working for the party, life was not going to be easy. My wage as a toolmaker was three times what a party organiser was supposed to get – "supposed" being the correct word, for, as my experience was to confirm later, party wages were usually much less than this, or even non-existent.

Yet, although I felt that Kath had more to lose, it was she who was least hesitant. Her attitude was straightforward: the interests of the party had to be put before personal considerations, and if the party wanted me to work full-time, so be it. Although somewhat more hesitant, I agreed. Maybe my slight hesitation was due to the fact that I could see the elaborate and rosy plans we had worked out of what we were going to do in the first years of married life being shattered. But it was only a brief indecisiveness; it was an honour to be asked to work for the party and I was thrilled at the prospect of being a professional revolutionary once again. So, in October 1948, I started work as East Midlands Organiser of the Communist Party.

But to return to the A.E.U. election. Here was a predicament. I was in the second ballot for District President, but now didn't want to win. Both the party and our engineering group discussed this, and we decided it might cause some demoralisation if I withdrew after so many members of the union had been working on my behalf, and with such hopes. The result we wanted was a good vote, but not a winning one. This would be a sound basis for fighting the election with another candidate next time. Merriman, the A.E.U. District Secretary got to know that I was working for the Communist Party, and was quick to inform branches of this – with the obvious intention of scuppering my chances. Even so, the result was surprisingly close, with only about twenty votes in it.

Mick Jenkins and I were faced with a difficult situation. The East Midlands District covered the five counties of Nottinghamshire Derbyshire, Leicestershire, Lincolnshire and Rutland, a rambling region stretching from the North Sea to the outskirts of Manchester, and from Chesterfield down to Market Harborough. Moreover, because of the ill health of the previous full-time workers, contact with the fifty branches had deteriorated and issues had been neglected. It was a question of rebuilding, and we were handicapped by the fact that we were both strangers to the district and the members – except, in my case, for Leicester. However, we had a strong Secretariat, which is what the party called the sub-committee that acted for the District Committee between meetings. It was akin to the executive committee of most organisations, but had more power. The Chairman was Les Ellis, who had gone back into mining after serving as a sergeant major in the army – he was later to become a full-time official of the Notts Area of the N.U.M. and a member of the union's National Executive. Other members of the Secretariat were: Bert Wynn, an official of the Derbyshire Area of the N.U.M., who was later to become its General Secretary and also a National Executive member; Frank Moore, a member of the National Executive of the railwaymen's union; Lloyd Harrison, an official of the

249

Nottingham Co-operative Society, soon to become its Chief Executive Officer and a leading figure in the C.W.S.; Bernard Shough, Convenor in the large Ransome and Marles factory at Newark; and several other well-known men and women who were mass leaders in their own field or who held positions in the party. At this time, the party in the East Midlands had about 1,600 members organised in fifty branches, but this under-states its real influence, for the members included many shop stewards and convenors of important factories, trade union officials and activists in almost every field of activity, as well as academics. The party certainly had clout.

Mick Jenkins was of Manchester-Jewish origin who had been in the Y.C.L. and the party all his adult life, and had already established himself as a political leader and a good organiser. His wife, Jessie, had been a Lancashire mill girl. Mick had a love of working-class history and was in the process of writing a booklet on Engels in Manchester. They had, of course, moved to Nottingham, and it was agreed that Kath and I would, in time, do the same.

In the meantime, my brother George, in London, was making his own contribution to history. He was well used to being victimised by the bosses, but now it was the Labour Government that was his persecutor. Responding to American pressure, Prime Minister Attlee initiated a witch-hunt against civil service workers who were members of the Communist Party or suspected of holding Communist or left-wing views. "Witch-hunt" was the right description, for the victims were not always told the source or basis of the judgement passed upon them. Although they were given the right to defend themselves, they were not allowed to be represented by their trade union. Communists in the civil service had never hidden their party membership – indeed, many were leading officials of their unions. Altogether, one hundred and thirty six were dismissed. Ironically, some members of Attlee's own party were among the first to come under the axe.

It was generally believed that the ban applied only to executive and administrative workers in the civil service – this was certainly the impression given to Parliament. Then, in September 1948, George was dismissed from his job as a fitter in the tank factory where he worked, because he was a member of the Communist Party – the first, and as far as I know, the only industrial worker to be victimised under the new reg-ulations. His trade union branch and the Esher trades council, of which he was an official, immediately protested, as did many other organisations, and the A.E.U. National Executive decided to fight the victimisation, making it a test case. The dismissal was changed to suspension while the case was being argued about. This took two years, during which time George was not allowed to set foot in the factory but was sent his wages, including the annual increases, every week – "the best job I've ever had," he wryly remarked. With the government moving ever further to the right, there was little hope of winning. A sad reflection of how Nye Bevan was also changing was that when my father appealed to him to help, he refused to do anything.

As the Labour Government neared the end of its term of office, disillusionment among wide sections of its supporters increased. Sir Stafford Cripps' budgets of 1948 and 1949 allocated massive and increasing amounts of money to the arms build-up. Cripps was heavy-handed on the need to cut social service expenditure and keep wages down, but feather-light when it came to touching profits. Although the T.U.C. marginally continued to support the wage freeze, it was being increasingly rejected by the rank and file, and sporadic strikes were taking place throughout the country, including one by 50,000 miners in Lancashire.

The most momentous action, however, was again by the dockers – although it was not directly about the wage freeze in this country, but on the issue of international solidarity. The Canadian dockers were striking against the freeze being imposed by their government and had appealed for international support. When a Canadian vessel, the Montreal City, with a scab crew, arrived in Avonmouth, dockers refused to unload it. The port employers declared a lock-out and the strike spread. As before, the government brought in the army, whereupon most ports came to a halt, with 15,000 coming out in London, 11,000 on Merseyside and similar action elsewhere. The strike was noteworthy for the hysteria of the government in its attempt to brand it as a Communist conspiracy. It ended when the Canadian dockers won concessions and withdrew the call for international support.

On September 18th 1949, after a visit by Bevin and Cripps to Washington, the pound was devalued. The consequence was a cut in real wages; the price of bread, for instance, immediately went up by thirty three per cent, later falling to twenty five per cent. It came just after the annual conference of the T.U.C. It was later revealed that the decision to devalue had been taken before the Congress met, but that the announcement had been deliberately held back in order to help the right-wing

251

union leaders win support for government policy – which they succeeded in doing, but by a small majority.

The Cold War was now getting under way, and in response to this the World Peace Council was set up to campaign for peace in all countries. Needless to say, the Labour Party leadership immediately banned any of its members from taking part in it. In April 1949 we had experienced the frightening power the government and the media had to play on pseudo-patriotic feelings. It was also the nearest I have ever come to being burnt at the stake – or at the platform! It happened like this. In China the Kuomintang forces of Chiang Kai-shek were in headlong retreat before the Chinese People's Army, which had reached the Yangtse River. Kuomintang forces were on one side of the river and the People's Army on the other side. The fighting was across the river. Suddenly, a British sloop, the Amethyst, sailed up the river between the two armies and was put out of action by, it was alleged, Communist gun fire. Seventeen of its crew were killed and twenty injured. Instead of asking what a British warship was doing there at such a time, all hell was let loose in Britain over the fact that the Communists had killed British sailors. It got even worse when another British ship arrived and received similar treatment, with more casualties.

Here in Britain Communists bore the brunt of the jingoist feelings that were whipped up. Harry Pollitt was attacked and injured at a meeting in Dartmouth, and at all our open-air meetings there were rowdy scenes – usually, it must be said, organised by small groups of avowed anti-Communists taking advantage of the situation. This was the situation when I spoke in the Bull Ring at Grimsby, but we carried the quite substantial meeting through to the end (the report in the local paper spent more time describing how neatly I was dressed, for a Communist, than on the event itself!). I wasn't so lucky the following Sunday, when I was supposed to be speaking in Loughborough. The local comrades had not told me that at the time our meeting was to take place, the town would be occupied with soldiers of the Leicestershire Regiment, attending the opening of a new war memorial only a few hundred yards from our meeting place. To make matters worse, they were bound for Hong Kong, being sent there because of the tense situation caused by the Amethyst incident. I didn't know this until afterwards: if I had, I certainly wouldn't have stuck my head so calmly into the lion's mouth. When I mounted the portable platform, it did seem to me that there were an unusually large number of soldiers about, an observation that was soon confirmed.

Before I started speaking the platform was surrounded by a sea of khaki. We used no loudspeakers in those days, but even if I had one, it's doubtful whether it would have been of any use.

The problem was now not whether to hold the meeting, but how to end it! I was hemmed in by the crush of bodies and couldn't even get down from the platform. One or two soldiers had picked up stones, which wasn't exactly reassuring. Then a couple of bright sparks had a better idea: they collected newspapers and started to light a fire underneath the platform. The wood started to burn, but fortunately, before I emulated Joan of Arc in coming to a fiery end, rescue came in the form of a battered old car driven by a comrade who ruthlessly forced her way through the crowd. After a struggle I succeeded in getting aboard, and, to much banging and shouting, we forced our way out. I shall always remember Joyce Phelps. She was a young teacher and always gave the impression of being the most timid member of the branch; but on that occasion she was to me the most courageous of comrades.

The Communist Party had to decide its attitude to the coming general election. In 1945 it had fielded only three candidates, believing that the election of a Labour government committed to the programme of "Let Us Face the Future," was vital for Britain and for the working class, and because – in common with most people – it had overestimated the danger of a Tory victory. The situation was much different now. The government had veered more and more to the right, was totally subservient to the anti-Soviet foreign policy of the Americans, and had turned against the working people who had elected it. Whilst preventing a Tory comeback was still crucial, there was also a great need to present socialist policies to the electorate – something that certainly would not be done by Labour. Indeed, the return of the Labour Government largely depended on the extent to which the faith of the workers in the future could be maintained. Consequently, the Party decided to put forward a record one hundred candidates. Clearly, there was no possibility of most of these being elected, but at least it would enable Communists to put forward the socialist case on a national scale.

We were asked to contest four seats in the East Midlands, and after a great deal of discussion we decided which they were to be: North West Nottingham, with Arthur West – a well-known campaigner on local issues – as the candidate; Mansfield, with Les Ellis; Chesterfield, with Bas Barker – shop-stewards' convenor at an important local factory; and North East Leicester, with myself as candidate. I was opposed to standing because it had long been accepted that if ever we fought in Leicester, the candidate should be Margaret Stanton. Margaret had established for herself a well-deserved reputation in the city for her sterling work on social issues and had received respectable votes in local elections. However, Party Centre and the District Secretariat were adamant that one of the four candidates should be a full-time party worker. This was the first occasion I was personally confronted with the rigid discipline that passed as democratic-centralism within the party. It was made quite clear that I was not to disclose my dissenting views even to the District Committee, and certainly not to the Leicester comrades or to Margaret. The reason given was that it would cause divisions, when unity was important. This upset me personally, as it did Kath – for Margaret was her closest friend – but such was our belief that iron party discipline was a basic principle for Communists that we loyally carried out the line. It was particularly hard because for a while it soured relations between Margaret and ourselves. However, good comrade that she was, she did not allow her feelings to affect in any way our political co-operation. I have given this explanation, not only because it is a small example of how the party then operated, but because, distant though the incident is and unimportant though it might now appear, it has rankled with me all these years; so I am using this opportunity to set the record straight, particularly as Margaret is still a valued friend and politically active (although she has not been a member of the Communist Party for some years). In 1976 she was awarded the T.U.C. Gold Medal for services to the trade union movement.

The election took place on 23rd February 1950. This was the first of the five times I would stand as a Communist Parliamentary candidate, among the most exhilarating and satisfying experiences during the forty years I was a party organiser. N.E. Leicester was a strong Labour constituency, which had Terence Donovan as its Labour M.P. He was a dry-as-dust lawyer who was later to achieve fame as the chairman of the government commission that produced the ill-fated Donovan Report on wage bargaining. Our campaign had hardly started when we were informed by the head postmaster for Leicester that he had vetoed the free distribution of my election address because we had enclosed with it a copy of the party's national election manifesto, and this included a call for electors to read the *Daily Worker* – which he construed as commercial advertising! My agent, Jack Adams, and I went round to his house and pointed out that he was taking on a heavy responsibility, for his deci-

1946-1951: TIME OF HOPE - AND DISILLUSIONMENT

sion could have national repercussions. He was saying, in fact, that it was illegal for one hundred candidates throughout the country to have their addresses delivered by the post office. Whether this frightened him, or whether the Home Office intervened – for I had phoned George Matthews, the Party's National Election Agent – I don't know, but he quickly capitulated. My election address was the best of all the candidates, technically as well as politically, because the owner of one of Leicester's largest printing firms was a close friend of the party, and Jack was one of his managers.

Of course, raising money for the campaign was a big problem, but we thought that at least our £250 deposit was taken care of when one of our members, a woodworker, won £10,000 just at the start of the contest. A strong deputation consisting of Harry Brown, Jack Adams, myself and the organiser of the woodworkers' union, the N.U.W., went round to see him. He met us on the doorstep and nervously told us that his wife and his mother-in-law had already decided to use the money to buy a business, but that we could rest assured we would get something. We did a few days later: a ten pound note and his resignation from the party!

There was an occasion during the campaign when I considered I was justified in resorting to a minor act of personal terrorism. Housing conditions were appalling in parts of the constituency and one night Jack and I were passing what we thought was a derelict pub in one of these areas, when we heard a child crying and on investigation found one room occupied by a woman and four young children. It had been one of the bar-rooms, and was dirty and dark, with a cold stone slab floor, and windows that were either broken or boarded up. There was no furniture, only an orange box, and no lighting or heating. In the middle of the floor was a large hole where a trap-door down to the cellar had been, and two of the children were crawling on the floor dangerously near it. When I shone a torch into the cellar, there was a scurry of rats. At one side of the room were some old bedclothes and coats, and lying there being comforted by her mother was a little girl who was obviously in a high state of fever. There was no husband – we learned that he had deserted them some time before. We thought that the mother was squatting, but she told us she was actually renting the room and was paying a pound a week for it – not a small amount at that time. Apparently a doctor had been to see the little girl earlier in the day, but had only give her medicine. I phoned him and expressed in no uncertain terms my feelings, letting him know I was a Parliamentary Candidate. He came round at once and this time took her to hospital – and not before time, since it turned out that she had rheumatic fever.

Obviously, we wanted the family moved as soon as possible, but were so angry at the callousness of the landlord that we decided to pay him a visit. He lived on his own in a gloomy house outside Leicester, a notorious money-grabber who preyed on the weak and lived on the exorbitant rents from the slum houses he owned – and, indeed, he looked the archetypal Dickens' villain: in his fifties, shifty, stooped, shabby and with a permanent scowl on his face. We demanded that he immediately find a decent place for the family to live, and that until they settled down he should charge no rent. He blustered and threatened to call the police, but we countered with threats of our own. "I'm the Communist candidate," I said, "and you've heard what ruthless people we Communists are. Unless you do what we ask, you'll be getting another visit – and this time it won't be two of us and it won't be just to talk." To our surprise, I must admit, this did the trick; he was obviously frightened and agreed to all our demands. "We'll be checking," were my departing words, trying to put on my best gangster voice!

The next morning I visited the town hall and asked to see the housing manager. "He is too busy," his secretary told me. "Tell him," I said, "that I am a Parliamentary candidate and unless he sees me at once, I shall issue a statement about a case of housing neglect that will not do his reputation any good." He saw me at once. Quite reasonably, he argued that he was in an impossible situation, trying to cope with a problem for which at that moment there was no solution. He showed me hundreds of cases of families in Leicester forced to live in the utmost squalor and preyed upon by property sharks, a consequence of the acute housing shortage. He agreed, however, that the case I had brought was particularly bad and said that he would look into it as a matter of urgency. Within a fortnight the family were found other accommodation. More surprising still, the rack-renter had visited the mother the morning after we had seen him and had not only cancelled her rent, but had actually started renovating the pub. So, in this case, terrorism achieved results. Incidentally, on all occasions I was a Parliamentary candidate, I found that it was an open sesame to official doors and to officials who dread getting unfavourable publicity.

I received three hundred and twenty seven votes, and the total Communist vote throughout the country was 91,746. Unfortunately, because of constituency boundary changes the two Communist M.P.'s,

William Gallacher and Phil Piratin lost their seats – a truly bitter blow after their great record in Parliament. Labour's massive majority disappeared, and the government was left with an absolute majority of only six. But the total Labour vote was a million more than in 1945, indicative of the fact that although there was widespread disillusionment with many of the policies of the government, there was still a determination to defend the gains won. The trade union movement as a whole rallied in a united effort to keep the Tories out of office, and the effective propaganda campaign of the Communist Party, both in the constituencies where it had candidates and generally, was a further positive factor. However, there was a substantial increase in the number of people voting, which meant that Labour's share of the vote dropped, while the Tories' and Liberals' share went up.

It was obvious that with such a slender majority the government existed on a knife-edge. What was needed was to use the period up until the next General Election, which could not be long away, to increase popular support. Instead, Attlee carried on as before; indeed, his policies were even more right-wing, for he argued that he now had to appease the Liberals.

30. NOTTINGHAM

Just before the election, Kath and I had moved to Nottingham, to a house found for us by an old party member, an estate agent, who specialised in rather run-down working-class properties. Alf Marshall was a well-known Nottingham "character." He had once been in the I.L.P. but, when I knew him, he was one of the mainstays of the famous Cosmopolitan Debating Society – the "Cosmo." Our new home was at Old Basford and was at first quite depressing. It was a small terraced house with a tiny scullery equipped with an ancient and dilapidated earthenware sink. There was no hot water (until we put in an Ascot gas sink-heater) and only an outside toilet. The two small downstairs rooms were damp in the winter and every morning we had to clear slugs that had wandered into the scullery from the garden. That area of Basford had once been a swamp, and I discovered when I lifted some floorboards in the living room that there was eighteen inches of water underneath. The house cost £875, far more than we could afford, but Kath's parents lent us the money for the deposit. Fortunately I enjoyed D.I.Y. and spent my occasional periods of free time renovating it, putting in cupboards, etc. In time, we were able to make the house reasonably comfortable, and all of our four children were born there. An advantage was its proximity to a small park that had a day nursery and a nursery school adjoining it.

Much to Kath's annoyance, she had been unable to play a full part in the Leicester election campaign because she was in the final stage of pregnancy, and soon after moving to Nottingham our first child was born. It was in March, and arriving home from a Secretariat meeting at about 10 o'clock one evening, I found the house in darkness and no sign of Kath. On the table was a scribbled note, "Sorry, couldn't wait!" I phoned the Firs maternity hospital and discovered that Glyn had arrived. Believing the birth was imminent – which, in fact, proved to be the case – she had phoned for an ambulance rather than taking up time trying to contact me. This was typical of Kath: making the least fuss about anything, especially if it interfered with party work. My sister-in-law had earlier introduced her to what were then the pioneering "natural childbirth" ideas of Dr Grantly Dick-Read, and she had been convinced by them. She put the comparatively easy birth of Glyn – and, indeed, of our other children – down largely to following them.

The district office of the party was at 4 Fletcher Gate, which bordered on that part of Nottingham called the Lace Market. This is the oldest part of the city; indeed, it was the site of the original town when King John's reputedly villainous sheriff continually plotted the capture of Robin Hood. "Fletcher" was, in fact, the medieval name for an arrow-maker. The small factories nearby, most of them old, produced the lace that Nottingham is famous for, and at the end of the street was the narrow ally where D. H. Lawrence worked as a youngster. We occupied the top two floors of office accommodation, which was found for us and rented to us for a nominal payment by a sympathetic Jewish owner of a small textile factory. At that time the standing of the party among many Jews was high because of our long anti-fascist record. Dessau has long been dead, but the firm he started is now a large and well-known company. Unfortunately, his descendants were not as progressive as the old man.

We had about eight hundred members in the city, organised in eighteen branches, and we had converted one of the rooms into the only progressive bookshop in Nottingham. This meant that there was a continuous flow of people to the district premises – so much so that we had to set Saturdays aside for talking to comrades and friends who popped in to discuss problems, give reports, exchange information or just for a chat. There were party branches in many workplaces, including Raleigh's, Players, Boots, Ericson's, in a few hosiery factories, the railways and at several pits, and party members played leading roles in the Co-op and in some of the main unions. The Nottingham Trades Council was one of the strongest in the country and its two most influential members were both party comrades – Lionel Jacobs, its President, and Jack Charlesworth, its Secretary.

After Harry Brown had left, Mick Jenkins and I were the only two political workers, although there was also a clerical worker. We badly needed someone to manage our bookshop, which occupied one of the rooms, so we advertised the vacancy in the "*District Bulletin*" of the party. The only application we received was from John Peck, the secretary of our Scunthorpe branch. John worked in the office at one of the steel works and had been a bomber pilot in the R.A.F. during the war. The Secretariat accepted his application and John moved to Nottingham with his wife and two children. Some time later he became Nottingham Area Secretary, so we again needed a bookshop manager. On the recommendation of a comrade at Party Centre, we offered the job to a London branch secretary. It was not the most inspired suggestion. Joe was a lovely character, good-natured and hard-working; but running a bookshop was certainly not what he was qualified to do. He was a skilled jewel polisher who had led a strike in that most exclusive of professions, as a result of which he had been blacklisted. His other somewhat exotic distinction was being a European fencing champion. He had not been in Britain long enough to have a thorough grasp of our peculiar money system, so one of the first things he did was to hang up a memo card above the till – "12 pence = 1 shilling; 30 pence = 2/6d; 20 shillings = £1; 240 pence = £1" – not the sort of spectacle to inspire prospective customers with confidence. Branches began to complain about the astronomical bills they were getting. He found our weight and postage system almost incomprehensible, and as the job entailed sending out large numbers of parcels a week, there was usually confusion. No doubt Joe would soon have mastered all these technicalities, but he felt it wasn't the job he was best suited for, and we agreed that he return to London.

One of the problems facing Mick and I was how to pull the District together after a long period without effective leadership. Then Mick had the idea of staging a massive public event, involving the entire District, which, we hoped, would give inspiration to comrades. As it happened, 1949 marked the five hundreth year of the granting of a Royal Charter to Nottingham and there were to be official celebrations around it. We decided to organise an alternative Quincentenary commemoration, stressing the struggles of the people throughout the period. In a short time, over five thousand copies of the pamphlet we produced were sold, many more thousands of leaflets were distributed and meetings held. It culminated in a colourful march through the city with tableaux depicting Robin Hood, the Chartists, the Reform Bill struggle, the Luddites, the Hunger Marchers, etc. William Gallacher was the main speaker on Town Hall ("Slab") Square. Our celebration eclipsed the official one.

Getting to know the East Midlands, the branches and the members proved extremely interesting because of the region's diversity. Sometimes I would borrow a car, and with a Nottingham comrade, Eric Cogging as my driver, spend a few days touring Lincolnshire. We usually came back with a good supply of produce from party members working in the food industries. There was a dour old comrade who was a foreman on the fish docks at Grimsby; as he sorted out the fish, fresh from the trawlers, he would pick out some large plaice, deftly fillet them, wrap them in newspapers and hand them to me without a word being spoken. Another comrade owned a large market garden and I could always be sure of going away with half a sack of leeks and some tomatoes.

It was not always easy for comrades to work openly in the small towns and villages of Lincolnshire. There was one occasion when, after having enrolled about a dozen members in and around Louth, we decided it was time to set up a branch. We called a meeting in a comrade's house, which was attended by our members and some supposed sympathisers, and the branch was established. One of the "sympathisers" was obviously not what he purported to be, for a few days later, the Louth weekly newspaper not only reported the formation of the branch, but published the names of all who had attended the meeting – and even some addresses. Of course, this was particularly serious because of the nature of the area: comrades losing their jobs would find it extremely difficult to get alternative work. Several members did resign, and it could well have been because they were threatened by their bosses. The branch, however, survived. A more positive experience was that of our small but very active Spilsby branch, which was officially praised for its help in rescuing people from tidal floods that engulfed the Lincolnshire coastal region.

While a lot of my work was spent in the cities of our district – Nottingham, Leicester, Derby, Lincoln and Grimsby – I soon found that I was most at home in the mining villages and towns of Notts and Derbyshire, working with comrades with whom I could easily identify because of my South Wales roots. Mining communities are remarkably similar, wherever the coalfield, and this affinity is world-wide. It arises from the strong bonds formed by the nature of mining, the dangers faced by those who work the mines, the fact that cooperation is vital for the safety of all, and the fact that the communities are often self-contained and based around a pit. Mining was also the industry where the party in the East Midlands was strongest and had most influence. I shall write later about the many fine comrades in the industry with whom I worked and who became firm friends in subsequent years.

Like most young parents, Kath and I revelled in the joy of having our first child. There were acute problems. We were stony broke and my wage was very low, yet we did not want Kath to resume teaching for some time. And my determination to make a success of the job of party organiser meant spending many evenings and weekends away from home. I chafed at this, for it meant Kath having to bear the main respon-sibility of parenthood, as well as having more opportunity to savour its pleasures. Nevertheless, we did enjoy it, although it was physically harder work then than it is today. We had no washing machine or hot water, and disposable nappies were unheard of. Usually, my last chore at night was washing the day's nappies by hand in a bucket. But it was all so very worth while, for Glyn was a healthy and happy baby, and it was so rewarding to see him develop towards childhood. The free supply of vitamins for babies and children, started during the war, was still in force, and was much appreciated by us as by all parents.

Then, when Glyn was almost nine months old it all came to an end, by a totally unexpected and cruel turn of events. He had become irrita-ble one morning, and later in the day was sick, with some diarrhoea. In the afternoon, Kath phoned our surgery and, unfortunately, as we were later to discover, the doctor on duty was a junior member of the practice. This was his first job and he was not very experienced. After examining Glyn, he was quite dismissive, saying that it was only a mild tummy upset and nothing to worry about. I arrived home from work not long afterwards, and it became obvious to us that Glyn was getting worse, so we phoned the senior partner at her home. She came immediately, and after asking why we hadn't phoned for a doctor earlier, rushed him to hospital with suspected gastro-enteritis. Glyn died soon after admission.

Only those who have experienced the totally unexpected loss of a specially loved one can appreciate the agony of the grief that over-whelms all feelings and erases all other emotions. It truly seemed that our world had come to an end. We could not bear to go back to the house

261

and face there the reminders of Glyn, and we spent most of that terrible night wandering aimlessly in the drizzle around the streets of Basford until dawn and sheer exhaustion forced us home. It seemed so incomprehensible, so unfair, so unreal and quite impossible to accept. Arising out of my own experiences, at this time and in later years, I believe that of all the deep-felt emotions, grief of such an order is the most profound and most difficult to come to terms with.

We were later told that after an internal inquiry the young doctor had been reprimanded for his mistake. When the loss had become more bearable and the bitterness had diminished we began to feel a little sorry for him, for we recognised what a tragic start it was to his career. One Sunday morning there was a knock on the door, and it was him. He told us that the error he had made had haunted him and although he didn't know what reception he would get from us, he wanted us to know how deep was his remorse. In later years we came to know him quite well, and when he left the practice, Kath even gave him a small parting gift.

A few months later Kath went back to teaching and, in the summer, Party Centre offered us a free fortnight's holiday at Bucklers Hard in the New Forest. With a few other comrades we stayed at a lovely house with its own grounds and lake; it had been put at the disposal of the party for such a purpose by its sympathetic, well-off absentee owner. When we returned, we threw ourselves into the political fight, finding this the best antidote for depression.

31. THE RETREAT CONTINUES

As we had expected, the new Labour government had learned nothing from the experiences of the first five years. It continued with the same disastrous policies that had resulted in Labour's massive majority being almost wiped out – indeed, it was more committed than ever to them. Its determination to continue the wage freeze received a blow when the Trades Union Congress rejected a General Council motion pledging modified support, and, instead, carried a motion calling for control of profits and prices. But this didn't change its policy. There were strikes in many industries, notably on the railways, but the main struggle was over the use of "Order 1305" against strikers. This was an Order made in 1940 as a wartime measure making strikes virtually illegal, but during the war it was handled very carefully, and in 1945 the government gave a pledge to end it. Instead of doing this, it now started to invoke the Order. During a strike of gas workers, ten of the leaders were prosecuted under the Conspiracy and Protection of Property Act 1875, and Order 1305. They were sentenced to one month's imprisonment, later changed to a fifty pound fine each. This caused widespread anger, and as a result a Joint Trade Union Defence Committee was set up to campaign against the Order.

It was just in time. Unrest among dockers was rising because of the failure to bring in the Dockers' Charter, a modest list of proposals that had been drawn up by the unions in 1945. In February 1951 dockers in Manchester, Merseyside and London came out on strike, and, immediately, seven leading members of the unofficial Port Workers' Committee, led by Communist, Ted Dickens, were arrested under Order 1305. The effect was electric. Nine thousand men immediately stopped work and huge demonstrations were held in all the major port towns. To follow one stupidity with another, the Attorney-General, Sir Hartley Shawcross, directly committed the Government by deciding to conduct the prosecution himself at the Old Bailey. Large crowds of dockers demonstrated outside the court when the case was being heard, and to their great joy and Sir Hartley's chagrin the jury demonstrated its independence and good sense by finding the defendants "Not Guilty" on the main charge. Faced with such a defeat, Shawcross ignominiously dropped the lesser charges. Order 1305 was totally discredited and in August the Government annulled it. It was a fine victory.

In the field of foreign policy Attlee clung more firmly than ever to the coat-tails of Uncle Sam. Anti-Sovietism was now the undisguised guiding principle of American foreign policy, and the recent alliance against fascism was hushed up as an unpleasant memory. Symptomatic of the change was that the first steps were taken to rearm Germany. The death sentences on twenty one Nazi war criminals were commuted and the sentences of seventy others reduced. Probably the most outrageous act by the Americans was to hand back to Alfred Krupp the vast fortune he had made out of supplying the Nazis with arms during the war, much of it made by the use of slave labour. The original plan to nationalise his factories was ditched and they were restored to him. Rearmament in the West was soon well underway.

Despite Britain's economic problems, in July 1950 the Government announced that it planned to spend a massive 3,600 million pounds on defence over the following three years – an increase of forty nine per cent. Two months later National Service was extended from eighteen months to two years and the U.S. bomber force in Britain was increased

263

from one hundred and eighty to one thousand. It was no great surprise that, when Parliament was asked to endorse these measures, the Government received the enthusiastic support of the Tories.

These moves had been decided some time before, but a dramatic escalation of the Cold War was seized upon as partial justification for them. On 25th June the Korean War started. Since 1945 Korea had been divided along the 38th Parallel between the northern part of the country liberated by the Red Army, and the southern part liberated by the armies of the United States. When the occupying forces withdrew, each area had its own government. Although the declared aim was reunification through democratic elections, it soon became clear that the only reunification countenanced by the Synghman Rhee Government of South Korea was absorption of the North, if necessary by military means. And it was equally manifest that behind Rhee was the U.S. Administration, obsessed with the need to "contain and defeat Communism."

As far back as October 1949, Synghman Rhee had said, "I would wage war, but for that American help is needed." On 1st November 1949, the *New York Herald Tribune* reported a speech made by Rhee's Defence Minister when visiting the U.S. Fleet. In it he expressed confidence in his ability to wrest power from the Communists. "If we had our own way," he said, "we would have started already, but we had to wait until they (the American government leaders) are ready." "They keep telling us, no, no, wait. You are not ready." He boasted that he could take Pyongyang, the northern capital, within a few days. In May, five weeks before hostilities started, the Appropriation Committee of the U.S. House of Representatives was told that 100,000 officers and men of the South Korean army, equipped with American arms and trained by an American military commission, had completed their preparations and "can start war at any moment." Proposals of the Soviet Union for free elections under international supervision were turned down. A week before the outbreak of war, the paranoiac anti-Communist, John Foster Dulles, Republican adviser to the American Secretary of State (he was later to take over the job himself), flew to Korea and had discussions with Rhee. Addressing Rhee's National Assembly, he said, "The eyes of the Free World are upon you. Compromise with Communism would be a road leading to disaster." He then flew to Tokyo for discussions with General Douglas MacArthur, Commander in Chief of the US forces in Asia. It seemed obvious to many of us that the stage was being set for the next act in a truly frightening drama.

And so it was. On 25th June, the United Nations Commission on Korea sent a message to the U.N. which began, "The Government of the Republic of Korea states . . . " and then went on to report Rhee's allegation that North Korean forces had invaded the South. Those first words are important. Although official histories now all state as a matter of fact that the North invaded, there never was, nor has there ever been, independent evidence that this is what happened – as distinct from border incidents, of which there were many on both sides. Indeed, the Commission made it clear that it had seen nothing, made no investigation and knew only what it had been told by Rhee. Yet, on this hearsay evidence alone, without any attempt to find out the facts or to call for mediation, Washington immediately declared that an unprovoked act of aggression by the Communists had taken place and that it was giving the Synghman Rhee government immediate military help. The People's Democratic Government of Korea (North Korea) declared that Rhee's forces had crossed the 38th parallel in force. It appealed to the world for support against the invaders, but this was totally ignored by the capitalist powers.

There then followed an incredible charade, the aim of which was to turn an American war into a United Nations conflict. An emergency meeting of the U.N. Security Council was called, which, in a few hours, passed a resolution condemning the "invasion" of South Korea, again without making any effort to ascertain the truth or to offer conciliation. In fact, the so-called resolution and the subsequent actions that stemmed from it were in total violation of the Charter of the U.N. This lays down that any military action taken on its behalf must have the "concurring vote" of all the Permanent Members of the Security Council – the "principle of unanimity," insisted upon by the Americans when the U.N. was set up. The Permanent Members were, and still are at the time of writing, the Allied powers that defeated fascism: the U.S.A., the Soviet Union, Britain, France and China. But in June 1950 the Soviet Union was boycotting meetings of the Security Council in protest over the fact that the People's Republic of China was not represented, China's place being usurped by the discredited Chiang Kai-shek regime which had fled to Formosa (Taiwan). It might be argued that the Soviet Union was outmanoeuvred; even so, without its vote the decision was obviously invalid. The flimsy "justification" was that there was unanimity of the four represented at the meeting – which included, of course, the Chiang Kai-shek rump. This was accepted by Britain, even though Attlee had

265

privately made it clear to Truman that he believed China's seat on the Security Council should rightly be held by the legitimate government.

The war didn't go well for the South Korean army. After its initial advantage, "the best army in Asia," as the American State Department had called it, was soon in headlong retreat, and the retreat swiftly turned into a rout. It looked as if the war would be over before the United States Cavalry arrived. But arrive it did, under the command of arrogant, blustering, fire-eating General Douglas MacArthur. American troops, with massive air support, poured in through the only beachhead left in the far south, and by overwhelming military superiority were soon able to reverse the position.

Apart from Washington, governments of other countries were singularly unenthusiastic about the war, sending relatively small token forces. When it was debated in the House of Commons, the left-wing Labour M.P., S. O. Davies, moved a motion opposing the war, but with leaders of the Tory and Labour parties subserviently following United States policy, it never even went to a division.

Then, suddenly, the war took a truly dangerous turn. MacArthur landed forces north of the 38th parallel and began to advance towards the Yalu River, the border with China, against undertakings given to the U.S. allies. The Chinese had already announced that if the advance continued, in its own defence it would support the North with arms and men – and did so. Until then, it had been generally accepted that the only foreign troops in Korea were those supporting Synghman Rhee. But now there was no controlling MacArthur. He publicly advocated taking the war into China and bombing Chinese industrial centres, even with atom bombs, and it was clear that he had strong support in the Pentagon. When Truman gave a press conference supporting this line, Attlee flew to Washington to express the opposition of the British government to any moves that would risk starting a third world war – "fighting the wrong people at the wrong place and at the wrong time" (Attlee's rather interesting words). MacArthur was sacked and recalled to the U.S.A., but it is worth correcting another historical myth. He was not sacked because of his policy – which Truman basically agreed with – but because he had become dangerously paranoiac, could no longer be relied upon to obey orders from Washington and, probably most important of all, because he and his Republican friends at the White House, were now openly criticising Truman for what they alleged was his hesitant attitude to the war against Communism. He had become a political threat to the

Administration, and that could not be tolerated.

The Americans were driven back, but the war dragged on until the end of 1951, when a cease-fire agreement was signed restoring the 38th Parallel as the border between North and South – back to the position at the beginning of the war, but hundreds of thousands of casualties, immense suffering and many devastated towns and villages later. It was an unpopular war in Britain and in most countries. A little of the frustration felt by American G.I.'s forced to take part in it is conveyed by the writers of the TV series "M.A.S.H.," particularly through its central character, "Hawkeye" Pearce.

During this period I was, of course, involved up to the hilt in the campaign against the war. Although the war was not popular, there were occasions when things were difficult. Britain had sent out a contingent of the Gloucestershire Regiment, and when it was involved in action, jingoist feeling was whipped up about the "Glorious Gloucesters," and we felt the brunt of this at our open-air meetings. At the time of crisis, when MacArthur was threatening to cross the Yalu river and use atom bombs against China, I was on my own at the district headquarters, everyone else being on holiday. I organised protest meetings throughout the East Midlands and persuaded a number of prominent personalities to sign telegrams to the White House and to Attlee.

During 1950-51 – which included the period of the Korean war – the peace movement in Britain and other countries took on a new impetus, concentrating most of its attention on the urgent need to remove the nuclear threat. In March 1950, the World Peace Council initiated the Stockholm Appeal, which called for the prohibition of atomic weapons. A campaign to collect signatures supporting the Appeal was launched throughout the world. Despite being condemned by the leaders of the Labour Party and the T.U.C., the campaign was a tremendous success. In three months, 823,000 signatures had been collected in Britain. At the conclusion of the campaign it was announced that 330,000,000 people had signed throughout the world – although, of course, most were in the socialist countries. Kath had become secretary of the Nottingham branch of the British Peace Committee and was very much involved in organising the petition in the city and the area around.

The malevolence of the Labour Government towards the peace movement was dramatically demonstrated in the latter part of 1950. After successful international meetings in Prague and Paris, the World Peace Council decided that the next World Peace Congress should take

267

place in Sheffield, one of the great steel centres of the world. In response to U.S. pressure to ban the Congress, the Home Secretary made a sanctimonious statement that although the Government was opposed to it being held, Britain had a strong tradition of free speech and would keep to this tradition. It, therefore, did not intend prohibiting it. Weasel words indeed. All the arrangements were being made and delegations from the various countries were starting to arrive when the Government showed how much it really valued the tradition of free speech. Hundreds of delegates, including even those with visas, were refused entry into the country on the grounds that they were persona non grata. These included the famous French scientist, Professor Joliot-Curie and author Louis Aragon. Picasso and the Soviet composer Khachaturyan were allowed in but had to kick their heels waiting in Sheffield. It soon became clear that the Government had effectively sabotaged the Congress by preventing it being a gathering truly representative of all countries. On the invitation of the Polish Government, which supplied a passenger liner to transport the delegates, the Congress was moved to Warsaw.

However, before the delegates left Sheffield there was a great rally at the City Hall, at which Kath and I were fortunate to be present. There was no feeling of defeatism: on the contrary the enthusiasm of the audience as we listened to Picasso and the other speakers was sharpened by the anger we felt that a British Labour Government had acted in such a vile manner.

Speaking at the dinner of the Foreign Press Association a week before the Sheffield Congress for Peace was due to take place, Attlee had delivered an abusive speech against its supporters. The World Peace Movement, he declared, was part of that "evil phenomenon," the Soviet Union. He thus anticipated by thirty-five years the notorious "evil empire" speech of American President, Ronald Reagan.

32. THE BRITISH ROAD TO SOCIALISM

Within the Party there was another matter that concerned us very much as Marxists, and about which we had endless and heated discussions. It was related to the developments taking place in Eastern Europe. They raised important theoretical questions for the international Communist movement, for they appeared to run counter to Marxist thinking on the form of the state in the period leading to socialist revolution. The Marxist view of the state is that it is not politically neutral or impartial, as most people, including the Labour leaders and even many on the left believe.

268

On the contrary, in capitalist society it is an instrument moulded to the needs of the ruling class and the system, and is used to maintain the economic and political domination of that class over society. For example, in Britain, the state, in other words Parliament, the civil service, the police, the judiciary, the armed forces, and, indirectly, the education system, is geared to the preservation of capitalism, helped by the manipulation of public opinion through the capitalist-controlled media. Workers on strike or people demonstrating soon come to realise how "impartial" the police and the courts really are.

One of the conclusions Marx drew from the failure of the Paris Commune of 1871 – the very first time that workers took political power into their own hands – was that "it is not possible for the workers to take over the ready-made (capitalist) state machine and wield it for their own purpose." They have to create a new state, controlled by the working class and geared to a new task, building socialism. Acting on this conclusion, after the Russian Revolution Lenin insisted that the form of the state should be based on the workers' and peasants' councils that had developed (the Russian word for council is "soviet"). This seemed quite a likely possibility in other countries. Indeed, this was the experience in several countries where there were popular insurrections after the First World War. These insurrections were brutally crushed, together with the infant soviets. In Britain, there had been occasions, and particularly during the General Strike – a time of sharp class confrontation – when "Councils of Action" of the workers involved in struggle naturally sprang up and acted in many areas as local governments. It didn't require a great stretch of the imagination to envisage, in a period of great crisis, such councils being the basis of a national workers' parliament.

There was another reason why this concept took hold. The Soviet Union was the only country where there had been a successful socialist revolution, and it was understandable that its experience should be reflected in the strategies of other Communist parties. The Thirteenth Congress of the British Communist Party, held in 1935, adopted a programme, "For Soviet Britain," which, although it rejected the sectarianism of the "Class Against Class" period, also rejected any idea of using Parliament to change society.

Yet, here we had "People's Democracies" established in Eastern Europe, with Marxists in the lead, and with the declared aim of building Socialism – and none had adopted a soviet form of government. The forms were diverse, but most were based on the broad anti-fascist resistance movements that developed in the war against the Nazis. The countries had been liberated by their own resistance fighters aided by the Red Army. In France and Italy, Communists were ministers in coalition governments. China was working out its own distinctive form of a workers' and peasants' state.

It was obvious that these were momentous new experiences that Marxists had to take into account. Being a scientific ideology, Marxist theory must all the time be tested and reappraised in the light of objective reality – by what is actually happening in the real world. Every scientific theory, in nature and in social relationships, is only an approximation, based on the knowledge existing at the time. When more knowledge is acquired, often gained through new experiences, the theory usually has to be modified to bring it in line with the known facts. This applies to Marxism as to other fields of scientific understanding.

More important to British Communists were the profound experiences of the anti-fascist struggle, of post-war events – including the Labour Government – and the special character of our labour movement. It was felt that these should be reflected in the programme of the party. We needed a programme, a strategy, said Pollitt, that would clearly indicate how we are going to move from the Britain of today, to a Britain where Socialism would be on the agenda. After a great deal of discussion, The British Road to Socialism (B.R.S.) was adopted at the Twenty Second National Congress of the Party in April 1952. One of the most significant statements in the programme declared:

Britain will reach Socialism by her own road. Just as the Russian people won political power by the Soviet road which was dictated by their historical conditions and background of Tsarist rule, and the people in the People's Democracies and China won political power in their own way in their historical conditions, so the British Communists declare that the people of Britain can transform capitalist democracy into a real People's Democracy, transforming Parliament, the product of Britain's historic struggle for democracy, into the democratic instrument of the will of the vast majority of her people.

Although giving Parliament a positive role was new, the demand for a vast extension of genuine democracy had always been a demand of the party, which had also consistently stressed the great progressive traditions of struggle of the British people. Subsequent editions of the B.R.S. put forward the concept of a "broad alliance," led by the working class, of all people being hit by capitalism. Subsequently this was changed to an "anti-monopoly alliance." The aim was to win a socialist majority in Parliament, but the crucial importance of extra-parliamentary struggle as a means of achieving this was stressed.

The programme won acclaim from Communists throughout the world and was the model for similar programmes in other capitalist countries. *Pravda*, the organ of the Communist Party of the Soviet Union published it in full, as did the periodical of the international Communist Information Bureau. It has since been stated that Pollitt had put some of the original proposals to Stalin, but if this were so we were not told, and therefore it didn't enter into our discussions.

I have mentioned that there was a great deal of discussion within the Party prior to the adoption of the B.R.S. As District Organiser, I attended many packed branch meetings called to discuss the draft – and what lively meetings they were. No other political party could get near to the high level of political debate that took place. And this applied to most issues of importance. Yet, deriders of the Communist Party have always tried to portray most Communists as mindless fools, submissively accepting "the line" handed down from on high. By definition, Communists are natural rebels. This is why they join the party in the first place. It would be against the character of most of them to meekly fall into line just because they are told to do so. Debate and discussion has always been an essential feature of Communist Party practice. I know several Communists who have left the party and joined the Labour Party, and their common complaint has been the absence of political discussion in their ward and constituency organisations. Just before he died, the famous historian, E. P. Thompson was interviewed on television. He admitted that what he missed most after leaving the Communist Party was the stimulating, even brilliant discussions he used to participate in as a party member; "This was so," he said "even during the Stalinist period."

33. VISIT TO CZECHOSLOVAKIA

In 1951 Kath and I visited Czechoslovakia as members of the first group of tourists to visit a socialist country since the end of the war. Most of these countries were too preoccupied in repairing the damages of war to receive tourists, however much they wanted Western currency. Czechoslovakia was in a better position than the others, but there was an additional reason. The visits were sponsored by the Cumberland Area of the National Union of Mineworkers. In 1947, one hundred and forty seven miners had been killed in a tragic pit accident at Whitehaven pit in

271

Cumberland and Czechoslovakian trade unionists had collected £40,000 for the relief fund. However, the money could not be sent because of currency restrictions. A scheme was worked out for the money paid by tourists to be retained in this country and transferred to the miners, with the Czech authorities meeting the cost of the visits. The trips were being organised by Progressive Tours, a tourist agency that had been established by the British Communist Party primarily to raise money. It was accepted that there could be no restrictions whatsoever on who could go, but there was some worry that the British media would jump at the opportunity to send in undercover journalists to collect material for anti-Czech propaganda. This might appear paranoid, but some nervousness could be understood in light of the sustained campaign conducted by the media against the Czechoslovak Government since 1948 – part of the Cold War hotting up. It was therefore decided that travelling with each tourist group of a few hundred should be a few experienced British party members, who could look out for possible press infiltrators. I was asked to be one of these, and it was agreed that Kath accompany me.

Then came the snag. The group was to go by train, but about a week before we were due to start we were informed that the Americans, who occupied the zone of West Germany we had to cross, had refused to give transit visas to Bill Alexander and myself. Bill was the Midlands District Secretary of the Party, and had fought in the Spanish Civil War. He had the unique distinction for a Communist of having gone through the Sandhurst Military Academy and winning the Sword of Honour. During the war he was a Captain in the army in Italy. No explanation was or ever has been given as to why we were singled out. What made it ludicrous was that our group included Marjorie Pollitt, wife of the General Secretary of the British Party, and several other well-known Communists, most of them full-time workers. Indeed, of the seven hundred and fifty tourists who visited Czechoslovakia that summer, Bill and I were the only ones who were refused visas by the U.S. authorities. A great honour, but at the time distinctly awkward.

The party protested to the Foreign Minister, and I asked Ian Winterbottom, a Nottingham Labour M.P. to take it up, but to no avail. Although Kath was over five months pregnant, and the long train journey was not going to be very comfortable, no power on earth would have stopped her going – with or without me. The problem was resolved when the Czechs offered to transport Bill and me by air. We were the only two passengers in a plane loaded with freight, and eventually we arrived at

Marianske Lazne and joined the rest of our travel-weary fellow tourists. Marianske Lazne, formerly Marienbad, is a famous spa town, once patronised by the European aristocracy, including Britain's royals. From the sixteenth century its waters have had the reputation of possessing healing properties, and it wasn't long before we dutifully joined the large groups of earnest visitors wallowing in the baths or drinking the water, hoping that it really was the elixir of life and that ten more years would be added to our lives. During our stay we visited other places and spent a couple of days in Prague. This is surely one of the most beautiful cities in Europe, with its picturesque medieval buildings still intact around King Wenceslas Square, the many and varied bridges across the Vltava river, its ancient library and the view from the President's Palace.

But we were interested in talking to people. Three years earlier an event had taken place that had infuriated the capitalist powers. When the war ended parliamentary democracy was restored to Czechoslovakia and in the first general election the Communist Party emerged as the largest party – a testimony to the resistance it had organised against the Nazi occupation before and during the war. With the socialists, they constituted an absolute majority and a government could have been formed based on the two parties. Instead, the capitalist parties were invited to join in forming a government of national unity. The pre-war president, Dr Eduard Beneš, became the new president, with Communist leader, Klement Gottwald as prime minister. The government embarked on a programme of economic reconstruction along socialist lines, and much was achieved in the first two years. Obviously, many of these reforms were not liked by those who wanted Czechoslovakia to pursue a capitalist path. When the Communist and Socialist parties proposed further reforms, including more nationalisation, the distribution to the peasants of large estates owned by one person and differential tax changes in the interests of the workers, the differences came to a head. On 20th February 1948, twelve Ministers representing these pro-capitalist forces suddenly resigned. The pretext they gave was the removal of some police chiefs who had proved disloyal to the regime, and their replacement by working-class militants. The constitutional way of resolving differences would have been to raise them in Parliament; the action they took was clearly aimed at precipitating a crisis which would undermine the position of the Communist and Socialist parties. The Government was obviously in a difficult position. Key sections of the economy and the state were in the hands of people who had been trained under the old regime and had no sympathy with socialism. They managed the banks, ran the civil service and the police, and had the necessary expertise. The pre-war Czech Communist Party had not been large, and half its members had lost their lives in fighting fascism. Both the party and its Socialist Party ally were desperately over-stretched and lacking experience.

The Government and the Communist Party believed that the resignations were part of a plot to destabilise the country and bring about the Government's downfall. It acted quickly. New Ministers were appointed, which Beneš reluctantly swore in – reluctantly, because he was sympathetic to the plotters yet recognised that their replacement was fully in accordance with the constitution, which he was responsible for upholding. Gottwald went on the radio and called for massive demonstrations of support in cities, towns and workplaces. He appealed to workers: "The future," he said, "is now in your hands!" In some factories, workers broke into arsenals and armed themselves in preparation for any possible coup. In fact, the attempt to bring down the Government soon collapsed. Predictably, in the capitalist countries these events were stigmatised as a "Communist takeover." Soon afterwards Beneš resigned as President and was replaced by Klement Gottwald.

We found it interesting to talk to workers who had taken part in these events. We stopped a policeman in a park, and he explained to us that he had been a lathe operator at the time. He and his mates worked with rifles by the side of their machines, and when a call for volunteers to join the police force had come over the factory tannoy, he had volunteered. Others who we met with in a local pub told similar stories. There was a real feeling of jubilation over what they had achieved.

By accident, we met the Prime Minister, Antonin Zapotocky – in the public Lido at Marienske Lazne. It was a stiflingly hot day and the pool was crowded with locals, when this tallish elderly man appeared in bathing trunks, and was immediately surrounded by people who wanted to shake his hand. We were told who he was, so Marjorie Pollitt introduced herself and told him who we were. He politely spent a few minutes with us, but was obviously more keen to get in the water. Zapotocky was a Communist veteran, one of the founders of the Czech party, and had been imprisoned during the war. When Gottwald died in 1953, he became the country's President. Although there were two security guards in the background, it spoke volumes for his feeling of security that, Prime Minister though he was, he should choose to spend an afternoon enjoying himself in a public swimming pool with hundreds of his fellow-citizens, and without any announcement or fuss. The purges in the Soviet Union stemming from Stalin's paranoia with conspiracy from within were now being paralleled in other socialist countries, including Czechoslovakia, but we were not then fully aware of this. Yet, only a year later, Rudolf Slansky, the former General Secretary of the party and a foundation member, was to be unjustly executed for treason. It would be comforting to believe that if we had known this we would have enjoyed our holiday less, but it would not have been true. When, later, the news of the purges were revealed, Kath and I were uneasy, but – like most party members – we rationalised them as, at best, based on evidence we didn't know about, at worst, a regrettable but understandable paranoia arising from the overwhelming need to protect the socialist system.

But how about the job we British Communists were supposed to be doing – that is, trying to root out agents of the British anti-Communist media. I regret to say that we were utter failures. Inept would probably be a better word. There were about three hundred tourists in our group, a large proportion of them teachers and professional people. Naturally, they were very curious, asking questions wherever they went and taking hundreds of snapshots, as, indeed, we did. We would meet for an hour in the evening and exchange notes – rather melodramatically, I thought. But without results. One suspicious character who several of our group hived in upon, a cantankerous old chap who seemed to ask an inordinate number of critical questions and made copious notes, turned out to be a British Party member. It turned out that there really was a reporter from the *Daily Express* among the tourists who kept her identity secret, and none of us spotted her. Worse than that, she became very friendly with one of our full-time Party organisers who was supposed to be looking out for such infiltrators. We didn't know this until a few weeks later, when the *Express* carried a series of articles by her about this first excursion behind the "Iron Curtain." Probably because of our ineptness, there was no attempt to repeat this exercise on subsequent occasions.

On the return journey, Bill and I had to change planes at Brussels airport, and while we were waiting in the lounge, a close comrade of mine, Les Ellis, a member of the Party's National Executive Committee, came in. He glanced at us but gave no sign of recognition. However, while queuing for coffee, he did manage to slip a note to Bill asking us not to recognise him. We discovered the explanation for this odd behaviour when we arrived home. The World Youth Festival was taking place in

275

Berlin and the Americans were doing their damnedest to wreck it. British, French and other delegates on their way to the Festival had been turned off the train at Innsbruck, in Austria, and had been held on the railway track at bayonet-point while the authorities decided what to do with them. Les was the Party's fraternal delegate to the Festival and wasn't taking any chances of being held up. Because of American obstruction only sixty five of the 1,640 British delegates were able to get to Berlin for the start, although most of the others did succeed in getting there later by taking circuitous routes through Italy and the Soviet Zone in Austria.

CHAPTER VII

THE 1950's: A DEFINING DECADE

34. A DEFINING DECADE

The years of the 1950s saw changes that were to have a profound impact on the rest of the century. The Cold War was given legal sanctification with the formation of the North Atlantic Treaty Organisation (N.A.T.O.), leading to its counter-organisation, the Warsaw Pact. The H-bomb first cast its dark shadow over humankind, bringing with it the threat of total obliteration. The Treaty of Rome established the Common Market and laid down the plans for the eventual economic and political capitalist integration of Europe. The ignominious debacle of British imperialism in the Suez War dramatically exposed its weakened position in the world. Britain's desperate struggle to hold back the forces of independence in Malaya, Kenya, Guiana, Cyprus, and other colonies ended with a Tory Prime Minister having to admit in its final year that "the winds of change" were too powerful to stop. This was also revealed by the historic defeat of the French colonialists by the Vietnamese people at Dien Bien Phu and the failure of the Americans to impose imperialist domination over the whole of Korea.

The death of Stalin and the subsequent exposure of his crimes and the negative role he had played in the development of socialism forced communists in all countries to re-examine many of their cherished ideas. Yet, it was the failure by communists in the Soviet Union and other socialist countries to grasp all the lessons and act on them that was to be a primary cause of the shattering reversals that were to come. But at the time the negative features of Soviet society then revealed did not in any way diminish our belief in that society. This was given an enormous boost in October 1957 when the launch of Sputnik, the first artificial satellite, took humanity into the space age and seemed to demonstrate the superiority of Soviet science. The decade also saw the fall of Batista in Cuba and the foundations being laid to build a new socialist Cuba, led by Fidel

Castro. So much of what happened in the 1950's was to define developments for the rest of the century.

In 1951 the Tories regained power in Britain. In the flush of Labour's victory a mere six years before, this had seemed utterly impossible. Apologists pointed to the increased Labour vote, but the hard fact was that the Tory vote went up even more. Although there was widespread disillusionment at the government's retreat from its early promises, the organised working class was prepared to give it a second chance. However, millions of hitherto politically uncommitted electors were repelled by the harsh and unpopular measures that had now become so much a part of Labour's policies. The tragedy was that the government had so much going for it. The post-war reorganisation of industry was continuing and there was full employment. Yet, it obsessively sought to ensure, by means of successive wage restraint policies under various names, that the absence of a "reserve army of labour" and the advantage this gave the trade unions would not result in higher pay. Only six months before the General Election, in order to pay for increased defence spending, Hugh Gaitskell, Chancellor of the Exchequer, re-imposed charges for prescriptions, dental and other health care, leading to the resignations from the government of Aneurin Bevan, Harold Wilson and John Freeman. Three basic factors led to Labour's defeat: its determination to strengthen the capitalist basis of British society; its subservience to the United States and to the demands of the Cold War; and its desperate attempt to hang on to the empire and Britain's imperialist position in the world. These led to ever-increasing sacrifices being demanded of the working class. It also meant that the capitalist class, which had been somewhat demoralised after the war, was stronger and had recovered its confidence. However, there was a powerful challenge to the right-wing within the Labour Party. Originally used by the Tory press as a term of abuse, the loosely-organised group of left M.P.'s gladly took over the name "Bevanites." It became the most powerful left-wing grouping there has ever been in the Labour Party. Many of its members were associated with *Tribune*, of which Bevan had been editor for a time.

Although now little more than a drink-sodden, doddering old fool basking in past glories, the ruling class granted Winston Churchill his cherished desire to be the peace-time prime minister that he had thought he was going to be in 1945. The Tory Government continued the same basic policies begun by Labour. Churchill, who had officially launched the Cold War with his infamous Fulton speech in 1946 when he stole from Goebbels the term "iron curtain" to justify the West's anti-Soviet policies, enthusiastically cooperated in the creation of N.A.T.O. The war against the liberation forces in Malaya continued, and a new struggle developed to crush the independence movement in Kenya, a movement led by Jomo Kenyatta. Using alleged Mau Mau atrocities as a pretext, Kenyatta was put on trial, and was defended by the eminent left-wing Q.C., D. N. Pritt. He was imprisoned, but, as was the pattern in so many cases, was subsequently to become the first president of his liberated nation. In 1953 troops occupied Guiana and the constitution was suspended – officially, "to prevent a communist takeover," but in reality because the independence movement led by Cheddi Jagan was receiving mass popular support.

As the post-war "boom" came to an end new attacks were made on the working class. Real wages in 1952 actually bought six per cent less than in 1947. But there was a powerful fightback; the following year over one million engineering and shipyard workers staged a day's strike in support of a fifteen per cent wage increase demand.

35. THE MINERS – SPENCERISM AND THE AFTERMATH

Soon after our trip to Czechoslovakia, Gwyneth Mary was born. We had decided from the first that we would give each of our children a Welsh and an English name, leaving it to them to decide in future by which name they wanted to be known. In fact, they have all stuck to the Welsh name. Gwyneth, and our subsequent two children, were born at home, and I was more directly involved than I had been with Glyn. As the crucial day grew near I would make sure that my bicycle was well-oiled and in good working order, because my scheduled task when the contractions indicated that the crucial moment was near, was to cycle madly around looking for the midwife – who was never at home. It was some years before we had a phone. Of course, Kath had to give up work, but finances were so tight that she was forced to go back to teaching before being really fit enough to do so. The wage I should have been getting as a Party organiser was only about half the average industrial wage but I was not getting even that. There were weeks when there was no pay at all. Fortunately, because of the shortage of teachers they were given priority in placing their children in nursery schools. One of them was two to three miles away, and I would take Gwyneth in the push-chair before going into work. Kath would collect her after school.

Because of my factory and trade union experience, I had been in charge of the Party's industrial work in the East Midlands from the start. I was active in my A.E.U. branch, and we had a good engineering advisory committee and party branches in several engineering factories. These included Rolls Royce at Derby, Hucknall and Mountsorrel, Raleigh, Plessey and the R.O.F. in Nottingham, Ransome and Marles in Newark, as well as others in most of the main cities and towns of the East Midlands. We also had branches in some hosiery factories, on the railways, at Boots, at Players, and at the big British Celenese (now Courtaulds) factory at Derby. In most of these places, Communists played a leading role as shop stewards, and, in some cases – as in Derby, Hucknall and Mountsorrel Rolls Royce, Derby Rails Workshop, Players, Qualcast, International Combustion, Brush Electric, and Ransome and Marles – as convenors. Interestingly enough, some of the firms recognised the existence of party organisation, accepting it as the norm, even though they didn't approve of it. The management of Players, Nottingham's famous tobacco company, approached the party branch secretary – who was also the convenor – objecting to it being called the "Players" branch, because "Players" was a registered trade name. With their agreement, we henceforth called it the "Tobacco Branch"! Having to familiarize myself with so many different industries, including the large-scale capitalist agriculture of Lincolnshire, smallholder farming – we had several small farmers in the party – and deep-sea fishing (Grimsby's main industry) gave me a much fuller perspective on the complexities of working-class organisation.

Nottingham had a long tradition of working-class struggle and had thrown up many great working-class and progressive leaders. During the English Revolution of the seventeenth century it had been a parliamentary stronghold and Feargus O'Connor, the Chartist leader, had been one of its M.P.'s. It had a powerful trades council with several Communists playing a leading part in it. Jack Charlesworth, its Secretary, was also the full-time General Secretary of the Hosiery Finishers' Association. A well-known and capable comrade, he was one of the leaders of the unemployed struggles of the 1930's and for many years was the National President of the Labour Research Department. His first office was in a street adjoining where we lived, and Kath and I would often drop in for a chat. When he died in 1993, at the ripe old age of ninety three, I was proud to be asked to make the funeral oration.

Jack worked closely with Lionel Jacobs, who was President of the

Trades Council two out of every three years – the change required under the rules – and President of the North Midlands Federation of Trades Councils. Lionel came from a well-known London East End Communist family, his brother Julius (universally known as "Julie") being Secretary of the London Trades Council for many years. He had volunteered for the International Brigade during the Spanish Civil War but had been captured and imprisoned by the fascists almost as soon as he crossed the Pyrenees. Even when in prison he helped to organise his fellow prisoners in making things as difficult as possible for his captors. When I first met him in 1947, Lionel was the Nottingham Area Secretary of the Communist Party and on the District Committee. A master of procedure, he was impatient with incompetents and had the reputation of being a difficult bloke to be opposed to – he could wreck any meeting or conference with usually well-founded "points of order." But his main ire was directed against the class enemy, and he has never wavered in his devotion to the cause of working-class emancipation. Lionel died after a long illness soon after these lines were penned.

Of the many other comrades worthy of mention, Ernie Cant stands out. Born in 1891, Ernie was a speaker and lecturer in the socialist movement when a teenager and took part in the negotiations that led to the formation of the Communist Party in 1920. He was one of the twelve Communist leaders arrested before the General Strike in 1926. Ernie was always ready with a good story – often directed against himself. He attended several meetings of the Comintern, and once related how, after a fraternal "booze-up" with some of the other delegates, he woke up the next morning in bed naked with one of the German women delegates. "What irked me," said Ernie, "was that I couldn't remember anything that took place!" When the party was reorganised in the early 1930's, Ernie was removed as London Organiser, and he used to tell the story of how the congress ended with the singing of the "Internationale," but when delegates came to the words, "Now at last ends the age of cant" the congress broke down in laughter. He could never come to terms with the later denunciation of Stalin, who he had met several times and whose personality, as he experienced it, didn't square with the image presented by the denouncers. No doubt this was influenced by an incident when, according to Ernie, Joe had directly intervened to help him at a difficult time. After having to give up his job as London Organiser, he couldn't find work – he was too well known as an agitator. Around about this time, Stalin asked William Gallacher what had happened to the comrades who had been removed from their full-time positions in the party, and when Willy said he didn't know, Stalin was highly critical. "They are still comrades," he said, "and the party should help." As a result, Ernie became a manager for R.O.P. (Russian Oil Products). Later, he became a respected and popular figure in the Nottingham labour movement, and for some years was on the Board of the Co-operative Society. He was ninety one when he died in 1982 and again, I was privileged to give the funeral oration. Typical of him, he didn't want the party to spend anything on a funeral, a request I am afraid we didn't accede to, and in a letter he gave me to be opened after his death he wrote, "I hope, Fred, that throughout my life I have helped to make the world a happier place for some people." This, Ernie Cant certainly did.

However, it was coal mining that more and more came to occupy my attention. Ninety eight thousand were employed in the four mining areas of the East Midlands – Nottinghamshire, North Derbyshire (usually called Derbyshire), South Derbyshire and Leicestershire. It was technically the most advanced and most profitable coalfield in Britain, but as far as the miners were concerned Notts had a somewhat notorious history. It was the home of Spencerism, the scab union that emerged after the defeat of the miners in the 1926 lockout. With the connivance of the coalowners, Labour M.P. George Spencer set up an "independent industrial trade union" in opposition to the Notts Miners' Association (N.M.A.), which was affiliated to the Miners' Federation. Because of the favourable geological conditions and the high profits arising from this, the Notts coalowners had been able to offer special concessions to their workers if they broke away from the miners in the rest of Britain. But the concessions were quickly eroded once the miners' power to resist had been weakened. There followed years of bitter struggle. The majority of the Notts miners never accepted the Spencer union, but membership of the N.M.A. had to be kept secret for fear of victimisation – eight hundred were victimised at Welbeck colliery. N.M.A. branches had to meet in secret and their members were always under threat from informers. Known militants were sacked, but they remained active keeping the union going. At times there was virtually a reign of terror conducted against the N.M.A. Yet, with outstanding tenacity and great personal sacrifice, the struggle against the scab union was maintained and gradually built up. The climax was reached in 1936 at the pit and village of Harworth, in the north of the county. Sparked off by the sacking of twenty five N.M.A. members, nine hundred men at the pit came out on strike.

After a demonstration in the village, eleven of the strike leaders were arrested on a charge of "incitement to riot." Chief among them was Mick Kane, the chairman of the N.M.A. branch and a foundation member of the Communist Party. Mick was sentenced to two years' imprisonment, which he spent in Lincoln prison.

But the back of Spencerism had been broken. After a coalfield ballot, conducted by the T.U.C., resulted in an overwhelming vote in favour of the N.M.A., Prime Minister Stanley Baldwin was forced to initiate talks to achieve unity. The resultant agreement restored the N.M.A. and the M.F.G.B. as the sole union recognised by the employers. Yet, it caused much bitterness among those who had suffered in the struggle and who found it extremely difficult to accept the compromise, including many Communists. The party produced a pamphlet, "Notts United," putting the case for unity. For a limited period, all the Spencer union officers kept their positions but within the N.M.A., and Spencer himself became a member of the Executive Committee of the Miners' Federation. These were indeed bitter pills to swallow, but, as Arthur Horner said at the time, they were temporary compromises in order to achieve a much bigger prize – the unity of all mineworkers.

There was an international campaign to release Mick Kane, and he regained his freedom after having served fourteen months. Of him, Page Arnot, the official historian of the miners' union wrote: The freedom of organisation of miners in Nottinghamshire had been secured. But in the case of Mick Kane, words like those uttered to the Apostle Paul could have been applied: "At a heavy price obtained I this freedom."

I shall be writing more about Mick, a truly wonderful comrade who became a dear friend of mine. He helped to initiate the process that, in form at least, ended the federal structure of the miners' organisation and replaced it by one union – the N.U.M. This was achieved at a special conference in Nottingham on 14th August 1944.

During the war coal was vital: it was needed to produce the energy required for arms production. Yet in the first years wages remained low compared with other industries, and there was an acute shortage of manpower.

The unwillingness of the coalowners to spend money on technical developments had left the industry in a sorry state. Eventually, even such a long- standing friend of the coalowners as Churchill was forced to recognise that the output required could only be achieved if the mines were placed under full government control. The union was represented on the

283

national and regional advisory boards, and pit consultative committees were set up at every colliery. This machinery continued up to nationalisation in 1947.

Nationalisation was greeted with enormous enthusiasm by the miners who saw it as the fulfilment of a long dream. Alas, it was not long before disillusionment set in as it dawned on them that they still had no say, let alone control, in the running of the pits where they worked. The old worker-employer relationship had not ended, although the struggle to improve wages and conditions was now with the National Coal Board and not with private owners. Profits were still the main concern. The huge compensation payments to the old private owners and the interest on loans needed to modernise the industry placed a crippling burden on the miners. Ironically, the value of the shares of the former private coalowning companies was higher after nationalisation than they were before.

The contribution and the sacrifices made by Communists and other militants in the Nottinghamshire coalfield who fought against Spencerism and for a united miners' union is, in my opinion, very much underestimated in the many books and articles written about the mineworkers of this period; regrettably, this includes some works written by progressives and even by one or two academic Marxists who seem not to have troubled to include Notts in their source material. The Notts miners had the toughest fight of any body of miners in Britain. They and their families were persecuted, victimised and hounded, in a manner reminiscent of the treatment endured by the early trade union pioneers of the 19th century. They should be remembered and honoured. I am proud to have known so many of them, and welcome this opportunity to place on record a small part of the contribution some of them made to the cause of working-class emancipation. Alas, in the confines of these memoirs, I can only deal with those who played a major leadership role in the struggle of the miners. It isn't a diversion. They are very much part of the history of the time I'm writing about.

Mick Kane has already come into this narrative. He always protested that he was not a foundation member of the Communist Party because he joined a year after it was formed in 1920. For the rest of us this was near enough, but his concern at not claiming any kudos he was not entitled to was very typical of him. For a working-class hero he was a very modest man, a refreshing contrast to so many trade union and political leaders I have known who have been addicted to wallowing in self-importance and whose often justified progressive reputations have been sullied by their embarrassing egocentricity. The Kanes were a remarkable family of rebels, ten in all, who emigrated from Ireland to Scotland in 1912. Young though they were, the four boys soon became known as militants in the West Lothian coalfield, and for leading a successful eleven-week strike of four hundred men Mick was barred from all Scottish pits. The family moved first to Yorkshire and then to Derbyshire. Again he was victimised by the coalowners, who evicted him and the family from the 'tied' house they occupied. Mick then led his own and eleven other families to the Chesterfield workhouse, where they lived for three months. Mick's younger brother, John ("Jock"), also a Communist, became a much-loved leader of the Yorkshire miners.

I had, of course, heard of Mick Kane as far back as the 1930's, and had taken part in a small way in the campaign to get him released from prison; but our first meeting was in 1947, when we were both members of the Party's East Midland District Committee. He was then secretary of our Staveley branch. My responsibility for mining threw us together a great deal and he went out of his way to help me all he could. He was totally dedicated to the working class, the miners and the Party, but apart from his hatred of capitalism and all injustice, he was a most gentle man who lived simply and was always prepared to help anyone in need. Again, unlike many who rise to higher positions in the movement, no task was ever too menial for him if it helped the movement, and he never asked others to do what he was not prepared to do himself. Even when he became a full-time official of the Derbyshire Area of the N.U.M., he still organised sales of the *Daily Worker*, collecting the papers from the newsagent, distributing them to sellers and taking part in selling them. He did this until ill health, brought on by his work in the pits, prevented him continuing. Before he died, Mick gave me his personal papers, documents and photographs to look after, including the hundreds of cards and letters sent to him from all over the world when he was in prison. Although these have been used by students, one day I hope they will be the basis of a fuller appreciation of a man who, as I said at his memorial meeting, is the finest example of a working-class fighter and a socialist revolutionary. Mick never married, but he was looked after by his devoted sister, Bridget, another wonderful character and the matriarch of the Kane clan, who died in June 1996 when approaching her 102nd birthday. Right to the end she had an alertness and political perspicacity that would put many youngsters to shame.

Another outstanding immigrant to the coalfield was Dai Ley. As a youngster working in a South Wales pit, Dai was victimised after the 1921 strike and moved to Notts two years later. He soon became a union branch official but was blacklisted for the second time after the defeat of the miners in 1926. However, when feelings cooled he started work again at Pleasley pit, only to be thrown on the dole in the 1930 depression. He threw himself into the struggles of the unemployed, becoming Notts and Derbyshire District Secretary and a National Executive member of the N.U.W.M. He took part in every national hunger march of that decade. Like Mick Kane, Dai was a foundation member of the Communist Party, and in 1937 was elected Communist councillor in Kirkby-in-Ashfield. While working in the building industry during the war he recruited three thousand workers into the T.G.W.U., for which he was awarded the union's Gold Medal.

He went back to the pits in 1943, and was soon elected checkweighman in a spectacular victory over fifteen opponents, and when he himself was not working at the particular pit. Two years later he was on the Executive Committee of the Notts Area. He received the highest accolade from his fellow miners when he was elected, first Financial Secretary and then Area Chairman – a lone Communist working with three right-wing officials. He was not the first Communist to be in this position; for many years Harry Straw had been a miners' agent, but unlike Dai, Harry was not very well-known as a Communist and played little part in party activities. For many years Dai was a member of the party's District Committee.

Everyone knew that there was corruption in the Notts miners' union, but its extent could only be surmised. When Dai became Financial Secretary he was appalled to discover its magnitude. This was a carry-over from the Spencer era. In order to buy off the union leaders, the old private coalowners had set up a fund, making contributions to it based on tonnage, which was administered by their representatives and full-time union officials. The entire set-up was surrounded in mystery. The members of the union itself had no say whatsoever in how the money was spent – indeed, Area Council delegates were not even allowed to ask questions about it. Officially, it was called the Allocation Fund, to be used for some vague 'special purposes;' but it was more popularly know as the "didl'um fund," and the 'special purposes' included giving sizeable 'perks' to the officials. When the mines were nationalised, the Coal Board took over from the old coalowners and the backhanders continued.

Direct cash bribery was suspected but couldn't be proved. Certainly, a multitude of more devious methods were used to benefit the officials. Generous additional payments were made for meetings with Coal Board officials, even though they were held in office hours. Hotel expenses were lavish, first-class fares paid for travelling second class, gardeners were supplied and furniture bought for their private houses, whisky and cigars supplied regularly. When it couldn't be hidden, the explanations were as unconvincing as they were devious.

Unfortunately, the canker had penetrated downwards throughout the union. Quite deliberately, though not so extensively, many of the branch officials were indirectly benefiting from the corrupt set-up. Thus it was that when Dai, soon after being elected Financial Secretary, called at the Party's District Office to tell Mick Jenkins and me the whole gruesome story of what he had unravelled, and indicated that he was planning to publicly blow the gaff, we had to caution him to hold his horses. Neither he nor the Party was in a strong enough position to launch such a head-on attack. The union branches, Area Council and members had to be won to fight the corruption.

Although Dai was well versed in socialist theory, he was also, like Mick Kane, tempered in the school of struggle, particularly direct action. They could well hold their own in any formal debate, but preferred discussions with their fellow workers at the pit-face or the union branch. They were certainly much more at home on the picket line than in an office. In later years, when Dai became President of the Notts N.U.M., he had the job of writing a foreword to the printed Area Committee Minutes that went out to the branches every month. Dai disliked the task, so soon after every Area Committee meeting my phone would ring and Dai's slow Welsh voice would say, "Fred, can you come up?" I would catch a bus to the miners' headquarters at Basford, and would write the foreword, which he would approve. I don't think the other officials, all dedicated right-wingers, nor the Area Council, ever suspected that the words of wisdom that went out under their auspices every month were written by the Communist Party's District Organiser!

The first Communist Party official I met when I came to the East Midlands in 1947 was Les Ellis. He came from a family of miners. His father and three sons all took part in the 1926 lockout, which led to Les being blacklisted from Notts pits, so he had to take whatever other jobs were around, including window-cleaning. He was elected Vice-President of the Bassetlaw Divisional Labour Party and a director of the Hucknall

Co-op, and he became very much involved in working-class education, lecturing for the National Council of Labour Colleges. It was in this period that he met the future leader of the Labour Party, Hugh Gaitskell. Margaret Cole has recalled Gaitskell telling her and her husband of the great importance to his political development of the year he spent teaching at Nottingham University, where, for the first time he met "working members of the working class" and miners in particular. "Up to that time he had scarcely set eyes, effectively, on an authentic working man." He was appalled to discover the conditions miners worked under. Gaitskell was later to acknowledge the help he received from Les Ellis. In 1934 Les joined the Communist Party, following his brother Frank who was already an active member. Their mother had joined in 1929. Les was very much involved in the struggle for peace, attending the World Peace Conference in Brussels in 1936.

When the East Midlands District of the Communist Party was formed in 1940, he became its first District Secretary until he was called up into the army. He was demobbed in 1946 with the rank of Warrant Officer and in that year stood as a Communist candidate in the local elections. Ninety four of the men in his unit – seventy five per cent of the total personnel – signed a statement "commending him to the people of Hucknall" for his ability and fearlessness.

In 1947 he went back into the pits. He scorned a surface job and insisted on working at the coalface, a courageous decision considering that he was forty five and had been out of mining for over twenty years. He later confessed to me that that first month hewing coal at Linby was physically the toughest experience of his life, and that there were times when he didn't think he could continue. But there was method in his decision. Face-workers were the elite among miners, and at that time it was difficult to get anywhere in the union if one was employed on the surface. And Les had plans involving the union. It wasn't long before his fellow workers made him checkweighman, and in 1951 he was elected to be a full-time agent for the Notts miners, replacing Dai Ley, who had recently died. In the final ballot (it was the single transferable vote system) he received 13,195 votes, winning over twenty five other candidates.

Les Ellis stood head and shoulders above the other officials in ability, understanding and forcefulness of personality. He was an exceptionally imposing character, a fine speaker and always decisive in an argument. His faith in his class was uncompromising and he was an outstanding tactician in its struggles. Much to the chagrin of the right wing, it wasn't long before he was elected to the National Executive of the N.U.M. However, in the atmosphere of the Cold War and anti-Communist hysteria, the Notts right wing succeeding in getting through the Area Council a resolution banning Communists from holding any of the three top Area positions in the union. It was an occasion when I seriously thought that God had moved to our side. The leading anti-Communist, an official, moved the resolution and then went to the toilet – where he dropped dead! Unfortunately, no heed was taken of this obvious sign. For many years, Les was Chairman of the Party's District Committee and on its National Executive Committee, but it was to his beloved miners that he was most devoted. Whatever subject the Party leadership discussed, be it the situation in Timbuktu, women or culture, Les always managed to weave the problems of the British coal industry into his N.E.C. reports to the District Committee! The party benefited in another respect: the regular substantial contribution he made to its funds from his very first week as a miners' agent – certainly the highest proportion of a salary I have ever known a trade union official make to the party. At the 1950 General Election, when I was standing as Communist candidate in North West Leicester, Les stood in Mansfield.

It is no disrespect to Les to say that he was more respected and admired than he was popular. It seems a contradiction, but the public figure who never held back from a fight when workers' interests were concerned was, privately, a somewhat retiring man who didn't make personal friends easily. Outside his family, Kath and I were probably as close to him as any; he used to call at our home at Basford on Sunday mornings for a chat, often about personal matters. We didn't know his first wife, who had died some years before and to whom he was obviously deeply devoted, but on one Sunday morning he told us he was thinking of marrying again. This second marriage proved disastrous and ended in divorce. He wed a third time, but this time it was more a marriage of convenience for both partners, and it turned out very well.

Les was only sixty three when he died. Typical of him, soon after going into hospital he persuaded another patient in his ward to take the *Daily Worker*. I saw him the day before he died and he obviously knew that the end was not far off. He delivered a little lecture from his bed, enjoining me to pay special attention to the young miners who were coming forward in the party and the movement, naming them and stressing that these were cadres the miners and the working class badly needed. His loss was a blow to me, but, more important, it was a loss for the miners, for the working class and for the Communist Party. Often misunderstood and underestimated, even by some Communist miners' leaders outside of the East Midlands, Les Ellis towered above most trade union officials, including progressives. His dedication to his class and his cause could not be surpassed.

Frank Ellis joined the Y.C.L. as a teenager in 1933, and moved from there into the party. In both organisations he was most active, and when the call was made for volunteers to defend the Spanish Republic, he joined the International Brigade. He was captured, and imprisoned in a Franco jail. During World War II, Frank was a machine-gunner and rose to the rank of Captain in the famous First Airborne Division. He and his men were dropped by glider at the ill-fated battle of Arnhem. He served later in Burma. After the war he, like Les, went to work at Linby, which was soon to be the centre of resistance to the right wing and the still strong Spencerite influences in the county. Frank became one of the most popular rank-and-file leaders in the Notts coalfield, with a knowledge of the industry that was arguably better than Les's. He was chief author of the *Linby Manifesto*, which became the programme of the left in the coalfield for many years. There was great pressure for him to stand for full-time office in the union, and his standing was such that he could have won any election; but he preferred to stay at the pit-face and be a rank-and-file leader. Later, he did stand, but by then the anti-communism of the Cold War had made the position of communists more difficult.

Some time after Les had established himself at Linby and, together with Frank, had built a strong and influential party pit branch there, he said to me one day, "We've a promising youngster at the pit and I've per-suaded him to join the party." The "youngster" was Joe Whelan, who was to become the most charismatic and popular leader the Notts miners have produced – as well as a close friend. Joe's roots were obvious as soon as he opened his mouth. He was born in 1925 at Dun Laoghaire, near Dublin, and his childhood was extremely harsh. He once described to me how his mother used to make clothes for the lads out of flour bags and how he and the other children would scour the markets for cast away fruit and vegetables. This is why James Plunkett's graphic novel, *Strumpet City* was a bible of his, for although it deals with a slightly earlier period, it evoked memories of the Dublin he had known as a child.

During the war, at the age of 18, he came across the water and joined the R.A.F. He met Ethel, a Hucknall girl, they married and settled down in the Notts coalfield. There was an acute shortage of coal, so there was no problem in getting a job at Linby. Ably tutored by Les Ellis, in a year or so he became branch secretary. He moved upwards and in time become a full-time Area Agent, a member of the National Executive Committee of the N.U.M. and eventually Area General Secretary. The election for Area Agent was notorious for the scurrilous campaign against him by the right wing of the Labour Party. Before voting day, every pit was flooded with two leaflets, neither with a publisher's imprint. One leaflet read, "Stop the Notts Area being controlled by Communists. Keep Whelan out." The other gave the names of the candidates who were members of the Labour Party and read, "Vote for a Labour candidate. Keep the Communists out." We soon found out who was responsible for this blatant interference in a union election. Frank Ellis was friendly with the printer who did the leaflets, and he had no compunction about revealing that the order and payment came from the East Midlands Regional Secretary of the Labour Party. It made Joe's victory all the more significant for there wasn't a miner who voted for him who didn't know he was choosing a Communist.

Joe was very much an all-round character and enjoyed playing the guitar and singing – especially Irish songs. He never forgot his roots and was an active member of the Connolly Association – indeed, he started the Nottingham Branch and always had copies of the *Irish Democrat* available. Fulfilling the role of "father confessor" was not always easy for me and he gave me quite a few headaches over the years, but this fades into insignificance compared with the reward reaped by our friendship and the very many enjoyable evenings I recall spending with him and Ethel at their N.U.M. house at Ravenshead. Needless to say, he was a committed Communist and served on the party's District Committee.

Up until the 1950's, the Derbyshire Area of the N.U.M. was also very much under right-wing influence, but there were two outstanding Communists among the full-time officials. Mick Kane was one, and the other was Bert Wynn, who was later to become the Area Secretary. Bert had been victimised after the 1926 miners' lockout and after a spell as a Labour County Councillor, joined the Communist Party. Upon becoming union secretary, he set himself the aim of transforming the political stance of the union in Derbyshire, and through this of influencing the situation in the rest of the labour movement. Bert saw the need to help and train young union activists who were also committed socialists to become the future leaders of the miners and the Labour Party in the area. The fact that North Derbyshire was to become a bastion of the left, with such outstanding M.P.'s as Tom Swain, Dennis Skinner, Tony Benn and Harry Barnes is largely the result of the foundation laid by Bert, Mick Kane and their close colleagues during those years. He was particularly concerned with working-class education and worked with Sheffield University in organising schools and classes for miners. Bert followed Les Ellis as Chairman of the Communist Party's District Committee but left the party after the events in Hungary in 1956. He did not, however, turn anti-Communist, as did so many, nor did he ever make any public criticism of the party, but continued to work closely with it. My friendship with Bert continued, and we would regularly meet and exchange views on mining and the political situation. Presumably, recognising my organising capabilities, he asked me to organise an important broad peace conference in Derbyshire under the auspices of the N.U.M. – which proved to be highly successful. Harry Wynn, his son, was for many years the secretary of the party's Chesterfield branch. When Bert died in 1966 a solid basis had been laid for another left-winger, Peter Heathfield, to step into his shoes.

One of Bert's failures, and the failure of the left in the political field, was Eric (now Lord) Varley. It didn't seem so at the time. Eric was a youngster working at the mining area workshops, and showed great promise. His views were very much on the left and he attended several meetings of the Y.C.L. After one discussion I had with him, he agreed to seriously consider joining the Party or the League. Subsequently, he signified his intentions to do so to his dad, a well-respected N.U.M. member, who told Mick Kane what then happened. Apparently, Eric mentioned it to Bert Wynn, and Bert, now in the Labour Party, stepped in to forestall the move. He told Eric of the plans he had for North Derbyshire and held out the carrot that he could well become a miners' M.P. Needless to say, Eric took the bait. When George Benson, who for twenty five years had misrepresented Chesterfield in Parliament, announced he was retiring, the miners put Eric forward as prospective Labour candidate for the 1964 General Election. It was by no means a foregone conclusion that he would be chosen, for the Chesterfield Labour Party was at this time not very progressive and there were three other nominees. Every obstacle was put in his way, and it was only because of a well-organised campaign by the miners, helped by the A.E.U. – for Eric was a member of both unions – that he was finally chosen. As A.E.U. members, Bas Barker and I – but particularly Bas, who was President of the union's district committee – threw our weight behind the campaign to get Eric accepted. We did so because he espoused left policies, even though it soon become apparent that he had no real ability and was not a fighter.

Varley did, indeed, prove to be a great disappointment. Within weeks of being elected his voice changed. He lost his Derbyshire accent and spoke as if he had pebbles in his mouth – the result, it was rumoured, of elocution lessons. He became one of Harold Wilson's poodles and was rewarded with ministerial positions. In exasperation, I once asked him at my trade union branch meeting whether there was any issue on which he would publicly oppose Wilson. "Yes," he replied, "on joining the Common Market." This was soon to be put to the test in the referendum on Britain's entry, when the government urged people to vote "yes." There was not a peep out of Eric during the entire campaign period, nor did he play any part in the effective campaign we conducted locally for a "no" vote. Then, on the eve of the poll, at a public meeting in Chesterfield's Market Hall which he couldn't very well avoid attending, and when it was too late for him to influence the vote, he expressed some conditional doubts about Britain joining. The reason for his reticence soon revealed itself: the next morning Wilson announced that Eric was to replace Tony Benn as Minister of Industry. Eric must have known about this, of course, but he never mentioned it to Bas or me when we went for a drink in the "Yellow Lion" after the public meeting. In 1984 he resigned as M.P. and become Chairman of the Coalite Chemical Group, the Bolsover-based company that owned most of the Falkland Islands. He allowed his membership of the Labour Party to lapse but rejoined and subsequently was awarded a peerage. He has never played any active part in the local labour movement since he resigned as M.P. – not even in the subsequent bye-election when Tony Benn was elected his successor.

There was another fight over who was to represent the North-East Derbyshire constituency. The National Executive of the Labour Party wanted Morgan Phillips, the party's General Secretary, and brought all the pressure it could locally to get him selected, but it proved no match for the miners and Bert Wynn. Tom Swain, an active member of the N.U.M. was chosen and became a very popular M.P. who kept his roots firmly among the workers. The constituency is now ably represented by Harry Barnes.

In the post-war years coal was undisputed King. Those growing up in the period after the decimation of the industry by the Tories may find it difficult to imagine what coal meant to the nation. It was Britain's largest industry, employing around 700,000 men – and even this fell far short of what was required. More important, not only was it the basis of the power produced to heat and light homes, but it was essential to keep the rest of industry going. Without a thriving coal industry, factories would grind to a halt, trains would stop running and people would shiver in their homes. This was demonstrated during the freeze-up of 1947 and was to be proved again in 1972. There was an intense drive to recruit youngsters to take up mining as a career and to increase the productivity of every pit.

It was understandable, therefore, that the Communist Party gave a great deal of attention to the coal industry. There were other reasons. The militancy, solidarity and class feeling of the miners were legendary, and they had long been rightly recognised as being in the leadership of the organised working class. Miners also had a strong socialist tradition, and this was reflected in the fact that the Party was strongest in the mining areas, particularly South Wales and Scotland. There was a closer affinity between the Communist Party and mineworkers than existed in any other industry. The welding together of the Party's Marxist ideology and the expert knowledge and experience of hundreds of class-conscious miners, many holding leading positions in the union at all levels, put the Party in a unique position when it came to working out correct policies on mining and influencing the struggles of the miners. N.U.M. General Secretary, Arthur Horner, the Scottish Miners' leader, Abe Moffatt, and the Secretary of the Welsh miners, Will Paynter, were all on the Party's National Executive Committee. Such was the importance attached to mining, that Harry Pollitt for some time took on personal responsibility for the Party's work in relation to the industry.

It must have been in 1952 that Les Ellis and I attended a meeting at King Street (the Communist Party head office) to take part in a discussion to define our Party's policy regarding the urgent problems then facing the industry. Leading mining comrades were there from all over Britain. Harry Pollitt chaired the meeting and Arthur Horner made the opening statement. The acute shortage of coal had continued after the war and had intensified the problems facing the Labour government in carrying out its programme of post-war reconstruction.

The N.U.M. was fully behind the drive for increased production, and the Communist Party decided to continue to support it. However, the wage restraint policy of the government was a major obstacle, both in maximising production and in recruiting youngsters to work in the pits. Compulsory arbitration was an obstacle to the development of the struggle to improve wages and conditions.

One of the topics that was foremost in the discussion at the meeting was how to strengthen the unity of the miners. When the N.U.M. was formed, it preserved almost intact the old area structure of the Federation; indeed, each area was virtually an autonomous union with its own set of rules and its own organisation. It was intended that eventually these would be superseded by one national union structure. In fact, this was never really achieved, something that the miners were to pay dearly for in the future. At the time, a major obstacle was the pay structure in the industry. There was a multitude of grades and big discrepancies between wages in coalfields like South Wales and Scotland, where geological conditions were bad, and areas like Notts, Yorkshire and Derbyshire where coal was relatively easier to extract. There were also historical differences. In the case of Notts there. was the heritage of Spencerist ideas and attitudes still prevailing.

These differences inhibited the development of any national struggle, particularly around wages. While basic rates were negotiated nationally, more important in some areas were what miners could win additionally on their own. So while recognising the need for a continuous fight to preserve the industry and improve wages and conditions in all coalfields, stress was laid on creating a national wages structure that would place the emphasis on national negotiations and weld the areas more firmly together.

A National Day Wage Agreement was eventually signed in 1953. Will Paynter was General Secretary of the N.U.M., and he said later that he regarded it as one of the finest achievements of his years in office. It was a tough fight bringing it about, and it was thanks above all to the leadership given by Communists. We had a particularly hard fight in Notts and Derbyshire, because it meant persuading the miners in these areas to accept smaller pay increases than their fellow-workers in other areas until such time as wage rates throughout the country were equalised. The right wing were not slow to play upon sectional feelings, accusing Communists of holding back the wages of miners in the East Midlands' coalfields.

There was another factor separating the miners of Notts and Derbyshire from the rest of the country. Technical changes were taking place at an accelerating pace. Revolutionary new coal-cutting machinery was being introduced, and it was the Notts coalfield that was being used most as the hot-house for these developments. This meant that our comrades were faced with an unprecedented set of problems in negotiating piece-work rates, safety provisions and conditions at the mechanised pits. The agreements reached in Notts eventually became the model for the industry as a whole.

The policy of the party in different industries was always worked out by comrades who actually worked in the particular industry. They then "advised" the Executive or District Committees; surprisingly enough, they were called Advisory Committees. We had a powerful Mining Advisory in the East Midlands, with about twenty comrades from Notts, Derbyshire and Leicestershire – all comrades who had real mass influence in the pits and the unions from branch to area level and could bring forward the views of comrades not on the committee. Often there were long and sharp debates before a policy was agreed, but once a decision had been reached all were expected to fight for it. Indeed, it was only through such discussion that consensus and conviction could be achieved. Working in this organised, basically democratic and collective manner is one of the reasons the party has always been able to exert an influence far greater than its membership would seem to justify. This simple explanation is something our enemies have never been able to accept and is why they have had to explain our influence by inventing conspiracy theories that portray a sinister, ruthless leadership deciding policy in secret and imposing an unquestioning discipline on the rank and file. In all my many years working as a Communist in or connected with industry I cannot recall a single instance of a policy relating to a particular industry being "imposed" on an advisory committee against the opinion of the majority of comrades working in it.

36. STALIN, KHRUSHCHEV AND HUNGARY

In March 1953 Joseph Stalin died. "Stalin, the Architect of Socialism is Dead," was the banner headline in the *Daily Worker*. It is difficult to convey to those who have come into the communist movement since, what a void was created by his death. My generation had venerated Stalin as the man who triumphed against all odds to establish the world's first socialist state. The Five Year Plans, which he started, lifted an abysmally backward country into a twentieth century industrial nation. We correctly saw him as contributing far more than Churchill, Roosevelt or anyone else, to the victory over Nazism. Indeed, in that struggle, Stalin's name had inspired millions who were not Communists. "Tanks (or planes, or coal) for Joe!" were popular slogans in factories and pits during the war. But we also felt that the world had lost a Marxist theoretician, a worthy successor to Marx, Engels and Lenin. We had been brought up studying his Foundations of Leninism, A Short History of the C.P.S.U. and his other shorter works. Every pronouncement he made was the subject of study. He had a simple style of writing, often with the liberal use of anecdotes, similes and metaphors which made him easier to read than the other classical Marxist writers. This quality later led to him being denigrated by some of his erstwhile uncritical academic devotees; they belatedly discovered that he had in fact been a "mere populariser." Be that as it may, he certainly introduced many youngsters to Marxism.

A greater shock was to come. Six months after Stalin's death, following a short internal struggle in the leadership of the C.P.S.U., Nikita Khrushchev became First Secretary of the party and adopted a relatively more open and innovative style of leadership. In February 1956, at the Twentieth Congress of the CPSU, he made his famous speech denouncing Stalin as a megalomaniac who had ruled by terror and who had been responsible for the deaths of countless numbers of people, including loyal and devoted members of the Communist Party. These included many old Bolsheviks who had worked alongside Lenin in the revolution.

I first read the speech in the leaked version that appeared in *The Observer*, but I had little doubt that the report was substantially true. This was the general feeling, although there were some comrades who did not believe it, or thought it was grossly exaggerated, reflecting a new power struggle. It caused intellectual turmoil among comrades and raised sharply a number of uncomfortable questions. How could it have happened. What had the C.P.S.U. been doing to allow it to happen. Where was democratic centralism. Did it mean that our estimate of Soviet society was wrong. What were the implications for Communists in other countries, including ourselves. It was not difficult to rationalise the stress on centralism since the revolution. For sixty years the Soviet Union had faced a desperate situation – the civil war and wars of intervention, the need for rapid industrialisation and vast agricultural expansion, and then the threat of invasion, followed by a devastating war, and the massive task of reconstruction afterwards against the background of the Cold War and the nuclear threat. It was always a race against time and firm leadership and discipline was essential. We in Britain experienced something of the need for this when we were faced with invasion during the war – including the cult of personality around Churchill. The Soviet Union had been in a comparable situation for the whole of its existence. But these were not satisfactory answers to all the questions posed.

Most of us could honestly say that we were not aware of the lack of inner-party democracy and collective leadership in the Soviet Communist Party or Soviet society. Uncomfortable though some of us may have felt at the excessive adulation of Stalin, we explained it away by referring to the Russian tradition and the Soviet people's recognition of his brilliant leadership and what he had achieved. We certainly knew nothing of the crimes he was responsible for. The trials in the 1930's of honoured comrades of Lenin, like Bukharin, Kamanev, Radek and Zinoviev, had been hard to come to terms with. It seemed quite bizarre that they were "agents of imperialism" and "fascist collaborators," but we accepted that men of such proven courage would not have pleaded guilty of treason in open court had they not indeed been culpable. Confirming this belief were the reports of eminent non-communist western observers at the trials who declared they were convinced that the accused were speaking the truth. Indeed, I had been in the Labour Party during the first trials and found an acceptance of their validity even among critics of the Communist Party. We did not suspect that the evidence against them had been fabricated and that they had pleaded guilty in order, as they saw it, to protect the Soviet system they had helped create. Some of them believed that Stalin was not involved in their prosecution.

What dominated our attitude was the enormous progress the Soviet Union had made since the revolution, emerging from extreme backwardness to becoming a super-power. As I heard Willie Gallacher say at many of his public meetings, "they had to pull themselves up by their boot laces" with no help, indeed, facing unremitting hostility and sabotage from the surrounding capitalist countries. They then had to bear the main burden of defeating the greatest military power on earth. From 1919, when the famous American writer, Lincoln Steffens proclaimed, "I have seen the future, and it works," through a long line of distinguished investigators like Bernard Shaw, Sidney and Beatrice Webb, the Dean of Canterbury, and hundreds of trade union delegations which included avowed right-wingers, there had been unstinting testimony to the progress being made, particularly in the fields of grass-roots democracy, social benefits and economic advance.

There was no rich, exploiting, employing class, no unemployment, and the elderly, sick and infirm were cared for. Trade union delegations from capitalist countries waxed lyrical about the extent of workers' control at workplace level. The care of children and education was a priority. Hitherto oppressed nationalities had been liberated. This was proof that socialism worked. It was also, as we saw it, a testimony to Stalin's leadership. Our attitude was reinforced by the hysterical anti-Sovietism of the capitalist media and the trotskyists.

We communists had every right to share in the pride over what was accomplished, and I certainly do not in any way apologise for my whole-hearted, even uncritical, support of the Soviet Union over the previous twenty years. As a socialist living in a capitalist country, I saw it as my prime duty to defend the first workers' state against the relentless criticisms and propaganda of a capitalism hell-bent on destroying it. I accepted that there were weaknesses and that mistakes were made, but the ones we knew about paled into insignificance compared with the achievements, and the historical importance of a new socialist society in the process of being created.

Yet, the great positive achievements could not excuse or justify the rise of a personal dictator with uncontrolled power and the evils that stemmed from that power. Nor did the fact that he was revered by millions of Soviet men and women, many of whom met death in the war with the name of Stalin on their lips. Something had gone badly wrong with the way the party operated and the way socialist society was run. It was deeper, much deeper than Stalin. It was not good enough to put it all down to the "cult of the individual" – the phrase coined by Khrushchev and the C.P.S.U. As the leader of the Italian Communist Party, Palmiro Togliatti, stated at the time, "At one time, all that was good was due to the superhuman positive qualities of one man; now all that is bad is attributed to him. Both judgements are un-Marxist." And whilst we Communists outside of the Soviet Union can protest that we knew nothing of what was happening, can we so easily rid ourselves of any share of the blame. I agree with Joe Slovo, General Secretary of the South African Communist Party, who later, in his autobiography, wrote:

"But if we throw our first stones at these sinners only (the other one was Mao Tse-tung), we are ignoring an enquiry of a social process of which they must have been instruments. By attributing to these two leaders a monopoly of sin, we are also perpetuating cultism. No cult (whether of the personality or otherwise) has ever left its mark on history without the blind devotion of congregations of worshippers. We all share in the guilt

299

and the starting-point of any assessment must be ourselves."

We were also to learn that for some time serious divisions persisted in the Central Committee of the C.P.S.U. Molotov, who for many years had been Soviet Foreign Minister, Malenkov, who had followed Stalin as General Secretary and Kaganovitch were the central figures in a move to dismiss Khrushchev. An emergency meeting of the Central Committee rejected the motion and, instead, took measures against the dissidents. An interesting feature about this event was that it must have been the last time that the C.P.S.U. went to some pains to inform the British Communist Party (presumably along with C.P.'s in other countries) of a crucial development in advance of the news being released to the world press. An extended meeting of our Executive Committee, which I attended along with Mick Jenkins, was called to hear a statement read out by John Gollan. This was followed by District Committee meetings, and then by special branch meetings. At our District Committee meeting I upset Mick and other comrades by abstaining on a vote expressing support for the action of the C.P.S.U. I did so, not because I supported Molotov and Company, but because I felt we had insufficient information to pass judgement.

The discussion about the role of Stalin and the revelations of his crimes and conduct was to go on for many years – indeed is still going on – but I want now to deal with their immediate impact on the British party, particularly in the fields where I was directly involved.

The response of the C.P.G.B. was to express shock at what had been disclosed and to "welcome the fact that errors, abuses and injustices have been so fearlessly laid bare by the present leadership of the C.P.S.U. We see this as a demonstration of Communist honesty and integrity. "The statement went on to say that, "on the basis of false information we, in all good faith, made a number of mistakes . . . "

Membership meetings were held throughout the country. At a packed meeting in Nottingham, Palme Dutt received a stormy reception, largely because he appeared to gloss over Stalin's crimes and because *Labour Monthly*, which he edited, had done the same. The main emphasis of the criticisms was on the lack of democracy in Soviet society and in the C.P.S.U. that had been revealed, and on our own party leadership for not being aware of what had been happening. But there was also a demand that the C.P.G.B. should examine its own organisation and methods of work. This was raised particularly by academics throughout the country and was highlighted by the publication of a paper, *"The Reasoner"* by two Yorkshire university lecturers, E. P. Thompson and John Saville. There was an unusually open presentation of the arguments for and against "*The Reasoner*" in the pages of *World News*, the official periodical of the party. Because they refused to abide by party rules, Thompson and Saville were first suspended and then expelled from the party. The Executive Committee appointed a commission to visit the Soviet Union to have discussions with Soviet comrades and to convey the views of our party. The commission included severe critics like Professor Hyman Levy, who had been particularly concerned at the evidence of anti-semitism. A leading member of the party in the East Midlands, Ida Hackett, was also a member.

Not surprisingly, we lost many members, but not as many as our opponents anticipated. Ironically, the most serious loss in the East Midlands was from our thriving Eckington Branch where almost all the members, including Horace Kay, our only Communist Councillor, left in protest at the criticisms being made of Stalin!

The revelations at the Twentieth Congress prompted questioning in other developing socialist countries. The system of suspicion and Stalin's paranoia had been transported to these countries, and many communists had been falsely imprisoned and some, such as Rudolf Slansky, the General Secretary of the Czechoslovakian Communist Party, had been executed. Those who were still living were gradually released; those who were dead were posthumously rehabilitated. But the Twentieth Congress also gave encouragement to those who wanted greater democracy and economic changes. This came to a head in Poland and Hungary in October. In Poland there were strikes and demonstrations. One of the demands was for the return of Wladyslaw Gomulka to lead the Polish United Workers Party. Gomulka had a fine revolutionary record and, as Secretary of the underground Communist Party, had played a leading part in the Polish resistance movement during the war. However, he fell under Stalin's suspicion and was imprisoned – and would probably been executed but for Stalin's death. He was released from prison in 1953 and was now restored to his position as First Secretary of the P.U.W.P. He immediately initiated a far-reaching programme of economic and political reforms, and in a short while the protest movement died down.

Hungary was a different story. It had been the world's first fascist country. A working-class revolution had been brutally crushed in 1919, and afterwards the White Terror – as it was called – under Admiral

Horthy, mercilessly persecuted communists, socialists, trade unionists and Jews. Thousands were tortured and put to death. When, in 1944, dictator Horthy agreed to the country being occupied by the Germans, the reign of terror became even more ferocious. This was the historical background to the first free elections, held soon after the country was liberated by the Red Army. The former fascist ruling class had been destroyed and those of its supporters who remained in Hungary were completely demoralised. The Small Landowners' Party emerged as the victor of the election, and a coalition government was formed in which only four of the eighteen members were communists. However, the then small Communist Party, based as it was on the industrial workers and peasantry, quickly won mass support for its policies. Mass pressure led to the banks and heavy industry being nationalised. In the 1947 general election the Communist Party received nearly forty per cent of the votes and with its allies constituted an absolute majority. Its democratic credentials could hardly be denied, even according to Western criteria. In 1949, the coalition People's Front won an overwhelming victory. The country had been liberated by the Soviet armed forces and, in accordance with the peace treaty, Soviet troops were stationed there with the declared purpose of preventing the re-emergence of fascism and militarism. Its presence was also a barrier to outside military intervention aimed at preventing any development towards socialism, such as British military forces had succeeded in doing in Greece.

The Communist Party had emerged from illegality a small organisation with no experience of democracy or of government. Its membership quickly increased, but, of course, one of the drawbacks of this was that the majority of its members were still relatively backward politically because they had spent their lives under fascism. There had been no powerful liberation movement such as had existed in neighbouring Yugoslavia. Obsessed with the need to rapidly transform an extremely backward country totally devastated by war, the government concentrated on forcing the pace of industrialisation and the transformation of agriculture. This was done at the expense of consumer goods production and quick improvements in living conditions. It also meant a command structured economy, based on the Soviet model, rather than adequate popular participation in decision-making and implementation. Inevitably, there was widespread frustration and dissatisfaction for which there was no open outlet. This was the setting for the mass demonstrations that took place in October.

Initially, the demonstrations were not for a change of regime or against socialism. Led by students and journalists, the main demands were for freedom of the press and the end of Russian being a compulsory language in schools. Another demand was for the return of Imre Nagy as Prime Minister. Nagy had played an honourable part in the struggle against fascism and had spent many years as an exile in the Soviet Union. In 1953 he had been Prime Minister, but was removed from the position and expelled from the Communist Party as a "right-wing deviationist." The Communist Party vacillated, but on 23rd October, it gave way and restored Nagy as Prime Minister. The First Secretary of the party, Gero, was replaced by Janos Kadar. Kadar had been Secretary of the illegal Communist Party during the war, but in 1950, like Gomulka in Poland, he had been imprisoned, only to be rehabilitated after the death of Stalin.

By this time, there was plenty of evidence that counter-revolutionary elements were playing an important part in the protest movement. It would be naïve, indeed, to imagine that external forces, particularly the C.I.A., were not involved. Top army officers spoke at demonstrations; arms – including quite heavy weapons – mysteriously appeared on the streets and attacks were made on key places, like radio stations, bridges and Communist Party offices. Nagy called on Soviet troops to help restore order because, he said, "hostile elements had now joined the peaceful demonstrators." The evidence is that the Soviet military commanders were reluctant to intervene and only did so by making their presence obvious in the streets of Budapest. There was little, if any, military action at this stage and after five days the troops were withdrawn.

Even so, the open presence of Soviet tanks – later admitted to be a mistake – exacerbated the conflict. Instead of it resulting in a relaxation of the situation, it was used by the counter-revolutionary elements, who now played a decisive role in what had been a genuine and peaceful movement of protest, to increase the stakes. Increasingly, the demand now was for a return to capitalism. A veritable reign of terror began. Armed gangs roamed the street with the aim of exterminating Communists. Western correspondents reported bodies hanging from lamp-posts – the *Daily Mail's* Jeffry Blythe claimed there were four hundred in one night. Twelve communists were hanged in a row at one gutted party office. Many people were tortured. In the face of this, Nagy proved weak and powerless. The crunch came when he released from prison the notorious fascist collaborator, Cardinal Mindszenty, who had been imprisoned for treason after the war. The right wing were now demanding that he be made head of a new government. In his first broadcast on Budapest radio, Mindszenty called for the abandonment of communism, the return of land to the landowners and the replacement of nationalisation by private enterprise. He appealed to the western powers to intervene. This appeal was taken up by Nagy, who also renounced the treaty with the Warsaw Pact. The famous foreign correspondent Alexander Werth reported in *Reynolds News* that Hungarian fascist émigrés who had escaped abroad were pouring across the border into the country.

On 4th November, Communist ministers resigned from the Nagy government and set up a Revolutionary Government of Workers and Peasants of Hungary, with the aim of halting the advance of counter-revolution. Janos Kadar became Prime Minister. It immediately issued an appeal to the Hungarian people to defend the revolution. It condemned past mistakes and put forward a fifteen point programme of political and economic reforms. It called for military assistance from Soviet Warsaw Pact forces to help defeat the counter-revolution. After severe fighting over several days, this was achieved. Nagy went to the Yugoslav embassy and Mindszenty sought refuge in the United States embassy, where he remained until 1971. Thousands left the country, and although among them were the fascist émigrés who had returned, most were undoubtedly ordinary Hungarian men and women who had been caught up in the struggle. Quite a number no doubt took advantage of the western governments' generous offer of asylum, to come and live in the west. I had evidence of this later, when two Hungarians who had come to work in the Notts coalfield admitted that this was indeed so in their case. They said they had never been interested in politics, and certainly had taken no part in the events that opened up the opportunity for them to emigrate.

The Hungarian events can only be fully understood in the context of the sharpening Cold War. The declared aim of the western powers was to subvert what they called the Soviet bloc. The U.S. Congress had provided one hundred million dollars to "selected persons who are resident in or escapees from the Soviet Union, Poland, Czechoslovakia, Hungary, Poland, Bulgaria, Rumania or Albania, either to form such persons into elements of the military forces supporting the North Atlantic Military Alliance, or for other purposes." Head of the C.I.A., Alan Dulles, referred to the formation of "Operation X," with "strong-arm squads . . .

under American guidance. Assassination of key communists would be encouraged. American agents parachuted into Eastern Europe . . . would be used to co-ordinate anti-communist action." There was plenty of evidence to show direct C.I.A. involvement. It boasted of its long preparations to "produce revolutions in the countries behind the iron curtain" (General Lucius Clay), of the training given to émigrés to lead the countries when they were "liberated," and of having people "some in high places" who pass on valuable information. It requires no stretch of the imagination to see what a tremendous victory it would have been for imperialism if Hungary had changed sides. Conversely, it would have seriously weakened the Soviet Union and the socialist countries.

I have devoted some time to the Hungarian uprising because it was a traumatic experience for all communists and, together with the exposure of Stalin, set in motion an examination of many of our cherished ideas which was to have great consequences in years to come. It was shocking to see and read about the demonstrations, rioting, lynching of communists and shootings of civilians in Budapest. It was painful to see on our T.V. screens pictures of Soviet tanks and guns being deployed in the streets. But I accepted and agreed with the explanation of the leadership of the C.P.G.B. that, profoundly regrettable though it had been, the formation of the Kadar government and the intervention of the Soviet Union were objectively correct. This was the line taken, I believe, by every Marxist party throughout the world. Like most communists, I had no illusions about the bitterness of the class struggle, nor of the ruthlessness of capitalism in crushing workers in struggle and opposing socialism. Imperialism was intent on destroying socialism and was quite prepared to adopt any method to achieve it – including using the justifiable discontent of people in the countries struggling to build socialism. I have already explained that in this autobiography I try to describe my views and feelings at the time, and not to use hindsight to edit them in order to present a more acceptable picture to today's readers – a duplicity, alas, that so many biographers are guilty of. But having said that, and having examined the Hungarian events again, I still believe that the line of the international communist movement at the time was correct. In the objective conditions of the time, which included the harsh reality of the Cold War, there was no viable alternative.

Many comrades didn't see it this way. Reeling under the "double whammy" of Stalin and Hungary, they began to question the fundamental role and organisation of the Communist Party. The use of Soviet armed forces in another country was totally unacceptable, even though it could be argued they were legally justified by treaty obligations as being necessary for security and to crush counter-revolution. Many argued that the threat of counter-revolution was exaggerated. It is true to say that all comrades, whatever line they took, felt shattered. The simplistic certainties of the past had gone. Our idealistic picture of events was blemished.

I was awakened early one morning by a phone call from Bert Wynn, Secretary of the Derbyshire miners. He had just heard on the radio of Soviet tanks being used in Budapest, and was extremely agitated. For me, this presaged a period of intense discussion when feelings ran very high. Branch meetings had never been so well attended. I recall a meeting of our largest branch, Chesterfield, which was packed – standing-room only. Bas Barker chaired it, and I was the speaker. Another comrade, the convenor of one of the largest factories in the town, came along prepared to hand in his party card, but changed his mind after the discussion. One comrade was in tears, such was the emotional atmosphere. All felt a personal hurt. That week, Bert announced to the Area Council of the Derbyshire N.U.M. that he had left the Communist Party. What was most significant about that Council meeting, however, was the applause given, not to Bert, but to veteran miner and communist, Mick Kane, when he declared he was proud to be a Communist and had no intention of deserting the party now the going was tough.

While all this was going on, British imperialism was having its own problems. Its economic and political domination over Egypt, weakened after the Second World War, was now being directly challenged on a crucial issue – control over the Suez Canal. In July 1952, the puppet playboy king, Farouk – the butt of many bawdy Eighth Army songs – had been deposed. Although it was a military coup, led by General Neguib, it reflected both the rising tide of the national independence movement in the colonial world, and the disintegration of the old colonial system. Neguib was replaced by Colonel Gamal Abdel Nasser, who launched a programme aimed at transforming Egypt into a modern capitalist state. A key part of the plan was to construct the Aswan High Dam on the Nile, which would power a big hydroelectric station capable of supplying electricity to Egyptian industry. In July, Britain and the U.S.A. announced that they would not give financial aid for this to be done. Nasser responded by proposing that it be paid for by the nationalisation of the Suez Canal Company, whilst guaranteeing the canal's status as an international waterway. Generous compensation was offered to shareholders, mainly British and French. As was admitted later, by secret agreement with France and Britain, Israel occupied the canal zone. This gave Britain and France the excuse for invading Egypt on the pretext of protecting the right of international free passage of all ships through the canal – never actually threatened. On 31st October, Egyptian airfields were bombed and paratroopers landed.

There was immediate world-wide outrage. An attempt to "legalise" the aggression by getting the support of the United Nations was vetoed by the Soviet Union, and the groundswell of popular opposition grew rapidly. Trafalgar Square saw one of the largest demonstrations ever held there, addressed by Aneurin Bevan and a wide range of speakers. Yet, the attitude of the Labour leaders was despicable. Gaitskell and Morrison immediately backed Prime Minister Anthony Eden, and it was only later as a result of the widespread opposition throughout the labour movement that the Shadow Cabinet partially shifted its stand, not by condemning the aggressive policy of the Tory government, but by arguing that the invasion should first have had the support of the United Nations.

Indian President Nehru launched a bitter attack on Britain and France, and other national leaders followed suit. The United States maintained the imperialist common front in condemning Nasser but at the same time was quite ready to see its imperialist rivals weaken their position in the Middle East to its own future advantage. By the middle of December Britain and France were forced to beat an ignominious retreat. It was the end of Eden. A few weeks later he resigned as Prime Minister and was replaced by Harold Macmillan. A footnote: the Aswan High Dam was ultimately built with Soviet financial and technical help.

There is no doubt that the Suez crisis took a lot of heat out of the public reaction to events in Hungary. We played a full part in the campaign to end the war and continued to hold our regular open-air meetings in town centres and at factory and pit gates. The response we met with was not seriously diminished by Hungary. Over one thousand copies of a special broadsheet were sold in the East Midlands and 10,000 leaflets immediately distributed. Petitions were initiated by the party in several pits and factories.

Party members played a key role in mobilising protests from the labour movement against Tory policy. These included resolutions from the Notts and Derbyshire N.U.M. Area Councils, and every important trades council in the District.

Of course, there were other issues that also took up a great deal of our time. In the United States, anti-Communist hysteria had reached new heights with McCarthyism at its centre. We couldn't do much about that, but we did take part in the campaign to save Ethel and Julius Rosenberg from the electric chair. They had been accused, on evidence that later proved to have been forged or non-existent, of spying for the Soviet Union. As well as initiating resolutions from the labour movement, we worked hard persuading many well-known citizens in the East Midlands to send telegrams to the White House. Despite appeals for clemency from many heads of state and the Pope, the Rosenbergs were judicially murdered in March 1953.

Yet, the party suffered greatly from Hungary and many members left even as the debate over it continued. Some of those who left were the least active, those who took no part in the discussions and who were therefore more vulnerable to the anti-communist hysteria of the capitalist media. But we also lost valuable comrades about whom this could not be said. Many were communists who were active and who played an important role in their own field, particularly academics. In the East Midlands, there was a marked contrast between the relatively low membership losses in the coalfields and the greater losses in the cities, where there were many more teachers, lecturers and professional people. Nationally, the membership fell from 32,681 at the end of 1955 to 24,900 after the Twenty Fifth National Congress in April 1956, a drop of twenty four per cent. In some cities, over a third left the party.

The Twenty Fifth Congress was the climax to the debate. It was certainly the most dramatic Congress I ever attended both because of the clear divisions on issues of vital importance and because of the sharpness and eloquence of the speeches from both sides. The opposition to the leadership included many well-known and respected comrades who pulled no punches. General Secretary John Gollan called on the delegates to take a firm line against "the wave of revisionist ideas that had emerged," and attacked those who wanted "to retreat from Marxist-Leninist conceptions to social-democratic, even capitalist ideas on the state, democracy and the class struggle," whilst at the same time warning against sectarianism. The delegates overwhelmingly supported the line of the leadership. Some months before, a Commission had been appointed to examine how to improve democracy in the party, and the majority proposals were accepted. A report submitted by a minority of the commission (which included the historian Christopher Hill) which wanted, among other things, to legalise factions, was rejected. Congress also adopted a new version of the *British Road to Socialism*, which reiterated the basic Marxist-Leninist standpoint of the party and an internationalist outlook that recognised the Soviet Union as central in the struggle against imperialism. At the same time, in my view, it made concessions to the minority viewpoint that were to strengthen the revisionist trends in the party and were ultimately to have dire consequences.

Following the Congress, most of the critics left the party. Of course, the capitalist media wrote the party off. Hungary was the mortal wound from which it could never possibly recover. It wasn't long before, for the umpteenth time, they were proved wrong. At the Twenty Sixth Congress in March 1959, Gollan was able to announce an increase of 2,500 members. In view of what was to happen in years to come it is interesting to note the reasons he gave. The party had:

"rejected all the dissolutionists and compromisers who would have turned the party into a spineless talking shop or abolished it altogether," because "it rejected the revisionists and reformists' illusions of a reformed capitalism," because it rejected the revisionist attempt "to undermine our proletarian internationalism. They (the revisionists) wanted to take a stand that would have separated us from the world Communist movement."

It is worth noting that by the Twenty Eighth Congress in 1963 all the losses of 1956-7 had been wiped out, and at 34,372 the membership was actually higher than before the Hungarian crisis.

37. COALFIELD ORGANISER

Because of the importance of mining, round about 1953 Harry Pollitt came up with the idea of having full-time Party organisers in the areas covering some of the main coalfields. Dave Priscott became organiser in the Rhondda, Frank Watters in South Yorkshire, a comrade in Midlothian and myself in the East Midlands. As I was District Organiser we did try a few other comrades, but they didn't prove suitable. One, a full-time London comrade, disappeared after a fortnight, and when we investigated, we found he had returned home because "the job was too difficult." He had probably been used to a compact London Borough and not the widespread pit villages and towns of a coalfield, and tough, insular miners to deal with. My wages were for a short while paid largely out of contributions made by our full-time trade union comrades, who also covered the expenses of me attending some of the annual N.U.M. conferences as a visitor.

I still worked from our Nottingham office and took part in the general activity of the district. We did an enormous amount of propaganda work, including regular Sunday market-place meetings at about ten of the main towns, and a weekly routine of lunch-time meetings outside many of the main factories. There were some prime sites for our Sunday meetings, when we could always guarantee a good audience – "Slab Square" in front of the town hall in Nottingham, "The Pump" in Chesterfield market place, The Bull Ring in Grimsby and the market places in Derby, Leicester and Mansfield. Apart from other aspects of propaganda, arranging rotas of speakers over such a big area was quite a job, and for a period when Kath was not teaching she worked part-time in charge of district propaganda. Nationally, the word "propaganda" had been replaced by "publicity," but I'm afraid it was a euphemism we hardly ever used.

These public meetings were a training ground for aspiring orators. We usually had a less experienced comrade speaking or chairing a meeting with a seasoned campaigner. Preparing their speeches helped political understanding, and speaking – especially at meetings where there was a great deal of heckling – helped them to think on their feet. Open-air speaking of this sort is a skill in itself, as anyone who has ever heard great exponents of the art like Donald Soper, Phil Piratin or Solly Kaye perform at Speakers' Corner in London's Hyde Park knows very well. It's a great pity that politically active youngsters today do not have the opportunities to develop as public speakers that we had. The regular open-air meeting is a rarity. Indeed, public meetings themselves are far fewer than was once the case: sound bites on T.V. are now considered more important by politicians of all parties. And the ending of the regular one-hour lunch break has almost destroyed factory-gate meetings.

Needless to say, our meetings were often quite rowdy affairs. I have already mentioned a meeting in Loughborough that was broken up. Another one I recall was at one of my regular appearances outside the Ericson electrical factory at Beeston. A group of fascists in the factory laid in wait, and as soon as I started they charged the platform and roughed me up. Our comrades who also worked in the factory were taken by surprise, but were determined to counter-attack. The next week I spoke there again, but this time had a cordon protecting the platform – not that it was necessary, for the whole factory turned out. It was one of the biggest factory-gate meetings I ever held! Did these meetings do any good? A testimony that they had some impact has come from an unexpected source. Alan Sillitoe's first novel, *Saturday Night and Sunday Morning*, was based on his experiences when a worker at Raleigh's, in Nottingham. His hero ponders on what the Communists who speak outside the factory say, and, he thinks, they do make a lot of sense. I must have been one of the first speakers to use a portable public address system. It was made for me by a Derby comrade, Ivan West, who was something of an electronic whiz-kid and had constructed it from ex-service transistors and other components he had acquired. Once, when I spoke outside "W. B.," the well-known loudspeaker firm in Mansfield, I was delighted to have a group of their technicians in the audience. Alas, all they were interested in was my apparatus, which, at the close of the meeting, they asked if they could examine!

38. A GREAT FIND

Finding a very rare and important book is the sort of thing most of us dream about. Yet this dream became a reality for me and two other comrades. Nottingham used to boast one of the best second-hand bookshops in the Midlands. It was called Woores, and my lunch-times were often spent poring over the thousands of old books stacked up to the ceiling in every room. Many a bargain did I get, but none such as was acquired one day early in 1952. Two comrades came into the office and told me that a fresh consignment of political books were on the shelves, including many Marxist classics. We went down there posthaste, and sure enough there were a good number of books on socialism and the labour movement. Among them were three leather-bound copies of Marx's Capital in German. When I opened them, I could hardly believe my eyes. The frontispieces of each of them were signed "Samuel S. Moore" and "F. Engels," seemingly in Engels' handwriting. I knew that Moore and Engels were the translators of Capital into English, but could hardly credit that these volumes had actually belonged to Engels himself. I handed over 7s 6d and took them back to the office.

Although we were fairly certain the books were genuine, we wanted to confirm it. Mick Jenkins had written a pamphlet on "Engels in Manchester" and there was a good chance that he would have a photograph of Engels's signature, so we went to collect him from the British Restaurant where he was having his lunch. He went home and came back with a photograph that verified that the signature was authentic. What could we do with such an important find? First of all we had to be absolutely certain that the books were what they seemed; so we entrusted

311

Mick with the task of handing them over to Dona Torr when he next visited King Street, she being the acknowledged expert on the history of Marxism.

Some months later, Dona Torr gave her report. The books were almost certainly the long-lost volumes of Capital that Engels had used to translate the third volume into English. If they were put up for auction they would fetch a considerable amount, certainly running into many thousands of pounds, but the chances are that they would go to an American collector. The three of us who found them, Marjorie Jacobs, Pat Jordan and myself agreed to present the books to the Marx Memorial Library and Mick concurred. This was done at a ceremony in July 1952, and as far as I know the volumes are still there. There was a photograph in the national press some years later of Khrushchev looking at one when he visited Marx House.

Unfortunately, there was a sour aspect to the affair. Either there was a misunderstanding that Mick didn't correct, or – sadly – he took credit for the discovery. Consequently, he was acclaimed as the finder and alone invited to a hand-over ceremony, while we who actually found the volumes were ignored. We were naturally somewhat aggrieved at this and mildly protested. Eventually, the Marx Memorial Library did send us each a facsimile of the frontispiece and a short note of thanks for "our contribution."

Some time after the discovery, I told the manager of Woores the story and asked him where the books had come from. He said they were part of a private library belonging to an old Manchester socialist, which he had bought for £40. He also said that the relatives had burnt a considerably quantity of his papers. It is sad to think of how many precious documents were destroyed and are destroyed through ignorance of their true historical value.

39. DIVISIONS

Nineteen fifty four began with Bronwen being born, to be joined by Emrys in October 1956. He arrived precipitously and very much sooner than we expected – a fact we attributed to Kath having tripped on the stairs not long before. I arrived in the office after doing a factory-gate meeting at Raleigh's and was told that Kath had phoned and appeared to be upset, though she hadn't given any reason. Call it premonition or telepathy, but I sensed at once that something was seriously wrong and did what I wouldn't normally have dreamed of doing – phoned for a taxi.

When I arrived home, Kath was standing at the phone trying to contact the doctor, with the newly born baby in her arms, umbilical cord still attached. He came at once, but then there was a frustrating hour of waiting for help to arrive, when the incredibly tiny piece of humanity that was to become Emrys was rushed to the premature-baby unit of the hospital, where he was to spend the first week or so of his life in an oxygen tent. Bronwen – then two and half years old – still boasts of the fact that she saw her brother being born.

The following year was one of the most difficult periods of our married life, politically and personally. Since 1947, when we had both taken over in the East Midlands, Mick Jenkins and I had worked well together as District Secretary and District Organiser. I very much respected his experience and his qualities of leadership. But now our relationship was becoming somewhat strained. The root cause, I believe, was that Mick resented serious criticism or any expression of meaningful independence on the part of his subordinates. Kath and I had come up against this in a small way in 1947, soon after we knew him. In all innocence, we had written an article for the party journal, *World News and Views*, on the situation in the hosiery industry. Mick was furious, not with the article, but because, he said, it should have been published under his name. I had cause to disagree with him on a number of occasions, and once or twice had even taken my disagreement to the District Committee. Worst of all, I had even expressed doubts about some decisions of the Executive Committee. Mick was very much a professional revolutionary of the old school, where unquestioned discipline was everything. I can never recall a single occasion when he stood out against Party Centre, even when he thought he was right. There was one occasion when he had laboured for a week preparing the keynote speech he was to make to a District Congress. The evening before the Congress, the National Organiser, Bill Lauchlan, who was to attend the Congress, came up, read the speech, and insisted on Mick staying up all night re-writing it, like a schoolboy being instructed to re-write a bad essay. And Mick took what I thought was an unjustified insult without a murmur.

Probably what he resented most of all about our relationship was the fact that in the coalfield and among mining party members, I was regarded as the leading full-time comrade – in other words, I seemed to represent a challenge to his authority. I also had greater personal contact and was in good standing with branches in Leicestershire and Lincolnshire because I frequently visited them, whereas he didn't. Indeed, one of my criticisms of him was that he tended to lead from the office. Nor did he always have a very sympathetic approach to comrades – a fact that led to two full-time workers resigning. He insisted on the Secretariat formally censoring one of these young comrades who enjoyed a good argument because he had had the temerity to invite a Trotskyist into his home to argue with!

The other factor that soured our relationship was the role played by John Peck. Peck had been the secretary of our Scunthorpe branch and worked in the offices of a steel company. He had been a bomber pilot and had been awarded the D.F.C. after he and his crew had completed the requisite number of flights over enemy territory. Around about 1950 we had advertised in our bulletin for a bookshop manager, and he was the only one to respond. After spending a stint as manager, he became Nottingham Area Secretary of the party. Understandably, he was very inexperienced and for a while, at Mick's request, I attended the Nottingham Area Committee to help protect him from the vitriolic criticisms of the more experienced and sometimes intolerant comrades on the committee. He lived next door to Mick, and as one would expect, a close relationship developed between the two families. Unfortunately, it went further than that. Peck was the archetypical "yes-man," totally uncritical, even obsequious to Mick and the leadership of the party. Although Mick often privately expressed to me his exasperation at some of Peck's more stupid actions, the close association between the two grew as both seemed to feed on each other's uncritical support. Mick saw Peck as his protégé and pushed him forward on every possible occasion. It became obvious that he was grooming him as his successor. Mick, and his lovely wife, Jessie – a former mill girl – hankered after Manchester; he once told me that they wanted to return there while still politically active.

Peck was a first-rate public speaker, although with a somewhat arrogant style. However, although a fine propagandist, he was not a deep thinker and his understanding of Marxism and politics in general remained shallow throughout the years I knew him. He never seemed to read deeply and very seldom tutored at classes on anything other than practical subjects. Later, he was to find his forté in local activity, where he established a deserved reputation for case-work, which led eventually to him becoming a Communist councillor. It was no surprise to many of us that some years later he was to switch allegiance to the Green Party. One of his greatest weaknesses was an inability to build an effective collective around himself. He was an individualist, respected by many, but never able to build the warm relationship with a wide circle of comrades over a long period of time that I was fortunate enough to enjoy.

Matters came to a head at a Secretariat meeting in April 1958. Without any warning Mick delivered a prepared statement proposing that because of our financial problems we should shed one full-time worker. The one to go should be me, and Peck should replace me as District Organiser. I was quite dumbfounded. What particularly angered me was the manner in which it was done. As usual, Mick and I had spent the entire morning in his office amicably going through the matters to be discussed at the evening meeting, and he never hinted at the bombshell he was going to deliver only a few hours later. He obviously intended using the tactic of surprise, aiming to catch me and the other comrades off-guard. It didn't work. Most members of the Secretariat were as astounded as I was. He didn't offer a single political or organisational criticism of my work. The only argument he advanced was that, being a skilled toolmaker, I would find it easiest to get another job. The real reason was quite transparent. There was an acrimonious debate, in which two of the most respected members of the committee, chairman Les Ellis and National Executive Committee member, Ida Hackett, were particularly outspoken in opposition to the move to get rid of me. In fact, the tables were turned. Mick had presented such a strong case for reducing staff, that this was agreed to, but to his chagrin the majority believed that Peck should be the one to go! Mick, who was a good tactician, then retreated from his insistence on an immediate decision and proposed we sit on it for a week. He then got to work to strengthen his position. As they told me later, he visited Les and Ida individually to try to pressurise them to change their position, but to no avail. He then asked Party Centre to intervene in his support, something they invariably did for District Secretaries. The National Organiser, Bill Lauchlan, came up and met the four full-time comrades. Lauchlan quickly realised that Mick was on to a loser. There was no way the Secretariat, even less the District Committee, would agree to me going. But there was the possibility that Peck would go, so he put forward a compromise proposal that the fourth full-time worker, Bill Messom, should be the sacrificial lamb. Bill was a young ex-miner and a very promising party organiser who eventually ended up as a full-time W.E.A. organiser. At the time he had become our Coalfield area organiser. I urged Bill not to accept dismissal, but eventually he gave in. In a letter to me he stated that he was resigning because

315

he was "totally disillusioned with the conduct of Mick and John, which did not come up to the high standards he had expected from responsible communists." He was also bitter at the lack of help he was getting from them and felt he could no longer work with them. Lauchlan insisted that the full-time workers present a united front in the Secretariat and that the Secretariat do the same at the District Committee meeting – another example of the rigid and quite wrong way that democratic-centralism, the organisational principle of the Communist Party, was interpreted.

Unfortunately, that was not the end of the matter. Peck became District Organiser, and I became responsible for the coalfield area, but Mick and John soon demonstrated their resentment at their failure to get rid of me. The atmosphere in the office became extremely chilly and I was spoken to only on matters from which I could not very well be excluded.

What engendered some bitterness on my part was that Kath and I were going through one of the most difficult periods of our married life. Because of illness, Kath was not working, and we had a young family, including a premature and delicate child, to care for. I was getting almost no wages and our meagre savings had gone, which meant we were desperately short of money – indeed, for food and household requirements we had to rely on the generosity of the friendly family who kept the neighbourhood shop and who allowed us to run up a substantial bill. This lasted about a year, yet not once during this entire period did Mick or Peck enquire how on earth we were managing with no income. On the contrary, there was increased pressure on me to raise more "quota" for the District from the coalfield branches.

It should be explained that at this time all full-time workers, from the top down, were equal with regards to the wages they were supposed to receive . . . but some were more equal than others when it came to getting them. Everyone at Party Centre received their full wages regularly. So did most District Secretaries. But the poor sods below, especially area organisers, were in a different category. In the East Midlands, at least, the strict priority task was to get branches to pay a monthly sum – a "quota" – to the District, from money received from donations, money-raising events and a share of the low contributions. The District paid a quota to Party Centre. The wages of area organisers came out of what they could raise after such quotas were paid – which was usually little and often nothing. Some of us felt the injustice of this and often protested against it, but to no avail. We felt that as we were all comrades and employees of the party, wages should be paid centrally, with no discrimination. We knew nothing then of the help the party was getting from the C.P.S.U., or our protests would, perhaps, have been stronger! In fairness, it must be stressed that no-one gained financially from working for the party. The pay of all full-time workers, from the General Secretary down, was less than the average wage of a skilled industrial worker. It required dedication and conviction to be a party organiser at whatever level.

Difficult though things were for her, Kath was fully behind my resolve not to succumb to the move – I am tempted to write "plot" – to sack me as a full-time party worker. In fact, she was probably more determined than me, for I was continually beset with misgivings about her health and the disproportionate burden she had to bear. When I attended my union branch meeting and compared the wages skilled toolmakers were getting with my woeful pittance I could not help but be tempted. If she had any doubts, I would probably have packed up, even though I have a stubborn disposition which makes it difficult for me to give in if I feel I am in the right. Despite problems, when she was well Kath insisted on playing the maximum part she could in the work of the party, including continuing to serve as a fully functioning member of the District Committee and acting as tutor at party classes. Eventually she was able to go back to work – sooner than she should have – but we were only able to bridge the month before she drew her first pay by accepting a loan of one hundred pounds from two friends in the party to help pay the nursery charges and other expenses.

Personal problems and differences though there were, there were no major disagreements on the need to fight for the policies of the party. My growing belief that some aspects of party organisation and the way authority was exercised were not as perfect as once I thought was strengthened by these experiences. However, these were minor defects in relation to the role of the party as a revolutionary organisation fighting for socialism. Personality problems arise in most organisations, and we know now that they had often existed in the national leadership of the C.P.G.B., but because of the discipline of the party they never became widely known. In the East Midlands, not many outside of the secretariat knew of our differences – they were not even revealed to the District Committee!

However, Kath and I felt it would be best for all if we moved outside of Nottingham. We would be happier and it would be more politically rewarding if we were away from the negative atmosphere that pervaded the district office. Neither of us felt any attachment to Nottingham; indeed, we didn't particularly like living there. As the comrade responsible for work in mining I felt it would be more convenient to live in the coalfield. But what probably influenced me most was the close and friendly relationship I had established with our mining comrades, and the fact that it gave me a firm political base from which to work.

Kath and I were both small-town people and never really felt at home in what we saw as the impersonality of city life. Chesterfield seemed the ideal place to move to. Though a large branch, there was a great community spirit, and its members were genuine friends as well as comrades. We already knew some of them very well and got on with them personally. An added bonus was that it was so close to the lovely Peak District. We were fortunate in getting a house in what was then a quiet street in Whittington Moor on the outskirts of the town. It had a well-kept lawn that had once been a tennis court, surrounded by flower beds and with a small orchard attached. An added bonus was a small office, the previous owner being a local wool trader. With a bathroom, running hot water and two toilets – one up and one down – it was a palace indeed after the house we left. What a joy it was to dispense with the tin bath and not to have to go outside on a cold winter's night to meet the calls of nature. At £1,750 it was above the ceiling we had set, but it was so much what we wanted that we decided to take the risk of trying to meet the high eleven pounds a month mortgage payment. An added complication was that we sold the house in Nottingham (for slightly less than we paid for it) to a Spanish immigrant family who could neither afford to pay cash nor get a mortgage. They offered to pay in monthly instalments, which we accepted.

40. VISIT TO THE SOVIET UNION

Negotiations for buying the house had hardly started when we were offered the opportunity of spending four or five weeks in the Soviet Union. During the summer months the C.P.S.U. invited groups of comrades from other countries to visit the Soviet Union for a holiday, a health check-up and to see something of the country which meant so much to all communists. Those who went were mainly, although not exclusively, full-time party workers. In our case, it was Party Centre that decided who were to go, and apart from political considerations some preference was given to active comrades who could not otherwise afford such a holiday. We were very excited at the prospect of meeting people whose historic attempt to build socialism we had so long championed. Then came a snag. The negotiations for purchasing our new house could not be completed before we were due to leave. There were other prospective buyers ready to take our place if any snags cropped up, and probably prepared to offer more. Acting on the time-honoured precept that possession is nine-tenths of the law, and having got hold of the keys from the estate agent, we decided to move in at once. Our solicitor, a party member, warned us that this was illegal and could land us in trouble, but we thought the risk was worth taking. We occupied the house two days before we were due to leave for the Soviet Union, arranging for relatives to take the children. A nearby Chesterfield comrade and personal friend, Win Clark, about whom I shall write later, and her daughter, Kate, valiantly helped us get the carpets down and the curtains up. The rest, mainly boxes of books, had to wait for our return.

At that time there was no direct flight to Moscow, a reflection of the Cold War, so we had to fly on a Vickers Viscount to Prague and change there to an Aeroflot TU104. There were only seven of us: James Klugman, Jack Pascoe and his wife, Bill and Phyl Earle, Kath and myself. James was a member of the Executive Committee and editor of *Marxism Today*, Jack was an official of a building workers' trades union and Bill and Phil were active members in their branch. We were met at Moscow Airport by representatives of the Central Committee of the C.P.S.U. and our interpreter, Yuri Ivanov. Yuri spoke perfect English, with an Australian accent – having lived in Canberra when his father had been an official in the Australian embassy. What gave him away was his constant use of the word "golly," which he obviously thought was modern English usage. James could speak Russian fluently and Kath was learning it and could get by reasonably well. We were flown to a large country house (dacha) in a beautiful silver-birch forest outside of Moscow. That evening a magnificent "spread" was put on for us, and we became acquainted with the Russian convention of proposing a toast between the numerous courses – in vodka, of course. After a couple of hours we tottered off to bed. The next morning I had an appalling hangover and Jack had lost his false teeth down the toilet. He had a new set made in a few days. Still, we had learned a valuable lesson – to be restrained in accepting one feature of Soviet hospitality. On future visits it wasn't necessary because the Soviet Party and the government were campaigning against excessive vodka drinking.

We had a meeting with the Central Committee representative in which he asked us to work out a programme of where we wanted to go and whether we wanted to have discussions about anything or with anyone. "For a month," he said, "The Soviet Union is yours." In addition to Moscow, we decided to visit Leningrad and Stalingrad, and one of our comrades expressed a desire to see the Volga-Don Canal and a collective farm. I wanted to visit engineering factories and have discussions with workers and shop stewards. The first few days were spent looking around Moscow, visiting the Kremlin and museums, and going to the theatre. In the Kremlin, we were shown the treasures of the Tsars, not usually open to visitors. In stark contrast was the modest little room where Lenin worked, kept as it was when he used it. We made the obligatory visit to the Mausoleum in Red Square and saw the embalmed bodies of Lenin and Stalin (later, his was to be removed). We also had a thorough medical check at the central "polyclinic." In response to my request, we visited the "Red Proletariat" machine-tool factory, where we spoke to workers and had a discussion with the trade union committee. At the end, the director asked for my impressions. A criticism I ventured to make concerned the cluttering up of floor space, which could be a safety hazard; but I acknowledged that an aircraft factory is somewhat differently organised. On the positive side I was impressed by the generally informal attitude among the workers and the control they had over the production process.

We then flew to Leningrad, where we stayed at the party hotel near the Smolny Institute, the headquarters of the Bolshevik government during the revolution. Leningrad is a far more attractive city than Moscow, with its wide streets, wonderful old buildings and intertwining canals. Looking down the Nevski Prospect, one could not help feeling that Leningrad's founder, Peter the Great, had an inspired insight of what would be needed to meet the traffic problems of the Twentieth Century. As Communists, we were particularly interested in seeing the places, the names of which were so familiar to us from reading about the 1917 revolution. We travelled out to Rasliv, near the Finnish border, and went in the cottage where Lenin had hidden, masquerading as a peasant, in the weeks prior to the revolution.

It has since been encased in a massive and ugly glass structure, which takes away something of its romantic impact. Of course, the Winter Palace was a must. In November 1917 it was the headquarters of the Provisional Government of Kerensky, and its storming by the Red Guards was the high point of the insurrection. Now it is the world-famous Hermitage Arts Museum and we were escorted through some of the spectacular displays by a prim but resolute guide explaining the treasures in the manner of a school-mistress and in rapid but quite good English. She told us it would take several years to examine all the exhibits in the thousand rooms, and after about two hours of increasingly aching feet we grew seriously worried in case she was intent on forcing us to accomplish the task. Of course, we had to go aboard the battle cruiser Aurora, moored in the Neva nearby. It was a cannon shot from the Aurora that gave the signal for the storming of the Winter Palace. During the Second World War it was brought into active service again.

The next day we met an elderly man who was actually near the spot when history was being made – and had not taken a blind bit of notice of it. As a teenager, uninterested in politics, he was walking his girl along the Neva embankment opposite the Winter Palace when they heard the cannon shot and a lot of shouting. They thought something odd might be happening, but were too much preoccupied with themselves to worry about less important matters. It reminded me of the story the American journalist John Reed told of the park gardener in Petrograd, as it then was, who went on doing his job totally unconcerned about the revolution taking place around him.

We took a short boat trip to the island where stands the Peter Paul Fortress, and visited the cells where famous political prisoners, including Dostoevsky, had been incarcerated. The tombs of some of the Tsars are in the Fortress, and we were intrigued to see a candle burning on the tomb of Peter the Great. It was replaced every day as a tribute to the city's founder. In the evening we went to the Kirov Theatre to see a performance by the world-famous ballet company. But the most moving episode was visiting the graves of the 200,000 Leningrad men and women who had perished in the year-long siege of the city by the Germans – many of them having died of starvation. We placed a wreath near the foot of the statue of a mother-figure. I noticed that the war memorials I saw on this and subsequent visits to the Soviet Union were never martial in character, as they often are in the West, and usually portray a mother weeping for her lost children.

We had asked if we could have discussions with a leading party comrade, and were pleased to be invited to the Smolny one afternoon to meet a member of the Leningrad Party Committee who was also Chief

321

Inspector of Schools. We were fortunate in having James Klugman as the leader of our group, because he was known and respected for his writings, and this gave our group some prestige. Normally, the Smolny was not open to visitors, as it was the working headquarters of the Leningrad party. We were first shown around the building, including visiting the hall where the workers' and soldiers' delegates had been meeting when Lenin proclaimed Soviet power and had ordered the arrest of the Provisional Government. Standing in the hall stirred my imagination; it was easy to picture the epic event, so vividly described by John Reed in *Ten Days that Shook the World*.

We then had a two-hour discussion with the party secretary. Before going I asked if we could visit the homes of workers. He immediately agreed. He suggested that we make our own choice. When we visited the big Kirov turbine factory the next day, he proposed we ask one of the workers if we could go home with him. We decided to split our forces and choose two. My group picked on a middle-aged maintenance fitter repairing one of the machines. He was a little abashed by the request, but agreed. Even more disconcerted was his wife when her husband returned home from work with four foreigners in tow. We were the first British people she had ever met. Even so, we spent an extremely enjoyable evening exchanging information and views about our respective countries. Anton had fought in the war and many of his and Maria's relatives had died. When we mentioned that there were people in our country who saw the Soviet Union as a military threat, he was genuinely angry. "After what we have been through," he said, "only madmen could even think that we wanted another war." We were shown around their neat and reasonably well-equipped three-roomed flat. They had moved there after their children had married and moved to flats of their own. They seemed reasonably well off, and Anton explained that one-third of the workers in the factory had a plot of land outside of the city which they could use either to build a small dacha on, or to grow fruit and vegetables for their own use. This is what he was doing. I mentioned that I had a few apple trees and was plagued by boys "scrumping" the fruit. Anton just grinned and admitted he had the same problem but added magnanimously, "How can we blame them: haven't we all done it in our time?"

The Kirov factory was old; its workers had played a crucial role in the revolution. A statue of Stalin still stood outside it, although showing signs of neglect. What impressed me most about the factory was the easy relationship between workers and management. My experience as an engineering worker was that when the top manager walked around the factory, especially with visitors, we would at least appear to be concentrating on our work. At the Kirov, workers were obviously curious and groups gathered to eavesdrop on our discussion, even asking questions, seemingly oblivious to the presence of the manager. I left the main group to chat to some of the workers, and there were certainly no sign of inhibitions. Later, we had a formal discussion with the trades union committee. I was impressed by the explanation of collective discipline, including the fact that no worker could be dismissed without the agreement of the factory committee. It was also the first time I had seen computer-controlled machines automatically producing complicated parts, such as turbine blades and propellers, without anyone in attendance. I only realised its significance when, many years later, we read of the technical stagnation that developed and became one of the major factors in the collapse of the Soviet system.

We spent a few days at a sanatorium about twenty miles out of Moscow. One morning Kath and I went for a long walk through the forest and came across a village straight out of Tolstoy, with a higgledy-piggledy collection of wooden cottages in a large clearing, all differently designed and decorated. One was in the course of construction, and we were told it was for a young couple who had just wed. The state supplied building material free if they, with the help of neighbours and friends, did the construction.

From Moscow we flew to Stalingrad, an odd-shaped city straddling the Volga for eighty miles. Understandably, part of our time was spent re-living the famous battle, including talking to many who had fought in it. One such comrade took us to the site of one of the bitterest engagements, where shrapnel still littered the ground. The magnitude and significance of the battle is little appreciated by post-war generations in the West, and was deliberately played down in the commemorative events in the United States and Europe marking the Fiftieth Anniversary of the victory over fascism. To give some idea: more took part in the battle of Stalingrad than all the soldiers on both sides who fought in the North African and Italian campaigns. The defeat of von Paulus's Sixth Army was where, in Churchill's words, the Russians "tore the guts out of the German army" and was the turning point of the war. Only fourteen years before I had stood on another killing field, Cassino, and I could not help feeling an anger that cannot be expressed in mere words at the abomination of war and the wasteful loss of so many young lives. For the

Russians, it was the loss of an entire generation, a generation that, would, perhaps, have changed Soviet history in the dark years to come.

We visited the tank factory that had continued to function throughout the battle, although it was now making tractors and employed 15,000 workers. We next saw the giant Volga hydroelectric power station under construction – it was to be the largest in the world. A small town had been erected for the workers and their families, with workshops where they could be trained in new skills for when the power station was completed.

Wherever we went we were followed by a host of kids, who kept shouting what appeared to be rude remarks at us. It seems they were intrigued by the way we were dressed and were shouting the Russian equivalent of "Teddy-boys." Before we left we gave them some small presents and postcards.

In the morning of the third day we embarked on the Volga-Don Canal in a large ship which must have had about one hundred passengers. Overlooking the start of the canal was an enormous two hundred foot statue of Stalin. The journey through the sixty mile long canal and along the Don took two days and a night. It was delightfully restful, but it also gave us the opportunity to meet and talk to our fellow passengers, some of whom we got to know quite well. A picture I shall never forget is of James Klugman desperately trying to win games of chess on deck. His opponent was a ten year old lad. We stopped at two steppe villages on the way and were able to look around. The villagers were as interested in us as we were in them, and they plied us with questions about Britain.

Our programme at Rostov was almost wrecked on the first day. It happened this way. We spent the morning and part of the afternoon being shown around the gigantic "Lenin" collective farm, covering 28,000 acres and home to almost one thousand workers and their families. At the end of the tour, the chairman of the farm committee invited us to have a meal with him and the farm committee. Trestle tables had already been laid out in the open air, which we all duly sat at. We were served with giant dishes of borsch, the delicious Russian national soup made from beetroot, and then the Chairman proposed the usual toast. In front of us were large glasses of what we innocently thought was water. Of course it was vodka – and, as we discovered to our cost, an extremely potent spirit made on the farm. It was the tradition, so Yuri, our inter-preter, whispered to us, that for this first toast of friendship the glass be emptied. We dutifully complied. Immediately, our glasses were filled again, but fortunately we could now eat. It was a tremendous meal, made entirely with food grown on the farm. The problem was that between the interminable courses there were more toasts, each side taking turns. We drank to Soviet-British friendship, to peace, to the success of the collective farm, to the health of the Chairman and any other subject we could think of. As the meal progressed we were getting more and more befuddled until James whispered to Yuri that we just couldn't go on. "You mustn't offend them," Yuri said, "you have to be diplomatic. I suggest that the next one who proposes a toast begin by saying that how difficult it is to tear ourselves away, but in proposing this last toast, etc." This task fell to me, and we did eventually get away. We tottered back to our hotel, but had to cancel the theatre visit planned for the evening. Incidentally, there were two who kept sober throughout it all and were never pressurised to join in the drinking: Kath, who explained at the outset that she never drank spirits, and Sasha, the Regional Secretary of the Party, who they knew was a teetotaller.

The next day we were shown round a grape farm, interesting because of the manager. He was fine old character, an old Bolshevik who had fought in the revolution and also in the war. He made no secret of having a soft spot for Stalin.

Kath and I had an interesting experience when we were taking a stroll in one of Rostov's parks. Walking alongside us was a young couple with a small child in a pushchair. They kept glancing at us, and eventually the woman came across to us and said hesitatingly that she heard us talking and wondered if we were English. We temporarily put aside our nationalist scruples and told her we were indeed. She told us she was a schoolteacher and taught English but had never met an English person. As she obviously felt this was a heaven-sent opportunity for language practise, we spent an hour with them, which was useful from our point of view because it enabled us to quiz her. One remark she made was, "you know, we are very proud of our country," and she said it so naturally, without any self-consciousness, that it made an impression on both of us.

We spent ten days at the holiday resort of Sochi, on the Black Sea. We stayed at a "sanatorium," but the name means something different from its English equivalent. The Russian sanatorium is a rest and health centre with only loose medical supervision. Most of our time at Sochi was spent resting, swimming or rowing in the sea. The main beaches were packed with holiday-makers and our white skins stood out like sore thumbs against the bronzed torsos of everyone else. What made our stay partic-

325

ularly interesting was that we were able to have long talks with communists from other countries who, like us, were invited guests, as well as with Soviet families. One memorable event was a visit to a nearby Pioneer camp. It was occupied by children from Magadan, a town in the extreme far east of the Soviet Union. The four hundred children had been flown over four thousand miles at the state's expense to spend a month's holiday. They made a great fuss of us and put on a concert, unfortunately insisting that we sing some English songs in return.

We had a day in hand in Moscow before our return flight, and, by a majority vote, we opted to go to a football match. Moscow Dynamo was playing Athens in the huge Lenin Stadium. There was one price and seating throughout, and the stadium was packed. There was some light relief when the electronic system broke down for half-an-hour. First the scoreboard starting registering fantastic scores – 102-27, 170-35 – and then the floodlights failed, all to the great hilarity of the spectators. Some jeeringly lit newspapers and held them above their heads.

I have dealt at some length with this first visit to the Soviet Union because it was a profound experience for both Kath and myself. It strengthened our belief in socialism and our confidence in the Soviet system as we saw it.

It was before decline and stagnation had set in. Living standards seemed reasonable and were rising, and we sensed a wonderful feeling of faith in the future wherever we went. We were overwhelmed by the friendship shown to us. In later years I was to visit the Soviet Union again under similar circumstances and was to detect signs of changes for the worse taking place compared with that first visit. We were fortunate in being a small group on this occasion, and in having James Klugman with us. We had met James before, but the four weeks we spent with him cemented a friendship, especially between him and Kath, that was to last until he died.

41. CHESTERFIELD

Our first job on our return was to endorse the completion of the sale of the house and get settled in. Fortunately, the Junior School for Gwyneth and Bronwen and the Nursery School for Emrys was within walking distance of the house, and when Kath started teaching at Westfield Secondary School, at Eckington, we were able to afford for Doris Parsons, the mother of a party member, to come each day to do some of the housework and collect the kids from school. "Auntie Doris," as they knew her, travelled by train each day from Ilkeston and was truly devoted to the children – as they were to her.

Thus began our life in Chesterfield, a move we never regretted. The Communist Party branch was well respected in the labour movement and many of its members held influential positions in the workplaces, trades unions and progressive organisations of the town. Our closest friend was Win Clark. If ever a statue is warranted for someone who has given service to the people of Chesterfield, it is Win. Yet, she was unassuming to a fault. She shunned self-publicity and was content to work without pause and without recognition for the causes of socialism and peace that were so near to her heart. It isn't the famous, the great and the good, those who have biographies written about them or who write autobiographies, that have built our labour movement and on which it depends. It is the countless thousands of men and women who devote their lives giving unstinting service to the cause in which they so passionately believe, who distribute the leaflets, sell the literature at the workplace and on the doorstep, maintain grassroots organisation often when the tide is very much against them, and who act in accordance with their beliefs expecting no reward other than the satisfaction that they are helping their fellow creatures. As individuals, they pass by usually unrecognised and unrecorded – and not expecting it to be otherwise. Win was indeed such a person.

Coming from a staunch Mansfield trades union and Co-operative family she became involved in socialist politics in her early teens, joining the I.L.P. Guild of Youth in 1927, when she was nineteen. She and her husband Wilf resigned when Labour Minister of Labour, Margaret Bondfield, introduced the "not genuinely seeking work" condition for unemployed men and women claiming benefit. She attended the first National Summer School organised by the National Council of Labour Colleges. In 1936 Win and Wilf were expelled from the Chesterfield Labour Party because of their opposition to the witch-hunt against Communists and others on the left, and soon afterwards they joined the Communist Party. She was an indefatigable campaigner in support of Spanish democracy and the other great movements of the pre-war years; she also helped form and was active in a local Left Book Club Theatre Group. Like her mother, Win was a keen member of the Co-op Women's Guilds, for thirteen years being Chairperson of the Whittington Moor Guild. When a ban was imposed on Communists holding any position, her Guild refused to apply it – even threatening to dissolve itself if any attempt was made to remove her. She was the first secretary of

Chesterfield C.N.D., although an active peace campaigner long before the C.N.D. was formed. Yet, none of this gives a real picture of Win. She combined a selfless and caring personality with a hatred of all forms of injustice. And she acted on her principles, never hesitating to undertake any task that needed doing. She stood as a Communist candidate in local council elections on many occasions and although never elected, her votes by no means reflected the great personal respect in which she was held throughout the entire labour and progressive movement in Chesterfield.

It was Wilf's job that brought them to Chesterfield. He was an engineering worker who "rose in the ranks," starting out as a teenage apprentice and ending up as General Manager of the important Sheepbridge Stokes engineering works, employing over two thousand workers. He did this through sheer ability, without in any way compromising his Communist principles. After the rise of Hitler, he helped to smuggle into Germany thousands of flimsy rice-paper leaflets for passing on to the clandestine anti-fascist trade unionists who were resisting the Nazi jackboot, and for some time he was a member of the Party's District Committee. He was keen on Marxist education and for almost twenty years was a voluntary tutor for the National Council of Labour Colleges (N.C.L.C.), covering North Derbyshire and North Nottinghamshire. When the war started, Wilf had already proved his supervisory abilities at the firm's Mansfield plant and was eventually made manager of its main factory. Untypically, the firm recognised that having a competent person in charge of an important armament factory was more important than political prejudice.

For most of the war years Wilf was in a unique position, combining superb management skills with deep political convictions in the drive to increase war production. The particular role of Sheepbridge Stokes was to produce cylinder liners for the absolutely vital Rolls Royce engines. The end of the war, followed by the Cold War and the changes that this imposed, eventually led to the firm getting rid of Wilf, but not before he had wrung out of the company a moderate sum as conscience-money, giving him the capital to start a small engineering plant of his own. Wilf was a tough personality, sharp of tongue and not suffering fools gladly, but he retained throughout his life an unswerving devotion to the working class and the Communist Party when so many others would have compromised their principles for the sweets that capitalist conformity offered.

When we moved to Chesterfield, the branch secretary was Harry Wynn, a hard-working and thoughtful comrade who loved a discussion on any subject, particularly if it was over a quiet pint. He was the son of miners' leader Bert Wynn and worked for the National Coal Board. When I first knew him, he and his wife, Glenda – also an active comrade – lived with Bert's family in the living premises attached to the Derbyshire Miners' Offices. The branch had about one hundred members, and there were also two small factory branches, at Sheepbridge Stokes and at the Chesterfield Tube Works. The two main industries of Chesterfield were mining and engineering. Communists were influential in the unions covering both industries and were also on the trades council. The Chesterfield Trades Council did not have a very auspicious history. In 1949 the TUC had revived the ban on trade unions electing Communists to official positions, including representing their unions on trades councils – the infamous Black Circular. This was increasingly ignored, but Chesterfield Trades Council was among the last to apply it. There had been the ludicrous position where two of the leading N.U.M. Agents, the chairman of the A.E.U. District Committee, the convenors in the two main factories, and many other shop stewards and pit representatives were not allowed to be delegates to the Trades Council. A successful campaign had been conducted against the ban, and when we arrived in Chesterfield Communists were playing an important part on the Trades Council.

Being based in Chesterfield made an enormous difference to me. I now had a small office at home, but it meant that I was not as office-bound as in Nottingham because it was easier to get out to the pits and to visit comrades in the pit villages without interference. In addition, it was satisfying being able to play a part in an important and active branch. One of the problems in getting around the coalfield was having to rely on public transport. The coalfield was made up of numerous pit villages, significantly often called "compounds," built around a pit. Although public transport was better than it is now, it was irksome having to spend hours travelling to a pit to sell about twenty copies of the *Daily Worker*, or to visit comrades – who were often out or on the wrong shift. I once estimated that I was spending about a third of my time on buses. This is what prompted us to get a second-hand car – that, and the threat that I would get a motorcycle, vehicles which Kath regarded as bats from hell. My first driving test was a disaster. Unfortunately for me, there was a bitter vendetta between my driving instructor and the particular examiner it was my lot to have. Before the test began an unholy row started between the two of them, with my instructor insisting on sitting in the

329

car while the test was being taken because he believed the examiner was totally incompetent to do the test. Understandably, my self-confidence was totally sapped before I had turned the ignition key. It didn't help when, not knowing Chesterfield, I immediately succeeded in getting the car stuck for ten minutes between two stationary buses in a street serving as a bus terminus. Fortunately, the next time I took the test was less traumatic, and I passed. What annoyed me was the thought that when in the army in Italy I had had the job of issuing driving licenses to men in my unit, yet I never thought of giving myself one, obviously not being farsighted or optimistic enough to appreciate that one day I might reach the dizzy heights of owning a car.

Two or three days a week I would visit a pit, driving into the pit yard and parking in the car park. Often with another comrade, we would stand outside the canteen, covering the morning shift coming off and the afternoon shift going on. Although we were on Coal Board property, usually there was no interference by the management. Occasionally, though, an officious-looking trumped-up clerk would come up to us and ask if we had permission. The exchange would then go something like this:

Me: "We don't need permission."

TUC: "You do."

Me: "We don't. We are never stopped at other pits."

TUC: "Well, it's different here. The management doesn't allow trespassing."

Me: "Go and fetch the manager, I'd like to hear it from him."

He would then trot off and we would continue distributing our literature or I would continue speaking. Of course, the manager hardly ever deigned to put in an appearance. If he did, we would pack up, because my policy was not to provoke the Area Coal Board into making a ruling that would ban us from all pits. On one occasion when I was prevented from selling, a comrade at the pit who had just come off his shift and had listened to my altercation with the deputy manager, without a word took the quire of *Daily Workers* from me and, in front of the under-manager, quickly sold them all to his workmates – doing a far better job than I would have done!

What was common to all mining villages, whatever the coalfield, was the strong sense of community. I found Notts and Derbyshire to be remarkably similar to South Wales in this respect, which, no doubt, is why I felt a special affinity towards them. The main reason, of course, was because they were welded to one industry, often one pit, with the menfolk working in the same dangerous occupation, an occupation that depended so much on mutual trust and co-operation. The life of the community was conditioned by this fact. In the pubs, the social clubs, out shopping, men and women met neighbours who shared the same lifestyles and the same experiences. It was a precious culture that enriched the wider culture of the entire working class. Its destruction by the vandals advancing under the flag of free-market economics, and the way it was done, will be condemned by history – of that I am sure.

I found mining comrades particularly generous in their hospitality. The problem often was persuading them that I wasn't on the bread-line and didn't need two or three cooked meals a day. Among the older women comrades in particular there was the pre-conceived conception that no amount of argument would shift, that working for the party was synonymous with being starved. Often, soon after arriving, the lady of the house would appear with a steaming hot plate, and would peremptorily issue the order, "Get that down you!" There was one comrade, Hilda Crompton, the widow of a miner in Alfreton, who just ignored all protestations that I had eaten, and would, whenever I called and whatever the time, insist on preparing a massive meal, which I had to force down. No doubt this was a throwback to the days when party organisers did have to rely on such generosity. When I lived in Caerphilly I was told of the veteran comrade, Bob Stewart, who had come down from Scotland as an organiser in the 1920's literally penniless and with no income whatsoever. He would eat at a different comrade's house each day.

CHAPTER VIII

1959-1975: THE SHADOW OF THE BOMB

42. THE STRUGGLE FOR PEACE ENTERS A NEW STAGE

"You've never had it so good!" This is what the sixteen sheet Tory posters assaulted our eyes with prior to the 1959 general election. It was the slogan on which "Supermac" Harold Macmillan fought the election and which led the Tories to their third consecutive victory. Undoubtedly, there was a "feel-good factor" among some sections of the people and it was translated into votes. Capitalism was going through a short period of relative stability; wages were increasing and living conditions for many improving. Just before the election the official unemployment figure was below 400,000 – in reality probably over half a million. Unacceptable though this was, it did mean that the shortage of labour in some industries gave unions a lever to wrest concessions from the employers. Indeed, a constant cry from bosses' organisations such as the Confederation of British Industry was that "unemployment is too low" – meaning that they needed a more effective reserve army of labour as a weapon to keep down wages.

As before, the Labour Party failed to put forward a socialist alternative. But now powerful right-wing ideologues launched a new offensive against socialist ideas in the labour movement. They were collectively called the "New Thinkers" and the most influential was C. A. R. Crosland, whose book *The Future of Socialism* is still something of a bible among right-wingers. The essence of their argument was that capitalism has been transformed since Marx's day – and has changed for the good. Crosland argued that we now lived in a "post-capitalist society" where power was no longer in the hands of a capitalist class; some industries were nationalised and those that were not were run by managers on behalf of large numbers of shareholders. "The function of decision-making," he wrote, "has been transferred to a largely non-owning class of salaried executive . . . the classical capitalist class of entrepreneurs has largely disappeared, at least from large-scale industry". Nor are workers any longer a coherent exploited class. The creation of surplus value, of profit, no longer means exploitation, as Marxists argue, but is necessary and desirable, since it now benefits the whole of society. As for socialism, he maintained that it has never been clearly defined, nor can it be. It is quite wrong to see capitalism and socialism as opposed systems, for what is happening is the gradual development of a more equal society. From which readers will discern that the "new thinkers" of the Blair era are not nearly as new as they may think they are. In fact, right-wing "new thinking" is a malady that has broken out many times in the history of our labour movement. It is a malignancy that confuses and weakens the movement, undermines socialist resolve and justifies class collaboration.

The end of the decade marked what is arguably the most critical point in the entire history of intelligent life on this earth. The very genius of humankind had created a technological monster that was now capable of totally destroying all life on the planet. In 1952 the United States had tested a new weapon – the H-bomb. In one blast it released the power of ten million tons of high explosives – far greater than all the explosives used by both sides in the Second World War. A year later the Soviet Union tested its first H-bomb and in 1954 the Americans dropped a super H-bomb on the Bikini Atoll in the Pacific. From then we have lived under the shadow of the mushroom cloud. The Americans were confident they could keep ahead in the production of these ever more poisonous weapons, but on 4th October 1957 they reeled under a most unexpected shock. The Soviet Union launched Sputnik, the first artificial satellite. Most people applauded this historic first step on the part of humanity to extend its understanding of the cosmos, but the US administration immediately saw the military significance of the event and the revelation that it was so far behind in the conquest of space. The full extent of the panic in the Pentagon was only revealed years later. Enormous resources were directed to the space programme, with Kennedy setting the goal of America landing a man on the moon in ten years. It is interesting to note that official western propagandists now use this event, not the launching of Sputnik or Yuri Gagarin's historic flight in 1961, to mark the date when the space age began. This, despite the fact that the Soviet Union not only placed the first man – and the first woman – in space, but was first to photograph the far side of the moon. This was followed by sending two unmanned moon vehicles, Luna Fourteen and Luna Fifteen, around the moon – all before the U.S. Apollo landing. It is worth noting, in view

333

of current mythology that the United States "won the race to the moon," that the Soviet Union announced at the time that it did not intend joining such a race because it did not consider the cost worth it in view of the fact that unmanned probes could just as well be sent.

When, at the beginning of 1955, the Tory government announced that Britain was building an H-bomb, the Labour Party leadership predictably supported it – although seventy M.P.'s did abstain in the vote endorsing government policy. One of these was Aneurin Bevan, who three years later as Shadow Foreign Secretary was to stun delegates at the Labour Party Conference with a withering denunciation of unilateral nuclear disarmament as government policy. Opposing the unilateralist resolution, he uttered the long-remembered words,"If you carry this resolution . . . you will send a British Foreign Secretary, whoever he was, naked into the conference chamber!" While the right was delighted, the left, including some of his closest friends, were shocked at what they saw as a betrayal by their idol. It marked an end to the name "Bevanites," although the organised grouping around "Tribune" continued.

Every action produces a reaction. The catastrophic character of the nuclear threat provoked the most extensive and powerful broad popular movement seen since the days of the Chartists. In February 1958, a meeting of distinguished personalities that included philosopher Bertrand Russell, writer J. B. Priestley, historian A. J. P. Taylor, journalist James Cameron, and the Dean of St Paul's, Canon Collins, met at Collins' house and formed the Campaign for Nuclear Disarmament. Soon the inspired, simple semaphore emblem of C.N.D. was to become the most easily recognised symbol throughout Britain and was eventually to be seen on walls and placards all over the world as a testimony of those struggling to save humanity from the madness of nuclear destruction.

I don't think it has been sufficiently recognised that the C.N.D. was largely built on the foundation laid by the British Peace Committee (B.P.C.). It was the B.P.C. that led the struggle for peace in the first difficult years of the Cold War, and that really did bring many thousands of people into action. The Stockholm Appeal (and the great petition following it) and the Sheffield Rally have already been referred to, but the B.P.C. also conducted continuous local actions, and organised inspiring national demonstrations. And it was part of an organised international movement for peace. The World Peace Council united peace organisations of all countries and had many distinguished international personalities on its ruling Council, including scientists of international repute like Professor

J. D. Bernal, Professor Joliot-Curie and Professor Peter Kapitza. This all-embracing character was held against it by some who argued that because the peace committees of the Soviet Union and the other socialist countries were associated with it, it could not possibly be independent. It is true that the Communist Parties in this and other countries strongly supported the B.P.C. It was put on the Labour Party's list of "proscribed organisations," bodies that Labour Party members were supposed not to have anything to do with.

In the East Midlands Kath had been secretary of its quite strong Nottingham Branch, and Win Clark held the same position in Chesterfield. For some time the B.P.C. and C.N.D. existed and worked together, but as the issue of nuclear weapons came to dominate the struggle for peace, C.N.D. became the main force in the peace movement. Nuclear disarmament was a simpler and more emotive issue than the struggle for peace on very many fronts necessitated by the Cold War, which is the struggle that the B.P.C. sought to advance.

The 1960's began dramatically with significant victories for the left at the 1960 Scarborough conference of the Labour Party. Hugh Gaitskell, who was now the leader of the party, tried to get rid of Clause Four from the Labour Party's constitution (the clause committing the party to bringing under public ownership the means of production, distribution and exchange). This attempt failed and the party's socialist purpose was reiterated. To rub salt in the wound, a call was made for increased nationalisation. A proposal by the right-wing to reduce the sovereignty of the conference over the Parliamentary Party was defeated. But the biggest upset was the success of a resolution supporting unilateral nuclear disarmament. This really did send shock waves throughout the establishment. In *Labour Monthly*, Palme Dutt warned against premature rejoicing, but being human we did rejoice. Unfortunately, Dutt proved to be right. Gaitskell was not prepared to accept defeat on such a crucial issue. In a rare show of passion, the man who Nye Bevan had called "a desiccated calculating machine" declared that he would "fight, fight, and fight again to save the party I love" from the unilateralists. By the next conference the right-wing had mobilised all their big guns in the trade union hierarchy to reverse the decision – leaders of three of the biggest unions even defying their own conferences' pro-unilateralist decisions.

43. THE CUBAN MISSILE CRISIS

The razor's-edge on which the world was so finely balanced between

335

existence and obliteration was soon to be dramatically revealed by the Cuba missile crisis. For several nerve-wracking days in October 1963 we lived under the threat that U.S. President J. F. Kennedy would succumb to the pressure of the hawks in Congress to push the nuclear button and go to war against the Soviet Union. The ostensible reason was that the Cubans were building missile sites supplied by the Soviet Union and that this threatened the security of the United States. Kennedy claimed that they were "offensive" weapons, but this is a term he invented. The categorising of weapons as "offensive" or "defensive" is not internationally recognised, and by a strange twist of logic, the American bases and rockets targeted on the Soviet Union, including those in Turkey and other countries near to the Soviet Union, were "defensive." In any case, the idea that a small and poor country like Cuba could pose a threat to its rich and powerful neighbour was quite ludicrous.

The reality was the very opposite. It was the United States that was threatening the security and independence of Cuba, and under international law Cuba had every right to take measures to defend itself against possible aggression. Nor was this a fanciful idea. Almost since the new regime was established in Cuba, the American ruling class was hell-bent on destroying it. Motivated by pathological anti-Communism, the very idea of a socialist state so near to its shores provoked an unreasoning hysteria. After all, it could well be an example that other countries in Central and South America might decide to follow. In defiance of international law and the U.N., the United States imposed a trade boycott and blockade. In April 1961 its war department connived with Cuban émigrés in planning, training, equipping and even transporting an invasion force against Cuba. U.S. planes bombed Cuban airfields in advance. The attempted invasion at the Bay of Pigs was an unmitigated disaster for the Americans. Instead of the Cuban people rising against Castro, as had been fondly hoped, they rallied to the defence of their socialist motherland, and the invasion collapsed ignominiously. Even so, there were plenty of voices in Congress urging a better prepared repeat and accusing Kennedy of timidity.

This, then, was the backdrop to the events eighteen months later. The United States government demanded the immediate dismantling of the missile sites and announced that its navy would fire on and board any ship delivering supplies – in other words, Soviet ships. This was a gross violation of international law, and the Soviet Union announced that any attack on its ships would be regarded as an act of piracy, an act of war,

336

and would be resisted. As Soviet ships approached the blockade zone, the world held it breath. Had the moment of truth arrived? Was this the countdown to the first action of the Third World War, the first direct military conflict between the two superpowers? Few were in any doubt as to what the appalling consequences would be.

There was a universal sigh of relief when, with only hours left, Khrushchev ordered the Soviet ships not to enter the blockade zone and proposed negotiations between himself and Kennedy. In the talks that followed he argued that the strengthening of Cuban defences was made necessary because there had already been one attempt at invasion, and ever since its failure the United States government had not ruled out the possibility of destroying the Castro regime by force. He proposed that Kennedy give a firm pledge that neither the United States nor any of its American allies would ever invade Cuba. If this pledge were given, the missile sites would no longer be necessary and would be dismantled. To the fury of the hawks in Congress, who called Kennedy "soft," this was what was agreed. It is strange – or perhaps it's not – that the perceived wisdom today is that Kennedy saved the peace; but this is not how it was seen by most people at the time. This was best expressed by Bertrand Russell, who, in a remarkable tribute to Khrushchev, said:

"I say to Premier Nikita Khrushchev that mankind owes him a profound debt for his courage and determination to prevent war due to American militarism. Under the public threat of a Great Power, he has ignored the dictates of false pride, the infantile code which leads men of power to put aside the interests of humanity for their own muscle-bound prestige. I cannot praise sufficiently the sanity and magnanimity, the willingness to do all required to solve this overwhelmingly grave crisis."

And Hella Pick, *The Guardian's* United Nations correspondent, reported that:

"The almost unanimous view of the African and Asian countries was that the Cuban government was justified in going to almost any lengths to ensure its defence against American invasion . . . including building missile bases . . . Premier Khrushchev's decision again shows that the U.S.S.R., unlike the U.S., is willing to negotiate rather than move by force."

There is no doubt that one of the decisive factors was world outrage, expressed in marches, demonstrations, telegrams to the White House, deputations to American embassies, etc. In Britain, the Tory government acted as the abject apologists for Kennedy, and the Labour leaders – in line with their bipartisan stand on foreign policy – were little better. Yet, there was a tide of protest that embraced all sections of the people, including some Tories. What happened in Chesterfield and the East Midlands was a microcosm of what was taking place everywhere. When the crisis broke, our Communist Party branch secretary, Win Clark, was knocking on my door at 8 a.m., upset, but typically full of fighting determination – Win was never one to wallow helplessly in negative emotions. We drew up a plan of campaign that included a telegram to Kennedy signed by as many local dignitaries as we could get hold of, phone calls to others urging them to send similar telegrams, a leaflet to be given out at workplaces and a public meeting the following evening with a broad platform of speakers. We decided to personally visit the dignitaries, and the response exceeded our expectation – I don't think we had a single refusal. As well as the Mayor, several Aldermen, other local politicians and trade union leaders, we even persuaded one of the Robinson's – well-known Tories and owners of the large family firm that bears their name – to sign. Five hundred leaflets were given out at Markham, the main local pit, that afternoon. In the evening the Sheffield Star published a statement from the party. We visited every branch committee member and called an emergency meeting of the committee for the evening, and the next morning every important factory was covered with leaflets; altogether six thousand leaflets were given out in three days. The public meeting, although organised at such short notice, was well attended and had an atmospheric urgency about it. This was Wednesday, and it was agreed to call another public meeting on Sunday, this time with twenty five sponsors, including the M.P., eight Labour Councillors, the Derbyshire Miners and the other main trade unions, and church ministers. The previous day a poster parade with forty participants walked through the town centre. The same sort of activity was taking place in other towns of the East Midlands and, indeed, throughout the country. In most cases, it was the Communist Party that took the initiative.

An interesting footnote: when it was all over, the girls in the sixth form of Chesterfield's main girls' grammar school, St Helena's, sent a letter to Khrushchev signed by them all thanking him for saving peace. This was typical of the thousands of messages he received.

Kath and I never went on any of the Aldermaston Marches – the great annual event organised by the C.N.D. – although we often made the Easter pilgrimage to London to greet the marchers when they arrived at Trafalgar Square or Hyde Park. They were great occasions, long to be savoured, for at their peak there has never been anything like them either before or since. Each march seemed endless, swollen by fresh participants as it neared London. Throughout the morning and afternoon the marchers would be arriving, and when the information periodically came over the loudspeakers telling us how many miles away the tail of the march still was, it would be greeted by a great cheer from 100,000 throats. Every year the march looked more colourful, more broadly based and more international. There were Buddhist monks in their saffron robes, contingents in national costumes, groups from virtually every religion and walk of life and from every political party in Britain – even enlightened Tories. The American and Soviet contingents were particularly warmly applauded. Although the purpose was serious, it was also a joyous occasion, with well known and little known bands and singers performing from floats and on the plinth of Nelson's column throughout the day. People's power was being demonstrated, and it is little wonder that our political masters were disturbed by it – as has since been admitted. On one occasion we were pleased to meet Betty and Tony Ambatielos again; they had come over from Greece soon after Tony had been released from prison, where he had spent many years for his part in the struggle for democracy.

At the beginning of the 1960's we were sorry to say goodbye to a close friend, Rose Smith. Rose was a foundation member of the Communist Party and in the 1920's and 1930's had been a star *Daily Worker* journalist. When she retired, she came to live in Chesterfield, only a couple of streets away from us. We became firm friends and she often used to drop in for a chat and regale us with stories of her eventful life. Her rather severe appearance belied a gentle personality and a keen sense of humour. She established a rapport with our children and soon became one of our chief "baby-sitters," often collecting them from school. Of course, she played a full part in the work of the branch and would come with me to sell the *Morning Star* at pits. When she decided to go and live with her daughter in Australia I organised a farewell dinner for her at which Johnny Campbell, the former editor of the *Star*, and veteran reporter Walter Holmes were the chief speakers. There were many messages from those who had worked with Rose, Labour Party personalities as well as Communists.

Eventually, she moved to China, and worked as a "polisher" of English language translations. She settled there, and was much honoured, becoming a friend of Foreign Minister Chou En-Lai. She re-visited us a few years later and tried to persuade Kath and me to join her in China –

to which she had clearly become deeply attached. She targeted Kath more than me. In an all-night discussion she eloquently explained why China's universities needed politically dedicated English lecturers, clinching her argument with the carrot – "you won't have to do any housework." When I asked what my position would be, she responded, rather dismissively, "we'll find something for you to do!" We weren't tempted. We felt that there was too big a job to be done in this country. Sadly, some time later, when the rift between the Soviet Union and China had widened and the Chinese press was continuously attacking what it called the "revisionism" of the Soviet leaders and those Communist Parties who supported them, Rose wrote an article in *Peking Review* attacking the British party for its support of the Soviet position and citing how good comrades in Chesterfield were being misled – including even a stalwart like Mick Kane. The last time I saw Rose, was a surprise encounter at a bus stop in Chesterfield. She was on her way back to China. She had come over for a few weeks before making up her mind where to end her days and had concluded that she wanted it to be in China. We can only speculate as to why she had not contacted any of her old comrades when she was over. She died soon afterwards.

44. AGAIN THE SOVIET UNION – UZBEKISTAN

In August 1964 we visited the Soviet Union for the second time. This time I was leader of the delegation, which included two veteran Scots comrades, Finlay Hart and Arnold Henderson, and the Secretary of the Belfast Trades Council, Betty Sinclair. Finlay and Arnold were Communist councillors, and when we were asked on the first day if there were any places any of us would like to visit, Arnold asked to see a sewage farm. This was not first on our list of holiday attractions, but apparently the disposal of sewage was something he was interested in, it being one of his responsibilities as a councillor – and Communist councillors are nothing if not conscientious. His request was granted but, not surprisingly, he went alone.

Most of us wanted to see more distant and exotic parts of the Soviet Union than Moscow and Leningrad, so when it was suggested that we travel to Uzbekistan we jumped at the proposal. We flew there from Sochi, 1,800 miles across the Caspian Sea and the Kara-kum desert, and on arrival were based at the modern party hotel in Tashkent. In 1966 Tashkent was partially destroyed by an earthquake and the entire city centre had to be rebuilt. Years later, we met the City Engineer who was bold enough to assert that if a similar disaster occurred again the new buildings would stand up to it. He made an interesting point: the main damage was done to buildings above and below seven storeys. So seven storeys seemed to be the optimum safety height. Tashkent is a truly beautiful city, with open spaces, gardens and many pools and fountains – which surprised us, for it is, we were told, an "oasis city" and has a very low annual rainfall. Water has to come from the distant mountains. The fountains and pools had a utilitarian purpose in that they moistened the normally dry air. It was certainly extremely hot, but not all that unbearable, and the evenings were pleasantly cool. It was then that Kath and I would go for long walks around the streets and in the public gardens.

From Tashkent, we travelled two hundred and fifty miles along the ancient route of the "golden road" to Samarkand and Bukhara. En route, we stopped at a state fruit farm and were the guests of the Chairman, a huge, jovial chap who had an encyclopaedic knowledge of English football. The fruit farm was on irrigated soil that had not long before been a desert. He and Finlay vied with each other in drinking vodka and, much to our surprise, Finlay seemed to be winning – until we discovered that our interpreter was filling his glass with water. Samarkand is 2,500 years old – one of the world's oldest cities – and was the ancient capital of Tamerlane, the fourteenth century Mongol ruler, whose tomb we visited. His grandson, Ulagbeg, was a remarkable philosopher and scientist, and we were able to examine his observatory containing the remains of a giant sextant with which he measured the length of the year. He was only four and half minutes out. The year before our visit, the world astronomical conference had been held in Samarkand as a tribute to Ulagbeg.

But what I remember most was the breathtaking beauty of the ancient Moslem buildings, the walls and domes of which were covered with thousands of brightly coloured tiles making up complicated geometrical patterns, gleaming in the bright sun and seemingly as fresh as when they were put in position. The most impressive was the perfectly preserved Shir-Dor medresseh – an ancient religious university containing hundreds of student cells, and the Sha-I-Zinda mosques. We were not allowed to enter the "mausoleum of the living prophet" because it was sacred to Moslems and contained the remains of a relative of Mohammed. Considering the problems it was faced with, it is noteworthy that only a year after the Revolution, the new Soviet government allocated money to help preserve the buildings. We saw how extensive was the restoration work still going on – indeed we spoke to some of the workers, for whom it was obviously a labour of love. One explained that they were still unable to match exactly the permanent blue of some of the original mosaics. The region, of course, has a large Moslem population. The Tashkent City Engineer had told us that in deference to the wishes of older adherents, when they rebuilt the city after the earthquake, they constructed many homes in the Muslim style of an open box, with no windows facing outwards.

Bukhara is even older than Samarkand. We arrived on market day when the town was teeming with people hustling and bustling between hundreds of stalls selling a great variety of goods, food, fruit, clothes, furniture, household goods, second-hand and new, even some animals. Free enterprise that Thatcher would have approved of! It was a kind of Chesterfield on flea-market day, except that the clothes many of the people were wearing would give the game away. In contrast to the western clothes of the young, many older men wore baggy trousers and turban-type headdresses, and those that didn't, men and women, wore the distinctive Uzbek hat. The desert association was indicated by the camels tethered to posts. We visited the Emir's palace and several ancient mosques, including a minaret that is the tallest medieval structure in central Asia. When it was finished, the Emir had the hapless architect thrown to his death from the top in case he was tempted to make a copy for a rival ruler!

The physical differences between Uzbeks and the minority Russian population are quite distinct. Uzbeks are darker, with black hair and distinctive features. All wore the traditional round soft brimless hat – plain for the men, coloured for women. Most of the younger women wore very colourful cotton dresses and silk scarves, with conventional Uzbek designs, and their hair was done in a multitude of plaits. At our request, when we were passing through a village, we paid a "spot-check" visit to the homes of an Uzbek and a Russian family. They were neighbours, but the contrasting living styles were striking. The Russian living-room was quite orthodox western, but the furniture of his neighbour consisted only of a small low table and a T.V. set – discreetly covered with a coloured drape. There were cushions on the floor and beautiful carpets on the walls. In the garden just outside the back door was a covered platform – a tea-house – where they served tea. Larger public tea-houses were common in the towns and we sampled a few. We would have to remove our shoes and squat at a low table, when the attendant would serve us with green tea and unleavened bread, to break and eat while drinking. Rather like pubs in Wales, there was a time when women were not allowed to use the tea-houses and – we were told – some older Moslems still resent their use by both sexes.

One of the biggest problems facing Communists after the revolution was breaking down the harsh discrimination against women in Moslem areas like Uzbekistan. In the 1920's, members of the Young Communist League literally risked their lives in spreading education and conducting propaganda among women, urging them to fight for equal rights with men – Jennie Lee visited the region during this period and wrote a graphic account of the problem. The great breakthrough came in 1928, when a big demonstration of women gathered at Registan Square in Samarkand and publicly threw off their veils and yashmaks. Possibly because of the high profile given to women's rights, Uzbekistan was the only Soviet republic where the majority of M.P'.s in their parliament were women. So was the Regional Secretary of the party, who was in charge of us.

However, we had one experience that rather besmirched this bright picture. We visited a large cotton factory and had a discussion with the Party Secretary – a man. Kath had made women's rights her issue during the entire trip, and she therefore proceeded to question him about the situation in the factory.

Kath:"What is the proportion of women employed here?"

PS: "82 per cent."

K:"How many women are on your committee?"

PS:"None."

K:"How do your account for this?"

PS:"Most party members are men, and women don't want to stand for the committee."

K:"Don't you think this is odd? Why are they not prepared to be on the Committee? Have you ever discussed it with them? How can the party give leadership when the majority of the workers are not represented on its leading body?"

PS (Now clearly embarrassed): "I will see that it is discussed and that the points you make are put to the Committee."

One final point about this fascinating visit. I noticed that everywhere notices, posters, road signs, etc were in two languages – Russian and Uzbek. All public announcements were in the two languages, and either could be used in the courts, in the Soviets and public bodies. We were told that in Uzbek schools, Russian was the second language, and in Russian schools, it was Uzbek. Being Welsh, I particularly appreciated

343

this. I had a nephew who was an active member of the Welsh Language Society and who spent a considerable amount of his time campaigning for Welsh to be recognised in the same way in Wales. Even now, this has still not been completely achieved.

In light of these experiences I have found it difficult to understand or fully believe the stories of extreme Uzbek nationalism directed against the Soviet regime. The Uzbeks and their culture were savagely suppressed under Tsarism. They were a non-nation without a recognised language or culture. The Revolution changed all that. Their nationhood and culture were restored and encouraged, and with them their self-confidence. If the reports are true – and I must confess to reservations about them – I can only assume that the present generation is making comparisons only with the immediate past and is translating the economic hardship suffered by all the peoples of the Soviet Union regardless of nationality, into national terms. There is also, of course, the religious dimension. The events of the past few years have demonstrated that Marxists have underestimated the tenacity of religious ideas as well as national feelings. In a country like Uzbekistan, where Islam has been the dominant ideology for a thousand years it is surely too much to expect its influence to be fundamentally weakened in a mere seventy years. Moreover, the determined struggle for women's rights created a special conflict of interests between the Soviet government and the particular fundamentalist branch of Islam that existed in Uzbekistan.

At Kiev and at Leningrad, in discussions with party officials Kath brought up the issue of the position of women. What concerned her was the fact that although women had legal equality with men and that such equality was clearly seen in many spheres throughout society, it was not reflected in the political field – where power really lay. The C.P.S.U. leadership, for example, was very much male-dominated – there was only one woman on its Political Committee. The responses were enlightening. The Kiev Party Secretary, a sixty year old veteran shrugged off the question with grin, "Well, you know what women are like; they prefer doing their things . . ." There's no need to enlarge on how that response was received! He would not accept that there was a serious problem. In Leningrad, the keen, very young Party official we spoke to responded in an entirely different way. He readily agreed that it was a serious problem, and he didn't believe the party was paying enough attention to it. Equality could not be achieved by legal or administrative measures alone: it was a question of aggressively changing the inbred reactionary attitudes of men. In Leningrad they had made a start with education directed at male comrades. It had been made clear that it was totally unacceptable that when a husband and wife were both party members, that it was the husband who attended meetings and took part in party activity. He was not optimistic about any quick transformation of the position.

One of our delegates was a *Morning Star* journalist – I believe it was Tom Spence – and he, Kath and I had an interesting discussion with Ukrainian writers at the Writers' Union offices in Kiev. They had recently held a seminar on Kafka and wanted to know our views on this famous Czech writer . . . unfortunately we had to confess our ignorance as not one of us had read any of his books! Incidentally, I had not long before read in our Western press that Kafka was banned in the Soviet Union. When we visited the newspaper Pravda, Tom tackled the editor about the paper's condemnation of the Beatles in a recent article for being "decadent." "Have any of you here ever heard them?" he asked. The editor hadn't, of course, but he did offer to publish a letter from Tom answering the criticism. Whether or not Tom did so I do not know.

Our Soviet hosts committed a faux pas on our last evening in Leningrad, when they put on a farewell dinner for us at the hotel where we were staying. Spaced out along the tables were miniature Union Jacks. I didn't like this and asked for them to be removed, but by then Betty Sinclair and the Irish comrades had walked out and refused to come back until they had been taken away. I could well understand why; it was as if they were being asked to sup with the symbols of the devil. The scene was watched with interest by that most obnoxious English right-wing politician and journalist, Woodrow Wyatt, who was sitting at a nearby table, and who was curious to know who we were. He and his companion – a glamorous young woman half his age – had been seated in front of us at the Kirov theatre the evening before. I suggested to our host that if they wanted to do a service to the British working class they would arrange for him to be dumped in the Neva that evening. He looked at me gravely, and said: "Comrade, getting rid of British reactionaries is your responsibility, not ours!"

45. THE VIETNAM WAR

Soon after we returned from the Soviet Union thirteen years of Tory government came to an end. The October 1964 general election resulted in Labour being returned to power, but only just. It had a knife-edge majority of four. This, and the fact that it inherited a parlous economic situation, was predictably seized upon by the right-wing as an argument for going slow on any radical proposals. These were few indeed. Labour had fought the election on a bi-partisan foreign policy, giving full support to the joint Tory-U.S.A. Cold War strategy, which included German rearmament, building the nuclear arsenal and virulent anti-Sovietism. The right-wing sought to dampen down the wages struggle by playing on the anti-working-class record of the previous Tory administration and using the threat that it could easily make a come-back unless the trade unions were "disciplined" and "responsible."

In the meantime, ominous events were taking place in the Far East that were to cast a dark shadow over the world for many years ahead. In August, the Americans had alleged that North Vietnam torpedo boats had fired on one of their destroyers in the Gulf of Tonkin. In undue haste and without producing any satisfactory evidence of the veracity of the allegation, U.S. planes bombed North Vietnam naval bases. Within six months, regular bombing of North Vietnam cities had started and American soldiers began disembarking in South Vietnam.

Lyndon Baines Johnson, who had taken over from Kennedy when the latter was assassinated the year before, was elected U.S. President in November. He was soon to prove his mettle as defender-in-chief of imperialism. It has since been admitted that the "Tonkin incident" was a deliberate set-up, engineered for the purpose of giving the United States a pretext for attacking North Vietnam. Of course, this was suspected at the time, but the beans were well and truly spilt when former government employee Daniel Hellsberg published highly classified documents that became known as the "Pentagon Papers." These were serialised in the *New York Times* and revealed, in the words of the newspaper, that for many years the government had ". . . consistently lied to the American people about Vietnam." It was admitted that if Tonkin had failed, another pretext would have been found for attacking North Vietnam. This was confirmed in 1999 when the transcripts of presidential phone conversations at the time were published.

But why was it so important? American strategy, refined by Kennedy's Secretary of State, the notorious John Foster Dulles, was to "contain" and then "roll back" the power and influence of the socialist world. Dulles was a paranoiac anti-communist who invented the word "brinkmanship" – being prepared to risk going to the brink of war in order to win a diplomatic victory. In Vietnam, the Americans were faced with a reversal of their grand design. In 1954 a conference was held in

Geneva; of Britain, the Soviet Union, China and Vietnam (with the United States attending as an observer) which agreed to the "temporary" division of Vietnam into north and south. The division was conditional on free elections taking place in July 1956 to ensure the unification of the country. In the meantime, neither side was to enter into international alliances or to receive military assistance from outside: "no military bases under the control of a foreign state may be established in the regrouping zones of the two parties." In the north there was formed the Democratic Republic of Vietnam under the leadership of Ho Chi Minh. In the south, U.S. imperialism established a government more in line with its position. As the time approached, North Vietnam pressed for elections to take place in accordance with the treaty, but the U.S. and its puppet government began to put obstacles in the way, claiming, for instance, that free elections could not be guaranteed in the north. The truth, admitted in Eisenhower's memoirs, was that if elections had taken place they would have resulted in an overwhelming victory for the Vietnam liberation movement.

There were already 16,000 U.S. "advisors" in South Vietnam, helping to build the military forces of the pro-American, anti-Communist government. In July, all pretence of not wanting to be involved in conflict ended and 125,000 American troops landed. A rain of bombs were dropped daily on the towns and cities of North Vietnam from one hundred and sixty heavy bombing planes based on the American Seventh Fleet and from bases in Guam and the Philippines. The greatest military power on earth was intent on punishing a country, poor though it was, that had had the temerity to break away from grip of imperialism and join the socialist world. "The Vietcong are going to collapse within weeks. Not months, but weeks," said National Security Advisor, Rostov. One of history's finest example of ignorant over-confidence. The war was to drag on for almost eight years and to end in ignominious defeat for the United States.

The Vietnam war provoked the greatest world-wide movement of protest in history. In virtually every country, demonstrations and marches became routine. It was not just the war itself, but the barbaric methods used by the Americans, particularly the extensive and indiscriminate use of napalm – jellied petrol – defoliants and the burning of villages. Blanket bombing of civilians in the cities of North Vietnam took place nightly.

When Johnson arrived at Heathrow on a visit to this country he was greeted with a crowd, chanting "Hey, hey, L. B. J. How many kids have

347

you killed today?" But great though the demonstrations were in Britain and other countries, the most impressive developments were in the United States itself. As the war dragged on and the bodies of G.I.'s being brought home for burial increased, public emotions became more and more hostile to the "dirty war." Young people, particularly students, were in the forefront of the campaign to end it. In August 1968, a violent demonstration took place outside the Republican Convention in Chicago. A year later several million demonstrated across America for a "peaceful moratorium." The following April, 200,000 marched in Washington and 12,000 were arrested. There was outrage when armed police opened fire on a peaceful student demonstration on the campus of Kent State University in Ohio, killing four and injuring many more. The students had been protesting because their government had extended the war to Cambodia.

By the end of 1967, there were about half a million American troops in Vietnam, and U.S. generals were confident that they had crushed the N.F.L. – the National Front for the Liberation of Southern Vietnam – insultingly called Vietcong by the U.S. They were soon to be disillusioned. On 30th January , the time of the Buddhist "Tet" holiday, the N.F.L. counter-offensive was launched against US bases, and the hundred towns the Americans had proclaimed as being totally safe – including Saigon itself. Underground units of the N.F.L. in the towns joined up with their advancing comrades, town after town was taken over and in a short time the U.S. and South Vietnam forces were in full retreat. Later, it was revealed that Nixon, who had replaced Johnson as president in 1968, was appalled at the false information he had been given by his generals. It was when he learned that his military had misinformed him that he realised that the United States could not possibly win. What sharpened this realisation was a great upsurge in anti-war feeling as the truth of the Tet offensive became known, and the bitter realisation spread that all the lives lost and all the sacrifices had been in vain.

Over the next few years the number of American troops in Vietnam was gradually reduced (although the bombing of North Vietnam continued and was even extended into Cambodia). By 1975 the last remaining U.S. officials were besieged in their own embassy. The world watched on T.V. the incredible spectacle of them scuttling in disorder by helicopter from the roof of the embassy, leaving hundreds of South Vietnam officials whom they had promised to take with them, futilely hammering on the locked gates of the embassy, left to their fate. With the departure of the Americans and the surrender of the South Vietnam government, the way was at last clear to unite all the people of Vietnam into one nation. But the leaders of the most powerful and richest nation on earth would never forgive Vietnam for the humiliation of their defeat. No reparations were ever paid for the ruined bombed cities and industries of the North, for the thousands of villages razed to the ground, for the tens of thousands of square miles of forests and fertile land made barren by chemical spraying, let alone for the hundreds of thousands of men, women and children killed and maimed. The people of Vietnam were left to pull themselves up by their own bootstrings and what help they received from the Soviet Union.

Needless to say, for the entire war the leaders of the Labour Party were servile apologists for American policy, defending even the worst atrocities. I still recall with anger the scene in an Oxford Union debate on T.V., with Patrick Gordon-Walker, Labour Foreign Secretary, justifying all that the Americans were doing, and justifying it with such enthusiasm. The Labour right-wing has always sought to prove itself as the staunchest defenders of imperialism – as is being demonstrated as I write, when it enthusiastically takes part in the criminal bombing of Yugoslavia.

For Communists – and, indeed, for most progressives – those eight years of the Vietnam war was a challenging and stimulating period. It polarised the struggle between socialism and capitalism, between the warmongers and those who wanted peace, between the people of the former colonial countries struggling for independence and a brutal imperialism determined to strengthen its domination of the world. It was rightly called a dirty war, and it was an unpopular war. In Britain, there were great national marches and demonstrations and hundreds of smaller ones in most towns and cities, and millions of leaflets were given out. The mood of the public was sympathetic, despite the servile attitude of the media – with the exception, of course, of the *Morning Star*, which played a magnificent role. In the East Midlands, Vietnam was central in our public activity, in the factory and pithead meetings and the regular open-air Sunday meetings we held in the main towns of the district. Wanting to do something different, Nottingham Y.C.L.'ers and party students decided to hoist the Vietnam flag on the flagpole of famous Nottingham Castle, overlooking the town. Very early one Sunday morning, experienced climbers ascended the very high flagpole, replaced the existing flag – and cut the rope so that it wouldn't be easily detached.

349

The flag was proudly flying in the breeze all day and aroused a great deal of interest – and publicity. My modest contribution was to be one of the "look-outs." There were also broadly-based meetings, such as when Peter Heathfield returned from North Vietnam where he had been one of a miners' delegation. Peter was able to give a graphic description of the blanket-bombing by the Americans and the determination of the people in the face of it. As elsewhere, the students of our region's universities were in the forefront of the campaign. The Y.C.L. had a publicity van, which toured the country, and the organisation for medical aid for Vietnam equipped a large van with a travelling medical team collecting blood. The response in Nottingham was far beyond our expectation.

46. CZECHOSLOVAKIA

Elation at the outcome of the Vietnam war was to some extent tempered by events nearer home. In August 1968 we were spending a family holiday in Ireland, and on the last day were on the Ring of Kerry returning to our caravan at Bantry when I caught snatches of news on the car radio that seemed particularly important. The kids were making a hubbub in the back of the car and I shouted to them to shut up, and pulled into a lay-by. The announcer was talking about Soviet tanks in Prague and about demonstrations that were taking place. We were to spend the last week of the holiday in South Wales, and I called in at the Welsh district office in Cardiff, where Bert Pearce, the Welsh party secretary, filled me in on the serious developments that were unfolding in Czechoslovakia. I knew that John Peck, our District Secretary, was also on holiday, so I phoned Brian Simon, one of the East Midlands E.C. members. On his advice, I decided that no useful purpose would be served by curtailing the rest of our holiday. The kids were to spend two weeks at a Woodcraft Folk camp in Pembrokeshire, and I had planned to visit my family and friends in Tredegar.

Those weeks in August 1968 were a traumatic experience for communists throughout the world. We held up Czechoslovakia as one of the jewels in the socialist crown. Before the war it had been a developed capitalist democracy with a strong industrial base, and an experienced and organised working class. It was the first industrialised country to tackle socialist reconstruction. After the 1948 events, socialist planning resulted in a rapid growth rate and with living standards higher than any other socialist country. It was the first to open its borders to foreign tourists, the number increasing to almost two million a year – forty three per cent from capitalist countries (I was in the first group to go). However, in the late 1950's stagnation and then deterioration set in. A 9% growth rate in 1961 dropped to 0.6% three years later. Living standards declined and unrest spread. It was clear that a crisis situation was developing. At the Twelfth Congress of the C.P.C. in 1964, decisions were taken to analyse and rectify the situation, but there was a reluctance by a section of the leadership to initiate changes, and as a result Antonin Novotny was eventually replaced as Party Secretary by Alexander Dubcek. In April 1968, the Central Committee launched an Action Programme. It argued that there were many reasons for the setback, but chief among them were inexperience, lack of knowledge and dogmatism. A centralised command structure that was justified when it was a question of fighting for survival was continued when it was no longer necessary and became ossified. It led to a strengthening of the centralised bureaucracy both in the party and the state, and a weakening of democracy in both. Decisions had been taken that bore no relation to possibilities, both in economic aims and in the demands made on workers. Technical developments in industry slowed almost to a standstill, and so did productivity.

Like the other socialist countries, Czechoslovakia suffered from the rigid copying, even imposition, of the Soviet model. On the instigation of Stalin, purges had taken place that had led to the unjustified and tragic execution of some of the finest of Czechoslovak communists, including Rudolph Slansky, its General Secretary. Novotny, who replaced him, was a conformist who had neither the political insight nor the imagination nor ability to successfully tackle the big tasks of reconstruction.

The Action Programme was in many ways truly imaginative and presented economic proposals that might have taken Czechoslovakia out of the crisis. It also proposed ending the traditional rivalry between Czechs and Slovaks by proposing a federal state structure that would give autonomy to both ethnic groupings that constituted Czechoslovakia. But it also included political proposals which many communists, particularly those in other countries, were unhappy about. The programme correctly saw that advances could only be guaranteed if there was an expansion of democracy and a more open society. But in the opinion of its critics, the measures adopted went too far too quickly, accepted the bourgeois interpretation of democracy, and seriously risked weakening the socialist state and strengthening counter-revolutionary forces within the country. Censorship was abolished and anti-socialist, even anti-Soviet propaganda,

351

was permitted. Whilst this allowed the public expression of criticism and dissent by loyal and dedicated socialists, it also opened up the media to those whose more sinister aim was to undermine the state. After all, there were still forces in Czechoslovakia that yearned for a return to capitalism: remnants of the old ruling class; the former landlords and factory owners and their hangers-on; the old police officials and civil servants, etc. And these groups had very articulate spokesmen among the intelligentsia who knew how to use the media to play on discontent. Immediately following the lifting of censorship, a "Two Thousand Word Appeal" was published, signed by seventy individuals, inciting attacks on state and party officials and calling for anti-government strikes, demonstrations and boycotts. One didn't have to suffer from conspiracy paranoia to believe that the C.I.A. was working overtime stirring things up; indeed the Americans have since admitted that a considerable sum of money was allocated for the purpose.

As was the case in Hungary in 1956, any meaningful assessment of the situation had to take account of the Cold War. Overshadowing everything was the threat of nuclear war against the Soviet Union and the socialist world. One has only to look at a map to see the vital strategic position occupied by Czechoslovakia, positioned between the capitalist and the socialist countries, bordering on East Germany, Poland, Hungary and pointing like a dagger at the Soviet Union. Just before these events, the Americans had sent 12,000 more troops to Western Europe and plans were underway for massive military manoeuvres.

Not surprisingly, the leaders of the Soviet Union and the other socialist countries were extremely concerned about the situation. They felt threatened. They believed that the situation was getting out of control and that there was a real danger of counter-revolution. Letters were exchanged between the Party and government leaders, followed by discussions. The fears were not allayed by the hesitation and perceived timidity of the Dubcek government to act along the lines agreed, and on 20th August Soviet tanks and troops from five Warsaw Pact countries entered Czechoslovakia – which was, of course, also a Pact member. The three main reasons given were (1) that a minority of "right-wing revisionist elements on the Central Committee . . . in alliance with imperialist circles abroad . . . were planning counter-revolution," (2) that the armed forces had entered Czechoslovakia "at the request of party and state leaders" and (3) that the country was "heading towards an open counter-revolutionary coup." It was emphasised that the occupation was a temporary measure aimed at defeating counter-revolution and the plans of the West to weaken the socialist world.

The reaction of the world communist movement was mixed and polarised. The majority of parties, mainly in the developing countries, but including the C.P.U.S.A., supported the action of the Warsaw Pact powers. Fidel Castro expressed full solidarity, seeing it as a regrettable but necessary action in the struggle against imperialism. The Communist Parties in most of the developed capitalist countries condemned the action and called for the immediate withdrawal of Warsaw Pact troops from Czechoslovakia.

This was the position of the C.P.G.B. Within twenty-four hours, the Political Committee of the party issued a statement condemning the "military intervention," which, it said, "plays into the hands of anti-socialist and anti-Soviet elements." It expressed solidarity with the Communist Party of Czechoslovakia. This policy was endorsed by a special meeting of the Executive Committee held on 24th August. The E.C. stated that the intervention "had no support from any leading body of the Communist Party of Czechoslovakia or state and is opposed by them . . . Equally deplorable is the intervention from outside the country to remove some of the leaders of the Czechoslovak Communist Party and to prevent them carrying out their duties, less than three weeks before the Party Congress on 9th September . This is a gross violation of the democratic rights of the Czechoslovak communists." In a fuller analysis, at the next meeting of the E.C., International Secretary Jack Woddis maintained that no concrete evidence had been produced to support the three reasons given by the Warsaw Pact powers for their intervention, and that the intervention was a gross violation of a basic communist principle – the equality and independence of socialist states. The armed forces had not been invited in by any group. Although it was true that there had been inflammatory right-wing activity, it could easily be handled by the Czechoslovak communists, and the threat of an imminent counter-revolutionary coup was exaggerated.

The sudden presence of foreign tanks and troops on the streets of Prague and the occupation by them of state and party offices understandably produced an enormous reaction, mainly (although not entirely) hostile. Perhaps surprisingly, there was little violence and few casualties: twenty-five dead was the maximum quoted for the whole of the country during the entire period. Students and others argued with the soldiers, but there was also some fraternisation, and there was no significant hostile reaction from workers in factories and pits throughout the country.

Dubcek and other party leaders were forcibly taken to Moscow, where discussions started between them and Soviet leaders that eventually ended in an agreement to scrap most of the Action Programme, particularly those parts seen as a threat. The proposal for a Czech-Slovak federal structure was, however, retained. It was agreed that military contingents from the other Warsaw Pact countries be stationed in Czechoslovakia. The following April, Gustav Husák replaced Dubcek and became Party First Secretary.

Needless to say, the party membership in Britain was very much divided. Whilst the majority supported the line taken by the leadership, there were many misgivings about the immediate unqualified condemnation of the actions taken by the Warsaw Pact countries. True, as Napoleon once said (I think it was Napoleon), "it is sometimes better to risk taking a wrong decision than to take no decision at all," and admittedly this was one of those situations on which a stand had to be made quickly. But many of us felt that the policy was presented so dogmatically that any subsequent modification would have been difficult if new evidence emerged. Like so many others, I felt that I didn't have enough hard facts to be certain, particularly as there was so much conflicting evidence published and so many contrary statements being made daily. Under the circumstances, my gut reaction was to give the benefit of the doubt to the Soviet Union. True, this was partly an instinctive emotional response, based on years of what some would call conditioning but which I would call a class attitude, reinforced by the realities of the Cold War and the fact that the western capitalist media unanimously condemned the Warsaw Pact "invasion" and praised to the skies those Czechoslovak communists whom, a little earlier, they had condemned as villains. Suddenly they were transformed into patriots and heroes. I recalled a comment once made by Harry Pollitt, that if he awoke one morning and found the capitalist press praising him he would seriously suspect that he had done something wrong. Even so, despite my reservations and whilst expressing them, as a party organiser I was duty bound to put the party line to the branch meetings I attended, and this I and the other full-time comrades did – apparently much to the surprise of Reuben Falber, who, many years later, in an article in the *Socialist History Journal*, commented on the fact that even a "hard-line district" like the East Midlands didn't oppose the policy. (Incidentally, at the time John Peck – a conformist if ever there was one – was our district secretary).

At the National Congress, when Czechoslovakia was discussed, our delegation was split, but Ida Hackett was chosen by the Arrangement Committee to be one of the five delegates to oppose the resolution endorsing the line of the leadership. It was carried by two hundred and ninety two to one hundred and eighteen.

To the credit of the party's leadership, it did allow full and free discussion of the party's policy, both in the pages of the *Morning Star* and in *Comment*, its periodical. However, such tolerance was not general. Some of the leaders of the Y.C.L. in particular went overboard in their condemnation of the critics of the line, at times verging on the hysterical. They took over from the Trotskyists the term "tankies" to describe comrades who refused to condemn the intervention.

Sadly, there are people who are arrogant enough always to make lightning decisions as to what is right, however complex the situation, and who will never admit even the slightest modicum of doubt to sully the righteousness of their position, nor tolerate anyone who dares to question it. These are the real dogmatists.

47. PARLIAMENTARY ELECTIONS – MANSFIELD

In 1966 I had been election agent in North Nottingham, and in 1970 I was chosen to stand as Communist candidate in Mansfield. It was the first of the four times I was to stand there, although I had stood once before in Leicester. For the sake of convenience I will deal with the Mansfield contests together – Leicester I have already described.

Among the most satisfying and stimulating experiences as a political activist was fighting parliamentary elections. This might seem strange considering that on the five occasions I stood in general elections there was not a snowball's chance in hell of my getting even within sight of the winning post. There was, of course, the excitement of the hustings at a time when public interest in politics was at its highest; but added to this was the fact that for a few weeks one could escape from internal problems and the deadening daily routine of office work and concentrate with gay abandon entirely on public activity – on doorstep discussions, pit, factory-gate and street meetings, evening rallies, mass leaflet distributions and torch parades. I felt that this is what politics is all about. Comrades were brought together in positive action; even addressing the thousands of election envelopes became a happy and meaningful social event.

Mansfield was and still is a strong Labour constituency in the heart

355

of the Nottinghamshire coalfield. There were ten pits either in or on the border of the constituency and another ten slightly further afield – one of the biggest concentration of miners in Britain. It was one of the safest Labour seats in the country. In 1966, Bernard Taylor, who had been the M.P. for twenty-five years, was made a life peer, and another miner, Don Concannon, became the Labour candidate. He was a former guardsman and was to become a junior minister for Northern Ireland.

We had a strong and long-established party branch in the town as well as three influential pit branches, and many local Communists had honourable records and were held in high esteem. In 1950, Les Ellis, one of the most respected leaders of the Notts miners and someone who had received massive votes in union elections, had stood as Communist parliamentary candidate and had polled only four hundred and eighty two votes – very low compared with the other candidates. This is an example of what has always been a fundamental problem in Communist election strategy. When workers elect someone to represent them at workplace level or in the trade union, the choice is between individuals and they vote for the person they consider will best serve their interests. The party allegiance of the candidate is not usually regarded as being of prime importance, despite occasional smear campaigns to make it so by some right-wingers. But the choice in local and parliamentary elections is between political parties, and in constituencies like Mansfield loyalty to Labour was, and still is, deeply rooted. The argument that we were not really anti-Labour and that every Communist vote strengthened the socialist forces within the Labour Party was not very convincing.

I found little real antagonism to the Communist Party or myself, neither in canvassing nor at meetings. Sharp differences, yes, but no bitterness, and a great deal of friendship shown. A common attitude was, "I agree with your election address and think that you are the best candidate, but I've always voted Labour. Besides, it would be a wasted vote, for you'll never get in." We maintained good relations with the Labour Party, and I with Concannon – in the confident knowledge on his part, of course, that I represented no real threat to his majority. On the contrary, the party's campaign, so much better than Labour's, did a lot to demolish the Tories and strengthen Labour's vote.

I was particularly fortunate in having Ida Hackett as election agent. She had often stood for the local council, and although never elected, did more work for the community than any councillor. Indeed, I often thought that she should have been the candidate. The weight she carried at the council offices led us, in 1970, to having what was probably the finest election headquarters in Britain. Ida was demanding that the council find us premises for our central committee rooms, and the town hall official was stonewalling, protesting that they had nothing to offer. Exasperated at Ida's persistence, he rather rashly said, "You suggest somewhere!" Ida promptly did. "We'll take the Health Centre," she said. The Health Centre was an attractive and spacious building near the centre of the town with many rooms and large windows – ideal for posters. It was also across the road from the Conservative Club, which was the Tory committee room. The Centre had just been emptied, waiting to be demolished to make way for a new road. Ida hardly expected her suggestion to be accepted, but the official capitulated right away, obviously preferring a quiet life free from the risk of daily harassment by the formidable Ida Hackett!

The Tory candidate in 1966 had been a hopeful young sprig of his party called Kenneth Clarke. In 1970 he was obviously being sent to Mansfield for a second time to add to his election experience, for there could hardly have been a more hopeless Tory constituency. There was certainly no sign that one day he would become a Cabinet Minister under Thatcher.

He was arrogant and contemptuous, looking for all the world as if he was slumming – which from his point of view I suppose he was. In the forum of all the candidates, he was appalling, and as Concannon was little better it was not much of an accolade to be told by so many Labour supporters and by the reporters that I was by far the best speaker. Indeed, at the forums, which were a feature of all the election campaigns, I was usually told that I put the case for a Labour government far better than the Labour candidate. The forums became established in 1966, when I wrote to the other candidates making the suggestion. The main local paper, the *Mansfield Chronicle and Advertiser* ("Chad"), took it up and offered to organise the event.

It was great, for once, to have the local media showing an interest in and giving publicity to the Communist case. Indeed, in all contests we had the grudging respect of the "Chad," whose chief reporter admitted that he liked to be with us. Our organisation and campaigns, he claimed, were far superior to the other parties and our workers most friendly.

One aspect of the campaigning that I particularly liked was speaking to schoolchildren. They were not yet indoctrinated with the prejudices of their elders and sincerely wanted to learn. At election time there is a

357

spate of parallel school mock elections, and at at least one secondary school the Communist candidate was victorious.

Another unexpected feature of election campaigning was the status being a candidate gave. On one occasion, I decided to try to hold a meeting in a pit yard, so I went along with Johnny Rice, a Leicester comrade. While he gave out leaflets I started speaking and a reasonable audience began to gather. As I expected, soon the deputy-manager came out and ordered me to stop or he would phone for the police. I wouldn't and he did, but much to his (and my) surprise they supported me continuing the meeting on the grounds that I was a parliamentary candidate. I have been stopped by the police numberless times, but this was the only time they supported me speaking!

I commuted from Chesterfield to Mansfield every day, seldom getting home much before midnight. They were long, exhausting, but exhilarating days. One night, I escaped by the skin of my teeth from being caught by a landslip when, after heavy rain, a big pit slag heap swept across the main road.

Raising cash to conduct an effective campaign is a major problem for a small party that has no rich donors or affiliation fees to fall back on. The £150 deposit (now £500) is not a barrier to eccentric candidates standing (its alleged purpose) providing they are rich eccentrics. When the party put up one hundred candidates in 1950 we first had to find £15,000 for deposits alone – a truly heavy burden. The amazing thing is that we always found the money to finance our campaigns, largely because our members and supporters were prepared to give generously when they saw us in action. 1974 was a particularly difficult year, for there were two general elections only ten months apart. Fortunately for the October election, our Mansfield campaign had an unexpected donation – from British Steel. As I explain elsewhere, I was working at its Staveley Works at the time, and the company ruled that employees who were candidates should be given time off on full pay for the period of the election campaign – quite a sizeable amount which otherwise we would have had to raise.

The final days before polling day, the climax of the campaign, seemed to be jinxed, for some crisis that had nothing to do with the election would inevitably crop up and need dealing with urgently. On one occasion I had an urgent call from Ethel Whelan telling me that Joe was in a very depressed state and that she was very worried. He certainly had cause to be depressed; he had been the target of considerable hate mail, and relations with the right-wing at work were not very good. He had recently been prosecuted for shoplifting – not declaring a piece of meat with the rest of the groceries he had bought at the local shop. With some justification, he felt that most of the local magistrates would be prejudiced against him and opted to be judged by a jury at the Crown Court. He was convinced that a jury would uphold his innocence, and rejected legal advice to plead guilty of what was a trivial offence. The shop concerned wanted to withdraw the charge, but the police insisted on going ahead. He was found guilty and fined, but the media made a meal of it.

I phoned John Gollan and suggested that he phone Joe to bolster up his spirits and that he also get Mick McGahey – for whom Joe had a great regard – to phone as well. This he did. I stayed with Joe and Ethel all that night and left in the morning straight into election campaigning again.

On another occasion, I had to appear at Dunstable Magistrates Court only a few days before polling day. Some time before, I had been driving along the M1 to attend a Party Congress in London, accompanied by Ida, Kath and a young Mansfield comrade, Royston Laycock, when we were caught up in a multiple traffic pile-up near Luton. It was a Friday evening and the motorway was crowded, with visibility very poor because it was raining heavily. Upon seeing flashing lights ahead, I slowed, keeping my distance with the car in front. The fast lane was closed. Suddenly, there was a crash as the car behind me collided with force, spun my car sideways and knocked me into the fast lane. By a miracle, no one was hurt. It turned out that twenty three vehicles had been involved in the pile-up and there had been one death.

All were advised to plead guilty to driving without due care and attention, but, despite a strong recommendation by my A.A. lawyer, I refused – the only driver to do so. I argued that I had done absolutely nothing wrong. The result was that I had to appear in court – the day before the election and one hundred miles from Mansfield. The A.A. solicitor was a dead loss and made it clear he thought it was a waste of time and that I would be found guilty. The first remark he made was, "How are you going to get back? Can one of your friends drive?" Fortunately, my witnesses – Kath, Ida and Royston – were not easily demoralised. They were quite superb in the witness box and the case was dismissed – the only one of the twenty three that was. The police had brought from the North of England the driver who had collided with me, but he proved to be a totally unreliable witness. It was all very interesting, but it had meant a day's lost campaigning at a most crucial point of our campaign.

The other occasion was not really on the same level. On Sunday morning, four days before polling day, Betty Reid phoned me from King Street querying, rather oddly, whether I had read the *News of the World* that day. I said it was not the Sunday paper I was in the habit of reading. "Go out and get a copy," she said. She explained. Under big headlines, "The Red In My Bed," was a scurrilous story about John Peck, based on an interview with his estranged wife, Roma, given some time before but obviously held back until it could do maximum damage. It was clearly part of the anti-communist campaign by the media, and could have possibly harmed us – particularly John. The paper had a big circulation and the story could have been taken up by the local media. Betty asked me to phone around and do everything possible to limit any possible damage. In fact, the local media did not take up the story.

48. THE EAST MIDLANDS AFFAIR

On another level, the period 1965 to 1971 was not a happy one for Kath and myself. There were the chronic financial worries arising from me not getting my wages, but this was a minor matter compared with the problems that had arisen within the district leadership of the party.

At the beginning of 1965 Mick Jenkins announced that he was resigning as District Secretary and moving back to Manchester. He proposed that John Peck replace him. This was the start of a bitter controversy, unique in the party's history, which was to last for several years. Its character and content was such that James Klugman, the official historian of the party, was later to remark, albeit only half-seriously, that it merited at least one chapter of its own in the third volume he was then preparing. The East Midlands Affair, as it came to be known, may now appear to be of no great consequence. If this chapter appears to be somewhat parochial and a little tedious in its detail to readers who were not concerned or around at the time – well, you can always skip it! But I have promised comrades involved that I will put the events on record. As a matter of fact, the affair does have some general historical significance in that it was one of the first expressions of collective dissent in the C.P.G.B. at some of the trends that eventually developed into revisionism, and it illustrates how the party leadership then dealt with dissent.

Mick sprung the proposition on us without warning. At the same time he revealed that he had had discussions with leading comrades at King

Street and they had endorsed his proposition that John Peck should replace him as District Secretary. The District Secretariat had been kept completely in the dark and resented being rail-roaded in such a crude manner. While little could be done if Mick was determined to leave, it felt it should have been told first. As for Peck replacing him as Secretary, the majority strongly dissented, arguing that there were three full-time workers, and electing a new District Secretary should be left to the District Committee in accordance with the rules of the party. Mick opposed this, and as no agreement could be reached the matter was deferred. At the next meeting Bill Alexander, the party's Assistant General Secretary, attended to lend his considerable weight to Mick's position. The choice was seen as being between Peck and myself. No political arguments were put forward, merely personal and practical ones that we had heard on the previous occasion they had tried to get rid of me: that Peck was four years younger than me, that I had to travel each day from Chesterfield and that I would find it easier to find alternative work because I was a skilled worker. Indeed, Bill conceded that I was certainly the most experienced comrade. The main argument put forward by Ida Hackett (District Chairperson), Barry Johnson (District Treasurer), other comrades and myself was that, while we considered the choice of Peck would be a serious mistake, it was not the issue at this stage. It was a question of principle, of abiding by party rules. Rule Eleven stated quite unambiguously that "the District Committee . . . shall elect District Officers and a District Secretariat. "It was quite revealing that Mick and the comrades at Party Centre were not prepared to allow the Committee to exercise this right unless they were certain in advance that the choice would the one they wanted. Left to its own inclinations, the choice of the Committee would certainly not have been Peck.

The next meeting of the Secretariat did not resolve the issue, and Bill thereupon attended the third meeting. In the meantime, considerable pressure was put on me to give way, particularly by Party Centre. Reluctantly, I did so, partly because there was still an ingrained discipline that made it difficult for me to oppose the national leadership, and partly in the mistaken belief that maintaining unity was all-important. Following my lead, the other members also withdrew their opposition. As had happened once before, we were instructed by the EC representative at the next Secretariat meeting that the District Committee must not be informed of the disagreements, and that no member of the Committee should be told in advance of the meeting that Mick was resigning and that Peck was being proposed as his successor.

This was the situation when the D.C. met. Not knowing that there was anything special about this meeting, there were more absentees than usual – in fact only sixteen of the thirty members were present. We dutifully acted out the charade. Although I travelled to Nottingham with the Chesterfield comrades, I never breathed a word to them about what was to take place. Ida, who was Chairperson, made a pre-arranged statement on "cadres work" during which she announced that Mick was leaving, and put forward the "unanimous recommendation" of the Secretariat that John Peck be the new District Secretary. She asked for a unanimous vote in favour. The Committee members were stunned. In the discussion many comrades expressed disquiet at being presented with a fait accompli, and I was nominated instead of Peck. I declined to stand and urged comrades to support the Secretariat recommendation. It was a travesty of democracy, yet it was the way the party worked then. If there was a clash, centralism took precedence over democracy. Peck was imposed on the District Committee and would never have been elected without the backing of Party Centre and the reluctant acquiescence of myself, Ida and other members of the Secretariat. It spoke volumes for the sort of person Peck was that he was prepared to accept the position, knowing that the majority of the members of his own District Committee did not want him. The basis was laid for a long and bitter inner-party struggle that did nothing to help the work of the party in the East Midlands and, in the eyes of many comrades, brought the national leadership of the party into disrepute.

I was genuinely sorry to see Mick Jenkins go. We had our differences, and at times I very much resented his conduct, but he was devoted to the party and the working class and had great ability. I often felt that he would have preferred to have devoted his time to writing working-class history. His "Engels in Manchester" was a well-researched pamphlet ("It should have been published as a book," said Harry Pollitt) which was thought highly of in the Soviet Union. When he retired he wrote a definitive work on the 1842 general strike. I certainly learned a great deal from him. Except for the one period I was in limbo, about which I have already written, even when we profoundly disagreed we could always have a chat over a cup of coffee. When I became District Secretary we invited Mick and Jessie to be guests of honour at a district party function, and whenever our paths crossed in later years we met as comrades and friends. But, like all of us, he had flaws. So far as the party was concerned, he was a rigid conformist, being almost obsequious to the national leadership; he found criticism hard to take, particularly from those working close to him, despite the fact that he could be ruthlessly critical of others, sometimes unreasonably and even cruelly so. And during the period in question he had an almost obsessively protective attitude towards Peck that blinded him to reality.

There was an immediate branch reaction to the procedure by which Peck was made District Secretary. Resolutions of protest came in to the District Committee from Chesterfield, Mansfield and Leicester, as well as from West and Central Nottingham (two of the largest branches in the area Peck was secretary of). At a fuller meeting of the District Committee in April a statement was passed declaring "that the D.C. members had not been adequately informed of the item at the February meeting that dealt with personnel changes. "Nevertheless, although feelings ran high, the decision had been taken. There were so many political issues and tasks for the party to do that we didn't want to dissipate our energies on internal differences. Don Devine replaced Peck as Nottingham Area Secretary and I became District Organiser, although continuing to be responsible for mining. Ernest Hackett became Coalfields Area Secretary on a voluntary basis.

The next four years were not happy ones. Peck was a born bureaucrat. Whereas Mick and myself always had an open-door attitude to comrades visiting the District Office, Peck tried to institute an appointments system. Nothing was supposed to be distributed, even by the District Organiser, until he had vetted it – an edict that I usually ignored. He imposed the most petty indignity on our wonderful voluntary worker, Edith Mock, who ran the bookshop single-handed until ill-health forced her to give up. Before she was allowed to take her meagre travel expenses – seldom totalling more than a pound for the week – she had to produce every bus ticket to and from work! We discovered later that he kept a record (we called it "the little black book") of all my movements. There was no informal contact with me or any of the other District officials. He drew his main support from the two national Executive Committee members from the East Midlands, principally Jean Stansfield. Jean had joined the party at a public meeting I had chaired when I lived in Leicester (the speaker had been the renowned anti-fascist and superb orator, Isabel Brown). Jean and I had been friends and always worked well together until she was elected to the E.C. Ironically enough, I had pushed her forward for the E.C. in the face of strong opposition from Mick Jenkins who

363

thought her too young and inexperienced. Once on the E.C., she became unaccountably antagonistic towards me and a staunch supporter of Peck. I was saddened by this, and put it down to pressure from King Street and the efforts made by Mick and Peck to influence her. The other E.C. member was Brian Simon, the well-known educationalist at Leicester University. He always accepted and fought for the E.C. line, although at a personal level I invariably found him friendly and helpful. I felt that he was uncomfortable in the role he was called upon to play.

Dissatisfaction with Peck grew, particularly from branches outside of Nottingham, who complained that they never saw their District Secretary. The Y.C.L. was especially critical, for he seemed to have difficulty in establishing a rapport with young comrades. Resolutions kept coming in from branches calling for a change, but these were put in abeyance because of the need to concentrate on political campaigning. In March 1966 there was a General Election. Both Peck and I were parliamentary candidates and had to concentrate on the fight in our constituencies. But in the following January Peck proposed that, because the financial situation of the party had deteriorated, we reduced staff from three to two, and that I give up full-time work and be replaced by Don Devine, the Nottingham Area Secretary. This last point was overwhelmingly rejected by the District Committee. Indeed, when it was argued by some comrades that if anyone were to go it should be Peck, he withdrew his proposal to cut staff, even though it was becoming obvious that it was inevitable. At the same time, the Committee carried a resolution calling on the Executive Committee to allow us to appoint our own District Secretary. Similar resolutions were sent to the E.C. from many branches. The E.C. stood by its position but opposed the cutting of staff unless there was no radical improvement in income.

If the E.C. thought that feeling over the issue would die down in time, they were very much mistaken; for such was Peck's ineptitude that he managed to alienate more comrades and branches. At the beginning of 1970 a meeting took place of Dennis Elwand (the National Treasurer), Peck, Barry Johnson and myself. Because there had been no improvement in income, it was recommended that we dispense with the services of one full-time worker. The Secretariat reluctantly agreed, but when it then went on to discuss the procedure for deciding which comrade was to go, Peck and Don Devine walked out of the meeting, arguing that the Secretariat had no right to discuss it. The remaining five members of the Secretariat then decided unanimously "to discuss the question of which full-time worker is to remain and which is to go at its next meeting on 12th February, and that we invite Party Centre to express its point of view." Chairperson Ida Hackett wrote to the E.C. conveying this decision.

The District Committee asked the Political Committee or the Executive Committee to meet the Secretariat in an attempt to resolve the problem (the P.C. was a sub-committee of the E.C., made up of its leading members, and with full powers between E.C. meetings). This request was turned down; instead Peck and myself were invited to a meeting of the P.C. At this meeting, Peck played his trump card. He alleged that the opposition to him was political, that I and those that supported me were critical of the political line of the party, particularly "The British Road to Socialism," whereas he was an undeviating supporter of the line. Among the charges he listed against me was that I had opposed the change of name of the *Daily Worker*, accused the national leadership of being "too staid" and often slow at taking initiatives, questioned our electoral policy, disagreed with parts of the "British Road," had reservations about the Party's policy over the Czechoslovakian events, supported the dissident group on the Surrey District Committee and (horror of horrors) had not supported four members of the Political Committee when they were nominated for the E.C. prior to the National Congress. He had never raised any of this in the District, and I had the distinct impression that it had been planned with some of the comrades at Party Centre.

It revealed the real reason why the leadership was so intent on keeping Peck as District Secretary. It had nothing to do with our ages, how far off we were from the office, ease of getting alternative employment, or any of the other spurious arguments that up to then had been put forward. George Matthews was my main interrogator and never once raised these points. He questioned me closely on my attitude to different aspects of party policy and to the leadership of the party. In reply, I declared that I had never hidden my views, which were also held by many of those who supported me, although by no means all. We were concerned at the direction the party seemed to be taking and about aspects of the "British Road." We felt that the party's revolutionary basis too often seemed to be compromised. Nevertheless, we had always accepted the decisions of the National Congress and had fought loyally and vigorously for party policy. Political differences had not been raised because we did not consider they were the issue in the context we were discussing. Was George now saying that no comrade who was in the least critical of the policy of the party or of its leadership could hold a

365

responsible position in it? The sole question we were raising was still whether the rules of the party were to be adhered to and the District Committee allowed to elect its own officers – critical or not. In his reply George Matthews stressed the importance of party unity, which was already being damaged by the dispute, and would be more so if they permitted a dissident leadership to be in charge of a district. John Gollan was present but played little part in the discussion. Not surprisingly, the Political Committee reaffirmed its support of Peck as District Secretary and turned down my appeal that we be allowed to elect our own officers.

However, the matter didn't end there. The decision was received with a great deal of anger in the district and the protests continued. The District Committee demanded that the Secretariat attend an Executive Committee meeting to put its case, but this was refused. Gordon McLennan, the National Organiser, attended the next District Committee to tell us the recommendation of the E.C.: "that we fight to maintain two full-time workers . . . that because it has no confidence that either Comrade Peck or Comrade Westacott could end the divisions in the District, both comrades should go off full-time work . . . and that a senior member of the Executive, Harry Bourne, Midlands District Secretary, be brought in as Acting District Secretary to resolve the problems." In the course of a heated discussion, McLennan shocked comrades by issuing a threat to the District Chairperson, Ida Hackett, when she declared she was putting the issue to a vote: "Ida, be careful what you move for your future in the party" He then made an impassioned appeal for unity behind the E.C. Ernest Hackett, of Mansfield, moved the rejection of all but the first point, seconded by Win Clark, Secretary of the Chesterfield Branch. Despite McLennan's appeal and the fact that the E.C. had now apparently dropped its support for Peck, the motion was carried by fifteen votes to thirteen, upon which Gordon declared that the recommendations would now be "decisions of the Executive" and would be imposed on the District.

Next morning we found we had become national news. King Street had released a press statement announcing our dismissal as party organisers, an event so unusual that B.B.C. radio and several newspapers carried the news. Surrey District Secretary, Sid French, later told me that when he heard it on his car radio he almost went off the road. Within a few weeks John Peck got a job with the Nottingham Co-op and I at a foundry in Chesterfield, of which I will write more later.

Harry Bourne was a fine comrade. We had something in common

insofar as we were both products of the struggles of the 1930's. Harry had fought in Spain and had been wounded. Although I didn't agree with the way he had been imposed on the District, we could hardly have had a more respected and able comrade. I and the other comrades made it clear from the start that we would co-operate with him in every way – which, indeed, we did. He didn't like the job the Executive Committee had given him, particularly the hidden agenda which we suspected and obtained proof of later. This was to resolve the problem by undermining my position and restoring Peck as District Secretary. Maurice Hookham, a respected University Lecturer in Leicester, later told me how Harry had visited him to persuade him to stand for the District Committee "in order to weaken Fred's influence and the support of the Coalfield comrades on the Committee." Unfortunately for Harry, when Maurice came on the Committee he found himself usually in agreement with me, and this applied to most of the others he brought forward.

I don't know what sort of reports Harry made to Party Centre, but if he was honest – and I have no reason to doubt that he was – he must have reported that the comrades around me were the best public campaigners in the East Midlands, and that – despite our political differences – he found himself more often working with us rather than with the Peck grouping.

It must be emphasised that we never allowed the inner-party differences to interfere with our political activities. Our public meetings, sales of the *Morning Star*, leaflet distribution and the fight for party policies continued unabated. In June 1970 there was another General Election, and once again I was candidate in Mansfield. Harry enthusiastically helped in the campaign – indeed, if his canvassing returns had been the measure of our impact I would have been elected with a thumping majority.

It was clear that the big trial of strength would be at the District Congress in November 1970. Gordon McLennan was the fraternal delegate from the E.C. and Ida was in the chair. There were resolutions from the Coalfield Area Committee and from the Chesterfield, Mansfield and Hucknall branches. The agreed composite read:

This Congress regrets the action of the E.C. in not allowing the elected leadership in this District to elect its own District Secretary in accordance with the Party Constitution and the Report on Inner Party Democracy. Whilst we recognise the overall authority of the E.C., we believe it was unnecessary for the E.C. to intervene, and the appointment of an Acting District Secretary can only produce a feeling of uncertainty amongst the membership. We request that the District Committee shall be allowed to elect the District Secretary at the end of the Card Exchange.

Barry Donlan, from Mansfield, moved the resolution. The debate was predictably one-sided. Whereas the resolution was supported in powerful speeches by three of the most able and respected comrades in the District – Barry Johnson, Joe Clark and Ernest Hackett – its opponents had great difficulty finding delegates to speak against. Eventually they did persuade a Derby comrade who knew nothing about the issues involved, to speak along with Peck and Jean Stansfield. I replied to the discussion. Before I spoke, in an unprecedented move, McLennan demanded the right to intervene in the debate. He had no right to do this, because he was not an elected delegate, and had already spoken in his capacity as fraternal delegate. He maintained that he just wanted to put some facts to the delegates, but in reality his speech was a poorly disguised plea to delegates to reject the resolution. It was a clever speech in which he stated that he had noted the strong feelings expressed and would report them to the E.C. He gave an assurance that the E.C. would seriously consider the points made, and ended by making an impassioned appeal to delegates to express confidence in the leadership of the party by leaving them to deal with the matter. There is no doubt that it had an effect, but even so the motion was carried by thirty six votes to twenty nine with one abstention. It must be remembered that this was after Harry Bourne had been in the District eight months and had visited every branch prior to the Congress.

The new District Committee met in January and dramatically demonstrated how much the combined forces of Peck, Harry Bourne and the E.C. had failed to change the situation. Harry reported that the Executive Committee had turned down the Congress resolution and was not prepared to change its position. The response of the District Committee was to pass the following resolution by eighteen votes to five with one abstention:

This District Committee regrets that the Executive Committee has rejected the resolution of our District Congress concerning the election of our District Secretary. It believes that a continuation of the present position prolongs the uncertainty and acrimony, and is harmful to the Party. The only way the situation can be ended and unity restored is by the District Committee electing its own District Secretary with a pledge by all comrades to accept fully the decision taken. It asks that a deputation elected by the District Committee should attend meetings of the Political Committee and the Executive Committee when our District is being discussed, in order to explain our views and take part in the discussion.

When it came to the election of officers and the Secretariat, Harry proposed that the respected Notts miners' leader, Joe Whelan, replace Ida as District Chairperson. Not only did Joe refuse to stand, but he urged support for Ida. Harry also proposed that Jean Stansfield replace Barry Johnson on the Secretariat. The voting was: for Barry twenty two, against two, abstentions two; against Jean fourteen, for eight, abstentions four. So the net result of all the hard work that Harry had put in over nine months was to increase support for me and what I represented. No wonder he was somewhat disheartened. He had never expected to be away from his home and from Birmingham for so long. He wanted to get back. Instead it looked as if he was here to stay. I believe it was at this stage that Harry decided to accept the reality of the situation and to recommend an acceptance of our position. By now he must have been acutely aware of the solid support I had, and that it was based on the most active and mainly industrial comrades. I felt that he was also disillusioned with Peck, his lack of qualities of political leadership, and the motley nature of the group supporting him. After the District Committee meeting, Ida, who was a former E.C. member with some standing, wrote to the E.C. appealing to them to take notice of the feelings of the members in the East Midlands.

At first there was no response from the E.C. to the District Committee resolution. Then, in March, Ida, Peck and myself were invited to appear before the full committee – an unprecedented event. We were each asked to make a statement, after which there were questions. Peck repeated what he had said at the P.C. meeting, with additional quotes from statements I was supposed to have made revealing my "political differences" with party policy and criticisms of the leadership. Some were true, others distortions. Ida gave a picture of the position in the District, stressing that we had co-operated to the full with Harry Bourne in developing party activity, but that this continued problem was not helping. In my statement, I reminded comrades that there would be a National Congress in November and expressed the hope that the issue would be decided by then "so that we would not have to raise it there." I also challenged the E.C. to take any measure they liked to ascertain the views of East Midlands Communists, including visiting the branches or even conducting a ballot of members. We were not allowed to be present for the discussion.

We were later informed by Harry that McLennan would be at the next District Committee to inform us of the E.C.'s decision. He passed word to me to "hold my horses" until I had heard what McLennan had to say. It was, in fact, a complete capitulation. Of course, it was not presented as such. In his short statement, Gordon tried to present a picture of an E.C. whose only concern had been to protect the interests of the District, but the long and short of it was that it now conceded our right to elect our own District Secretary. This was to take place at the next meeting on 18th April. In the meantime, every branch had to hold a meeting, preferably with Harry being present, to hear the report and express its viewpoint.

There was a tense atmosphere when the District Committee met. There was only one absentee and the preliminary agenda items were got through quickly and mechanically. We then came to "Election of District Secretary." Ernest Hackett nominated me and Don Devine nominated Peck. The result was: Westacott twenty, Peck four, abstentions four. Apart from his own vote, only the Stansfields and one other voted for him. Don Devine, who nominated him, abstained. Brian Simon had declined to stand for the Committee. A large number of Y.C.L.'s had gathered outside the District Office to await the result, and when they heard it there was noisy jubilation.

I was not sorry to give in my notice at Staveley. It had not been easy doing the most physically demanding job I had ever had and on a three-shift system with Saturday overtime, travelling to Nottingham for regular Secretariat meetings every week, visiting branches and conducting a fair level of political activity, whilst being a central figure in a highly-charged emotional atmosphere from which there was no respite. Without the help and unstinting support of Kath I could not have done it. She shared the strain with me, and was also a most effective participant in the discussions. She was usually a cool person, but at home after some of the most heated exchanges on the District Committee, she would show a blazing anger at the tactics of Peck and his supporters. She, also, never ceased being involved in normal political activity.

On 3rd May, 1971 I resumed my job as District Secretary. Harry Bourne was vastly pleased to put the East Midlands behind him. Before we left we had a long chat, during which he confessed that he had quickly realised that Peck would never have made a good District Secretary. "He is too small for the job," he said. "Bulwell is about his level." Bulwell is the area of Nottingham where Peck did his electoral work. Harry and I parted as the friends we had remained throughout the year. He had been put into a job he didn't want and given a task he had no heart in, but had accepted because he was a disciplined party member. The next time I went down to King Street, this time as District Secretary, John Gollan called me into his office and expressed regret at what had happened. He said "judgements had been clouded by some incorrect information" and he assured me that I could rely on his full support and co-operation.

Why did the Executive give way? In my opinion, it was because they were forced to realise that they were on to a loser. E.C. members, particularly Gollan, had been totally misled by its informants, particularly Peck, Stansfield and Simon as to the issues and strength of feeling in the East Midlands, and they had believed that someone of Harry Bourne's ability would soon sort things out. But it was also because of a hard-line attitude against any comrade and any group that had political differences – particularly regarding the direction in which the C.P.G.B. was beginning to go. It is ironic that people like Falber, Matthews and McLennan, who, after the collapse of the Soviet Union presented themselves as harsh critics of democratic centralism, were uncompromising in their interpretation of it before within our Party. Another factor was the approach of the National Congress and the wish to pre-empt a wider debate. The main credit for the decision, however, must go to the Coalfield Area Committee, the branches and the comrades who fought a principled battle in defence of party democracy. Peck always argued that his defeat was due to a factional conspiracy, but he could produce no evidence of this for the simple reason that there was none. I would not have agreed with such activity, but there was, in fact, no need for it because opposition to him and what he stood for was quite open and widespread. I must add that at no time did any national official or the Executive Committee make such a charge. Nor did Harry Bourne.

Unfortunately, however, although the district situation had been cleared up, there were still other developments connected to it. The E.C. still had a touching faith in Peck, particularly based on his electoral work, and later, as a consolation prize, they made him National Election Agent. In opposition to the District Committee, they took him on to the E.C., although Party Centre did agree that he would never be asked to give an E.C. report to our District Committee. Subsequently, he supported the revisionist faction in every move it made to undermine the party's

Marxist revolutionary role and weaken its organisation. Eventually, although elected as a Communist councillor for Bulwell on the Nottingham City Council, he left the party and joined the Greens. This came as no surprise to those of us who had known him for many years.

In an article written for the Socialist History Society in 1996, Falber characterised the restoration of democratic rights in the East Midlands as the district "falling into the hands of the hard-liners." The article dealt with the 1968 Czechoslovak crisis and the fight – as he saw it – for democracy in Czechoslovakia and the Czech Communist Party. Ironic, in view of the fact that he was one of the hard-liners who persisted in denying democratic rights to members and branches within his own party.

Ida Hackett has entered this narrative quite a few times, and it is about time I said a little more about this wonderful comrade, if only to place on record my gratitude for all the help and support she has given me over the almost half a century we have known each other. Ida and her husband, Ernest, were among our closest friends, personally and politically, from the time Kath and I first moved to Nottingham in 1947. The differences in their personalities augmented rather than impaired the close bond of affection they had for each other, which was strengthened further by their common outlook and joint participation in the fight for a better world. Ernest was a true working-class intellectual; he read widely and revelled in discussion and argument. Classical music was his great interest apart from politics, and to say he was an opera enthusiast would be a gross understatement!

Except for a period during the war when he was a petty-officer in the navy, he devoted his adult life to the working-class movement through both his union (he was a building worker) and the wider political struggle. On 7th November 1935, he and a small group of comrades formed the Mansfield branch of the Communist Party and Ernest became its first secretary. He was twenty at the time.

49. INCIDENT AT STAVELEY

When I was sacked by the party I was faced with the problem of finding another job, preferably at my old trade as toolmaker. This was not going to be easy in the best of circumstances, but it was many times more difficult in my case. No prospective employer takes kindly to employing someone fresh from being a full-time organiser of the Communist Party. However, within a couple of weeks Eddie Boyce and Bas Barker,

Chesterfield District Secretary and President of the A.E.U., used their influence to find me a job at the Staveley Iron Works, near Chesterfield, where Eddie was union convenor. It was not the job I would have chosen and a universe removed from the precision engineering I had been used to as a toolmaker. I started on the wrong foot by turning up for work on the first day wearing my yellow "smock," the loose coat worn by toolmakers.

Apparently, at Staveley these were strictly and only worn by foremen; the common herd wore navy blue dungarees, so I shocked everyone by apparently challenging the natural order of things and acting above my station!

The engineering was rough and ready, and a lot of the work was very heavy-going, man-handling and modifying large cast-iron mould boxes and getting them into position in the foundry in readiness for the moulds to be filled with molten iron from the ladles that were whisked around over one's head by the travelling cranes. The whole place seemed primitive to me, and the foundry was, of course, hot from the heated ladles, noisy, dangerous and full of acrid smoke. I know that foundry workers have always had to work under such conditions, but to me it looked like a preview of hell. Yet, there was some compensation in the generally easy atmosphere and the camaraderie of men who had worked together for most of their lives.

Despite the influence of Eddie and Bas, it soon seemed that my stay there would be brief. The Staveley Works was part of Stanton and Staveley, a division of the nationalised British Steel. Even so, we realised they would have doubts about taking me on with my record, so I gave a completely false account of what I had been doing during the previous twenty six years when I had worked for the party. Or rather, I was 'economical with the truth,' correctly naming the engineering factories where I had once worked, but being somewhat elastic regarding the periods I had worked there. To get over the recent insurance record, a comrade who owned a small engineering factory was prepared to state that I had been employed by him in the immediate period before.

This seemed to have worked alright. Not for long, though. One morning, three weeks after starting, Eddie came across to me and said the General Manager wanted to see us. The office buildings were away from the workshops and as we walked across to them we conjectured as to what on earth he wanted with us. When we went into the office, he was sitting at his desk with some papers in front of him.

373

"These are the employment particulars you wrote when you applied for a job here," he said to me. I looked at them and confirmed that they were indeed.

"They are not true. In fact, for most of the time you were working for the Communist Party."

"Who told you that?" I asked (as if I didn't know).

"I'm not prepared to say," he said.

"If I had written the truth, would I have got the job?"

"Maybe not, but that's beside the point. You deceived us."

"It's exactly the point. I wanted a job. I could do the job offered, as I have proved. But I knew that political prejudice would damn my chances of getting it if I had said I had been a Communist Party organiser. How can you justify that?"

"I don't need to. Your application was false and that's sufficient grounds to take action."

At this point Eddie came in. He had been listening to the exchange without saying anything. There were many who criticised him for what they saw as his softly-softly approach, but on this occasion he spoke forcibly and decisively, emphasising every word.

"Let me make the union's position clear, Mr Williams. If Mr Westacott is sacked because of his political opinions, which is what this amounts to, the entire works will be at a standstill this afternoon."

This obviously shook Williams. For a minute he was silent, then he said rather lamely, "Very well, consider yourself severely reprimanded."

I regret to say that my conscience was not overburdened by the reprimand!

There was a gratifying sequel to this a few weeks later. A General Election was called, and as I was Communist candidate in Mansfield I asked for leave of absence for the weeks of the campaign. The application had to go to the General Manager and there was some speculation among the lads as to whether he would get his own back by refusing me time off. However, the decision was taken out of his hands. The next day the Personnel Manager came searching me out to tell me that they had received a directive from British Steel that all parliamentary candidates employed by them must immediately be given time off on full pay until the election was over. It was the biggest financial contribution to our election fund!

When I restarted work there was a new manager. Williams had been sacked.

50. FAMILY LIFE

During the whole of this traumatic period family life continued as before. Kath was very much a leading protagonist in the struggle within the District; indeed, if anything she was more resolute than I was. If it had not been for her determination and that of other close comrades, I might very well have been so sickened by the whole affair as to have weakened. As it was, her conviction that we were right, the support she gave and the events that took place brought us even closer together – if that were possible. The children, of course, were not involved in it nor fully aware of what was happening. Preoccupation with them was a great escape, and fortunately we both had the ability to relax by reading. Apart from more serious books, we were both addicted to "who-dun-its" and I to science fiction. Kath was an exceedingly fast reader and could get through in a day an Agatha Christie that would take me a week. She never tired of classical novels, but had little interest in modern novelists.

Soon after we were married, she untypically became interested in photography, but all the equipment we had was a old Brownie box camera and some primitive equipment that enabled us to process our negatives by the old contact print method, putting sensitive paper behind a negative in a frame and holding it up to the light for a few seconds before plunging it into developer in a dark room illuminated only by a home-made red light. It could often be frustrating, but we extracted enormous enjoyment out of it.

Apart from reading, my main relaxation was woodwork, photography and do-it-yourself. A problem – if it is such – that I have always suffered from is the inclination to become involved in a wide variety of interests apart from politics. I qualify it as a problem because while those I have known whose entire world has been confined only to politics may have had a much simpler life pattern, they have also often been the most intolerant and narrow-minded in their general outlook. They suffer from tunnel vision, which obscures understanding of experiences outside of their narrow range of interests. Such self-centredness can be justified in many disciplines; indeed, in mathematics, science and the arts it is a common feature of geniuses. But in politics, where understanding people and society is a vital ingredient, it can distort that cognisance. Compounding my "problem" is an insatiable curiosity that compels me to find out what makes things tick. What makes a car go? How does a TV set transport pictures instantaneously into one's living room from across the world? How can aeroplanes fly or a computer do such marvellous things? I have

375

always found all aspects of life so absorbing. But finding things out can be so time-consuming! Fortunately, for most of my life I was blessed with a retentive memory and quite good powers of concentration – no longer the case, I must regretfully add.

Kath's main interest apart from politics was working with young children. She had an easy rapport with them, and it was the age group she preferred working with, which was why she later transferred from secondary to primary school teaching. She played an active part in the discussions among party educationalists on methods of learning English, centred at one stage on the respective merits of "look-and-say" and "phonetics." Based on her experience, she worked out a comprehensive innovative system of her own, which she hoped to publish but never got round to polishing. She proved many times that a major reason some children had difficulty in reading was the lack of individual attention. "Kids come to me," she said, "from homes where reading is not a normal activity in the family, where there is not a single book nor even a newspaper in the house. Often at school they are stigmatised as "backward," though in fact they are often quite bright. With forty or fifty children to a class, teachers were faced with an enormous problem trying to give such children the attention needed. Like other dedicated teachers, Kath tried to do it, using up her lunch time and staying on after school. She took enormous pleasure in telling me of the progress her special pupils were making, and enlisted me in making numeracy aids out of wood.

It was this love of children, and the belief that their attitudes as adults can be greatly influenced by their childhood experiences, that led to her starting a group of the Woodcraft Folk in Chesterfield. The Woodcraft Folk is the children's organisation of the Co-operative Movement. It was established in the 1920's, not in opposition but as an alternative to the Boy Scouts and Girl Guides. Its aim was and still is to instil into children a love of nature and a regard for humanity. Although not political in the narrow sense, it projects progressive ideas and values, opposing war and stressing the importance of co-operation (including trade unions) and social justice. It encourages links with children's organisations in other countries, and in the period I'm writing about it organised international camps to which were invited the children "pioneers" from the Soviet Union and the other socialist countries. It refused to compromise its principles in order to get government grants, although, regrettably, I understand that much of this has changed in recent years.

There had been a Woodcraft Folk group in Chesterfield many years before, but all traces of it had disappeared. Kath enlisted the support of another party member with children, Betty Heathfield. Betty was the wife of one of the leaders of the Derbyshire miners, and later became nationally well-known during the miners' strike of 1984-85 as an organiser of and spokesperson for the miners' wives. Together, they set up a local group of the Folk, linking up with an experienced Sheffield group led by a dedicated and able progressive, Ken Mayes. It soon took off and was taking up more of their time than they had bargained for. It was obvious that it met a real need. Fortunately, there was a good basis in the young children of party members, and as it became known other parents were only too pleased to enrol their youngsters. The kids participated with enthusiasm in the weekend camps, the activities around the campfire, the other outdoor events, and the fact that it was they, not the adults, that had much of the responsibility for running them. Co-operation and democracy was taught through practical experience. Because of my political commitments I played little part in the Woodcraft Folk itself, though I was much used to transport camping equipment and kids to the camp sites and perform other menial tasks. Our three children were enthusiastic participants in the Folk for many years, and it undoubtedly contributed a lot to their progressive social and political development. For some years Kath was elected to the Education Committee of the Chesterfield Co-operative Society and was instrumental in getting it to give regular grants to the Woodcraft Folk.

Because Kath was a schoolteacher our summer holiday had to be taken in August, and the question of where we were to go was always the subject of a prolonged family discussion. We always involved the children, even when they were small, being very much opposed to the autocratic set-up in many families where the children are expected to accept without question or discussion whatever their parents decide. Of course, when it came to important issues like holidays I shamefacedly confess that it was more appearance than reality: they were no match against two skilled political operators, and we could almost always persuade them that where we wanted to go was in fact their choice! The important thing, however, was that they felt they were participating as part of a family. They were usually caravan holidays, for as well as being cheaper they gave us more freedom to organise our movements. Most years we tried to fit in a week visiting my family in South Wales, or staying with George and Olive in Shepperton. The kids liked visiting relatives because there was a large gang of cousins of their own age; this was good for us, too, since it meant they were off our hands most of the time.

One of the most tiring experiences for us was when we decided one year to take the children to London, as part of their education. As parents don't need to be told, young children have an inexhaustible supply of energy. We did the usual round, including Madame Tussauds, the Planetarium, the Science Museum, Windsor Castle, Westminster Abbey and various other famous landmarks, and by the Friday Kath and I were eagerly looking forward to home and rest. On the last day we visited The Tower, then moved on to St Paul's where, of course, we had to climb to the Whispering Gallery. The Monument, Wrens memorial of the Great Fire, we were not allowed to pass before climbing the three hundred and eleven steps to its top, after which we made a tour of the *Daily Worker* premises at Farringdon Road. Flaked out, Kath and I were thankful to get to a Tube station, bound for home and glorious rest – while the kids ran back up the 'down' escalator as if they had been doing nothing all day.

51. THE 1970's

The 1970's began on a high note. The Vietnam War was coming to an end with a humiliating defeat for the Americans. It demonstrated that the ideological dedication and tenacity of a small country, backed by a world-wide mass movement, was more than a match for the strongest military power on earth. On 4th September, 1970, a Marxist, Salvador Allende, was elected President of Chile and a left-wing Government of Popular Unity established with a radical programme of progressive reforms. At home, the trade unions were still celebrating the defeat of the government's attempt to introduce far-reaching anti-union legislation.

In an attempt to keep wages down, the Labour government had passed, against strong opposition from the unions and from many Labour M.P.s, a "Prices and Incomes Act" ostensibly aimed at pegging both. In fact, it had no effect on prices and was directed almost entirely against wages. It provoked one of the biggest mass movements since the end of the war, with the Trade Union Congress coming out against it by a massive seven-to-one vote. But what disturbed the government most was that the Act proved to be a blunt weapon, for in industry after industry and in hundreds of workplaces militancy increased and resulted in workers winning pay increases despite the Act. It was in response to this that the government created the Royal Commission.

Harold Wilson and Employment Minister, Barbara Castle, had set up a Royal Commission under Lord Donovan (the very same bloke I had stood against in Leicester in 1950) to consider reform of the trade unions. The Donovan Report showed that the Commission had no doubts about what its main job was. Why had the government failed to keep wages down, it asked. The reason, it asserted, was that whilst it could exercise some measure of control over nationally negotiated wage rates, it had no control over local and workplace negotiated wage increases, and often these were more significant. Any shop steward could have told them this, but it was presented as a remarkable revelation. Therefore, what it called the "informal" system of wage negotiation on a local or workplace level must be ended, and – of crucial importance – the power of shop stewards should be drastically reduced. Despite strong opposition, and to the delight of the Tories, the government accepted the proposals of the Donovan Report and incorporated them in a White Paper, which was to be the basis of an Act. The White Paper was called "In Place of Strife."

It proved to be disastrous for the government. Whereas in the previous struggle there were many right-wing trade union leaders who were prepared to accept a measure of wage restraint "in the interests of the country," now, almost the entire movement rose in outrage against what was rightly seen as an attack on a fundamental part of trade union organisation – the shop stewards, workplace organisation and local autonomy. Meetings and demonstrations were held up and down the country, and thousands of trade unionists from all over Britain took part in a mass lobby of Parliament. In June, the T.U.C. called a special conference – the first for fifty years (the only other time had been in protest at military intervention against the new Soviet republic after the 1914-18 war). The government hadn't reckoned with this scale of opposition, nor with the strength and unity of the movement. It beat an ignominious retreat and withdrew "In Place of Strife." It was a great victory for mass action. The Communist Party had particular reason to be proud, for it and its members had been in the forefront of the battle against wage restraint. As for myself, I made a special study of the Donovan Report and "In Place of Strife," and as well as running a weekend school on the subject must have spoken to about twenty or thirty organisations, mainly trade union branches, explaining the implications.

The period of the two Labour governments from 1964 to 1970 again demonstrated the two contradictory forces at work within the labour movement. The leadership of the Labour Party desperately fought to defend dominant capitalist interests, as illustrated by "In Place of Strife," the main aim of which was to limit the power of workers to organise and fight. The unions, however, still constituted the mass base of the Labour party and had considerable clout, though they were usually held back by powerful trade union leaders who shared the philosophy of the Labour leadership. Its considerable strength sometimes showed itself when shop floor militancy asserted itself, as in the defeat of "In Place of Strife." This militancy asserted itself spectacularly when the miners defeated the Heath Tory government in 1974. In January the N.U.M. put in for a substantial wage claim and declared it would call a national strike if the claim were not met. Heath accused Mick McGahey of wanting to bring down the government and declared a general election for the 28th of February on the question, "Who Governs Britain?" The miners' strike was the pretext to close down large parts of industry, but the result was a complete victory for the miners – in fact they won more than they had asked for, despite the efforts of Joe Gormley, the right-wing N.U.M. President, to arrange a compromise. (Joe Whelan gave me a graphic description of the confrontation with a demoralised Heath at Downing Street. "Hullo Sailor!" he greeted Heath with when he came into the room, a reference to Heath's yachting prowess!) The Tories lost the election and Harold Wilson became Prime Minister, later to give way to James Callaghan. Another expression of trade union influence on the Wilson administration was the passing of a number of progressive measures, such as the Equal Pay Act, the Sex Discrimination Act, and the biggest reform of the state pension system since 1945, including a big increase in the state pension, the linking of pensions to earnings, the introduction of a Christmas bonus, and the establishment of a second contributory pension – the State Earnings Related Pension (S.E.R.P.S.).

Learning nothing from the past, Callaghan launched an attack on workers in the form of a harsh drive to keep wages down. The government's pay policy was rejected by the T.U.C. and the Labour Party Conference, but the warning went unheeded and led to widespread industrial action by trade unionists in defence of their interests. *The Sun* called it "the winter of discontent" and there is no doubt that those months of October, November and January 1978 did see an expression of anger that was unprecedented in both scale and its range (linking, as it did, diverse sections of the working class). The media launched a poisonous campaign of vilification of the trade union movement and workers on strike, using every incident of public inconvenience, however

380

small, to turn public opinion against worker. Thus a minor issue involving six Liverpool gravediggers who refused to dig graves became a major national scandal presented as the dead being left unburied.

This, but above all, the ignominious record of the Callaghan government and the widespread disillusionment arising from it, led to the start of the blackest ever decade in modern history, the decade of Thatcherism. The term Thatcherism implies that it was the personal product of one person and was peculiar to Britain, but this was very far from the truth. The unrestricted development of the capitalist market economy arose out of the needs of the trans-national global economy to do away with all economic and political barriers to its expansion. Its sharpest expression was in Britain because the problems of capitalism were greatest here, with the decline of industry, the lack of investment and the fact that our trade union movement was so potentially powerful. Thatcherism was the determination of the dominant section of British capitalism to force through radical policies in its interests and to defend, in particular, the supreme right to make profit without interference. John Maynard Keynes was finally disposed of and replaced by a new prophet, Milton Friedman.

52. POLICE SPYING

I was having my breakfast one August morning in the middle 1970's, full of the joy of life because I was on holiday and could look forward to a relaxing day, when my serenity was rudely shattered by the phone ringing. It was Edith, the comrade in charge of our bookshop. She was very agitated. The offices had been broken into overnight and a lot of damage had been done. The front door had been forced and the door to my room had been smashed. Unfortunately, she had reported it to the police, who had arrived with remarkable alacrity, so that when I turned up two cops were in my office. They had scattered white fingerprint powder over everything and taken a number of photographs, ostensibly of the damage. I got rid of them as quickly as I could, ascertained that nothing appeared to be missing – not even the little petty-cash coins in the drawer of my desk – and proceeded to tidy up the mess of papers scattered everywhere. The door was a write-off. And that appeared to be that. We were, of course, well used to petty vandalism, usually daubed insults or a brick through the big front window of the bookshop (until a comrade paid to have the glass replaced with unbreakable plastic); but this was one of only a few serious break-ins.

It is worth recounting because of the sequel. Some time later a bloke was browsing around the bookshop and asked to see me because, he said, he had an interesting story to relate. He was a mature student at Ruskin, but two years before he had been a civilian photographer employed by the Nottingham Police Department. "Can you remember," he said, "a break-in you had, when two plain-clothes policemen were sent to investigate?" I confirmed this, and then he told me the tale. When the call had been received at the police station, the address was at once recognised as being the district office of the Communist Party and was reported to the higher-ups. They immediately decided to send two local Special Branch C.I.D. officers. While one kept Edith talking in the bookshop, his mate took photographs in my office of all the lists of names and addresses he could find. "I know," he said, "because I processed the films when they came back." The officers were later commended for their initiative.

Sadly for them, what they didn't know – at least at the time – was that the lists they so assiduously photographed were quite useless. No addresses of party members were kept in the office, except those of branch secretaries, treasurers and District Committee members, all of whom were known Communists, anyway. The pages of addresses they apparently photographed could only have been lists of electors which had been copied from electoral registers for the benefit of canvassers in the Parliamentary election some time before, and which had no marking on them even to indicate whether they were our supporters or not. It must have given the cops an exaggerated idea of how strong the party was!

Of course, the Communist Party and active Communists have always been well used to such attention from the British secret political police (which establishment politicians and their media pretend doesn't exist) as well as from the local C.I.D.'s. Many tales can be told of such interference – some of them quite hilarious. During the war, the Party in South Wales held a weekend school on Marxism in Swansea, and during one of the sessions, Len Jeffreys, the District Organiser, noticed some wiring that looked suspicious. During the lunch break he investigated and found that it was connected to a hidden microphone. He traced the wiring through the window to an empty room in the house next door. On a table was an amplifier, with headphones, two policemen's helmets and notebooks – this was before the era of the tape recorder. Like us, the cops had obviously adjourned for their lunch. We confiscated everything, and, oddly enough, they were never claimed! We hoped the spies had benefited from listening to our discussion on Marxism. Incidentally, this was

382

when the Russians were Britain's allies and the Communist Party fully supported the war effort – a demonstration that, despite this, there was no letting up on anti-communist activity by the secret police.

As I've already recounted, I had written proof when I was in the army that I had long been under surveillance, but there were many indications before then. When, as a teenager, I went to the Government Training Centre at Bristol, I was told by a friend close to the administration that the management had been informed of my militant activities as soon as I arrived. Soon after joining the Communist Party, a private letter I received was accompanied by a scribbled note: "This letter has been opened and read by the police." It was signed, "Post office worker." When I was working in Southampton, my foreman told me that the police had been making enquiries about the articles I had written for *The New Propeller* – even though they were always anonymous. After starting work at the Staveley Works, it was obvious that it was the police that had supplied the management with my complete employment record since I came out of the army. We always assumed that our phones were tapped and became used to the odd clicks and noises that preceded connection or to the uncanny experience of hearing the words of one's conversation playing back in the background about half-a-minute after they were uttered. When some renovations were done to the King Street headquarters of the Communist Party, a hidden microphone and transmitter were found under the platform in the room where the Executive Committee met. It had been planted there some years before.

There are, or were, three levels of political spying. The operations of the local police are relatively crude. Whenever we held a public meeting we could always be sure of having an audience of two – the plain-clothed cops sent to check who else attended and that no subversion was spoken. The fact that we knew who they were didn't deter them. Our public meetings and marches, even local ones, were always well-photographed – and not only ours, but also demonstrations held by other progressive organisations. MI5 and the Special Branch were much more sophisticated and difficult to detect, although they can make abysmal blunders. Peter Wright, in his much-publicised book *Spymaster*, relates how on one occasion MI5 organised a slick operation. According to Wright, they had discovered that the records of Communist Party members were kept at the house of a middle-class comrade in London, and one night they burgled the house when the occupier was away and spent the entire night photographing all the records, thus obtaining the names and addresses of

383

every Communist in Britain. As a District Secretary at the time, I can testify that this is just a load of rubbish. No national lists of members were then kept. Members were registered each year by the district organisations, and all we had to do each week was to phone Party Centre with a figure of the number registered in the district and how many still had to register.

As every revolutionary knows, the use of agent provocateurs has always been a standard tactic of the ruling class from the time when "Oliver the Spy" achieved notoriety by his treacherous activities in betraying the workers of Derbyshire who took part in the Pentrich Rebellion in 1817. They either plant their agents in the organisation, or they use bribery or coercion to make use of existing members. Here are examples of both methods that I knew about. In a celebrated case in South Wales in 1932, four Communists were sent to prison for distributing copies of a paper called the *Soldier's Voice* to troops in Newport barracks, calling on them to follow the example of the sailors at Invergordon by opposing the cuts in pay. They were charged with "incitement to disaffection" and were defended by D. N. Pritt at the Old Bailey. Len Jeffreys was sentenced to three years imprisonment, spent in the notorious Parkhurst high-security prison, and the other three received from twelve to twenty months hard labour. (Len used often to regale us with stories of his life "inside"). The chief witness for the prosecution turned out to be the secretary of the Newport branch of the Party who had been coerced and bribed into becoming a police nark. An example of a "plant" during the war years was when the Cardiff organiser of the party came to suspect that the "comrade" who was responsible for Marxist education for the area and had worked hard for the party for a considerable time had, in fact, always been a police spy. The evidence was put before him at an Area Committee meeting, and he was forced to admit it.

We shall probably never know who the spies have been in the top leadership of the British Communist Party, but it is hard to credit that there have been none. For what it is worth, one ex-C.I.A. agent boasted that the C.I.A. had always had a contact in 16 King Street, the party's national headquarters. Our attitude has always been to take what precautions we can, but not to be paranoid about it; we accept it as a hazard of life in any organisation fighting the capitalist establishment, particularly if the aim is to change the system. Most of the spying, anyway, is quite useless to the establishment, and stems from the paranoia of the secret police. The Communist Party in Britain has always worked quite openly and within the parameters of our democratic system, limited though it is. There has never been any "secret agenda" or hidden policies to be dug up, and we have always eschewed the Trotskyist tactic of "entryism" – secretly burrowing into other organisations in order to control them.

There has been a lot of conjecture as to what part MI5 and the other branches of the British and American secret services played in the demise of the Communist Party of Great Britain. In my view, the main causes of the party's disintegration were political. But one need not subscribe to any conspiracy theory to believe that there were agents at work, stimulating and helping the process of disintegration, and that some of these "moles" were almost certainly in the leadership of the party. Your guess is as good as mine as to who they were.

There were two periods, in my recollection, when we had to take special measures to face the likelihood of the party being driven underground. The first time was at the beginning of World War Two. We now know from published Cabinet papers that in the early years of the war the British government considered following the example of the French government by making the Communist Party illegal. It decided against taking action out of fear of the unfavourable response such a move would arouse. However, bearing in mind the reactionary nature of the Chamberlain government, the Party had to take some obvious precautions. Shadow committees were appointed to take over in the event of leading comrades being arrested, and a shadow organisation set up, lists put in safe hands and duplicators and typewriters, etc. dispersed. We were told not to carry any names and addresses on us or keep them at our homes, and to obliterate even addresses on private letters. Fortunately, this proved to be unnecessary. The second time was at the height of the Cold War and the paranoiac anti-communist witch-hunt that took place mainly in the U.S.A. but was reflected in Britain. Our preparations, as I experienced them, were not as extensive as before and consisted in the main of taking precautions to safeguard our members. Veteran Communist, Bob Stewart, was sent around the party district offices to check on security. Our secretary, Meryl, was shaken one day when this burly man with a broken nose walked into the office and started rummaging in cupboards and drawers bulging with old files, and papers yellow with age. She ran to get Mick Jenkins, but before Mick could say anything, Bob barked, "You could have bombs planted on you here, and you wouldn't know a thing about it!" He made a rigorous check on what

385

records we kept, including phone numbers and addresses in our personal diaries.

Of course, it is now common knowledge that MI5 and the Special Branch penetrate the trade union movement as a matter of course. The exposure of how an agent was planted at the top level in the N.U.M. before and during the great miners' strike dramatically highlighted this practice, but such penetration has always taken place and still does. It goes along with the use of anti-working-class organisations like the Economic League and the Industrial Research and Information Service (I.R.I.S.). As I am writing this, the Cabinet papers for the 1960's have just been published. They reveal that Prime Minister Macmillan authorised payment of £40,000 – nearly £500,000 in today's money – to I.R.I.S., to engage in "undercover work" in the unions and to target left-wing activists. Ex-Labour Minister Shawcross, who ran it, boasted of how it had been used to influence elections in the N.U.M. As we in the A.E.U maintained at the time, it was this money that paid for the right-wing campaigns that led eventually to "Carron's Law" and the right-wing domination of the union. And these are the ones who claim to be the defenders of union democracy against the evil machinations of the militants!

53. THE DEATH OF KATH

"The best laid schemes of mice and men . . ." Kath had decided to retire from work early, and we spent many enjoyable, relaxing evenings mulling over plans about what we were going to do when we were both freed from the ties of having to work for a living – now not so far off. Of course, with lives spent as activists, neither of could countenance for a moment sinking into political inactivity: we would soon have withered away. "Retirement" is a senseless word for political activists. It is a new stage of activity, a period of new challenges. The main difference for us was that we would have some choice as to the fields in which we were going to meet them. Kath had plans of devoting herself to her real love – research work and writing. She had arranged discussions with Jock Kane, which were to form the basis of a book about his extended family to be called "The Fighting Kanes." She and Barry Johnson had discussed plans for jointly compiling a comprehensive reference book for the labour movement (still lacking), and I hoped to have more time for writing, while continuing my political and trade union activity locally. We both wanted to travel. We were going to spend a long holiday in Italy, a country with which I had become enchanted during my years in the army and about which I was always, at inordinate lengths, regaling her with stories. Neither of us had spent any length of time in Paris, an omission we intended to remedy. We were attracted by Rose Smith's standing invitation to visit her in China. Of course, we looked forward to spending more times with our children, and the grandchildren we anticipated. "Grow old along with me / The best is yet to be," were the lines of Browning I sometimes, rather flippantly, quoted to her.

During the school holidays in August 1975 we made arrangements to spend a fortnight in Scotland, staying for a few days with our dear friends in Edinburgh, Kate and Ricardo Clark/Figueroa. Afterwards, Kath was to visit her sister in Canada – the air ticket had been bought. On the way to Scotland, we decided to spend a night in York, a city neither of us had ever visited. Although she would not admit it, Kath did not seem well when we started out, and the next day she seemed much worse, so I insisted on us returning home. The news was shattering. She was diagnosed as having a brain tumour and was admitted to Sheffield Royal Infirmary for treatment. The torturous weeks that followed were punctuated by our having our hopes raised and then dashed. "The chances are that the tumour is benign," we were first told. The biopsy revealed it was malignant. "There are degrees of malignancy, and with luck it can be easily dealt with." It turned out to be very severe. "Even so, it may be possible to remove it without greatly interfering with the brain's function." After several operations I was told that it was too deep and that it would, in fact, critically change her, functionally and emotionally. And so the darkness grew blacker as the weeks progressed. There was little more the neurosurgeon, Mr Forster, could do for her, so after discussing it with him, I decided to bring her home – which was what Kath wanted. We decided against radiotherapy because, according to Forster, while it might prolong life for a few months the side effects and the frequent trips to Sheffield would make the time left more unbearable for Kath.

Kath's sister, Molly, came over from Canada to help look after her, and the children were truly wonderful. Emrys was at home and had started on his first job as a bus conductor; Bronwen was a music teacher in Nottingham, but came home whenever she could; while Gwyneth – who lived in Didcot – spent most of her time with us.

In a few weeks, Kath relapsed into a state where she could do nothing for herself. At first, she could chat, but in a strangely unemotional

387

way, so unlike her real self, and soon she gave up speaking altogether. We were not sure how much she was aware of what was going on around her, but we always included her in our conversations and Gwyneth read the *Morning Star* from front to back to her each morning. There were some indications of awareness, such as the very rare and precious occasions when she would suddenly respond to a remark someone had made. Talking to herself, Molly remarked, "I wonder if Kath would mind if I hung these wet towels over the radiator." From the settee where she was lying Kath said in her normal voice, "Not if they are too wet" – her first words after a week of silence. On another occasion, the rebel Clay Cross councillor, David Skinner, visited her, and when he and I were discussing a particular political problem, I remarked, "Stalin once said that it is sometimes better to risk taking a wrong decision than to take no decision at all." Kath had obviously been listening – and understood what we were talking about. She quietly corrected me: "It wasn't Stalin who said that; it was Napoleon!" Against all the evidence, these rare occasions always momentarily raised our hopes of a change taking place. She died in her sleep on 4th November 1975.

All sections of the Chesterfield labour movement were represented at her funeral, as well as her comrades from all over the East Midlands. Basil Barker delivered the funeral address, in which he said:

"Kath was, in the fullest sense of the word, a humane person – with unsurpassed qualities of tolerance, the ability to listen, to argue with reason, totally unselfish, but at the same time, in pursuance of or in defence of the principles and the cause and ideals she held dear, steadfast, determined and totally committed – but always with clarity and logic. Though small in stature, she will be remembered in the annals of the labour movement as a giant of strength and purpose."

Among the many messages was one from Athens, from Betty Ambatielos, whose husband, Tony, was then an M.P. in the Greek Parliament. It was she who had introduced me to Kath, and she recalled how they first met in South Wales (she was then Betty Bartlett) and shared a bond of friendship, having joined the Party at about the same time. She had always been impressed by Kath's integrity and humanity. Dennis Skinner wrote, "Kath's contribution to the creation of a socialist society cannot be measured in terms of honours she received but in principles honoured."

I was particularly moved by the fact that John Gollan paid a personal tribute by travelling up from London to attend the funeral. He said to me

388

afterwards, "it's a tragedy that we so often only fully appreciate comrades when it's too late." When Kath was ill, without being asked John had made enquiries about her going to the Soviet Union for treatment, and had arranged for me to see an eminent doctor friend of his, a party member, in London. He assured me that the neurosurgeon who was treating her in Sheffield, Mr Forster, had an international reputation for his work on brain tumours and that it was his opinion that nothing would be gained by moving Kath.

All who have sustained such a loss know what a devastating experience it is. The sum total of a deep and intimate loving companionship is far greater than the doubling of the psyche of either partner. Although each is a uniquely separate and different individual, living closely with and for each other in time produces an integration that cannot be truly separated and even now, twenty five years later, I still feel that a part of me is missing.

Hard though it was to lose Kath, I was glad she died when she did, and so were the children. It would have been obscene for someone as active and bright as she had been to continue existing as a vegetable. I know she would have agreed, for we had occasionally talked about such a situation in relation to other people. Soon after her death I drew up what is now known as a "living will," giving precise instructions regarding myself if ever I am in a similar situation. Apart from people with strong religious convictions, I cannot understand the aversion of otherwise sensible people to taking such a step. Basically, not to do so seems a quite selfish attitude, for it shifts responsibility on to surviving relatives to make a heartrending decision. In most cases, of course, no decision is needed, for nature takes its normal course. But if one is dying and in great pain, it is an intolerable burden to place on others – having to decide whether to cut off the life support system without knowing in advance that they truly have your blessing. Although not strictly connected with the above, I have always been a firm supporter of voluntary euthanasia. Providing there are adequate safeguards against its misuse, I think it is eminently reasonable for a person to decide when to depart this world, especially if the choice is between dragging out a miserable existence with no independence, or dying with dignity. Having said that, I frankly admit that I would find it difficult for two reasons: I would like to see my grandchildren grow up, and I have an insatiable curiosity concerning what the world is going to be like next year or in ten years' time. Indeed, as a life-long addict of science fiction, I had hoped that by now a process would have developed whereby one could be put to sleep for a hundred years. I would be the first to volunteer!

The trite saying that "time is the best healer" is only partially true. As the multitude of people in similar circumstances know, pain decreases but the loss remains. It is nigh impossible to get used to being on one's own, for me, not discussing the political situation with her, not mulling over problems and engaging in the inconsequential chit-chat that is so much a part of an everyday life lived together. It is hard to come to terms with the fact that she did not live long enough to know and revel in any of our eight grandchildren.

The East Midlands District of the Communist Party decided to commemorate Kath with an annual public lecture, to be held in Chesterfield in September – the month of her birth. As a tribute to her, the Derbyshire Area of the N.U.M. passed a special resolution offering the use of their fine Council Chamber for these lectures. The lectures ran for twenty one years and became something of an institution. It was appropriate that the first, on "Marxism and Reformism," was given by James Klugman, a close friend, particularly of Kath. He was very ill at the time – he died soon afterwards – and the tribute he paid her summed up one aspect of her life:

> I am very proud that you have asked me to come here to be the first speaker in this series of lectures. I remember Kath particularly in two ways. In relation to education in the labour movement. When I was in charge of Marxist education for the party, she was in charge for the District, and I remember her as a participator at one of the first women's schools that we organised. We often used to talk together about what we in a way used to describe as a tragedy of the British labour movement. Here was a labour movement two hundred years old or more, the oldest in the world, 200 years of consecutive struggle, with early trade unions and minor strikes as early as the 1760's, an enormous capacity for discipline, organisation and solidarity for struggle, but whose understanding of theory, consciousness as socialists was very, very low in the movement as a whole.
>
> Kath often used to discuss with me this question of the cream of the British working class who had come fighting to the labour movement and trade union movement as

kids, distributing leaflets as kids around the edge of the crowds, unknown soldiers giving themselves to the movement, living and dying for the movement, in harness, and yet so often having given their lives to building and maintaining the labour movement, died – died not really understanding the capitalism in which they lived, hating it but not understanding it, died not really understanding the sort of society they wanted to build, but knowing that they wanted a different society. Died above all, not understanding the tactics and strategy of how to get from the Britain of capitalism to the Britain of socialism. And we would discuss how could it be that a labour movement such as ours, a movement that is so old with such great traditions, could be so weak generally when it came to genuine socialist understanding.

Kath felt this profoundly, and, feeling this, devoted herself to changing it. She helped to show it in her own life by showing that the daughter of a mining craftsman could become a fine intellectual, by showing that the working class was totally capable of absorbing all the most complex ideas of society, by showing in practice by her own practice that it was possible to combine understanding, philosophy, theory, consciousness – socialist consciousness – with the activities and struggles of the labour movement. As a woman she combated another myth of capitalism – the inadequacies of women – the destiny of women to be delegated the more menial tasks in the struggle. She showed as a woman as well as a working-class person, that women can do everything with the same capacity as men in the labour movement. Kath's life in a way combated that false modesty of working-class people in their respect for "the best capitalist brains," of women in their natural respect for their menfolk, and showed that this false modesty was a weapon of capitalism and capitalist society.

CHAPTER IX

LIFE IN THE THIRD AGE

54. RETIREMENT AND INVOLVEMENT IN LOCAL POLITICS

After spending thirty years working as a "professional revolutionary," I retired in March 1982. Despite all the frustrations, disappointments and positively bad periods, I enjoyed working for the party, and I regarded it as a great privilege to be able to spend almost the whole of my working life not swelling the profits of faceless capitalist shareholders but devoting myself to the interests of the working class and the fight for socialism. Of course, retiring from full-time party work did not in the least mean giving up active participation in the work of the party, but not having the same responsibilities meant that I had greater scope in deciding what to do. Inevitably, more of my work concentrated on Chesterfield, and a lot of my time was now spent in the trade union field, particularly on the Trades Council.

Chesterfield Trades Council has become known nationally for its May Day Demonstration and Gala, which has become the largest such event in Britain, attracting men and women from far beyond North Derbyshire. For one day the town is taken over by the labour movement. A variety of concerts and other cultural events are held, competitions – outside and inside – organised, entertainment for children held, exhibitions displayed, and the market place is resplendent with stalls manned by dozens of labour movement and democratic organisations. Highlight of the day is the demonstration, with thousands of men and women marching behind about fifty banners and five bands, culminating in a political rally in the Market Place. It is truly a people's day, a joyous day, and the real meaning of May Day as an affirmation of faith in socialism and international working-class solidarity is kept very much alive. A measure of its success is that when we first started we had difficulty in getting national speakers; now they queue up for the privilege of being invited.

392

It was no easy task making our May Day Gala such an outstanding success. It is a tribute to the Trades Council, and the close co-operation built between it and the Borough Council. I am proud to have been involved from the start and to have been one of the team – and it was a team – that had the vision and the dedication to make it a reality.

After it was formed in 1883, the Chesterfield Trades Council had a respectable record in uniting and helping workers in struggle, particularly in mining, railways and steel. By the 1920's, however, its influence had declined, and for ten years after the General Strike it went out of existence. When it was re-formed it was handicapped by the operation of the "Black Circular," which the right-wing leadership of the T.U.C. had introduced in 1935 and which barred Communists from being elected as delegates to trades councils. Although it was at first rigorously applied, it had become largely inoperable during the war years. It was re-introduced in an altered form in 1948, and trade unions were threatened with "de-registration" unless they toed the T.U.C line. Some trades councils, notably London and Nottingham, refused to be intimidated and got away with it. Others quietly ignored it. To its shame, Chesterfield Trades Council was not one of them. On the contrary, it rigidly applied the ban. This reflected the right-wing character of the local Labour Party and was out of tune with a situation in which Communists were playing an outstanding part in the working-class movement in the area. Mick Kane and Bert Wynn were full-time officials of the N.U.M. (Bert was to become General Secretary of the Derbyshire Area); Bas Barker was shop stewards' convenor at Sheepbridge Stokes and a leading figure in the A.E.U.; Ernie Kelly was convenor at the big Chesterfield Tube Works and Secretary of the N.U.G.M.W.; and there were many others giving selfless service to their unions and to their workmates. Yet, all were barred from being elected delegates to the Trades Council. Chesterfield was one of the last trades councils in Britain to operate the Black Circular, but when the ban was eventually lifted Communists were soon playing a leading role on the Council.

I became a delegate from Chesterfield 7 branch of the A.E.U. to the Trades Council in the early 1960's. However, when I attended the first meetings in a small room in the Market Hall, I was frankly disappointed. Although now progressive, it didn't adequately represent the whole of the trade union movement of the town. There was also a sense of an "old boys' club" about it, an acceptance of things as they were – a hangover, no doubt, from the previous period. There could not have been more than about fifteen delegates present. It seemed to me that a real shake-up was needed. But when I suggested that we launch an affiliation drive, it was at first treated with polite tolerance as coming from a new boy who was speaking a little out of turn. In time, the suggestion was adopted, and the membership began to grow to the point where we had virtually every trade union organisation affiliated. Sixty to seventy delegates were now attending the Council's very lively monthly meetings. Just as important, it truly became the leadership of the organised working class and a recognised force in Chesterfield. Regrettably, it has declined in recent years due, in part, to the reduction in the number of unions through amalgamations, the destruction of mining in the area and the decline of engineering.

We decided to organise an annual May Day march on the first Saturday in May. For two or three years about a hundred of us marched through the busy town centre behind the new Trades Council banner – not spectacular, but it was a start. Then the Labour Government decided to make the first Monday in May a statutory holiday, beginning in 1978. When this was announced, I tentatively proposed that we should consider breaking away from our usual pattern. My idea was that the Trades Council should take over the holiday and transform it into a broad, people's event, celebrating May Day and retaining its political content. Nothing was done about it at the time, but some months later I raised it again. We decided to call an extended meeting, inviting leading trade union officials, representatives of the Labour and Communist parties and Labour Councillors. The meeting was divided. The main opposition to the proposal came from those who felt that it was too ambitious and that we should suggest to Sheffield Trades Council that it organise a gala in the city, with Chesterfield giving support. Fortunately, this was rejected, and we began to organise Chesterfield's first May Day Gala. How correct the decision was has been proved by the sad fact that Sheffield, like many other cities, seems to have abandoned the tradition of a May Day march.

We had one important advantage. Largely as a result of the work of Bas Barker and Eddie Boyce, President and Secretary of the Chesterfield District Committee of the A.E.U., the union now had an office and a full-time Secretary in Chesterfield. The first Secretary elected was Bill Mitchell, a fine left-winger and a former shop steward. He took over the preparatory work and threw himself wholeheartedly into the job. Bas had retired and was able to contribute the wealth of his own experience, working with Bill, and there were others who gave a great deal of their time and energy. Launching our first Gala was truly a collective effort. The Trades Council became a powerful influence in the area and played an important role in rallying support for the miners in the great 1983-84 strike, in organising support for other workers involved in struggle and in supporting the Clay Cross Councillors in their epic fight against the Housing Finance Act. An important initiative was setting up an unemployed workers' centre to give advice to the unemployed – the brain-child of Bas. At first this was run by a volunteer worker, Frank Troop, from the office of the G.M.W.U., but later a grant and other help from the Chesterfield Borough Council enabled us to have permanent premises and a full-time organiser. The Centre has become an important organisation locally and has initiated similar centres in other towns in Derbyshire and North Notts.

For some years I represented the Council on the North Midlands Federation of Trades Councils and, after reorganisation, on the Derbyshire County Association. For two years I served on the Chesterfield Police Consultative Committee (a most interesting experience) and for three years I represented the trade unionists of Derbyshire on the County Council Education Committee. When Bas retired as Trades Council President in 1981 there was strong pressure on me to take his place, particularly from Bill Mitchell, who was now the Trades Council Secretary. However, I decided against it because of my other commitments, particularly to the Party. We – that is, the left – decided to put forward Barry Johnson, who, although he didn't live in Chesterfield, was a lecturer at the Chesterfield Technical College. Except for one year, Barry has been President ever since. I was proud to be made an honorary life-member when I retired from being an elected delegate in 1990 – one of only four who have received this honour.

Bas Barker has been mentioned often in these memoirs, so I ought to say just a word about him. It is utterly impossible to do justice to a life packed with experiences in so many fields, but fortunately he has written his own autobiography, *Free, But Not Easy*. I knew him when I first became a C.P.G.B. District Committee member in 1947, and subsequently we became close associates and friends. He had been a party member since 1926, and during the General Strike of that year had acted as a teenage courier for the North Derbyshire strike committee. For a time he was a full time party organiser in Sheffield and attended the famous Lenin School in Moscow. When I first knew him he was shop-stewards convenor at Sheepbridge Stokes, an important Chesterfield engineering factory, and president of the A.E.U. District Committee. His ability and his national reputation as a member of the A.E.U. National Committee meant that he could easily have become a full-time officer of the union, but he preferred to remain on the factory floor, helping others climb the trade union ladder of opportunity. He would rather be king-maker than king. He was fully devoted to the labour movement and played an active part in all its fields. Before the war, when there was a parliamentary bye-election in Clay Cross and the national leadership of the Labour Party wanted to impose Arthur Henderson – a right-winger – as Labour candidate, the local party asked Bas to join the Labour Party so that they could chose him as their candidate – an appeal that he turned down. Although many years of his life had been spent in Sheffield, where he met and married Beryl – who became his life-long companion, politically as well as personally – he became so identified with Chesterfield and so involved in all aspects of its life that he became known as "Mr Chesterfield." In 1983 he was made a Freeman of the Borough, the first-ever trade unionist, let alone a Communist, to receive the honour. His autobiography is a striking testimony to his Marxist beliefs and his faith in the working class and the successful outcome of the struggle for socialism.

At the beginning of 1984 Eric Varley resigned as Chesterfield's M.P. and Peter Heathfield, Secretary of the Derbyshire Miners invited Tony Benn to put his name forward as his successor – Tony had lost his Bristol seat due to boundary changes. Unfortunately, Chesterfield Labour Party was not in any way progressive and Tony was not even short-listed. Obviously, something had to be done about this. We recognised that the setback was due to the fact that the unions, which represented the strongest section of the constituency party, played little part in its politi-cal life, and this was particularly significant so far as the N.U.M. and A.E.U. were concerned. By mobilising the delegates of the two unions who should have been at the selection conference, a recall meeting was demanded and Tony was put on the short list. This was a victory, but there remained the vital task of ensuring he was selected. It required organisation and a campaign to ensure that every bona fide trade union delegate attended the selection conference. With this in mind, a few of us met at the A.E.U. rooms and meticulously went through the list of del-egates and decided how best to approach them. In fact, there were few problems; it was simply a question of persuading them to attend. The NUM dealt with their own delegates and Bas Barker, Bill Mitchell and myself agreed to see the A.E.U. delegates. Other trade union delegates were similarly approached. As everyone knows, the result was that Tony Benn was selected as Labour candidate for Chesterfield and, after a rip-roaring campaign, elected M.P. As has been amply demonstrated, this proved to be probably the most important political event in the history of the town, for Tony has been more than an just excellent M.P.; he has been an inspiration and a stalwart fighter for the working class, for all progressive causes and for socialism.

55. LAST THOUGHTS

At the beginning of September 2001, I was diagnosed as having liver cancer, with the prospect of having much less time than I anticipated to finish this autobiography. Working against the desire to speed up and bring it to completion is the sapping of energy arising from the illness which makes it hard to concentrate for very long on writing (and I have never been very happy or efficient at using a tape recorder). But though I shall not be around if and when these memoirs are ever published, I hope that what I have written will be interesting and useful to those who are and who read them.

Regrettably, this unfortunate turn of events means that I shall not be able to deal with important political issues that I was looking forward to developing. These include the collapse of the Soviet Union and the other socialist counties of Eastern Europe, changes in the world communist movement, the growth of eurocommunism as a Marxist revisionist trend, the success of the revisionists in destroying the Communist Party of Great Britain and subsequent developments, the great miners' strike of 1984-85, the Clay Cross struggle against the Housing Finance Act and the pensioners movement. I have written about some of these in articles in the *Morning Star* and elsewhere.

In particular, I should have liked to have explained why, despite so many setbacks and a lifetime full of apparent disappointments, I remain as firmly optimistic about the future (given that the world survives an ecological Armageddon) as when I first joined the movement as a teenager. I refuse to believe that history ends with imperialism, global capitalism and the free market economy. Humankind has more to look forward to than that. Sooner or later a just society will be created. The basic contradictions of imperialism are as sharp as ever, and dialectics tell us that history can take sudden and surprising turns (as we have experienced in recent years).

POSTSCRIPT

To those of us who worked with Fred over the later years of his life, the memoirs leave a tantalising air of the incomplete. Certainly, the epic experiences that led to a life of working class struggle are there. So are the the main actors, both those who influenced Fred, and the much greater number who in turn were touched by him. It is tempting to see the memoirs finishing where they do as marking the end of a period of struggle. Nothing was further from Fred's mind. Fred was the first to decry those who saw in a lull an "end to history." He was the first to see new forms of struggle emerging where the employers and the state appeared to have gained the whip hand.

The loss of the Communist Party to reformist ideas, its gradual conversion to a discussion network, and its eventual dissolution as a party led to some bitter self-examination among communists, not least by Fred. When the issue came down to a struggle between the reformists who were trying to destroy the *Morning Star* and those who sought to defend and promote it (with the latter being disciplined within the Party), sides had to be taken. In welcoming and playing a leading part in the re-established Communist Party of Britain, an organisation dedicated to ensuring that the *Morning Star* survived, Fred was ever aware of the defeat it represented in terms of the split within the Communist movement. It is a tribute to Fred that in the East Midlands the party stayed essentially united and voted to back the C.P.B. rather than become a breakaway organisation.

The last two decades of Fred's life was a period of great ideological turmoil. The collapse of the Soviet Union forced the Communist movement to analyse the causes of this failure, to re-evaluate its own strategies, and to assess the implications for struggles throughout the world that had been supported by the Soviet Union or were protected by it from the full intervention of Imperialism. Fred was a tower of strength in these debates. Experienced from a multiplicity of struggles and wise from encyclopaedic study, he was ever-confident that in the end what was significant wasn't the fate of parties or political structures but the outcome of countless class, democratic and national struggles. He knew that it was these struggles that would eventually bring to an end the era of exploitation and lay the foundations for a new kind of society.

The range of Fred's interests was legendary. Apart from politics, they included carpentry, DIY, photography, science, electronics, computing, history, literature, and opera. A bibliophile and a born archivist, he built up a remarkable collection of documents and records relating to the

Labour Movement, He opened his library and archives to students of labour history, and several university theses were developed in Fred's sitting room and enriched by his oral supplements, for he was a great conversationalist.

The account Fred gives of his involvement in the Chesterfield Trades Council, the establishment of the May Day gala, and the selection of Tony Benn as the Labour candidate for Chesterfield gives some indication of how active he remained in retirement. But there is much that remains untold. In particular, Fred did a great deal of work in the pensioners' movement, work which won him a host of new friends and admirers. He regularly wrote articles for the *Morning Star* and letters to the *Derbyshire Times* on a wide range of issues, great and small. And, at the most local level of all, when the residents of Avenue Road got together to protest against the pollution coming from the factory next door to Fred's house, he acted as their spokesperson in presenting their case to the local authority.

In these last years, many of Fred's closest comrades died, and he was often in demand to officiate at funerals where his tributes recalled the best of their life's work. But Fred wasn't only called on by the elderly; his interests and erudition enabled him to appreciate and discuss the work not only of his children, but also of his grandchildren as they pursued their education.

New developments thrilled him to the end. He welcomed the anti-globalisation protests and wanted their ideas introduced into the main organisations of the working class, the trades unions and left-wing parties. At the same time, he was explaining the experiences and validity of trade union struggles to those presently outside them. As he opposed anti-trade union legislation in the past, he would today be challenging the restrictions on democracy allegedly necessary because of terrorism, but menacingly there to be used against any threat to profit or private property. In being a leading proponent of the unity of the working class, Fred had a very political concept of it, his every effort being to make it a unity of the class, not merely of groupings within it. But this concept was no mechanical measure of breadth or numbers involved. Every struggle was used to enrich the understanding of ordinary people, to help them see the need for solidarity and the development of independent working class strategies. Every experience would be used to promote the idea of Socialism, the necessity of Socialism if human society is to survive, and the practicality of Socialism amid the chaos of Imperialism.

APPENDIX I

Results of General Election contests in seats where I was a candidate

NORTH-EAST LEICESTER : 23 February 1950
Labour . . . . .Terence Donavan 25,305
Tory . . . . .H. A. Taylor 14,908
Liberal . . . . .M. J. Moroney .4,257
Communist . . . . . . .Fred Westacott .327

MANSFIELD : 31 March 1966
Labour . . . . .John Concannon 28,849
Tory . . . . .Kenneth Clarke 9,987
Liberal . . . . .Reg Strauther 6,628
Communist . . . . . . .Fred Westacott .590

MANSFIELD : 18 June 1970
Labour . . . . .John Concannon 30,378
Tory . . . . .W. Morton 15,027
Communist . . . . . . .Fred Westacott .628

MANSFIELD : 28 February 1974
Labour . . . . .John Concannon 34,378
Tory . . . . .J. Thompson 18,236
Communist . . . . . . .Fred Westacott .675

MANSFIELD : 10 October 1974
Labour . . . . .John Concannon 28,964
Tory . . . . .J.R. Wood 11,685
Liberal . . . . .D. J. Chambers 9,348
Communist . . . . . . .Fred Westacott .448

APPENDIX II

Kath Westacott Memorial Lectures – 1976 to 1996

All held in September and, except for the last one, all held in Chesterfield in the Council Chamber of the Derbyshire Area of the National Union of Mineworkers

1976   Marxism and Reformism
        James Klugman

1977   Trades Unions and the Fight for Socialism
        Dr John Foster

1978   Women, Class Struggle and Socialism
        Tess Gill

1979   Achievements of the Cuban Revolution
        Carlos Trejos

1980   60 Years of Struggle – The Communist Party
        Yesterday and Today
        Gordon McLennan

1981   Trades Unions and Socialism
        Will Paynter

1982   Towards a United Ireland
        Michael O'Riordan

1983   Which Way for the Labour Movement?
        Ben Rubner

1984   Communism and Freedom
        Dr John Hoffman

1985   Class Politics and the Left
        Fred Westacott

1986   The Struggle in South Africa
        Alan Brooks

1987   The Soviet Union and Perestroika
        Kate Clark

1988   The Irish Question
        Tom Durkin

1989   Women in the Fight for Social Change
        Elean Thomas

1990   The Future for British Socialism
        Tony Benn M.P.

1991   People, Profits and the Planet
        Dr John Cox

1992   The Media in the Fight for Socialism
        Tony Chater

1993   The Role of the South African Communist Party in the
        Struggle for a Democratic and Socialist South Africa
        George Johannes

1994   New Realism or Class Struggle –
        Which Way for the Unions?
        Arthur Scargill

1995   The Future of Socialism
        Fred Westacott

1996   Britain and the European Community –
        its Significance for Socialism
        Jim Mortimer